Moral and Spiritual Leadership in an Age of Plural Moralities

In crisis situations, such as terror attacks or societal tensions caused by migration, people tend to look for explicit moral and spiritual leadership and are often inclined to vote for so-called 'strong leaders.' Is there a way to resist the temptation of the simplistic solutions that these 'strong leaders' offer, and instead encourage constructive engagement with the complex demands of our times? This volume utilizes relational and dialogical perspectives to examine and address many of the issues surrounding the moral and spiritual guidance articulated in globalizing Western societies.

The essays in this collection focus on the concept of plural moralities, understood as divergent visions on what is a 'good life,' in an ethical, aesthetical, existential, and spiritual sense. They explore the political-cultural context and consequences of plural moralities as well as discussing challenges, possibilities, risks, and dangers from the perspective of two promising relational theories: social constructionism and dialogical self theory. The overarching argument is that it is possible to constructively put in nuanced moral and spiritual guidance into complex, plural societies.

By choosing a clear theoretical focus on relational approaches to societal challenges, this interdisciplinary book provides both a broad scope and a coherent argument. It will be of great interest to scholars of social and political psychology, leadership and organization, religious studies, and pedagogy.

Hans Alma holds an endowed chair in Contemporary Humanism at the VUB (Vrije Universiteit Brussel), Belgium, Department of Philosophy and Ethics.

Ina ter Avest is Professor Emerita of the Inholland University of Applied Sciences and was Senior Lecturer in Religious Education at the Vrije Universiteit in Amsterdam, the Netherlands.

Studies in World Christianity and Interreligious Relations
Series Editor
Frans Wijsen
Radboud University, The Netherlands

Editorial Board:
Michael Amaladoss (Chennai, India)
Francis Clooney (Cambridge, USA)
Fatimah Husein (Yogyakarta, Indonesia)
Diego Irarrazaval (Santiago, Chile)
Robert Schreiter (Chicago, USA)
Abdulkader Tayob (Cape Town, South Africa)
Anya Topolski (Nijmegen, The Netherlands)

The aim of this series is to publish scholarly works of high merit on relations between believers of various streams of Christianity, as well as relations between believers of Christianity and other religions. We welcome studies from all disciplines, including multi- and interdisciplinary studies, which focus on intra- and inter-religious relations and are non-denominational.

The Decline of Established Christianity in the Western World
Interpretations and Responses
Edited by Paul Silas Peterson

Religion and Social Reconstruction in Africa
Edited by Elias Kifon Bongmba

Catholic Missionaries and their Work with the Poor
Mitigating Market-Government Failure in Emerging Nations
Albino Barrera

Moral and Spiritual Leadership in an Age of Plural Moralities
Edited by Hans Alma and Ina ter Avest

For more information about this series, please visit: www.routledge.com/religion/series/WCIR

Moral and Spiritual Leadership in an Age of Plural Moralities

Edited by Hans Alma and Ina ter Avest

Routledge
Taylor & Francis Group

LONDON AND NEW YORK

First published 2019
by Routledge
2 Park Square, Milton Park, Abingdon, Oxon OX14 4RN

and by Routledge
52 Vanderbilt Avenue, New York, NY 10017

Routledge is an imprint of the Taylor & Francis Group, an informa business

British Library Cataloguing-in-Publication Data
A catalogue record for this book is available from the British Library

Library of Congress Cataloging-in-Publication Data
A catalog record for this book has been requested

ISBN: 978-1-138-48941-7 (hbk)
ISBN: 978-1-351-03762-4 (ebk)

Typeset in Sabon
by Apex CoVantage, LLC

Contents

Preface

In April 2016, an international expert meeting on *Moral and Spiritual Guidance in Liquid Times* was held at cultural center *Akoesticum* in Ede, the Netherlands. Participants reflected on urgent societal themes related to what Zygmunt Bauman has called "liquid modernity," from a relational and dialogical perspective. The meeting aimed at gaining deep insight into these themes from the shared experience of the participating academics and practitioners who work in different fields (psychology, religious studies, anthropology, humanistic studies, and education studies as academic disciplines on the one hand, and coaching, consulting, teaching, and spiritual care as practical areas on the other). During the meeting, research questions were formulated and explored, and the first outlines were drawn for a book that would both address theoretical issues and have a strong practical relevance.

The book you hold now is the result of that highly inspiring and challenging project. We decided to focus on what we called plural moralities and explore it from the point of view of both a relational ethic and the moral implications of dialogical self theory. We discussed issues regarding moral and spiritual leadership and wrestled with questions on what leadership could mean from an authentic relational point of view. We exchanged many ideas during the expert meeting and brought them home with us to digest them in the context of our own daily professional work. We read each other's contributions and related to them in our own chapter. In this way, a "web" was woven that manifests the main topic of this volume: building relationships in our complex and diverse globalizing world.

As editors, we would like to thank all the persons who contributed to the book: the participants at the expert meeting, the discussants who reflected on our presentations, the authors, and Jack Boothroyd from Routledge, who guided us through the process. We also thank *Kerk en Wereld* for its financial support. We share with this organization a strong commitment to justice, inclusiveness, and community building. We hope that this volume will contribute to both practical endeavors and academic research related to meaningful guidance and leadership in just societies in an age of plural moralities.

Hans Alma and Ina ter Avest

Contributors

Hans Alma holds an endowed chair in Contemporary Humanism at the VUB (Vrije Universiteit Brussel), Belgium, Department of Philosophy and Ethics. Trained in cultural psychology and psychology of religion at the Radboud University Nijmegen, her research focuses on the human search for meaning in life. She studied the ways people commit themselves to a religious tradition and the religious meaning of art. Her research also addresses worldview pluralism, especially the role of the imagination and the arts in coping with religious diversity and fluidity in a globalizing world. Using a process approach to worldview studies, she specifically analyzes the way humanism develops in this context. She is coordinator of the international research consortium SIMAGINE (Social Imaginaries in a Globalizing World) and is co-editor of a recent volume with the same title (De Gruyter, 2018).

Ina ter Avest is Professor Emerita of the Inholland University of Applied Sciences and was senior lecturer in Religious Education at the Vrije Universiteit in Amsterdam, the Netherlands. She did her master's at the Radboud University Nijmegen, the Netherlands, and graduated as a psychologist of Culture and Religion. In her PhD research she focused on the religious development of pupils (primary school) in an intercultural and interreligious context – a domain at the crossroads of psychology of religion and intercultural pedagogy. In her teaching as well as in her research, (religious) identity development is central: identity development of pupils/students, of teachers, and of teams of teachers in schools. In her private practice she combines her theoretical frame of reference of the dialogical self theory (she was trained as a consultant following the self confrontation method) with her education as a psychodramatist, and coaches individuals as well as groups.

Cok Bakker is Professor of Religious and Worldview Education in the Department of Philosophy and Religious Studies at the Faculty of Humanities, Utrecht University, the Netherlands. He has a background in Theology and Religious Studies (MA, 1988) and Educational Studies (1991) and holds a PhD from Utrecht University (1994). His research focuses on the relationship between education and worldviews and morality in the broadest sense. Additionally, his appointment at the university includes spending two days a week on secondment to the Hogeschool Utrecht, University of Applied Sciences as professor (*lector*) at the Research Centre for Learning and Innovation. His role there is to lead the research group that focuses on the theme of "Normative Professionalization." As part of a joint project by Utrecht University and HU University of Applied Sciences a research group of about 15 (PhD) researchers has been formed. The supervision of PhD research has thus become a key task.

Angel S. Buster is a PhD candidate at Tilburg University, the Netherlands, focused on identity challenges in family businesses using a dialogical approach. She has more than 15 years' experience in the field of personal change and leadership development. Currently, she works as a leadership consultant and therapist where, in both roles, she helps free the system(s) from sedimented positions in order to improve physical, mental, emotional, and spiritual wellbeing.

Kenneth J. Gergen is a Senior Research Professor in Psychology at Swarthmore College, USA, and the president of the Taos Institute. He is internationally known for his contributions to social constructionist theory, technology and cultural change, the self, and relational practices. His major writings include *Realities and Relationships: Soundings in Social Construction, The Saturated Self: Dilemmas of Identity in Contemporary Life, An Invitation to Social Construction*, and *Relational Being: Beyond Self and Community*. Gergen lectures throughout the world and has received numerous awards for his work, including honorary degrees in both the United States and Europe.

Mary Gergen is Professor Emerita of Psychology and Women's Studies at Penn State University, Brandywine (USA), special sections editor of *Qualitative Psychology*, as well as a board member of the Taos Institute, a non-profit organization dedicated to the integration of social constructionist ideas with diverse professional practices throughout the world. With a strong interest in feminist gerontology, she is a co-editor of the *Positive Aging* newsletter, an online publication, which is available in six languages. Her major works are involved at the intersection of feminist theory and social constructionist ideas. In 2001 she published *Feminist Reconstructions in Psychology: Narrative, Gender and Performance*. She has also been author or editor of nine other books, as well as over 100 articles and chapters for scholarly volumes. She has published pieces on aging, dialogue, gender, narratives, collaborative practices, performance, and qualitative inquiry.

Hubert J.M. Hermans is Professor Emeritus of Psychology at Radboud University Nijmegen, the Netherlands. His dissertation (1967) was on Motivation and Achievement and resulted in two psychological tests:

the Achievement Motivation Test for adults (1968; published in *Journal of Applied Psychology* in 1971) and the Achievement Motivation Test for children (1971). Both tests since then have been among the most frequently used psychological tests in the Netherlands. As a reaction to the static and impersonal nature of psychological tests, he developed a self-confrontation method (SCM) (Guilford Press, 1995). Application of this method in practice led to the establishment of the *ZKM Vereniging* (Association for SCM Consultants) that counted around 250 members in 2018. In the 1990s he developed the dialogical self theory (DST), inspired by the American pragmatism of William James and the dialogical school of the Russian literary scholar Mikhail Bakhtin. Hermans is considered a key figure in narrative psychology.

Julia Ipgrave is Honorary Senior Research fellow in the Department of Humanities (Ministerial Theology) at the University of Roehampton and associate fellow of Warwick Religions and Education Research Unit, University of Warwick, UK. She has a background in education, working in schools in various teaching and management roles from 1989 to 2004, and acts as consultant for a number of organizations with practical interest in the role of religion, interfaith dialogue, and intercultural education in schools. She has participated in a number of national and international research projects and, from 2013 to 2018, was principal investigator for the London strand of the Religion and Dialogue in Modern Society project of the World Academy of Religions at the University of Hamburg. Her research interests include religion in education, young people's religious understanding, interreligious engagement at the community level, and religion and political thought in the 17th century, subjects on which she has published widely.

Robin Knibbe studied humanistic counseling at the University of Humanistic Studies, Utrecht, the Netherlands. She obtained her master's degree with a study on meaning-making, intimacy, and sexuality in professional relations. Currently, she works at Victim Support Netherlands.

Jutta König is a coach and psychotherapist in her company Moving Experience, in talent management with Van Ede and Partners, and with REA coaching expats in the Netherlands. She enjoys working with executives, refugees, global nomads, and trailing spouses during their adventures of migration around the globe. She holds a PhD from the University of Humanistic Studies in Utrecht, the Netherlands. The subject of her thesis was "Moving Experience: Complexities of Acculturation." Growing up as a global nomad with her German diplomat parents in the United States, Australia, and Zimbabwe, later moving as a trailing spouse to Belgium and Singapore with her husband, she reflects on these experiences in her thesis and explores the intricacies of hybrid identities with a group of global nomads. She holds a master's degree in Clinical Psychology from Leiden University, a master's in Medical Anthropology from the University of Amsterdam, and a postgraduate degree in Movement Psychotherapy which she studied in Germany. She has published on dialogical culture coaching and the PEACE methodology.

Rens van Loon is Professor of Dialogical Leadership at the School of Humanities and Digital Sciences, Tilburg University, the Netherlands. He specializes in leadership, organizational change, and transformation. He has been a consultant for more than 30 years developing (global) leadership programs. His work extends the concepts of dialogical self theory to the leadership of organizations, drawing on social constructionism and leadership frameworks. Rens is a board member of the International Leadership Association (ILA) and is active in the International Society for Dialogical Science (ISDS) and the Dialogical Self Academy (DSA). He is the author of numerous books and articles. His main book is *Creating Organizational Value Through Dialogical Leadership: Boiling Rice in Still Water* (2017).

Toon van Meijl is Professor of Cultural Anthropology in the Department of Anthropology and Development Studies at Radboud University Nijmegen, the Netherlands. With a doctorate from the Australian National University (1991), he has been engaged in long-term anthropological research among the Maori, the indigenous population of New Zealand. His research concentrates on issues of cultural identity and the self, particularly among young people in multicultural societies, and on socio-political questions emerging from the debate about property rights, especially of indigenous peoples. Since his appointment to the chair of Cultural Anthropology in 2011, he coordinates the research program of the department that focuses on the relationship between cultural diversity and socio-economic inequality, with special attention paid to issues of citizenship, democracy, and dialogue.

Carmen Schuhmann is Assistant Professor in the Department of Globalization and Dialogue Studies at the University of Humanistic Studies in Utrecht, the Netherlands. Previously, she worked for several years as a humanistic counselor in the field of criminal justice. She started her career doing research in pure mathematics at the universities of Leiden and Essen (Germany). Her current research interests include existential, narrative, ethical, and political aspects of (pastoral/spiritual) counseling, meaning, and resilience.

Geir Skeie is Professor of Religious Education at University of Stavanger, Norway, and guest professor at Stockholm University, Sweden, and NTNU, the Norwegian University of Science and Technology, Trondheim. His research has focused on religion in education and religious education with both empirical and theoretical contributions. He has a particular interest in the challenges and possibilities for religious education raised by the diversity of religion and belief and, more broadly, by the socio-cultural context to which it belongs. Skeie has also done action research contributing to the development of religious education. He has had a leading role in several national and international research projects investigating religion and education. Presently he has initiated a development of systematic reviews in religious education research and has a leading role in the development of a new religious education curriculum in Norway.

Frans Wijsen is Professor of Practical Religious Studies and vice-dean of the Faculty of Philosophy, Theology, and Religious Studies at Radboud University, the Netherlands. He conducted fieldwork in Tanzania from 1984 to 1988 and worked as an assistant professor at the University of Theology and Pastoral Studies, the Netherlands, from 1988 to 1992, when he was appointed at Radboud University. He served as a Visiting Professor in Yogyakarta and Nairobi. Presently he is visiting professor in the Department of Sociology and Anthropology, University of Dar es Salaam, Tanzania. He is a board member of the Dutch Association for the Study of Religions (NGG) and a European representative of the African Association for the Study of Religions (AASR).

Edwin van der Zande has a background in Catholic Theology (MA, 2003). He is a teacher educator at the Hogeschool Utrecht, HU University of Applied Sciences Utrecht, the Netherlands. At this university he coordinates a minor program in Philosophy, World Religions, Worldviews and Spirituality. In this minor he primarily teaches Philosophy and Jewish, Christian, and Islamic Religion. He educates student teachers who want to specialize in teaching the subjects of Religious Education (RE) and Identity Formation at Catholic primary schools. As a PhD candidate he is a member of the research group "Normative Professionalization." His research project addresses the meaning of a personal worldview for Normative Professionalization. His interest lies with the dialogical process of meaning-making among students who come from different backgrounds, and the role played by religious and secular sources of wisdom within this process.

Introduction

Hans Alma and Ina ter Avest

'The times they are a-changin': after strong calls for democracy and freedom in the second half of the 20th century, many people in Western countries are inclined to call for 'strong leaders.' Is this a turn for good or for bad? Is the influence of leaders pivotal or marginal? And if leadership matters, how does it do so? These and related questions come to the fore in politics, in governmental institutions, and in non-profit organizations in different domains – for example, in education ('are leaders born or made?'), in the media (leading columnists influencing public feelings), and in the public domain (national and local governments taking the lead in discouraging segregation).

The call for 'strong leaders' is stimulated by the fear of terror attacks as a part of daily life, especially since the violent and iconic attack on the Twin Towers on September 11, 2001, which soon became known as '9/11.' As a consequence, a general feeling of fear for 'the other,' the foreigner, has become part of our existence. 'Us' versus 'them' dominates our thinking and divides our social world. However, this rough distinction easily masks a kind of intra-diversity in smaller groups of 'us' against 'them.' Even groups that at first sight present a homogeneous picture may upon closer inspection show a subdistinction among 'us' and 'them,' like baby boomers vs millennials, Moroccan Muslims vs Turkish Muslims, and so on.

The sense of 'us,' however, also opens up the possibility of bringing together different groups. For example, 'us' as born in the Netherlands includes people originating in Morocco, Turkey, Indonesia, and the province of Groningen. At the same time, when 'we' are pointing to 'them' as Muslims, 'them' includes people from Turkey, Morocco, and Indonesia, but definitely excludes the greater part of people from Groningen. This points to the complexity of identification, and the uncertainty regarding a sense of belonging. Gerd Baumann in *The Multicultural Riddle* (1999) speaks of cross-cutting cleavages. "What we thus find [in our age] is not a patchwork of five or even fifty fixed cultures, one definable without reference to the other, but precisely an elastic crisscrossing web of situational identifications" (Baumann, 1999, p. 123): a network society.

It is this crisscrossing that causes uncertainty and fear regarding people's sense of belonging. In this context no person or community "can be defined without reference to others," according to Baumann. He continues by stating that the practice of living together in a context of plural moralities is not "concerned with distinctiveness but with multi-relational thinking. The question that emerges from this relational thinking is 'Do we regard the so-called others as a necessary part of who we are?'" (1999, p. 124). According to Baumann, we have to rethink the dichotomy of 'us' and 'them': "The so-called 'others' form a necessary part of what 'we' think we are and want" (p. 125). Baumann favors convergence of different approaches regarding the (probably discordant) encounter with 'the other,' all pointing in the same direction, moving towards the same common point. In his 2004 publication, Baumann coins this common point as civil culture with its binding force of imaginary. The narratives of civil cultures, according to Baumann, building on Billig (1995, p. 42), are not "the result of grand designs by which scheming elites manipulate the populace: national imaginaries can work all the better when they use the trappings of banality: nationally propagated 'patterns of social life become habitual or routine: thoughts, reactions, and symbols are turned into routine habits and thus, they become *enhabited*'" (Baumann, 2004, p. 9). Civil culture and its narrative, Baumann states, are the result of the change from a mono-cultural to a plural context, resulting in the need to develop "a variety of ways to translate nation-state exclusivities into nationally specific, but productively inclusivist 'styles' (Anderson, 1991) of participation and identification" (2004, p. 3). People have to know about and recognize these dominant 'styles' – or 'voices' – in society and have to learn how to relate to and interact with them; a learning process of civil enculturation, of increasing understanding "that it is no longer about 'who you are,' for everyone has the right, at least in normative parlance, to cultural or ethnic difference, but about 'how one does,' for in that respect there must be some similarity of 'style,' regardless of the variety of 'roots'" (Baumann, 2004, p. 3). One of the new 'styles' people have to learn during this process of socialization in a civil culture is related to drawing boundaries between 'us' and 'them' – a matter of inclusion, exclusion, and expulsion – and the underpinning thereof. Civil enculturation on the one hand refers to the dynamic and flexible convergence to the same point between 'us' and 'them'; on the other hand it "strives hard at managing the seemingly paradoxical" of the integration of the specific loyalty of 'us' and the openness to all regardless of their identifications ('them') (cf. Baumann, 2004, pp. 12–13). Domination, Baumann stated in his earlier publication (1999) of either 'us' or 'them' in the focus on a common point on the horizon, or supremacy on the line of reasoning to arrive at that point, is unfit in terms of his view on civil enculturation and convergence. Each of the persons or groups follows an own and unique way of reasoning. For this process Baumann introduces the metaphor of the sextant, "an instrument of orientation in uncharted waters, but also such a precision instrument that it measures all things in relation of its user's position in historical time and space" (Baumann, 1999, p. 130). The sextant can be a helpful metaphor for moral and spiritual guidance in rapidly changing times. This line of thought can be traced in the work of scholars on innovative changes in all kinds of organizations and leadership styles in a context of plural moralities, as we will see next.

Liquid modernity

The uncertainty in today's societies is mirrored in all kinds of organizations – (non)governmental, healthcare, religious, educational, and societal – where changes are inevitable due for example to the migration pressure ('They grab our jobs!'), Brexit, the rising position of China in the world market, the rise of Evangelical movements and their political impact, and power shifts in global politics ('If mayors ruled the world'). In all cases people's call for strong leaders is a plea for an easy way out of the tensions resulting from the ongoing challenges that go with rapidly changing times.

With this book we address a pivotal theme in contemporary Western societies. Zygmunt Bauman (2000) coined the concept of 'liquid modernity' for the age we are living in. As people, information, ideas, weapons, and goods are 'on the move,' the meaning of boundaries changes. This is not only the case for boundaries between nation-states, but also for worldviews and religions, and for the boundaries between people of different hierarchical status in organizations. People have to find new ways for their life orientation, their moral and existential positioning. We witness an age of uncertainty and Bauman warns for a loss of sensitivity or 'moral blindness.'

Is there a way to resist the 'easy' solutions that (self) appointed strong leaders seem to offer, and to engage constructively with the complexity, vulnerability, and demands of our times? How can we strengthen democratic movements in societies and in organizations? Can education and pedagogical strategies, theories on moral leadership, and/or transformative dialogue offer ways out of these so-called easy solutions and seduce all persons concerned to living and working together in peace despite moral pluralities in the public sphere?

To respond to the challenges of the 'liquid modernity' in societies, various strategies at different levels of organization have been and still are developed to resist old solutions and to meet the requirements for dealing constructively with the entanglement and intersectionality of actual social situations. All these strategies focus on the dynamics of the group and by doing so more or less isolate the leader from the leader's team, which is hired to perform as well as it can to respond to problems and achieve a given target in line with the mission and vision of the organization. 'Agile leadership' is the newest offspring of the tree of leadership literature, but still with a focus on the leader's ability or inability to adapt flexibly to the needs of the group.

Ethics of organizing and organizations

In the voluminous publication *Images of Organization* (1986), Gareth Morgan takes a broad perspective and introduces an ecological approach of organizing, taking explicitly into account the relation with the context in which the organization establishes its activities. The question Morgan raises concerns the ethics of an organization, balancing on the tightrope of the organization's targets and profit and the contextual conditions. Morgan wrote for managers and professionals, inviting them to 'read' the situation-in-context that they tried to organize, or of which they were appointed as the leader. His approach, however innovative at that time, is mainly leader-oriented and focuses on the leader's moral judgment. Many years later, Edgar H. Schein, in his publication *The Corporate Culture Survival Guide: Sense and Nonsense About Culture Change* (1999), pointed to the imperative need for the leader to get to know the organizational culture – the artifacts, the espoused beliefs and values, and the underlying assumptions.

Schein, however, later shifted his emphasis from culture as a whole to a focus on leadership and its interrelatedness with the organizational culture. In *Organizational Culture and Leadership* (2004), Schein elaborates on the leader's interpretation of authority and the perception of conflict. It is particularly in conflictual situations that the ethical development and moral orientation of the leader is pivotal. Already in 2001, Joseph Kessels introduced the aspect of morality in the literature on leadership. In his public lecture at Twente University titled *Verleiden tot Kennisproductiviteit* (Temptation to Knowledge Productivity), Kessels works out in detail the ethical aspects of equality and equity, focusing on the leaders' capacity to establish a good relationship with the workers and to invite them to be partners on an equal footing in knowledge productivity.

This is not only of relevance for profit-organizations. For example, the non-profit initiative *Huizen van de Wijk* (Homes of the Neighborhood; Walraven & Witte, 2015) concentrates on shared knowledge productivity. To encourage autonomy, these 'homes' invite and give space to local inhabitants to organize the expertise and activities they need and to take responsibility. Activities range from pedagogical assistance for families to having a tea together, from religious prayers to football competitions or playing the typical Dutch play at shuffleboard. A strong ethics of shared responsibility and community engagement is at work here.

Whether the focus is on the context of the organization, the culture in the organization (de Caluwe, 2007), power relations (Witman, Smid, Meurs, & Willems, 2010), or the way to bring about change (Ardon, 2009), organizations mirror processes in all levels of society. In this volume we explore possible responses to the question of and in what way the ethics of organizing and leading innovative processes might initiate democratic processes in society-at-large in this age of 'liquid modernity' and plural moralities.

Existential concerns

Standing on the shoulders of previous scholars' findings regarding leadership in organizations, in this volume the authors explore the concept of 'leader' from diverse angles focusing on what guidance is needed in a time of plural moralities. This brings us to the next step in the reflection on leadership and leadership styles. The authors in our publication elaborate on (a) the moral and spiritual (potential) competencies of the person as a leader in that person's own 'society of mind' and/or of the appointed leader of a group, and (b) the way s/he approaches the plurality of life orientations and moralities that may cause feelings of uncertainty. The central question then becomes: How can leadership respond to the existential questions that go with the uncertainty of 'liquid times?' This question addresses a worldwide global uncertainty that is mirrored locally in societies, their institutions, and their organizations. We think these existential questions call for reflection and for the courage to create unusual responses in a world that suffers from the consequences of both neoliberalism, with its concurrent phenomena of consumerism, individualism, and worldwide exploitation, and (religious) radicalization, with its concurrent phenomena of intolerance, extreme violence, and discrimination of, amongst others, women and homosexuals. Not to mention the accompanying ecological crisis that may put an end to all ideological battles. We have to find new ways of living together in peace, working with the plurality of life orientations and their moralities. We must leave the well-trodden paths of 'easy' technical solutions and create innovative ways to live together, both with our fellow human beings and with the non-human world that not only surrounds us, but that has a dignity of its own. Our assumption is that we need new forms of moral and spiritual guidance that do not suffer from ideological and hierarchical 'superposition' of taken-for-granted moral and existential views. With this publication we expect to contribute to a thorough reflection on these issues.

We adopt a clear theoretical focus, choosing relational approaches to societal, organizational, and existential challenges. We address the issue of moral and spiritual guidance in 'liquid times' from both a relational and a dialogical perspective. We focus on relationships and practices that inspire people and tap their creativity in their search for meaning, and that foster democratic attitudes that reach beyond the limits of our current organizational, bureaucratic, and political systems.

Short description of the content

The driving force behind the volume is formulated in the question, how can we further develop theory and practice regarding moral and spiritual leadership, and/or transformative dialogue in the public sphere, in order to strengthen a democratic way of living together in a context of plural moralities?

In our view, 'plural moralities' are not so much about divergent beliefs about what is right or wrong behavior, but rather about encompassing views on the 'good life' as they can be found in late-modern societies. We choose the term 'moralities' (in plural) to leave space for different perspectives to be found in the volume: ethical, aesthetical, existential, spiritual. Of course, there is a difference between these concepts. Broadly speaking, moralities are about people's notions of the 'good' as they are imagined, articulated, and practiced in daily life. Conceptualization of and explicit reflection on these lived moralities belong to the field of ethics. We will see that several authors use related terms to do justice to the sensual and embodied dimensions of how people connect to the 'good' (aesthetics), to the ultimate concerns raised in this context (existential dimension), and to the experience of what people consider to be of ultimate importance, transcendent or holy (spiritual dimension). We will not give limiting definitions of these concepts, because we want to allow for free explorations of what plural moralities are about and what challenges for moral and spiritual leadership they pose.

We want to make clear from the beginning that we take a normative stance in this volume with a concern for democracy. We do not want to make the claim that democracy is the only way to live together in peace working with plural moralities. Our book does not offer a systematic comparison and evaluation of different societal forms that allow for such a peaceful living together. Yet, the authors come from and are committed to democratic societies. Many of them voice a concern for the way the democracies they live in are realized with undemocratic tendencies becoming manifest. Against this background, the central question of this volume is related to strengthening and improving democratic movements in the fields of organizations, education, and citizenship.

In the first part of the book, plural moralities are addressed from two theoretical perspectives: social constructionism and dialogical self theory (DST). With regard to social constructionism, the focus of Kenneth J. Gergen (Chapter 1) will be on developing a relational ethics that breaks away from normative ethical superiority and ethical relativism, and that considers the importance of relation and dialogue; ethics as an ongoing construction. From the perspective of DST, plural moralities will be addressed from the viewpoint of self as a society of mind and cultural multiplicity. The intention of Hubert J.M. Hermans (Chapter 2) is to further develop the DST approach regarding problems that arise in a glocalizing context and regarding issues of boundary-crossing (both literally and metaphorically), taking into account urgent themes as (de/re)radicalization and good leadership across boundaries of self, organization, and culture. Frans Wijsen (Chapter 3) explores the question, why and under what conditions are people no longer capable of shifting from one position to another, in accordance with different, and even contradictory situations? To answer this question, he consults and compares 'social identity' theory and 'multiple identity' or 'polyphonic self' ('dialogical self') theory, enlivening his argument with a case study. In the last chapter of this theoretical part (Chapter 4), Hans Alma relates people's search for meaning to the question, what do they consider to be good and meaningful in an aesthetical, existential, and spiritual sense? The search for meaning is discussed in terms of minoritization. Alma argues for a form of pluralism that rests on three pillars: justice as evenhandedness, building new connections that contribute to a sense of belonging, and moral imagination.

Next to these theoretical lines, in the second part of this book and with a focus on leadership, Ina ter Avest searches for '*good* leadership' and gives a short overview of different lines of thought. On her way from unilateral control to dialogical leadership, she arrives at the concept of relational leadership. This concept includes not only team members, colleagues, or subordinates, but also religious and secular worldview traditions, including their moralities. Ter Avest presents a reflection model for innovative leaders adjusting to plural moralities (Chapter 5). Rens van Loon and Angel S. Buster's focus (Chapter 6) is on *dialogicality* in leadership. Episodes of stories from Yann Arthus-Bertrand's movie *Human* are explored through the lens of dialogical self theory and dialogical leadership. All the narratives of the movie are expressions of explicit or more implicit moralities. According to van Loon and Buster, freeing space in the self allows for new perspectives to emerge, enabling one to lead oneself across the boundaries of self and culture. Questions of leadership are discussed by Jutta König in relation to *multicultural identity construction* (Chapter 7). She presents a case study illustrating the tensions of multiple belonging and how multiplicity and complexity show up in the multicultural identities of a multicultural person. Relational and dialogical interventions may be used, according to König, to help an individual refind focus. The case study also illustrates the tensions public and theoretical debates may cause within individuals.

The three following chapters focus on education. As a reaction to the statement of 'the need to improve the active promotion of Fundamental British Values' in English secondary schools, Julia Ipgrave (Chapter 8) explores the current promotion of these values. This is performed alongside different 'critical incidents' in recent history. Ipgrave argues that the concept of the relational self can provide a moral basis for communal living that each party can strengthen by interpreting it along the particular lines of their deepest understanding of the human being. The context of Dutch higher professional education is studied by Edwin van der Zande and Cok Bakker (Chapter 9). Van der Zande and Bakker argue that subjectivity is an integral and constitutive aspect of (normative) professionalization. They describe an educational minor program in philosophy, religion, and spirituality, in which students articulate their life orientation as a strategy for normative professionalization. They introduce concepts of the dialogical self theory in a narrative research into a moral and existential learning process as part of professionalization. Covering the Norwegian educational context, Geir Skeie (Chapter 10) discusses the possible contribution that issues of moral guidance, ethical reasoning, religious commitment and existential questions can have to education as a moral enterprise. An example is given from an action research project in upper secondary education, where dialogical approaches contributed to exploring questions of morality and existence both within and between students.

Toon van Meijl (Chapter 11) shifts our attention to a focus on citizenship in the context of the volume's central question about moral and spiritual leadership, and/or transformative dialogue in the public sphere. Van Meijl elaborates on the topical debate about the integration of people with a migration background in the Netherlands. He discusses the mechanisms of inclusion and exclusion and explores cosmopolitan sociabilities that are built on dialogue between participants of different ethnic, religious, and moral backgrounds. Politics of diversity in the public sphere are further explored by Mary Gergen (Chapter 12). She addresses the challenges of cohabitation when there are conditions of mutual loathing, disgust, and separation, as exemplified in various political, religious, and social venues in contemporary times. Relevant approaches are divided into three segments – Relational Engagement, Finding Common Ground, and Engaging in Transformative Potentials, and some concrete and challenging examples are included. Robin Knibbe and Carmen Schuhmann (Chapter 13) analyze what visions of the good appear in a refugee's narrative as orientation points, and the way in which the 'goodness' and the believability of these visions is questioned or negated in different relevant contexts. The case of a refugee woman connecting herself with a group of LGBTs (lesbian, gay, bisexual, transgender) is explored, focusing on (re)construction of this woman's moral orientation. The role of 'the other' (be it the real other or the other-in-the-self) is seen as pivotal in this process.

With our interdisciplinary and thematic approach as outlined here, this volume provides food for thought for all scholars and practitioners committed to leadership based on equality and equity – a dialogical leadership style in the face of a plurality of worldviews and value orientations.

References

Anderson, B. (1991). *Imagined communities: Reflections on the origin and spread of Nationalism*. London: Verso.

Ardon, A. (2009). *Moving moments: Leadership and interventions in dynamically complex change processes* (PhD thesis). Vrije Universiteit, Amsterdam.

Bauman, Z. (2000). *Liquid modernity*. Cambridge, Oxford, Boston, MA, and New York, NY: Polity Press.

Baumann, G. (1999). *The multicultural riddle: Rethinking national, ethnic, and religious identities*. London and New York, NY: Routledge.

Baumann, G. (2004). Introduction: Nation-state, Schools and Civil Enculturation. In W. Schiffauer, G. Baumann, R. Katoryano, & S. Vertovec (Eds.), *Civil Enculturation. Nation-State, Schools and Ethnic Difference in four European Countries*. New York/Oxford: Berghahn Books.

Billig, M. (1995). *Banal Nationalism*. London: Sage.

de Caluwe, M. (2007). *Managen van professionals? Niet doen!* [*Managing professionals? Don't do it!*]. Rotterdam, NL: Uitgeverij Scriptum.

Kessels, J. (2001). *Verleiden tot kennisproductiviteit* [*Temptation into knowledge productivity*]. Public Lecture Twente University of Technology.

Morgan, G. (1986). *Beelden van organisatie* [*Images of organization*]. Schiedam: Scriptum Books.

Schein, E. H. (1999). *The corporate culture survival guide: Sense and nonsense about culture change.* New York, NY: John Wiley and Sons Inc.

Schein, E. H. (2004). *Organizational culture and leadership.* Somerset, NJ: John Wiley and Sons Ltd.

Walraven, G., & Witte, T. (Eds.). (2015). *Lerende sociale professionals* [*Learning social professionals*]: *Werkboek Wmo praktijken* (pp. 44–59). Utrecht: Movisie, Wmo-werkplaatsen.

Witman, Y., Smid, G. A. C., Meurs, P. L., & Willems, D. L. (2010). Doctor in the lead: Balancing between two worlds. *Organization, 18*(4), 477–495.

Part I
Theoretical perspectives

1 Toward a relational ethic

Kenneth J. Gergen

Introduction

Several years ago I was having lunch with a philosopher friend, and described to her some of my theoretical work in social construction. The work focused on the way in which people together generate interpretations of what is real, rational, and good. As I explained, such ideas have been inspiring to many people, because they remove the rational grounds for any authority – whether secular or sacred – to dictate or determine what is true or good for all. A space is thus opened for the expression of all opinions. Yet, as I waxed enthusiastically about the implications of these views for science, education, and daily life, my companion grew quiet. When I paused for her reflections, I was met with a glowering silence. Finally, with clenched teeth, she let me know that she could no longer remain at the table with me. Dumbstruck, I pleaded to know the source of her irritation. As she explained, she had relatives who had died in the Holocaust, and the ideas I expressed offered no means of resisting Nazi atrocities. For constructionists, she reasoned, there was no commitment to an ethic that could stand in the way of such evil. This was intolerable.

We did work our way slowly through the entanglements of logic in such a way that we could complete the meal in relatively good terms. However, the experience was a powerful one, and its reverberations have continued to the present – now finding expression in the present offering. As I have now come to see it, we were caught that day within a tension of centuries' duration, reaching its zenith in the late 20th century. One might say we were still toiling with the outcome of the Enlightenment, in which the forces of reason and observation were set against religious beliefs. In the early 20th century, this tension emerged as the struggle between a secular and largely materialistic orientation to life and deep investments in spirituality, human values, and traditions of the sacred. As the century grew on, the Enlightenment echoes could be located in various forms of pluralism as against various efforts to sustain foundational values on the other side.[1]

Such dialogues continue, but now with a new and far more sinister edge. In my view, the emerging plethora of globe-spanning technologies of communication has radically intensified our differences. We have reached the point today at which values and beliefs have leaped from their geographical boundaries and are everywhere in conflict. Jet transportation enables one to relocate to virtually any other corner of the earth in less than 24 hours. By virtue of the World Wide Web, one may locate the like-minded in any geographical location, near or far. With email, one may remain in close contact with any acquaintance, no matter where they are. With smartphones we may instantly be in contact textually, auditorily, and visually. The result is that anyone seeking security in a tradition of value or belief can potentially locate around-the-clock support throughout the world. Communities of belief may thus engage in continuous reinforcement of their views, strengthening, intensifying, and expanding. With this solidification, all that is outside the wall of belief becomes alien, a potential threat. My luncheon colleague argued passionately, but hers is only one of myriad passions. As convictions spread and intensify, so the world becomes more deadly.

Paradoxically, however, these technologies that intensify a world of conflict also lend themselves to the deterioration of moral relevance. For large segments of Western culture, they undermine commitments to any belief or value whatsoever. Everywhere, individuals and organizations make strong claims to the moral high ground – in religion, politics, gender, race, and so on. All too often, such claims result in the demeaning, oppression, imprisonment, or murder of massive numbers of people. For those witnessing these effects, strong, passionate, or foundational claims to the good seem increasingly dangerous. Indeed, an inflexible commitment to any moral value seems childish or primitive.[2]

More problematically, a resistance to fundamentalism also lends itself to moral indifference.[3] Righteous claims to the good pose a danger. And if every group can make claims to 'the good' in its own terms, then no one's claims have commanding force – this includes the claims of government, the law, the church, one's parents, and so on. Thus "whatever I declare as good, is as legitimate as any other." Indeed, why should one bother inquiring into the good at all? Just live life as it comes, fulfill yourself, and don't bother with the rest. This is a world in which public lying, embezzlement, profiteering, fraud, intimidation, money laundering, tax evasion, and the like are not particularly shameful. The only significant problem is getting caught. Such views – often equated with moral relativism – find little resistance in the culture. There are no strong arguments against them, save those of yet another foundationalist enclave. Because of their alliance with the Enlightenment, and their need to remain non-partisan, our schools offer few resources for moral deliberation. Slowly, the resources for an ethical consciousness are bled from society.

We thus enter a period of history in which value commitments are moving in diametrically opposing ways. On the one hand, such commitments are moving toward an intense and globally threatening pitch; in stark contrast, in many enclaves of the world, value commitments are ceasing to be regarded or relevant. How are we thus to proceed? We cannot easily fall back on any of the traditional religions for an answer, because their very claims to moral authority contribute to the situation at hand. Nor can we in the West dip into the repository of ethical positions – from Aristotelian virtues, Kantian imperatives, or human capabilities – to sustain a universal imperative. All are byproducts of Western culture, and thus suspicious for those outside that culture. And, on what grounds could they establish moral authority? Whose tradition would justify these grounds? More directly relevant to world conditions are ethical positions that favor generalized love or care for others – for example, a feminist ethics of care (Tronto, 2005), or a Levinasian entreaty to attend to "the face of the other" (Levinas, 2005). But even here we are left with enormous ambiguities in how an ethic of care for the other would play out if 'the other' wishes to restrict education to males, abandon a two-state solution, expel immigrants, or segregate the races.

In what follows, I will open a space for an alternative orientation to ethics, one that could blunt the attempts to impose ethics that would silence all others, but that could simultaneously rekindle a concern with ethical deliberation. More precisely, I wish to generate an ethical standpoint that honors all visions of what is good or moral in human activity. At the same time, I will make no foundational claims for this meta-ethical standpoint. As ungrounded grounds, the proposal functions not so much as an imperative but rather as an invitation. Where will this take us? How would it benefit humankind or life on the planet more generally? What are we asked to sacrifice? The invitation to deliberation is inclusive. Yet, I do not view such deliberations as primarily conceptual in nature. The challenge here is not conceptual justification or a scholarly adventure into abstraction. Rather, the attempt is to explore the ethical implications in ongoing action. This means that neither a foundational commitment nor a relativistic insouciance will allow escape. The challenge lies in the way in which our actions play out together from moment to moment.

To explore what I shall call a relational ethic, I will first consider the origins of all moral orientations. This will invite an appreciation of the multiple and conflicting visions of the good now circulating the globe. It will also illuminate the closely related 'sources of evil.' This discussion sets the stage for considering the significance of relational process in giving rise to all moral orientations. Valuing this source of value thus serves as a meta-ethic. I then take up four domains of action that may ground the more abstract logic of relational ethics. This will allow us to confront the twin challenges of foundationalism and relativism.

The relational origins of good and evil[4]

The range of what humans have come to value over the centuries is virtually boundless – from the love of gods, community, country, love, self-realization, and equality, on the more sweeping side; to family, gun ownership, privacy,

and football on the more specific. One might even find values deeply insinu-
ated into every movement of the day – from the hour of arising, to the choice
of what one eats, to whom one speaks, to each of the websites visited as one
traverses cyberspace. To be sure, we find many speculations about universal
goods – for example, peace, benevolence, freedom, or sensual pleasure. But
for any value that one identifies in such efforts, there are people in various
conditions who will find war more desirable than peace, self-satisfaction
more appealing than benevolence, control more helpful than promoting
freedom, and asceticism more fulfilling than sensual pleasure. One is drawn,
then, to the ineluctable conclusion that moral values are specific to various
cultures or subcultures in various times and specific places.

Such a conclusion is no small matter because it reveals what may be
viewed as the primary source of values: human relationships. Whether any
activity is a good in itself – possessing intrinsic value – remains conjectural.
However, there is virtually no activity that some people at some time have
not resisted. The value of an activity does not emerge, then, from the activity in itself, but from the meaning it acquires in human interchange.[5] In this
sense, values acquire their meaning in the same way as language: participation in a social process. Virtually all relationships will generate at least
rudimentary understandings of 'what is good for us.' They are essential to
sustaining patterns of coordination. It should not be surprising, then, that
the term *ethics* is derived from the Greek, *ethos*, or essentially, the customs
of the people; or that the term *morality* draws from the Latin root, *mos*, or
mores, thus equating morality with custom. Our constructions of reality
walk hand in hand with our logics, and our moralities.

Let us view this movement from rudimentary coordination to value formation in terms of first-order morality. To function within any viable relationship will virtually require embracing, with or without articulation, the
values inherent in its patterns. When I teach a class of students, for example,
first-order morality is at work. We establish and perpetuate what has become
the 'good for us.' There are no articulated rules in this case, no moral injunc-
tions, no bill of rights for students and teachers. The rules are all implicit,
but they touch virtually everything we do, from the tone and pitch of my
voice, my posture, and the direction of my gaze to the intervals during which
students may talk, the loudness of their voice, and the movement of lips, legs,
feet, and hands. One false move and any of us becomes the target of scorn.
In effect, morality of the first order is essentially being sensible within a way
of life.[6] In the same vein, most people do not deliberate about murdering
their best friend, not because of some principle to which they were exposed
in their early years, and not because it is illegal. It is virtually unthinkable.
Similarly, it would be unthinkable to break out in a tap dance at a holy mass,
or to destroy a colleague's laboratory. To be sure, such ways of life may be
solidified in our laws, sanctified by our religions, celebrated in our moral
deliberations, and intensively articulated in ethical theory. We live our lives
largely within the comfortable houses of first-order morality.

It is at this point that we also join hands with writings on moral or value pluralism. As often attributed to Isaiah Berlin (1991), we recognize the possibility of a range of fundamentally different, incommensurable, and potentially conflicting traditions of morality. And, while pluralist writings are often equated with political liberalism – standing against fascism or absolutism of any kind – less is said about 'origins of evil.' But consider: whenever people come into coordination, first-order morality is in the making. As we strive to find mutually satisfactory ways of going on together, we begin to establish a local good, "the way we do it." Simultaneously, the emergence of 'the good' creates an alternative of the less than good. A range of actions are now featured as off limits, or forbidden – a door behind which lies mystery. All children know the joy of breaking the rules, whispering in class, laughing at a prank, stealing a cookie. And what is forbidden always invites the curiosity of "what if. . . ." Further, there is rebellion against the tyranny of the enforcer. "Why can't I . . .?" "Who says I can't . . .?" "I don't take orders from you."

The potential for immorality is furthered by the fact that most cultural traditions carry multiple values, variously important or emphasized depending on context. We place a value on working hard, and on playing; on freedom, and on responsibility; on obedience, and on disobedience; on fitting in, and on being unique; on pleasing others, and on autonomy; and so on. Thus the stage is set for choosing the good, and simultaneously being scorned or punished for being bad. One should care for one's family, but may be jailed for stealing to fill their needs; women should have the right to abort, but be ostracized for doing so; a president should not lie, but will be protected by his colleagues if the lie enhances the power of their party. 'Bad actions' may always seem to be a 'good idea at the moment.' And, of course, we now confront the clashes of civilizations, as deeply entrenched traditions of the good come face to face, often finding a threatening evil in the other.

Relational process: the ethical invitation

As I am proposing, as people coordinate their actions, creating a way of life that will optimally be harmonious and nourishing, they are laying the groundwork for what we call moral action. In this sense, moral action is always under production, whether unstated and little regarded, or articulated and staunchly defended. This also leaves us with the following paradox: the very production of first-order moralities also establishes the conditions for immorality. But whatever is immoral for one may be valued by another. In this sense, conflicting goods will always be with us. The challenge is not to achieve a conflict-free existence, but to locate ways of approaching conflict that do not bend toward mutual extermination. Given the challenge of moral apathy, are there means of inspiring moral engagement without the demands of singular commitment?

It is just here that we can return to the original source of moral commitment, and indeed, meaning of any kind: coordinated action. The value of harmonious relationships is scarcely new to ethical inquiry. However, almost invariably the ethic has restated on a fundamental assumption of separation. The ethically informed person acts toward others in a way that harmony will ensue: "*I* do unto *others*," "*I* am compassionate toward *others*," "*I* am caring for *others*," and so on. By focusing on the emergence of human meaning, we shift from this traditional concern with individuals to the more fundamental process of relating. Out of this process, the very idea of individuals is created. Human communication is essentially the outcome of coordination among persons. Like language, moral leanings are not the product of any single person. They depend on relational process. Without this process, we have no religion, science, political institutions, commerce, education, or organizations. There is nothing to care about or live for – big or small. Regardless of tradition – existing or in the making – the positive potentials of this process are vital. If we all draw life from this process, then it demands our collective attention. Here we may speak of what should be a universal concern, the grounding for a relational ethic.

Now consider the consequences of the paradoxical relation between 'good and evil.' Most typically, challenges to a moral order are met with resistance. As children we are encouraged to 'be good' through rewards, and our failures are met with irritation, lectures, correction, penalties, and physical punishment. In each case, a space of alienation emerges between the parties. Then there are the more heinous actions – robbery, extortion, rape, drug dealing, or murder. It is here we find a dangerous transformation in the quest for the good. In the case of these more threatening actions, an impulse toward elimination is often unleashed. This is typically accomplished through various forms of defense (surveillance, policing), curtailment (imprisonment, torture), or, more radically, through extermination (death penalty, invasion, bombs). This shift from alienation to elimination can be accompanied by a sense of deep virtue.

As we shift from alienation to elimination, we also undermine the potentials of positive coordination. Placed in jeopardy is the process of coordination, from which reality, rationality, and a sense of the good is derived. As the eliminative impulse is set in motion, and we move toward mutual annihilation, we approach the end of meaning. It is precisely here that a relational ethic becomes imperative. Required is participation in a process that can restore, sustain, and strengthen the possibility of morality making. In the embrace of a relational ethic, we sustain the possibility of morality of any kind.

From the standpoint of a relational ethic, there are no individual acts of evil, for the meaning of all action is derived from relationship. Holding individuals responsible for untoward actions not only is misguided but results in alienation and retaliation. In the case of a relational ethic, individual responsibility is replaced by relational responsibility, or a responsibility for sustaining the potential for positive coordination (McNamee & Gergen, 1999). To be responsible to relationships is to devote attention and effort to means of sustaining the potential for co-creating meaning. When the wheels of individual responsibility are set in motion, relationships typically go off track. Blame is followed by excuses and counterblame. In being responsible for relationships, we step outside this tradition, and care for the relationship becomes primary. In relational responsibility we avoid the narcissism implicit in ethical calls for 'care of the self' and as well, the self-negation resulting from the imperative to 'care for the other.'

One may argue that this proposal for a relational ethic simply reconstitutes the problems inherent in foundational ethics. Is this not equivalent to declaring that people *ought* to be responsible for the process of sustaining coordinated relationships? If so, is this not another hierarchy of the good in which the irresponsible are deemed inferior and in need of correction? Such a critique presumes, however, that lying beneath a relational ethic is some kind of moral authority, a bedrock on which it is established. There is no such foundation. The logics put forward here are themselves issuing from traditions of the good, no less socially constructed than all others. To be sure, the account provides a form of meta-ethic, but in the end it can only invite participation. It is not an authoritative pronouncement, but an invitation to re-coordination.

Relational ethics in practice

Thus far the proposal for a relational ethic is abstract and minimally explicated. Further development is needed, and this development should itself reflect the participation of many voices. To invite such discussion, what follows is an exploration of critical dimensions of ethical action. It is one thing to lay out a rationale for a meta-ethic, but what kind of actions would realize its implications? What is it to 'act ethically' from a relational standpoint? While this question may seem transparent enough, preliminary attention is required. As we shall see, the traditional relationship between ethical theory and practice – with abstract formulations dictating action – is problematic. Simultaneously thrown into critical relief is the concept of moral agency.

The philosophy of ethics has primarily been an exercise in language. Inquiries into 'what is the good' are exercises in discourse, with a reasoned account of ideal consciousness as the goal. An ethically informed consciousness should provide the grounds for ethical action. Yet, there is a major problem inhering in these attempts, one that threatens their relevance to cultural life. This is the challenge of deduction: how one is to derive from a general category of the good – or an ethical consciousness – a set of particular actions. The ideal category of the good provides no rules as to what counts as an instantiation. If one seeks to be kind, compassionate, tolerant, or appreciative, for example, what precisely is entailed in the way of action? What does one say, with what tone of voice, with what direction of one's gaze, and with what posture or movements of the arms and hands? We may all agree that it is good to 'love one another,' but what it means to love in terms of concrete actions varies dramatically – from a simple smile, to restricting a child's behavior, to smothering another in kisses, or smothering them with a pillow.

The relational account developed here adds a further level of complexity. One's actions in themselves do not count as kind, compassionate, or loving, for example. One's actions come into these meanings depending on the coordinated action of others. If one's self-considered action is 'compassionate,' and another reacts to it as 'condescension,' then it ceases for the moment to be compassion. Attention thus shifts from the traditional assumption of the 'moral agent' who engages in 'moral action' to morally rich processes of relating.

It is here that Wittgenstein's landmark work, *Philosophical Investigations*, is of special significance. Placed in question by this work is the traditional view of language as a picture of the world. By abandoning this view, the problem of deduction is also eliminated. If our accounts of love, compassion, care, and so on are not pictures of the world, then there is no problem of deducing what counts as instantiations of these accounts. In Wittgenstein's outline of a use-based account of language, our attention shifts to the pragmatic uses of ethical languages in ongoing social life. Ethical philosophy, cut away from 'contexts of application,' runs the risk of irrelevance. The most sophisticated theories of the good may undermine their potential through their very sophistication.

Thus, in what follows, I wish to explore four domains of ethical action from a relational standpoint. In each case, I attempt to wed conceptual ideals to practices of relationship.

Caring communication

If the primary value is placed on processes of relating that foster, sustain, and enrich the process of relating itself, then major attention shifts to our practices of communication. What forms of communication can achieve these ends? How can we relate with each other in ways that *care for the relationship itself*? When there is shared agreement on a way of life, common, civil communication may itself nourish relationship. The simple participation in a traditional way of life together symbolically honors 'our way.' To chat lightly with Emily, the cashier at the local grocery store, may seem a trivial event, but it is the kind of glue that holds the community together. At the same time, there is a sustained tendency toward fragmentation in any culture, with those sharing tradition drawing together in separation from others. On university campuses, for example, communication within departments of study far eclipses communication across departments. In corporations, there are separations in terms not only of management levels, but of the functions served (e.g., operations, marketing, R&D). Wherever people organize – in government, religion, hospitals, schools, and so on – there are tendencies toward separation. In effect, there may be care *within* various enclaves, but relations *among* them are threatened.

It is here that we may appreciate the ethical implications of far-reaching efforts to enhance collaborative practices. In universities, there is increasing reliance on collaborative research; in technology labs is now the major source of creativity; in classrooms collaborative projects are now common forms of teaching; many therapists now see their relationship with clients as a collaboration; in healthcare there is a shift toward collaboration across specialties, with the patient now included as part of the team; military top-down structures of command and control are giving way to linking collaborating teams; and in business, the practice the need for collaborative leadership is increasingly realized. To this we must add international collaborations to combat global warming, protect wildlife habitats, control the spread of diseases, coordinate air traffic, and much more. As practices of collaboration become instilled into the routines of daily life, we embody a relational ethic. For more on relevant practices of dialogue and collaboration, see Skeie (Chapter 10 in this volume), van Meijl (Chapter 11 in this volume), and M. Gergen (Chapter 12 in this volume).

Conscience: responsible to all

One might take a dim view of relational ethics on the grounds that it stands for so little in itself. Where are the hard questions of the world – questions of human rights, the rise of fascism, racism, and so on? To be sure, nothing within a relational ethic provides a foundation for voicing either support or resistance in such cases. At the same time, however, there are no foundational arguments against voicing preferences in any such cases. This is not for a lack of what might be called 'conscience' within the relational orientation. On the contrary, a relational ethic calls for an overflowing conscience. That is, to champion relational process is to treat with respect the intelligibility of all participants, even when other views are disagreeable. It is to carry the voices of all value orientations, to respect their validity within the circumstances in which those values were created. Every voice of value, no matter how heinous to others, carries the assumption of its own good. To be relationally responsible is to defend the rights of all to make themselves intelligible. One may surely resist what is seen as 'evil action,' but with a sense of humility –with respect to both one's own lack of fundamental grounds and the realization that, under identical circumstances, a similar choice could have been made.

What would this expanded form of conscience mean in action? It would favor, for example, supporting movements for social justice, for minority rights, or against tyranny of any kind, but without pathologizing those who might be targets of such movements. It would be to support those who speak out against sexual harassment, but respecting the possibility of alternative intelligibilities. In many cases, a relational ethic would lend support to the expression of multiple goods. Thousands are escaping the bloodshed and poverty in their home countries and seeking entry – often illegal – into other lands. The legal voice is relevant to such conditions, but it should function as only one voice among many. Here it is important that multiple expressions be set in motion, including those of the immigrants, citizen enclaves, economists, religious figures, educators, and so on.

Creativity: confluence in motion

A relational ethic is an ethic of improvisation and innovation. It is an ethic of improvisation because the daily challenge of sustaining harmonious relations with others requires continuous agility. At base, every conversation is a novel event. The words that are spoken, the way they are spoken, and the context in which they occur are always new. This means that all utterances harbor a certain ambiguity; one's interlocutors may shift the direction of their meaning in many ways. What seems to be a compliment may be construed by its recipient as a subtle criticism, a way of currying favor, a means of demonstrating superiority, an act of kindness, or something else altogether. And responses to this seeming compliment may also be construed in many ways. Whether the pair emerges from the conversation as caring companions or alienated acquaintances depends on coordination in improvisational skills.

A relational ethic also favors innovative action. This is so because all traditions of the good are limited in their forms of action. One may be taught from an early age that 'giving to the poor' is commendable. One may thus be drawn by the plight of the beggar on the street, and feel pangs of guilt in hurriedly passing by. It would not occur to one in this tradition that giving is an evil. And yet, for inner city workers attempting to reduce drug dependency, this is a warranted conclusion. Food and shelter are available to the homeless, it is argued. Money that is begged is likely to maintain a drug habit. The point here is especially important in terms of attempts to bridge contrasting moral traditions. If traditions are limited in their forms of action, then bridging work requires innovation – the creation of forms of action that may invite participation from differing traditions but be new to all. This is particularly relevant in the context of the global clash of moral traditions and the ensuing bloodshed. What Alma (Chapter 4 in this volume) calls a *moral imagination* is required. We may thus applaud the work of various groups – in peace building, community building, interreligious dialogue, mediation, witnessing, repatriation, and the like – attempting to create new forms of dialogue. Rather than settle for the "natural ways we talk with each other," they consciously set out to create new forms of interchange for building or restoring viable relations. Such efforts should not be limited to grassroots organizations, as they often are, but should also be shared by major institutions of business and government. Especially related to issues of leadership, see also ter Avest (Chapter 5 in this volume) and van Loon and Buster (Chapter 6 in this volume).

Continuation: process over outcome

There is a strong tradition in Western culture to seek decisive conclusions. It is within this tradition that *truth*, as a singular and universal account of the world, has had a prevailing sway. And it is within this context that the discourses of *principles, certainty, clarity, resolution, resolve, grounding, outcomes, solutions,* and *scores* have played a contributing role. All such discourse lends itself to final fixing, certain knowledge – ensuring a 'last word.' From a relational standpoint, a last word is no word at all, as its meaning will not be revealed until others coordinate with it in some way. A last word is the end of conversation, the end of communication, and thus the end of meaning. From a relational standpoint, then, the action focus is not on ultimate outcomes, but in the continuing conversation.

Here the work of Catholic theologian David Tracy is illuminating. As Tracy (1987) points out, there is a strong tendency in the major religious traditions to fix the nature of God, good and evil, the nature of human beings, the universe, and so on. Religious texts such as the Bible or the Qur'an are often used in this way. As Tracy argues, however, such texts always permit multiple interpretations. Not only are the texts inherently ambiguous, but the differing assumptions, values, visions, and so on that the reader brings to the text will permit or invite different interpretations. For Tracy, this is not a failing, but an invitation to increase the richness of the text. Thus, the readings of texts within various traditions "are different construals of Ultimate Reality itself" (Tracy, 1987, p. 90). For Tracy this is a clarion call to interfaith dialogue, as multiple construals add enriching laminations to our understanding and to the potentials for spiritual life (Tracy, 1991). For Tracy, engaging in such dialogue is itself a spiritual action. Also see Ipgrave (Chapter 8 in this volume) for a discussion of the significance of plural interpretation.

It is in this context that a relational ethic places a premium on the continuous process of relating. Issues of moral import should not be *solved*, thus permitting participants to retire with a sense of righteous satisfaction. Rather, recognizing the ambiguity inherent in such decisions, and the potential for multiple standpoints, there should be no principled end to the conversation. In terms of action, such a logic favors mediation over the structure of contention within the legal system. In the classroom, it also favors dialogic pedagogy with an emphasis on multiplicity in interpretation. Examinations and testing of students should be replaced by more relational processes that enlist multiple voices in an atmosphere of mutual respect. If properly conducted, it favors town meetings, and community-wide projects. In such practices we do not *apply* a relational ethic; we embody it in practice.

Beyond conclusions

My attempt in this offering has been to find a means of pressing toward an ethical form of life that would avoid the way in which competing ethical positions invite extremist intolerance and bloodshed on the one hand, and a moral lethargy on the other. The hope is that by bringing into focus the very origins of moral action, we might locate a process that could be embraced by all traditions. As proposed, moral action and ethical reasoning emerge within relational process. Thus, it is the life-giving potential within this relational process that must be placed in the forefront of concern. As also reasoned, ethical theory should not proceed, cut apart from the forms of life that might give it meaning. Thus, discussion was opened on various forms of action coherent with proposal for a relational basis of moral action.

To be sure, many issues remain unexamined in this treatment. It may first be apparent that in explicating a relational ethic, most of the discussions in the domains of practice concerned the challenge of moral or ethical conflict; how to bring people together, sustain dialogue, collaborate, and so on. Little was said about the twin problem of pluralism, namely a lethargic relativism. What does a relational ethic offer to those who simply shrug their shoulders in the face of moral issues? It is cavalier to suppose that, even if introduced into our educational systems, the reasoning offered here for a relational ethic would invite a transformation in ethical sensitivity. But, as advanced earlier, ethics in the abstract are little more than language games. The challenge is to embed the abstractions within forms of cultural life. In my view, the beginning of ethical consciousness lies, then, in participation in ethically relevant forms of life.

Most children learn at an early age not to lie, cheat, or steal, and for most, the lessons are sustained for a lifetime. Very few, however, would be able to provide an in-depth rationale for why these are unethical acts. Thus, in confronting the issue of moral lethargy, the primary emphasis may properly be placed on instituting forms of activity that privilege positive relational process. In education, as pointed out, pedagogies of collaboration are highly consistent with a relational ethic. Dialogic classroom practices can foster mutual understanding and tolerance, along with an appreciation for the creative outcomes of working together in groups. Much the same may be said of the increasing prominence of project learning, in which students work collaboratively toward a goal. Testing and grading practices generally work against generative relationships. They invite alienation and distrust among students, between students and teachers, and between students and their families. There is great advantage in replacing traditional assessment with practices of evaluation built into dialogic and collaborative processes, along with shared reflection on learning process (Gergen & Gill, forthcoming). In this case we build moral muscle not through declarations of the good, but through ethically informed practice.

A second significant silence in the present account concerns cases of illegal and/or onerous action. Consider here, for example, acts of pedophilia, murder, or terrorism. While illegal and detestable, the actor can offer arguments for their intelligibility. Now, much of the earlier discussion in this chapter presumed the possibility of interchange – the bridges for communication could be built between otherwise disagreeing parties. Mutual understanding and transformation might result. In the cases of actions of deep repugnance, such bridges would seem impossible. While one might come to understand why these acts were intelligible, they would still be roundly condemned, and incarceration enthusiastically endorsed. At the same time, such a conclusion would lead us into a *cul de sac*; it would suggest that a relational ethic is just fine until it isn't. Can we extend the ethic, then, to include cases of deep repugnance? Again, continuing discussion is needed; but again, we gain some purchase by considering realms of practice. The Truth and Reconciliation Commission in South Africa, healing the wounds of apartheid, is exemplary. The increasing numbers of restorative justice programs also point in a promising direction. And a relational ethic would entail abandoning the death penalty.

Yet, while opening a space for an overarching ethical orientation, the present attempt is scarcely complete. It cannot be complete in principle, because if the attempt is itself coherent with the ethic it espouses, it is essential to sustain multiparty deliberation. One might say that the proposal is for an ever-emerging theory and practice. The present account is but the beginning of a conversation.

Notes

1 See also Taylor (2007) on the rise of the secular age.
2 See also Stout (1988) on the failure of foundationalism and its contribution to moral malaise.
3 A resistance to religious foundationalism is scarcely the result of multiple and competing claims. The general drift of the West toward secularism, often traced to the period of the Enlightenment, is clearly relevant (cf. Taylor 2007). Many hold that the secularist drift is now prevailing globally. As Bullard (2017) reports in *National Geographic*, the "world's newest great religion is no religion."
4 A preparatory note: Concepts of 'the good,' the 'moral,' and the 'ethical' are closely bound. In my view, the sense of 'good' functions as a primitive (we may find it 'good' to have peace and quiet); when the sense of good is codified or articulated we speak of it as 'morality' (it is a moral good that we don't disrupt others' wellbeing, for example, by playing loud music); and when we provide a conceptual account of why such morality is imperative, we enter the field of ethics.
5 The remainder of this discussion draws from Gergen (2007, 2009).
6 Also see McIntyre's (2007) discussion of the way in which these ways of life are realized in individual identity and responsibility.

References

Berlin, I. (1991). *The crooked timber of humanity*. New York, NY: Random House.
Bullard, G. (2017). The world's newest great religion: No religion. *National Geographic*. Retrieved from https://news.nationalgeographic.com/2016/04/160422-atheism-agnostic-secular-nones-rising-religion/

Gergen, K. J. (2007). Relativism, religion and relational being. *Common Knowledge, 13,* 362–378.

Gergen, K. J. (2009). *Relational being: Beyond self and community.* New York, NY: Oxford University Press.

Gergen, K. J., & Gill, S. (forthcoming). *Relational evaluation: Beyond the tyranny of testing.* New York, NY: Oxford University Press.

Levinas, E. (2005). *Humanism of the other.* Evanston, IL: University of Illinois Press.

MacIntyre, A. (2007). *After virtue: A study in moral theory* (3rd ed.). South Bend, IN: Notre Dame University Press.

McNamee, S., & Gergen, K. J. (1999). *Relational responsibility: Resources for sustainable dialogue.* Thousand Oaks, CA: Sage Publications.

Stout, J. (1988). *Ethics after babel: The language of morals and their discontents.* Princeton, NJ: Princeton University Press.

Taylor, C. (2007). *A secular age.* Cambridge, MA: Harvard University Press.

Tracy, D. (1987). *Plurality and ambiguity: Hermeneutics, religion, and hope.* Chicago, IL: University of Chicago Press.

Tracy, D. (1991). *Dialogue with the other.* Leuven: Peeters Press.

Tronto, J. C. (2005). An ethic of care. In A. Cuddi & R. Andreasen (Eds.), *Feminist theory: A philosophical anthology* (pp. 251–263). Oxford: Wiley Blackwell.

2 Dialogical self theory in a boundary-crossing society

Hubert J.M. Hermans

Introduction

My purpose in this chapter is to present the historical background and basic concepts of dialogical self theory (DST) and to investigate its moral implications. The theory has been developed on the basis of the consideration that a dialogical self is a necessity in a globalizing society in which national, cultural, and regional boundaries are transcended as never before. In such a world, individuals and groups are confronted with their apparent historical and cultural differences, yet forced to communicate with each other as parts of an increasingly compressed world society. I will demonstrate that such differences and communications take place not only between people, but also within their own selves. An important implication of this view is that, in order to function in a boundary-crossing world, people are challenged to deal not only with different people, but also with the differences, tensions, and uncertainties in their own selves.

The central message of the present contribution is based on the observation that many of the social processes that can be observed in society at large, such as dialogical relationships and dominance struggles, also take place within the self as a 'society of mind.' In this view, the self functions not as an entity in itself, as something pre-given, with society as a facilitating or inhibiting environment; but as emerging from social, historical, and societal processes that transcend any individual – society dichotomy or separation. The self is not an entity separated from society. Instead, society works *in* the self, at the same time requiring an answer *by* the self (Hermans, 2018). As we will see in this chapter, the self, conceptualized as a mini-society of *I*-positions, functions as an integrative part of the society at large.[1]

DST weaves two concepts, self and dialogue, together in such a way that a more profound understanding of the interconnection of self and society is reached. Usually, the self refers to an internal state of mind, something that happens *within* the individual mind, while 'dialogue' is typically associated with something 'external,' processes that take place *between* people involved in communication. In the composite concept 'dialogical self' this dichotomy is transcended as bringing the external to the internal and, in reverse, transporting the internal to the external. This enables one to investigate the self as a society of '*I*-positions' and to consider society as populated, stimulated, and renewed by the selves of its individual participants. I believe that the self-society interconnection allows one to abandon any self-society dualism and any conception which regards the self as essentialized and encapsulated in itself. Moreover, it avoids the limitations of a 'self-less society' that lacks the opportunity to become enriched by the knowledge and creativity that the individual human self has to offer to existing social practices.

DST as inspired by James and Bakhtin

From a historical point of view, DST finds its origin at the interface of traditions in the social and literary sciences: American pragmatism and Russian dialogism. As a theory of the self, it is inspired by James's (1890) classic formulations on the workings of the self. As a dialogical theory, it elaborates on the fertile insights in dialogical processes proposed by Bakhtin (1984). (For extensive treatment of the influence of these theorists on DST, see Hermans & Hermans-Konopka, 2010.)

DST and James

DST assumes that the self is functioning as a dynamic multiplicity of *I*-positions in the self as a society of mind. Already James (1890), in his ground-breaking chapter 'The consciousness of self,' wrote "a man has as many social selves as there are individuals who recognize him and carry an image of him in their mind." He added, "he has as many social selves as there are distinct groups of persons about whose opinion he cares. He generally shows a different side of himself to each of these different groups" (p. 294). In agreement with these statements, DST assumes that the self is extended not only to other individuals, but also to a diversity of groups. When an individual or group is felt as significant to one's life, it is belonging to the self in the *extended* sense of the term. This extension has the advantage of opening the door to a conception of the self as transcending the limitations of the individualized container notion that has been so strongly emphasized in Western culture. For the *I*-position, as a theoretical concept, this means that it covers not only the first-person singular pronoun 'I,' but also its extension in the first-person plural pronoun 'we' and the second-person pronoun 'you' as referring to the other-in-the-self (see also Schuhmann and Knibbe, Chapter 13 in this volume).

In the line of the extended self proposed by James, DST makes a distinction between internal positions as part of the internal domain of the self (e.g., I as a man, husband, psychologist) and external positions that belong to the external domain of the self (e.g., my wife, my children, my colleagues, my opponent). Usually, the self contains relationships between internal and external positions (e.g., I as a father of three children, I as a colleague of John, or I as an opponent to demagogic political leaders).

DST and Bakhtin

The intimate relationship between 'I' and 'we,' as expressed by the extended self in terms of James, was also emphasized by Bakhtin (1984). Inspired by his reading of novelistic literatures, he proposed that all utterances are multivoiced and dialogical at the same time. In the act of speaking there are at least two voices: the voice of the speaking individual, and the voice of a social group (e.g., one's circle of friends, one's professional group, or one's dialect). In Bakhtin's view, the spoken word is 'half foreign,' as the collective voice of a social group is expressed through the mouth of the individual speaker (see also van Meijl, Chapter 11 in this volume). The speaker infuses the collective voice with her/his own intentions and expressive tendencies (e.g., I speak as a therapist or a scientist, but at the same time I combine it with my own opinion). The social languages are personalized and colored by one's own expressive and meaning-giving tendencies. The 'I' expresses an implicit 'we,' and the 'we' is personalized by the 'I.' In agreement with Bakhtin, DST considers the self as multivoiced and dialogical. Each position has an own specific view on the world and a different story to tell. As a voiced position, it is able to communicate with the world outside and with other positions in the self as an organized society of mind.

The spatial and temporal nature of positioning

The concept of 'position' has a spatial nature, and also dialogue is deeply spatialized. This can be illustrated by referring to the difference between logical and dialogical relationships (Bakhtin, 1984; Vasil'eva, 1988). Consider two completely identical phrases, 'life is good' and again 'life is good.' Considered from the angle of Aristotelian logic, these two phrases are related in terms of *identity*, because they are one and the same statement. From a dialogical perspective, however, the two statements are different, because they are expressed by the voices of two spatially separated people involved in communication, who entertain a relationship of *agreement*. From a logical point of view, the two phrases are identical; but as utterances, they are different because they are coming from the mouths of two people who have different positions in space. The first phrase is a statement, the second a confirmation. Similarly, the phrases 'life is good' and 'life is not good' can be analyzed. Within the framework of logic, one is a *negation* of the other. However, as utterances from two different speakers, there is a relation of *disagreement*.

There are spatial differences not only between two people in communication, but also between different positions and voices in the self of one and the same person. Two voices in the self have different spatial positions, and what they tell is determined not only by these positions but also by the nature of their dialogical interchange. When I'm involved in an imagined conversation with my mother, she is somewhere 'there' in my mind, located in a place in my self-space that is different from the place 'here' from which I address her. Somewhere she is in front of me, yet connected with me in my self-space. This spatial difference can be experienced not only in the imagined contact with a dear parent, wise adviser, or understanding friend, but also with purely imaginary figures, such as spirits, figures appearing in dreams, or imaginary companions in the fantasy world of playing children.

Positioning and repositioning

A conceptual advantage of the concept of positioning is that it is used not only in the active but also in the passive tense. I'm not only positioning myself towards another or myself (e.g., criticizing myself), but I'm also positioned by the other. I can look at myself through the perceived eyes of the other, a capacity of the self that Cooley (1902) had in mind when presenting his looking glass self. I can perceive the other as seeing me as friendly, nasty, cooperative, abusing, or a frantic freak. I perceive myself as positioned via the mirror in which the other appears to me.

At birth, or already during pregnancy, we are positioned as a 'girl' or a 'boy' with far-reaching consequences for our training and education. At a very young age we are positioned as 'sweet' or 'naughty,' or as 'good' or 'bad,' by significant others who impose these strongly emotional and morally loaded notions as influential qualifications on us. In cases of a religious or spiritual education, children learn from a young age onward what is 'good' or 'bad.' Although these ways of positioning can have a far-reaching influence on the later organization of the self, we are not purely determined by their evocations. On the contrary, we have the inherent capacity to *respond* to their positioning by taking counter-positions, such as agreement, disagreement, protest, opposition, or the generation of alternatives.

The process of positioning is not only spatial but also temporal. In the course of time, we may, in particular situations, *reposition* ourselves when, for example, we move from one position to another (e.g., from school to job, from one job to another, from single to married, from married to divorced). In addition, we may become *repositioned* via the signs and messages communicated by others towards us (e.g., in case of job loss, receiving a degree, as becoming old). Being positioned and repositioned by others influences, more or less, our identity in society (e.g., as immigrant, cultural other, racial other) which in turn evokes forms of counter-positioning and repositioning from the part of our selves.

All processes described in this section are part of the self as a dynamic multiplicity of *I*-positions in the society of mind. The dynamic-spatial manifestation of the *I*-position is in the process of positioning and counter-positioning.

Its dynamic-temporal manifestation is in the process of positioning and repositioning.

Difference with self-categorization and self-presentation

Positioning is not to be confused with what is known as self-definition or self-categorization. When I define or categorize myself as friendly, I see myself as a subject on my own to whom I attribute a particular personality trait or characteristic (friendliness). In contrast, when I position myself as friendly, I take a *stance* towards another person, that is, I direct myself or orient myself towards the other as an embodied being in a spatial configuration. When I categorize myself as a Dutch, I define myself as belonging to a specific group of people. However, when I position myself as Dutch in company with people from other countries, I place myself in relation to a representative of another nation. So, positioning is a form of addressivity towards a spatially located other. Because of this addressivity, a position is always questioned, confirmed, modified, or rejected by other positions. It can never escape its connection with other positions and, therefore, can never be considered purely as a thing-in-itself.

The words 'stance,' 'standing,' 'placing oneself,' 'orientation,' and 'addressivity' refer to a fundamental spatial-relational level that is absent in notions like self-definition, self-description, and self-categorization that are typically abstracted from their specific location in time and space. Positioning as a spatial-relational process is already significant in the development of children at the moments that they are playing with a doll, embracing a parent, enjoying the reciprocity of giving and receiving, or being involved in role-playing. These developments allow the child to take a multiplicity of I-positions and to look at the world from very different perspectives.

I-positioning is also different from self-presentation. In his classic work *The Presentation of Self in Everyday Life*, Goffman (1959) argues that a person is motivated to convey "an impression of reality that he attempts to engender in those among whom he finds himself" (p. 28). He illustrates this with the example of a student living in a dormitory who wants to impress the other students with her popularity by the number of telephone calls she receives. In this way, she aims to convey an image of herself to the outside world, in such a way that the addressee perceives this image as reality. I-positioning, on the other hand, refers not only to the positions people want to present to other people, but also to those that they take towards themselves. Indeed, internal forms of positioning may be entirely discrepant from external ones. The dormitory girl, who conveys impressive signs of popularity to her social environment, may internally position herself as 'somebody in whom boys are not really interested' or even as 'not worth a date.' In that case, the presented position may function as a compensation for a problematic positioning towards oneself. There exists a field of tension between one's interaction with the outside world and the way the self relates to itself. The two may be symmetrical but also opposed, and even contradictory.

Central concepts of dialogical self theory (DST)

DST includes some central concepts as elaboration of the spatial and temporal features of the process of positioning. In this section, I briefly discuss the following notions: centering and decentering movements in the self, third position, meta-position, and promoter position. I consider these concepts as particularly relevant to moral and spiritual leadership (see also van Loon & Buster, Chapter 6 in this volume).

Centering and decentering movements in the self

In a globalizing world in which people are crossing the borders of different cultures and countries, the self is faced with an unprecedented density of *I*-positions. As increasingly participating in a diversity of local groups and cultures, the individual position repertoire becomes complexly patterned and heterogeneous, laden as it is with differences, tensions, oppositions, and contradictions. Given the variety and speed of situational changes, the repertoire receives more 'visits' by unexpected positions and, as a consequence of the broadening range of social situations, there are more and larger 'position leaps'; that is, the individual has to make more and larger 'mental jumps' given the increasing diversity of situations in which the person is located (e.g., international educational contacts, immigration, tourism, social media contacts, living in diaspora).

The rapidly changing and diverse situations evoke decentering (or centrifugal) movements in the self. For sure, these movements create space for new possibilities and broaden the horizon of the self. However, when decentering movements become overly dominant, as typical of our globalizing society, they entail the risk of disorganization, confusion, and fragmentation. When the self becomes populated by an increasing number of contrasting and opposing voices, it may end up in a cacophony or identity crisis (see Arnett, 2002). Therefore, centering (or centripetal) movements in the self are needed in order to create the necessary balance. Working in the direction of coherence, consistency, and unity, these movements are able to restore the organization of the self when the existing order is challenged. Centering and decentering movements are not working in isolation from each other. Centering movements may profit from the new input introduced by the preceding decentering movements so that the self is prevented from becoming rigid and overly conservative. On the other hand, decentering movements need a centering counterforce, which prevents the self from arriving in a stage of disorganization or chaos. Basically, the two movements are mutually complementing forces, which need each other in order to find a balance between change, challenge, and innovation on the one hand, and consistency, coherence, and order on the other hand. In our contemporary society, it seems that this balance is compromised in forms of religious fundamentalism and political populism as far as these movements seek refuge in the establishment of 'super-positions' as highly centralizing and structurally dominating *I*-positions in their self-repertoire (see also van Loon & Buster, Chapter 6 in this volume).

Meta-positions: taking a helicopter view

For insight into the content and organization of one's position repertoire, the development of meta-positions is required. In order to clarify this position in the society of the self, a comparison with the macro-society may be helpful. Society is full of committees, investigative groups for 'staying on track,' and ombudspersons who review requests from individuals and groups. All of these attempt to gain insight into the complexity of a particular problem and to reach an overview of its different aspects. Aiming at a long-term view of the problem at hand, they may profit from taking a 'meta-position' that provides them with an overview of the various aspects of the problem including their patterns and inter-relationships (see also van der Zande & Bakker, Chapter 9 in this volume). Such a meta-position is not only indispensable for investigative groups or committees but also for any theory of the self that is concerned with a 'distance view' on the diversity and complexity of more specific *I*-positions and the ways in which they are organized. What is the nature of a meta-position, and which function does it have?

In order to illustrate the nature of a meta-position, take the example of a tennis player. As long as she is in the heat of the game, the best she can do is to keep her full concentration on the task at hand. Any moment of self-doubt or distraction would interfere with her performance. As long as she is fully involved, she is just *in* the position of playing the game. After finishing, however, she may reflect on her achievement and think about her position as a tennis player. She places herself *above* her performance as a tennis player, and at that moment she is on a higher level of positioning from which she looks down at the first level and reflects on it. She finds herself at a meta-position from which she critically evaluates her past performance. As a result, she decides to follow a different strategy next time. At some later point in time, she may move to a third, even higher, level where she poses questions about her future career. Does she go on to invest her best efforts in tennis? What is the view of her family members? At this higher meta-position, she considers the connection between her position as a tennis player and other significant positions – for example, she as a student gifted in math, as a mother of two children, or as interested in making a career in art. After her 'travel' across a broader range of positions, possibly enriched by a discussion with a wise adviser, she feels that she is able to make a decision about her future. Summarizing, the tennis player can move up and down between three levels: (a) being purely in the position; (b) moving above this position and reflecting on it; and (c) moving to a higher level from which a greater variety of positions are considered in their interconnections, so that adaptive or maladaptive patterns can be distinguished.

A meta-position has several specific qualities:

1   it creates an optimal *distance* toward other, more specific positions, although it may be attracted, both cognitively and emotionally, toward a more specific position (e.g., a critical position or a humorous one);
2   it allows one to take an *overarching* view of a multiplicity of positions, both internal and external ones, so that they are seen simultaneously and in their interconnections (helicopter view);
3   it enables one to see the *linkages* between positions as part of one's personal history and the collective history of one's group or culture;
4   it permits a *long-term view* of the self when past, present, and future positions are seen in their connections;
5   it leads to an *evaluation* of the several positions and the way in which they are organized – as a result of this evaluation, some positions become prioritized above others and the automaticity of positions is reduced;
6   it stimulates awareness of the *accessibility* of positions. Each position has an entrance and an exit. When the entrance is closed, it is difficult for the meta-position to know the specific needs, wishes, and values of this position. In contrast, a well-developed meta-position creates an open entrance to a broad variety of specific positions so that they can share their experiences and stories with the meta-position; and
7   the *direction of change* and the importance of some positions for the future development of the self become apparent.

In summary, the development of a meta-position with a broad scope and long-term perspective contributes, more than most other positions, to the cohesion and continuity of the self as a whole (Georgaca, 2001; Hermans & Hermans-Konopka, 2010).

At first sight, a meta-position seems to be a hard task to achieve. However, taking such a position is not a given but the result of a learning process. Particularly in educational settings, its development is crucial for people to learn what their own place is in a complex and increasingly globalizing society (see also Skeie, Chapter 10 in this volume). Moreover, moral and spiritual development may be stimulated by reflection on and discussion of meta-positions as guidelines for pupils and students to become aware of their moral contribution to their own social environment and to society as a whole.

Third position: from conflict to integration

I-positions are not isolated 'houses,' fixed somewhere in the space of the self. Instead, they interact with each other and are able to form new combinations with qualities that are more than the sum of its components. In the case of two conflicting positions, a third one may emerge (Figure 2.1) that is able, under certain conditions, to mitigate the conflict between the original ones. This has the advantage that the energy that is often usurped by the conflict can be invested in the third position and its further development. On the social level, this can be compared with an intermediator who assists conflicting parties in reaching a common position.

A clarifying example of the emergence of a third position on the level of the self is provided by the Brazilian investigators Branco, Branco, and Madureira (2008), who describe the story of Rosanne, a 25-year-old woman who found herself to be lesbian. She experienced a strong conflict between her sexual identity and the Catholic value system that functioned as a cornerstone in her life and that of her family. The case study shows how Rosanne was able to reach some level of integration of the strongly contradictory *I*-positions in the field of tension between the catholic society and the gay community.

Rosanne, who was well aware of the church's view on homosexuality, became involved in an intense self-dialogue in which she tried to justify herself as a good Catholic person, though lesbian. After many in-vain discussions with parents and priests, she started to develop a 'personal theology' in which the religious values of her upbringing and the affinities of her private, personal life were merging. She wondered if her religious virtues could offer her a way of life that could bridge the gap between two incompatible worlds that she felt as tearing her apart. At some point in this exploration, she started to talk about herself as a Christian woman who would like to help forsaken and lost people, including many gays and lesbians. At this

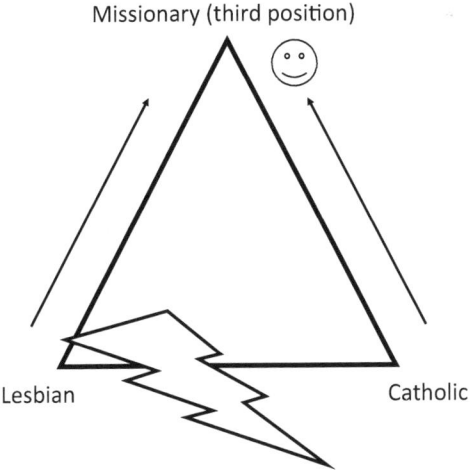

Figure 2.1 Emergence of a third position

turning point she realized that her mission was to help people to think about their lives in a way that would better fit traditional and Christian values and beliefs. From the perspective of her new position as a 'missionary,' she continued her presence in the gay community and could give space to her sexual identity. This third position helped her to accept her lesbian orientation and to reconcile the conflict between her original positions (see also Hermans & Hermans-Konopka, 2010).

The emergence of a third position is possible only under particular conditions. First, a person should know which *I*-positions are responsible for the conflict. This requires a certain degree of self-knowledge. Second, a third position may develop only if one position is not entirely dominant over the other. The self should be aware of the tension between the two identifiable positions without being totally absorbed by one or them. Third, both positions should open their boundaries to each other so that the energy can flow from the one to the other position. Finally, a meta-position is required with a distance large enough to take a stance outside the conflict zone so that the self is not blocked by the immediate pressure of the conflict.

Promoter positions: finding one's moral direction

Some people in society are granted the position of leader and they receive respect, admiration, influence, and even social power more than others. Typically, we perceive them as giving a noteworthy contribution to the development of a group, organization, or association. Such people are perceived as 'promoters' because they add value to the community, give it a sense of direction, and stimulate its further development. Such promoters do not work as purely outside figures. As 'promoters,' they can be adopted and even developed as parts in the extended domain of the self. Some of us are morally inspired by a person who reaches the status of an icon, like Mandela, Gandhi, Malala Yousafzai, an admired film actress, a pop artist, or an imaginary figure from a book. For others, it may be a person living in their immediate environment: a supporting parent, a grandparent, an uncle or aunt, a dedicated friend, or a psychotherapist. Such people are adopted as promoters in the virtual space of the extended domain of the self and become established as valuable sources of energy and inspiration.

Promoter positions are located not only in the external but also in the internal domain of the self. For some it may be 'I as religious,' 'I as an artist,' or 'my moral mission in life' (see also Wijsen, Chapter 3 in this volume). For others it may be 'I as a dedicated professional,' 'I as caring for the unprivileged,' or 'I as overcoming the limitations to which my father was subjected.' Over one's life-course, promoters may change, particularly when people arrive at a turning point in their lives (e.g., from 'I as a high achiever' to 'I as a mentor of young people').

Promoters in the self (initially proposed by Valsiner, 2004), have the following characteristics: (a) they organize and give (moral) *direction* to a diversity of more specialized *I*-positions that otherwise would go their own way in isolation of other positions; they have a 'compass function' for the self-system as a whole; (b) they have a considerable *openness towards the future* and have the potential to generate a diverse range of more specialized positions that are relevant to the further development of the self; (c) they *integrate* a diversity of new and already existing positions in the self, 'integration' used in the sense that different positions are brought together to form adaptive and productive combinations; (d) if sufficiently dialogical, they have the potential to contribute to the *democratic organization* of the self (Hermans, 2018), 'democratic' in the sense that the promoter gives each position a voice so that it can be heard; and (e) they function as 'guards' of the *continuity* of the self but, at the same time, they give room for *discontinuity*. Whereas continuity is realized by their ability to link the past, present, and future of the self, a certain degree of discontinuity follows from the fact that they are able to generate new positions. In this sense, promoter positions function as innovators of the self. Like meta-positions, promoters function as 'leaders' in the self. Meta-positions do so by their capacity to generate overview and long-term perspective. Promoters provide direction to the self and give an impetus to its further development.

My purpose in this section was to demonstrate that third positions, meta-positions and promoter positions represent *centering* movements in the self. They have the power to create a balance in the self that is otherwise subjected to strong *decentering* movements in a post-modern society. Such a society lacks the coherence that was typical of traditional communities, in which one's position repertoire was organized by firmly established stratifications based on class, age, ethnicity, geographic location, gender, and sex. Living in a post-modern society has the consequence that the boundaries of these stratifications have become highly permeable so that people are free (or forced) to move from one societal position to the other and, as a consequence, from one *I*-position to another *I*-position in the self. Boundary-crossing and globalization create an abundance of decentering movements that requires the self to answer with centering movements as a counterforce. Third positions, promoter positions, and meta-positions that are able to bridge differences, opposites, and conflicts have the potential of creating the necessary coherence and continuity in the self and function in this way as centering counterforces.

Fields of tension

Given the decentering movements in a multi-voiced self and the dynamics of a globalizing society, fields of tensions exist *between* positions (Hermans, 2018). In these fields the self is not simply located in one or the other position, but is moving in an in-between field in which new positions as hybrid formations can emerge. Such positions are not pre-given but emerge as a result of the interaction between existing positions. However, such fields are not only fertile ground for the blossoming of new positions. They can also be 'swamplands' for individuals who cannot find their way in these spaces such that they end up in disorganization or identity confusion. Fields of tension not only offer opportunities for growth and development, they also bring risks for individuals who are confronted with uncertainties for which they have no adequate response. In this section I will give two examples of identities in fields of tension: transcultural identities and transracial identities.[2]

Multicultural identities

An example of an adaptive answer to a cultural field of tension is given by Bhatia (2007), who investigated the identities of Indian Americans as one of the fastest-growing immigrant communities in the United States. Many of the participants of his research were educated as engineers, medical doctors, scientists, and university professors. In his participant observation and in-depth interviews, Bhatia found that these professionals perceived themselves as accepted members of American society because they felt respected in their professional capacities and contributions. At the same time, however, they noticed that they were seen as racially different and not 'real Americans.' They realized that they were not only different from but also similar to members of the American majority, which put them in a field of tension in their selves with a dialogue between two contradictory voices (e.g., 'I'm discriminated *but* I'm just as good as they are'). Although they and their children all were faced with racism, they seemed to simultaneously accept and reject their differences from the majority, in this way being involved in a 'double-voiced discourse' (Bhatia, 2007, p. 158) between their individual voices and the majority's dominant voice. On the basis of his observations, Bhatia argues that a dialogical view does not insist that conflicting positions or voices need to be replaced by harmonious ones. Apparently, conflicting or contradicting positions may form a hybrid identity, not very different from 'third positions' as discussed earlier. Apparently, such tension-loaded hybrid identity is helpful to coping with experiences of social discrimination (for similar results and conclusions of research in Ireland, see O'Sullivan-Lago & de Abreu, 2010).

Fields of tension between cultural positions not only offer opportunities but also carry psychological risks. An illustrative example is given by cultural anthropologist van Meijl (2012), who found that the impact of migration is nowhere so pervasive as in the Asia-Pacific region. Faced with limited prospects for economic growth and the effect of climate change, young people try to find their luck elsewhere, with many of them moving to New Zealand. As a result, these diasporic children and adolescents are located between two or more cultures, with migrants from Samoa and Tonga constituting the largest Polynesian groups in New Zealand. Placed in this field of tension, these youngsters develop multiple identifications with more than one cultural group in and beyond New Zealand. On the one hand, their Samoan identity is historically rooted in the culture of island-born members of their extended family or church community. On the other hand, their identity as a New Zealander is challenged by New Zealanders of European descent. They are faced with insecurity and lack of control, because the social and cultural attitudes of being a New Zealander conflict with the socio-cultural norms established by their Pacific identity. Their self-experience is divided between two cultural positions associated with inner voices that are contradicting each other to such a degree that identity confusion is the result. van Meijl's study demonstrates that not in all cases can the tension caused by contradictory voices in the self be resolved by an adaptive inner dialogue (see also König, Chapter 7 in this volume, for the development of adaptive dialogical relationships between cultural *I*-positions).

Multiracial identities

The opportunities and risks in fields of tension can also be illustrated in the area of multiracial identities. Since the legalization of interracial marriages in 1967, the number of multiracial children has grown exponentially, and people of multiracial backgrounds have become one of the fastest-growing minorities in the United States (Shih & Sanchez, 2009). This legalization happened in the context of changing views on race and racial differences. While during the late 19th century it was generally believed that race was carried in the blood and that group differences were heritable, the predominant view among social scientists today is that racial categories are socially constructed and are not fixed, immutable categories.

In their account of the history of racial opposites, Luke and Luke (1999) describe how the colonized, relocated, or dislocated object of modernism was perceived as the 'other,' that is, as being different from Anglo/European subjects who considered themselves as occupying the central position in the world. The 'other' was and is perceived as a deviation from the standard on which the legitimacy of the dominant part of the world depends. As the invisible center of normalization, whites produced, over the past centuries of colonization, regimes of truth about immutable racial differences. As subjected to a strategy of control and surveillance, the others were located in particular places (e.g., isolated areas, ghettos) separated from the spaces where principles of normalcy were produced and legitimated.

In their own research of multiracial families in Australia, Luke and Luke found that nothing is straightforward for the interracial couple. There are few role models for the organization of their lives. The cultural understandings of the wedding, family life, and education of children are for them not always useful guides to negotiate the unexpected and often confusing pressures and anxieties of family and community to which they are exposed. It is also difficult for them to deal with the negative public sentiment about 'race mixing.' These negative attitudes about race mixing, combined with the lack of positive models, function as obstacles to determining an adequate dialogical answer in the fields of tension in which they are located.

While Luke and Luke emphasize the identity struggles of multiracial individuals and their negative implications, other authors provide a more positive picture. The importance of a fluid and flexible view of race is emphasized by Rockquemore, Brunsma, and Delgado (2009), who propose the distinction between 'identity,' 'identification,' and 'categorization.' They define racial *identity* as the individual's self-understanding, racial *identification* as how others define an individual, and racial *category* as what racial identities are available in a specific societal context. They demonstrate that in a multiracial identity these self-definitions do not necessarily coincide and leave some space for adaptive responses in a field of tension.

One of their examples is Christy, a student who as part of her college application process has to check off a box designating her racial group membership. Although she defines herself as multiracial and is identified by others as white (because her physical appearance is more white than black), she checks off 'Black' as one of the available categories on her admission form because she thinks it will give her an advantage in the admission process. As this example suggests, Christy is moving between different racial positions and does so to her own benefit. She defines her own identity on the basis of her internal self, although she is identified differently by others. At the same time, she makes an adaptive choice between the identity positions provided by the institution. The interface between self and society functions as a field of tension between different positions in the self among which the individual can move, shifting from one to the other position and constructing a pattern of positions depending on self-definitions, other-definitions, and institutional opportunities and constraints.

At this point it is appropriate to emphasize (again) that DST is not a theory developed to study the *intra*psychic processes of the self. Instead, in its radical rejection of any self-society dualism, the theory conceptualizes the self at the *inter*face of self and society as a field in which society is an organizing part of the self and, in reverse, the self, in its response, co-constitutes social and societal relationships. An important implication of this view is that for the formation and development of self and identity and for both internal and external dialogues, it is necessary that the existence of racial prejudices and the impact of racial history are explicitly recognized. This is the central theme in Wekker's book *White Innocence* (2016), in which she deals with a central paradox of Dutch culture: the existence of aggressive racism and xenophobia alongside passionate denial of racial discrimination and colonial violence. She qualifies her book as 'iconoclastic' because whiteness is not acknowledged as a racialized or ethnicized positioning. Close to Luke and Luke's (1999) view, she observes that whiteness is generally seen as so ordinary, so lacking in characteristics, and so devoid of meaning that it runs the risk of being considered empty. Indeed, a field of tension can function only as fertile soil for productive dialogue, if individuals and collectivities are aware of the paradox between their self-image of being 'tolerant' on the one hand, and their past or present behavior that is guided by racial prejudices and discrimination on the other hand. Generative dialogue needs the acknowledgment of tension between positioning oneself as tolerant and behaving, in explicit or implicit ways, as intolerant. The generation of meaning needs *both* positions as constituting a field of tension where constructive dialogical relationships have a chance to develop. This problem poses an enormous challenge to education.

There is an essential difference between categories and positions. While a category is an abstract notion for classifying elements, a position as a spatial concept takes into account the space between positions. In this section, I argued that in a boundary-crossing and globalizing society, fields of tension between positions are becoming increasingly significant to understanding identity problems as multi-voiced constructions. I showed how multicultural and multiracial identities produce fields of tension that provide opportunities for self-integration and self-innovation in the form of third positions, hybrid identities, and adaptive combinations of positions. At the same time, these fields may function as 'battlefields' where disoriented individuals experience disorganization, fragmentation, and identity confusion. In order to stimulate dialogical relationships between positions in this field, awareness of contradictions, conflicts, and opposites between positions is needed.

Moral implications of dialogical self theory

In this final section, I address some moral implications of DST as a theory of multiple voices involved in dialogical relationships with each other. The focus is on three topics that are discussed as relevant to moral development: (a) the nature of *I*-positions; (b) dialogical relationships between voices that want to be heard; and (c) the acknowledgment of a human position as transcending ingroup–outgroup oppositions.

The moral significance of I-positions

As discussed in the beginning of this chapter, the dialogical self resists any self-other dualism that assumes the existence of the other person or group as existing entirely outside the realms of the self. Instead, the other is accepted and recognized as an intrinsic element of the self and co-influences its organization, at the same time evoking an answer from the same self. Moreover, the other is not considered as a self-*object* but as a self-*subject*. As we have extensively described in our earlier work (Hermans & Hermans-Konopka, 2010), the other is recognized as 'another I' in the space of the self. This means that in DST the other is granted a subject position that can be addressed in dialogical discourses with the possibility that this position gives an answer from its own specific point of view. My father and my mother are still living in my self-space, although they may have passed away a long time ago. I may not only remember them as significant persons in my past, but even bring them to life in my present self in the form of a promoter position in the external domain of my self. In my imagination I address them, and they address me, in verbal and non-verbal ways. As parts of this dialogical relationship, they are not simply 'mine' in the possessive meaning of the term, but they have subject positions, which invite me to take a receptive attitude towards them. This combination of construction and reception is typical not only of the relationship with my parents, but with all significant others in my life who have the potential of functioning as promoters of my self: my friends, my children, my colleagues, my spiritual guide, the spirits in my life, and even my opponents. The recognition of their existence as subjects in my extended self has a moral significance that goes far beyond the objectification of the other in cases of prejudices and judgmental evaluations or devaluations.

The moral nature of dialogical relationships

In its recognition of the other as another I in the self and in the significance of a receptive attitude, DST comes close to Buber's (1970) influential distinction between I and You. In his view, the I functions as a member of a pair that manifests itself in two fundamentally different ways: as part of an I-You relationship (subject-subject relationship) and as part of an I-It relationship (subject-object relationship). The term 'I' is not a single word in itself but rather part of the word pair I-You. This pair is distinguished from another word pair, I-It, which indicates a completely different attitude toward the world. Only in the I-You relation is an encounter possible. According to Buber, the encounter between I and You is unthinkable without a receptive attitude, which is the cradle for emergence of deeper meaning. From a DST perspective, the implication is that in their mutual communication, I-positions have the potential to address, from a receptive attitude, each other in their subject position, as persons within the person or, contrastingly, to speak about them in objectifying ways (as it-positions).

At this point, it may be noteworthy that self-reflection in the Jamesian sense assumes the distinction between the self as subject and the self as object. In this case, a particular position or combination of positions in the self is the object of self-investigation or self awareness. In the case of a dialogical relationship within the self, positions can be addressed as subjects and have the opportunity to talk back so that meanings can be explored and further developed in an ongoing dialogue. Strictly speaking, self-reflection lacks this ongoing play of question and answer, because an answer needs an addressable subject position. One reflects *on* something, one dialogues *with* somebody.

The moral nature of dialogical relationships was discussed in an earlier publication where we explored the temporal extension of the dialogical self with reference to the different phases in the collective history of human-kind: the traditional, modern, and post-modern self (Hermans & Hermans-Konopka, 2010). Whereas the autonomy aspect of the different positions in DST is inspired by the modern self and the multiplicity aspect influenced by the post-modern self, the moral aspect finds its roots in the traditional self. One of the central elements of the traditional model is the conception that the self is basically a moral enterprise because it is always embedded in a larger whole in which the human being realizes a moral telos. As Richardson Rogers, and McCarroll (1998) formulate: "Dialogic relations are always fundamentally ethical because in them we always are either acknowledged or ignored, understood or misunderstood, treated with respect or coerced" (p. 510). Not only dialogue, but also identity can be considered as a basically moral endeavor, as Taylor (1989) concludes in his philosophical investigation of the development of the self in the course of history:

> to know who I am is a species of knowing where I stand. My identity is defined by the commitments and identifications which provide the frame or horizon within which I can try to determine from case to case what is good, or valuable, or what ought to be done, or what I endorse or oppose. In other words, it is the horizon within which I am capable of taking a stand.
>
> (p. 27)

For the dialogical self as a society of mind, the first perspective (emphasis on self-extension) is on the different *I*-positions that are taking a stand towards each other. This stand is basically moral as the other position is acknowledged, is respected in its own specific point of view, and has the 'right' to speak with its own voice. *I*-positions have the right to be heard as participants in a dialogue both within and between selves.

In the second perspective (emphasis on dialogue), the focus will be on issues of dialogical leadership and the possibility of 'provocative guidance,' hybrid identities and the importance of coping with ambiguity and contingency, also with regard to questions of multiple religious belonging versus religious radicalization. The intent is to further develop the DST approach regarding problems that arise in a globalizing context, taking into account urgent themes as radicalization and good leadership across boundaries of self, organization, and culture.

The moral significance of taking a human position

One of the distinctive features of DST is that the self has the potential of making flexible movements from one to another position and to look at the world and oneself from different perspectives. This allows the self to explore and analyze a problem from alternative points of view. Is it possible to look at the world, not only from the position of oneself as an individual or as a member of a group, but also as a human being, beyond any ingroup versus out-group opposition?

In this respect, DST may learn significantly from self-categorization theory, developed by Turner and colleagues (1987), when we try to understand the identity implications of a globalizing and border-crossing world. Rather than perceiving inter-group dynamics as opposite ends of a bipolar spectrum – self versus other or ingroup versus out-group – these theorists characterize identity as operating at different levels of inclusiveness. They distinguish three levels of self-categorization: the subordinate level of personal self-categorizations based on comparisons with other individuals (personal identity), the intermediate level of the self as a member of an ingroup, distinctively compared with an out-group (social identity), and the superordinate category of the self as human being (or human identity).

Empirical support for this level distinction was provided by Wohl and Branscombe (2005), who performed research in groups of Jewish North Americans and Native Canadians. They posed the question whether increasing category inclusiveness, from the intermediate social level to the more inclusive human level, would lead to greater forgiveness of historical perpetrator groups. They found that human-level categorization resulted in more positive responses toward Germans and White Canadians as the result of decreasing the uniqueness of the past harmful actions toward the ingroup. The authors concluded that their experiments showed that negative group-based feelings toward the perpetrator category can be reduced by moving to the more inclusive human level of categorization. Such findings suggest that taking the position of 'I as human being' results in greater forgiveness than less inclusive positions of 'I as a Jew' or 'I as native-Canadian.'

From a moral point of view, it makes sense to translate self-categorization theory into the conceptual framework of DST. The hypothesis seems plausible that one's initial positioning to out-groups can be changed or complemented by climbing to a higher level of inclusiveness as a counter-positioning *answer* to one's reaction at a lower level (and vice versa). Allowing a space for moving between the ingroup position and the human position would create a field of tension where the initial (emotional) ingroup response could be mitigated and modified by taking a responding human position. Such a movement towards a human level of inclusiveness has an important moral implication: it stimulates the person to consider the other as an extension of oneself, which creates a condition to treat the other as one would like to be treated oneself.

At this point there is a coalescence of the flexibility regarding positioning and the moral telos of treating the other as an 'alter ego,' that is, the other is like me and different from me at the same time. In his book *Ethica Nicomachea*, Aristotle (1954) considers the other as alter ego as reflecting the highest form of friendship. Moving flexibly between personal, social, and human levels of inclusiveness, with a broader moral purpose in mind, prevents the self from sticking to any polarizing identity politics. From a moral point of view, it is good to recognize identity differences, but in order to make dialogue productive, one needs to go beyond them in order to search for connection. Without any doubt, the acknowledgment of multicultural, multiracial, and transgender identities has contributed considerably to the emancipation of these groups. In order to fully acknowledge their place in the world, the flexibility of moving to a human level of inclusiveness is part of a moral enterprise that touches the heart of a boundary-crossing society.

Finally, the three levels of inclusiveness allow the distinction of three kinds of responsibility: personal, social, and global. Responsibility has two components, 'response' and 'ability': the ability to give dialogical answers to others and oneself from one's personal *I*-positions (*personal* responsibility); to give dialogical responses to others and oneself from the we-positions of the group or social category to which one belongs (*social* responsibility); and to providing dialogical responses to others and oneself from the more general position of human being (*global* responsibility). This tripartite responsibility can be effective only if the self is able to develop the capacity to move in flexible ways between different levels of inclusiveness in agreement with the demands of the situation. A dialogical self with global responsibility finds a prominent advocate in Nelson Mandela who, at the occasion of receiving the Nobel Peace Prize for his long struggle against apartheid in 1993, said: "We need a globalization of responsibility as well. Above all, that is the challenge of the next century" (Mandela, 2000, p. 35).

Conclusion

Dialogical self theory is historically rooted in the American pragmatism of James and in the Russian dialogical school of Mikhail Bakhtin. In a most succinct form, the dialogical self can be defined as a dynamic multiplicity of *I*-positions in the society of mind. As a spatial construction, this mind can be depicted as a landscape in which a multiplicity of positions is moving around in search of a moral direction. At the same time, the mind functions as a soundscape because *I*-positions can assume a voice that allows dialogical relationships between positions to emerge. A moral implication of this view is that in the community of voices emerging in self and society, each voice has the right to be heard and to tell its own specific narrative. A central thesis in the theory is that in a boundary-crossing world, fields of tension emerge as spaces that provide opportunities for the construction of third positions, hybrid identities, and adaptive combinations of positions, but also imply the risk of disorganization and identity confusion. Located in these fields of tension, individuals need a moral telos as a compass that helps them to find their ways in a world of diversity and plural modalities. Starting from these considerations, three moral implications of the theory were discussed in particular: the other as another I in the self, the moral nature of dialogue, and the possibility of taking a human position as a way to transcend closed boundaries between positions at the individual or group level and to avoid or prevent the separating tendencies of religious or spiritual identity politics.

Notes

1 Since the first psychological publication on the dialogical self (Hermans, Kempen, & van Loon, 1992), the theory has led to the publication of several hundreds of books and articles in different fields of application. The interested reader may find an overview of theoretical, methodological, and practical developments in the *Handbook of Dialogical Self Theory* (Hermans & Gieser, 2012). Psychotherapeutic applications are collected in the *Handbook of Dialogical Self Theory and Psychotherapy: Bridging Psychotherapeutic and Cultural Traditions* (Konopka, Hermans, & Goncalves, 2018). Applications in the field of education are brought together in *The Dialogical Self Theory in Education: A Multicultural Perspective* (Meijers & Hermans, 2017). Different theory-guided methods for research and practice are provided by Hermans (2016).
2 This section is limited to a brief analysis of multicultural and multiracial identities. A more elaborate treatment of these identities, including transgender identities, is provided by Hermans et al. (2017).

References

Aristotle. (1954). *Ethica Nicomachea* (R. W. Thuijs, Trans.). Antwerp: De Nederlandse Boekhandel.

Arnett, J. (2002). The psychology of globalization. *American Psychologist, 57,* 774–783.

Bakhtin, M. M. (1984). *Problems of Dostoevsky's poetics* (C. Emerson, Ed. and Trans.). Minneapolis, MN: University of Minnesota Press.

Bhatia, S. (2007). *American karma: Race, culture, and identity in the Indian diaspora.* New York, NY: New York University Press.

Branco, A. U., Branco, A. L., & Madureira, A. F. (2008). Self-development and the emergence of new *I*-positions: Emotions and self-dynamics. *Studia Psychologica, 6,* 23–39.

Buber, M. (1970). *I and Thou.* (A new translation with a prologue "I and you" and notes by Walter Kaufmann.) Edinburgh: T. & T. Clark.

Cooley, C. H. (1902). *Human nature and the social order.* New York, NY: Scribner Book Company.

Georgaca, E. (2001). Voices of the self in psychotherapy: A qualitative analysis. *British Journal of Medical Psychology, 74,* 223–236.

Goffman, E. (1959). *The presentation of self in everyday life.* London: Penguin Books.

Hermans, H. J. M. (Ed.). (2016). *Assessing and stimulating a dialogical self in groups, teams, cultures, and organizations.* New York, NY: Springer.

Hermans, H. J. M. (2018). *Society in the self: A theory of identity in democracy.* New York, NY: Oxford University Press.

Hermans, H. J. M., & Gieser, T. (2012). History, main tenets, and core concepts of dialogical self theory. In H. J. M. Hermans & T. Gieser (Eds.), *Handbook of dialogical self theory* (pp. 1–22). Cambridge: Cambridge University Press.

Hermans, H. J. M., & Hermans-Konopka, A. (2010). *Dialogical self theory: Positioning and counter-positioning in a globalizing society.* Cambridge: Cambridge University Press.

Hermans, H. J. M., Kempen, H. J. G., & van Loon, R. J. P. (1992). The dialogical self: Beyond individualism and rationalism. *American Psychologist, 47*, 23–33.

Hermans, H. J. M., Konopka, A., Oosterwegel, A., & Zomer, P. (2017). Fields of tension in a boundary-crossing world: Towards a democratic organization of the self. *Integrative Psychological and Behavioral Science, 51*, 505–535.

James, W. (1890). *The principles of psychology* (vol. 1). London: Palgrave Macmillan.

Konopka, A., Hermans, H. J. M., & Goncalves, M. (Eds.). (2018). *Handbook of dialogical self theory and psychotherapy: Bridging psychotherapeutic and cultural traditions.* London: Routledge.

Luke, C., & Luke, A. (1999). Theorizing interracial families and hybrid identity: An Australian perspective. *Educational Theory, 49*, 223–249.

Mandela, N. (2000). The challenge of the next century: The globalization of responsibility. *New Perspectives Quarterly, 17*, 34–35.

Meijers, F., & Hermans, H. J. M. (Eds.). (2017). *The dialogical self theory in education: A multicultural perspective.* New York, NY: Springer.

O'Sullivan-Lago, R., & Abreu, G. de (2010). Maintaining continuity in a cultural contact zone: Identification strategies in the dialogical self. *Culture & Psychology, 16*, 73–92.

Richardson, F. C., Rogers, A., & McCarroll, J. (1998). Toward a dialogical self. *American Behavioral Scientist, 41*, 496–515.

Rockquemore, K. A., Brunsma, D. L., & Delgado, D. J. (2009). Understanding the struggle to build a multiracial identity theory. *Journal of Social Issues, 65*, 13–34.

Shih, M., & Sanchez, D. T. (2009). When race becomes even more complex: Toward understanding the landscape of multiracial identity and experiences. *Journal of Social Issues, 65*, 1–11.

Taylor, C. (1989). *Sources of the self: The making of the modern identity.* Boston, MA: Harvard University Press.

Turner, J. C., Hogg, M. A., Oakes, P. J., Reicher, S. D., & Wetherell, M. S. (1987). *Rediscovering the social group: A self-categorization theory.* Oxford: Wiley Blackwell.

Valsiner, J. (2004, July 11–15). *The promoter sign: Developmental transformation within the structure of the dialogical self.* XVIII Biennial Meeting of the International Society for the Study of Behavioral Development, Ghent.

van Meijl, T. (2012). Multiculturalism, multiple identification and the dialogical self: Shifting paradigms of personhood in sociocultural anthropology. In H. J. M. Hermans & T. Gieser (Eds.), *Handbook of dialogical self theory* (pp. 98–114). Cambridge: Cambridge University Press.

Vasil'eva, I. I. (1988). The importance of M.M. Bakhtin's idea of dialogue and dialogic relations for the psychology of communication. *Soviet Psychology, 26*, 17–31.

Wekker, G. (2016). *White innocence.* Durham, NC: Duke University Press.

Wohl, M. J. A., & Branscombe, N. R. (2005). Forgiveness and collective guilt assignment to historical perpetrator groups depend on level of social category inclusiveness. *Journal of Personality and Social Psychology, 88*, 288–303.

3 Religion, radicalism, relativism

Between social identity and dialogical self theory

Frans Wijsen

Introduction

Since the end of the Cold War, the 'clash of civilizations' scenario has been very influential in political science and international relations theory. The assumption is that, after political ideology, it is culture (including religion) that matters in human progress (Harrison & Huntington, 2000). Empirical evidence for this theory is robust, and it would be unwise to deny that there are ongoing clashes. The 'clash of civilizations' theory is supported by other theories, such as functional ethnocentrism theory (Sumner, 1906) and social identity theory (Tajfel & Turner, 1986).

These theories contrast with another body of knowledge that uses labels such as bricolage, syncretism, double belonging, popular, folk, liquid, and lived religion, multiple belonging, and polyphonic and dialogical self (Bakhtin, 1981; Bauman, 2000; Burke, 2009). I assume that the contrast between the understanding of intercultural encounters in terms of clashes or in terms of liquidity has something to do with the conceptualization and operationalization of civilization and culture, including religion (Hannerz, 1992; van Binsbergen, 2003).

In harmony with the positivistic paradigm in science, culture and religion are defined as entities that exist in themselves, independently of actors, that are shared by the members of the group, which unite them and distinguish them from others (Widdicombe, 1998, pp. 192–195). If this were true, a plural society would be a tragedy, and dialogue an illusion. Yet, most people in this world live together more or less peacefully, and understand each other at least partially (Pinker, 2011; Marshall, 2016). This insight brings me to study religion and identity in a relational and dialogical way.

Hypothesizing that people's identities, which I define as narratives of the self (Wijsen, 2013, p. 12), are multiple and polyphonic, dialogical, and democratic (Hermans, 2018, pp. 4–7), my main research question is: why and under what conditions are people no longer capable of shifting from one position to another, in accordance with different, and even contradictory situations; why are *I*-positions no longer perceived as compatible and fluid, but competitive and fixed? Put in different terms: why and under what conditions do dialogical and democratic selves become rigid and radical (Hermans, 2018, p. 27)?

By answering these questions, I aim to acquire insight into the relationship between 'social identity' theory and 'multiple identity' or 'polyphonic self' ('dialogical self') theory (Hermans & Hermans-Konopka, 2010, pp. 68–69, 74–75), particularly with regard to the 'software of the mind' and 'moral circles,' or the shared knowledge about what is considered to be 'real' and 'right' (Hofstede, Hofstede, & Minkov, 2010, p. 13). As we will see in greater detail, radicals deny or reject pluralism or the compatibility of different views of what is 'real' and 'right.'

I hypothesize that social identity theory with its 'us' and 'them' dichotomy is based on 'Western,' exclusive logic, and thus is culture-specific (Kim, 2002, pp. 159–166; Hermans, 2018, pp. 2–3). Also, that dialogical self theory is more adequate to interpret and to explain liquid, hybrid, or multiple identities, and more at home in 'non-Western' societies where 'relational selves' are dominant (Kim, 2002, pp. 72–76).

In this contribution I take a biographical approach (Tayob, 2017) to explore and test generalizing theories on religion and identity. I hope that my insights will be helpful to political and spiritual leaders who try to predict, prevent, and combat radicalism.

Seeds of conflict in a haven of peace

In the early 1980s I conducted a research project on popular religion and syncretism in East Africa. I concluded that believers there easily switch from one religion to another, or mix them according to their needs. In Tanzania, my interviewees said that they were totally Christian and totally African, and when they were confronted with crises in their lives, they moved back and forth between Christian and indigenous rituals, or freely combined them. In my view, there was a tradition of peaceful coexistence, symbolized by political ideologies of national unity such as *ujamaa* and *harambee*, by *taarab* music and ki-Swahili language (Wijsen & Tanner, 2002).

In the 1990s my research interest shifted to Islam and Muslim-Christian relations in East Africa. This was due to the growing rhetoric on religious, particularly Islamic, radicalism, and violent attacks on pork butcheries and churches in Dar es Salaam. When policemen opened fire on Muslims that gathered outside the *Mwembechai* mosque in the city on February 13, 1998, I realized that peaceful coexistence had changed, or that 'seeds of conflict' were there before but had remained outside my vision (Wijsen & Mfumbusa, 2002). Later that year, on August 7, 1998, the American embassies in Nairobi and Dar es Salaam were bombed; this was three years prior to the 9/11 attack on the World Trade Center in New York.

Between 2004 and 2007 I conducted fieldwork on these 'seeds of conflict' in Nairobi. The objective was to know how interreligious relations were dealt with, and how future religious leaders in Nairobi-based institutions of higher learning in theology and religious studies were being trained, five years after the attacks on the US embassies in Nairobi and Dar es Salaam. I concluded that religious education in Kenya was quite compartmentalized and that inter-ethnic and interreligious tensions were mounting. Consequently, I argued for a shift from religious studies to interreligious studies (Wijsen, 2007).

Soon after the results of my study were published, post-election violence occurred in Nairobi where 1,200 people were killed and 600,000 people were displaced. Yet, it is said that East Africa is a 'haven of peace,' and the violence that occurred did not match with my previous studies of double belonging and syncretism in Northwest Tanzania (Wijsen & Tanner, 2002; Wijsen, 2007, pp. 144–149). So, in 2007 I decided to continue with a study on (the construction of) religious identity and (the absence of) social cohesion (Wijsen, 2013).

Taking my inspiration from dialogical self theory (Hermans & Hermans-Konopka, 2010), I criticized theories about inter-group relations that hypothesize that loyalty to the own group necessarily leads to animosity towards other groups (Wijsen, 2013, pp. 12–13). Hofstede et al. (2010, p. 16), for example, state: "Social scientists use the terms *ingroup* and *out-group*. Ingroup refers to what we intuitively feel to be 'we,' while out-group refers to 'they.' Humans really function in this simple way: we have a persistent need to classify others in either group." The authors conclude, "our propensity as group animals is to bend our mental powers to our own, or our group's interests. We tend to believe anything that makes our group look good, such as being God's special favorites, rather than to be impartial about who we are" (Hofstede et al., 2010, p. 475).

These authors basically draw upon functional ethnocentrism theory, stating: "The relation of comradeship and peace in the we-group and that of hostility and war towards others-groups are correlative to each other" (Sumner, 1906, p. 12), and later variations such as social identity theory (Tajfel & Turner, 1986). The dichotomy between 'us' and 'them,' or ingroup and out-group, also dominates studies about the multicultural society as a drama (Scheffer, 2011), or about religion and violence (Jürgensmeyer, 2000; Selengut, 2003).

According to Jürgensmeyer (2000, pp. 6–7), religious violence "has much to do with the nature of religious imagination, which always has had the propensity to absolutize and to project images of cosmic war." And, in harmony with cognitive dissonance theory, Selengut (2003, pp. 57–58) argues that "(t)here is a an inherent human drive for cognitive consistency. . . . Essentially there are three solutions to the experience of cognitive dissonance and chronic religious disappointment: (1) surrender, (2) reinterpretation, and (3) militant transformation."

However, in globalizing societies, people are used to living with cognitive dissonance, and friendship with out-group members exists (Hermans & Hermans-Konopka, 2010, pp. 68–70). Assorted studies show that double loyalties or multiple and liquid identities are not exceptions but the rule

(Bauman, 2000). To a certain extent the two trends, liquidity and radicalism, are harmonized in the world (Hannerz, 1992; Barber, 1995; Robertson, 1995), and can be harmonized by one person. I have been interested in clerics who claim that they are 'fully committed' to their own faith and 'fully open' to the faith of others (Wijsen, 2007, pp. 161–165). This is the complexity and ambiguity of religion that I tried to catch in the title of my book *Seeds of Conflict in a Haven of Peace* (2007) and that I wished to explore further by using dialogical self theory.[1]

From social identity to dialogical self

Returning to my original question, it is good to define radicalism. Radicalism is an attitude (opinion, feeling, disposition to behavior) of (groups of) persons who hold absolutist beliefs, be they religious or not (Wijsen, 2007, pp. 151–153). Others are seen as complete strangers or potential enemies, and various worldviews as incompatible; there is no common ground or meeting point between them. Radical people deny or reject pluralism in the sense of compatibility of different views of what is 'real' and 'right' in accordance with various, and even contradictory situations. They are uncompromising and undemocratic in the sense that they impose their will on others (Hermans, 2018, pp. 23–28, 100–102). Since they see no meeting point and are uncompromising, conflicts in various degrees, from irritation or frustration to aggression and violence, are at stake.

Applied to conflicts between Muslims and Christians, usually there are two explanations for the origin of these conflicts. There are scholars who see causes of conflict in the religions themselves. For example, Jan Assmann (2003) argued that religious conflicts are caused by the distinction between true and false religion, which came about by monotheism that is based on the belief in revelation. Islam and Christianity are missionary religions that make absolute truth claims, so it is almost unavoidable that they collide. This is in harmony with the 'clash of civilizations' (Huntington, 1996) or 'culture matters' theory (Harrison & Huntington 2000).

Yet other scholars write that the causes of conflicts between Muslims and Christians are contextual (Maalouf, 2000; Mamdani, 2004; Abbas, 2011). They argue that conflicts between Muslims and Christians have little to do with religion, but with oil, gold, diamonds, water, and wood. This is in harmony with the 'realistic group conflict' theory. Sherif (1966) and others hold that inter-group conflict is caused by (perceived or actual) conflicting and incompatible goals, or competition for scarce resources.

Social identity theory

In social psychology there is a robust alternative to the 'realistic group conflict' theory, namely the idea that a positive attitude towards one's own (religious) group implies a negative, hostile attitude towards other (religious) groups. It was first propounded in the early 20th century by the ethnologist

William Sumner (1906) in his 'functional ethnocentrism' theory. Sumner (1906, p. 12) said: "The relation of comradeship and peace in the we-group and that of hostility and war towards others-groups are correlative to each other." This idea was developed further by Gordon Allport (1958) in his theory on prejudice and supported by social identity theorists (Tajfel, 1978). Social identity theory in turn draws on Festinger's social comparison theory and entails the following:

1   a person's identity or self-concept derives to a large extent from group membership;
2   people strive for positive self-esteem and therefore desire a positive social identity;
3   people are even willing to skew their view of the other negatively to enhance their own self-esteem.

Only the thought of the existence of another group, even if there is no lack or conflict of interest, strengthens the loyalty to and identification with the own group.

Social identity theory (Tajfel & Turner, 1986) claims that inter-group conflicts are caused by social categorization and group identification per se. Experiments show that even if there is no scarcity of resources, participants develop ingroup favoritism.

The limitations of this theory

Although there is quite some evidence in favor of social identity theory, it is problematic (Widdicombe, 1998, pp. 197–204; Wijsen, 2007, pp. 170–177) for several reasons:

1   it tends to see identity as realistic and objective;
2   it is not tested cross-culturally that much; and
3   it does not explain why the majority lives together peacefully.

In fact, if we look at the world today, there is less, not more, violence (Pinker, 2011; Marshall, 2016).

There are modifications of social identity theory in the field of religion that distinguish various dimensions of religion – in harmony with Ninian Smart – and argue that some dimensions of religion (e.g., dogma, law) are more exclusive than others (mysticism, ritual). But basically, these modifications do not solve the problem of exclusive thinking.

Dialogical self theory

Since 2007 (Wijsen, 2007, pp. 145, 176) I have been exploring an alternative theory, dialogical self theory (Hermans & Kempen, 1992; see also

Hermans, Chapter 2 in this volume). This theory combines the concepts of self and dialogue that come from two sources, American pragmatism and Russian dialogism (Hermans & Gieser, 2012).

First there is William James's notion of the extended self. James goes beyond the separation of self and environment (by Descartes) and distinguishes between 'I' and 'me.' 'I' is the self as knower or subject, and 'me' is the self as known or object. The self as known is composed of all that the person can call her/his own: my body, my clothes, my house, my wife, my children – i.e., people and things in the environment belong to the self to the extent that they are felt as mine (Hermans & Gieser, 2012, p. 3).

Second there is Mikhail Bakhtin's notion of the polyphonic novel. Analyzing Dostoevsky's publications, Bakhtin argued that in these publications there is not one author at work, namely Dostojevski himself, but a multiplicity of authors that are represented by the characters. In addition, there is a plurality of voices, which is later coined 'intertextuality' by Kristeva (1986).

Dialogical self theory assumes:

1 that the self can be conceived as a (mini) 'society of mind' or a multiplicity of embodied *I*-positions among which a dialogical relationship exists;
2 that the 'I' is capable of shifting from one position to another in accordance with different, even contradictory, situations (Hermans & Gieser, 2012, p. 2).

The self is not autonomous and unified but dialogical and multiple; so it is not substance but relation. And the other is not a total stranger, but already part of me. The question, then, is why and under what conditions are some people no longer able to shift from one position to another? Why do they become rigid and radical? Why and under what conditions do some voices become dominant and others peripheral?

I share with social identity theory the notion that people strive for positive self-esteem, but it is too simple to give mono-causal explanations for conflicts between (groups of) people (Taylor & Moghaddam, 1994; Roccas & Brewer, 2002). In some cases, positive self-esteem may translate into competition for scarce resources, and vice versa (Bourdieu, 1990).

I am interested in case studies of radicals (Tayob, 2017) who commit violent attacks but whose relatives and neighbors are surprised by this behavior and say that they are good neighbors, loving husbands, and caring fathers. I am also interested in the fact that some believers of a religion can become exclusive and extreme, saying that their religion contains absolute truth, while other believers of the same religion respect others, saying that God's truth is always bigger than their conceptualization. This is the 'ambivalence of the sacred' (Girard, 1977; Scott Appleby, 2000), or religion between radicalism and relativism.

From phenomenon to narrative

As mentioned earlier, I have been conducting research on (the construction of) religious identity and (the absence of) social cohesion in Tanzania since 2007 (Wijsen & Ndaluka, 2012). This research has extended to Indonesia (Wijsen & Cholil, 2014) and the Netherlands (Wijsen & Vos, 2015), interviewing some 400 people. The knowledge guiding interest behind this research has been a deep dissatisfaction with studies on Muslim-Christian relations thus far.

These studies have been conducted mainly from the 'World Religion' paradigm. This paradigm developed in the 19th century through historical and comparative approaches that systematized varieties of human beliefs and rituals into 'religions' that are clearly identifiable and have distinct characteristics (Masuzawa, 2005). By doing so, they 'reified' religions (Smith, 1963).

This led to the definition of culture and religion – e.g., the Christian or Muslim 'religion' – that I referred to in the introduction: religions as entities that unite the people who share them and that distinguish them from others. The differences between people and their moral circles are (almost) absolute and unbridgeable. Thus, a multicultural society is a drama (Scheffer, 2011), and a dialogical or democratic self that is able to shift from one position to another, in accordance with different, even contradictory situations and moral circles, an illusion.

An example is Catherine Cornille's book *The Impossibility of Dialogue*. Referring to the pioneers of interreligious dialogue in the second half of the 20th century, who believed that dialogue between religions might eventually lead to convergence between them, Cornille (2008, p. 209) writes that at present, "few would still share the optimism of these pioneers of dialogue. After some decades of significant effort at interreligious dialogue, there is little noticeable growth in religious traditions. In fact, one too often notes a contrary tendency to sharpen and reassert the boundaries of one's own distinctive identity in the face of religious diversity."

Cornille (2008, p. 2) writes: "As the history of religions amply bears out, the encounter between members of different religions leads to tension and violence more often than to peaceful coexistence and collaboration." But the empirical fact is that in most countries most Muslims and Christians live harmoniously together; and clashes or conflicts are 'ir-regularities' more than rule (Esposito & Mogahed, 2007; Marshall, 2016). So, maybe the main question is not the one that I started with, why and under what conditions are people no longer able to compromise, but why and under what conditions are people able to do so (Wijsen, 2013, p. 161).

To answer this question, I decided to start at the other end; not with the identity, or how religion is in itself, but with interaction, making a discourse analysis of how religious identities are constructed, reproduced, and transformed in social relations to gain symbolic or material profit. This is how identities are constituted through discourse (Wijsen, 2013, pp. 53–73). By discourse, I mean a shared language that (groups of) people use to construct (a vision of) social reality that is considered real, true, meaningful, and normal. Discourse analysis is a specific view of and way of doing social scientific research in which discourse is not only the object of study but also a theoretical perspective. According to Fairclough (1992, pp. 72, 80, 95), the aim of discourse analysis is not to show if language is true, but to show explanatory connections between language use and social realities.

When I look back to the research program that I mentioned earlier, both philosophical-theological and social-psychological approaches share the same conviction, namely that religion exists, independently of actors. This conviction is based on a distinction between known object and knowing subject (Flood, 1999). This is what Wilfred Cantwell Smith (1963) in his famous book *The Meaning and End of Religion* called the reification of religion. An attitude towards a reality (belief) became a reality itself, an entity. However, religion exists not in a reified way, but in a discursive way (Von Stuckrad, 2013; Von Stuckrad & Wijsen, 2016). The consequences of these different conceptualizations for our research are huge. If religion is an entity, it is fixed; if it is a construct, it is flexible and fluid. Let us look more closely at what scholars of religion study (object) and how they study it (method).

What do scholars of religion study?

There are endless debates about the definition of religion. Religion is said to be belief in spiritual beings, ultimate concern, relation with super-natural, super-human, or other worldly beings. But the basic question is: what makes a human practice, opinion, or artifact a religious practice, opinion, or artifact? A fact is that believers within and between religions do not agree on what is religious, and what is not. For ordinary Catholics, praying and burning candles at a statue of the Blessed Virgin is worship; for Protestants, this is idolatry. For Sufis, visiting the graves of saints is a religious practice; for orthodox Sunni, it is the opposite of religion.

From a social science perspective, this shows that human practices, opinions, or artifacts are not religious in themselves, but that they become religious because they are placed in a specific narrative context by the believers and is shared by the members of a speech community. A religious artifact or practice is what it is because believers say that it is what it is. They attribute a religious meaning to it (Von Stuckrad, 2013, p. 17). That is why the boundary between what is considered religious and what is not shifted in history; and that is why something that is considered to be religious within a speech community is not religious for people outside that speech community. Thus, in the same way as post-structuralist cultural anthropologists say that cultures do not exist, I tend to say that religion is not some 'thing' that exists 'out there,' but a construct in the mind of the scholar. As Jonathan Smith (1982) pointed out in his book *Imagining Religion*: "Religion is solely the creation of the scholar's study. It is created for the scholar's analytic purposes by his imaginative acts of comparison and generalization. Religion has no existence apart from the academy."

In keeping with this theory, we move beyond a reified understanding of religion as some 'thing' out there to a narrative one, without going to the other extreme of nominalism. 'Hinduism' was not 'discovered' but 'invented' by Max Müller. And what scholars now call African (Indigenous or Traditional) Religion was called idolatry, paganism, or animism; thus the opposite of religion, before. Thus, Hinduism and African Religion are to a significant extent constructs. This is not to deny that they exist (Fairclough, 2003, pp. 8, 14, 209). Millions of people position themselves as Hindu or African believers. But these 'religions' exist only if and to the extent that they are reproduced. This is what 'social facts' are all about (Fairclough, 2003, pp. 8, 15, 209).

So, unlike phenomenologists such as Gerardus van der Leeuw (1973), Bourdieu says that human beings are not religious by nature; religion is social through and through, produced and reproduced by language. Speaking about liturgy Bourdieu (1991, p. 116) said that language is effective if the speaker is considered trustworthy and addresses issues that are considered relevant by the hearers. I do not define religion in a phenomenological way, observing manifestations of religion and comparing them, and by doing so trying to grasp the essence of religion (Van der Leeuw, 1973). I define religion in a discursive way, starting from the idea that "religion is the societal organization of knowledge about religion" (Von Stuckrad, 2013, p. 17). Put differently, scholars of religion do not study religion, but the way religion comes about.

How do scholars of religion study religion?

The shift in understanding of religion from phenomenon to narrative equals the shift in the understanding of the self from realist to discursive. According to Fairclough (1992, pp. 23–25), discursive psychology has as advantage that it no longer sees the self as consistent; but it misses the social orientation. Consequently, in my work I link dialogical self theory as a research perspective and critical discourse analysis as a research method (Wijsen, 2013). Both these bodies of knowledge take inspiration from Michael Bakhtin's notions of 'voice' and 'polyphony' and are rooted in social constructivism with its dialogical and relational understanding of (social) reality (Flood, 1999).

According to Fairclough (1992, p. 56), any discourse has three levels, namely a personal (micro), an institutional (meso), and a societal (macro) level. For example, family interaction exists first as interpersonal relations between parents and children. However, the positions of 'father,' 'mother,' and 'child' go beyond the individual and are based on conventions that are shared and formalized, for example as family law (Fairclough, 1992, p. 65). Moreover, these positions and conventions are embedded in wider societal processes of democratization and commercialization.

Moreover, discourse always has three functions or aspects of constitutive effects (Fairclough, 1992, pp. 8, 10, 64, 238), namely subject positions or social identities ('selves'), social relations ('systems of dialogue'), and systems of knowledge and belief, or social cognitions ('mental maps'). The ideational function of a text is how the text signifies the world. For example, the way parents and children conceptualize 'family' determines whether they position themselves in an egalitarian or paternalistic relation.

According to Fairclough (1992, pp. 71–72), discourse analysis starts from three assumptions. The first assumption is that discourse is a practice just as any other practice; the only difference is its linguistic form. The second is that constitutive effects, or the relation between language use and social reality, are mediated through discursive practices, which are the production, distribution, and consumption of text. The third is that the relation between language use and social reality is dialectic. This is to say, language use influences social reality and vice versa.

In harmony with the three assumptions, discourse analysis has three dimensions, or stages (Fairclough, 1992, pp. 56, 73, 198–199, 231). The first stage is the analysis of discourse as linguistic practice, or formal features of text, also called 'description.' The second stage is the analysis of discourse as discursive practice, or production, distribution, and consumption of text, also called 'interpretation.' The third stage is the analysis of discourse as a social practice, or the social conditions and social effects of text, also called 'explanation'; this is the relating of text and context.

The case of Sheikh Ponda Issa Ponda

In trying to answer my question why and under what conditions are people no longer capable of shifting from one position to another in accordance with different, and even contradictory, situations – why and under what conditions are they not liquid and democratic, but rigid and radical – I draw in an exemplary way from fieldwork on Islamic radicalism in Tanzania (Wijsen & Ndaluka, 2012; Wijsen, 2013, pp. 75–90).

Discourse analysts can examine a whole corpus in broad terms, or give a detailed analysis of a small number of samples. Fairclough (1992, p. 230) prefers the latter, and I follow him in this respect by focusing on a particular outspoken figure who can serve as a metaphor for the whole Islamic radicalism discourse. By doing so, I link micro- and macro-level analysis, by showing how this discourse is influenced by, and in turn influences, wider societal discourses and realities. For this chapter I focus on one topic only, namely Muslims' perception of the Father of the Nation, Julius Nyerere. The interviewee was a 58-year-old adult male. His level of education is equivalent to form four, and he is a well-known Muslim leader in Dar es Salaam, secretary of 'Baraza Kuu,' a Muslim umbrella organization. In terms of religious education, he describes himself as an autodidact. He learned religion from various Sheikhs.

In the mass media, the interviewee, Ponda Issa Ponda (who agreed that his name could be mentioned), is positioned as a radical, extremist, and terrorist. He is an outspoken individual and is linked to the storming of the *Mwembe-chai* mosque in Dar es Salaam in 1999 where four Muslims were killed (Njozi, 2000, p. 9). He has frequently been detained as a threat to Tanzanian national security. Ponda Issa Ponda, who is labeled as 'sheikh,' is, in the words of one Western diplomat, "the public face of radicalism in Zanzibar," an important theological instigator for contemporary militant activism in both Tanzania and, more generally, in East Africa (Haynes, 2006, pp. 496–497). He is said to be responsible for a spate of violent incidents in 2002, including the armed takeovers of moderate mosques in Dar es Salaam and the firebombing of a tourist bar in Stone Town that left several people injured. A militant Islamic movement, *Simba wa Mungu* (God's Lion), was specifically singled out for fomenting much of the turmoil. This organization was alleged to take its lead from Ponda Issa Ponda, who was accused of actively inciting attacks against foreigners and 'morally corrupt' Muslims who failed to adhere to a purist Islamic line (Haynes, 2006, p. 496; LeSage, 2014, pp. 8, 9, 12).

Transcription of interview excerpts

When asked about the relations between Muslims and the government, the interviewee said that such relations were good during the common struggle for independence. Muslims supported the Father of the Nation in becoming the leader of the Tanganyika National Union. But after he became the first president, he started to marginalize them.

> For example, on the question of leadership, Muslims had their leadership in the past. They were in a good position, and they had expanded greatly to the level that it was no longer a national but instead, an international leadership, albeit limited to the three East African countries of Tanzania, Kenya, and Uganda. But what happened is that the government demonstrated that it was not comfortable with that unity because of a fear which has been explained by many authors, a fear which was rooted in religious foundations, especially in regard to the ruling leader of the time, Mwalimu Julius Kambarage Nyerere. And finally, the government disbanded that Muslim leadership without the consent of the Muslims themselves, and it blocked many projects, including educational projects such as the project of building an Islamic University at Chang'ombe in the year [19]64. Therefore, one can say that since that time the relations between Muslims and the Government have seriously gone down.

He continues,

> Therefore, I can answer that the relation between the Government and the Muslims is not very good. And it is not very good because the

government does not listen to Muslims and is not ready to sit down with them to listen to their grievances. Muslims feel that they are being oppressed, in this state of affairs; they are being denied their rights by the government. But one of the main violations of rights is the government's refusal to sit down with Muslims, so as to listen to their demands. This has not happened.

To further explain Nyerere's fear for Islam, the interviewee elaborates on his alliance with the Catholic Church:

For example, I read a translation of a book about Nyerere, written by Van Bergen. I belief its title is *Religion and Development*, or something like that . . . I read about it in an article. . . . The author says that there was a time that Nyerere softened his speech about ujamaa and self-reliance. The Catholic Church used to fear ujamaa and self-reliance because in general it [socialism] opposes God. Mwalimu [Nyerere] was accustomed to using the language of self-reliance to show that this was what he stood for. But also, the church was heavily reliant on Mwalimu (Nyerere) in the area of the growth of their faith and to get opportunities. Now, it is said that some of the leaders became doubtful and wondered if their son (Nyerere) was still their son. In [19]70 they sent a delegation to Mwalimu to make clear to him their doubts whether he was still their son, [whether he was still] their faithful, or [whether he had become] a communist.

He continues,

Now, according to what Van Bergen wrote, this is how Mwalimu responded to the church delegation . . . telling them: "I would like you to understand this issue and explain properly to the leaders of the church. I am just a mere lay person, but I try according to my ability and I will never betray my church. I want to give the church a good opportunity here in Tanzania so that it will not be blamed as it is being blamed in other catholic countries. Tanzania is not a Catholic country, but Catholicism is strong. Tell the bishops that I have set up a department of education in TANU and I have put a priest to lead it. He is not a professional politician but I have put him there on the basis of his faith and his humility. And on the main committee, I have put two representatives who are priests. I believe this is the right way of getting good people in the party."

Commenting on this, the interviewee says that,

when you consider that response and see what Nyerere did as president, you are forced to see that it is possible that the motivation for all this was religious. . . . So, you will realize that there were some secrets that Mwalimu had, which brings the understanding that those things were motivating Mwalimu . . . to do such fundamental things such as those.

After referring once again to Van Bergen's book, the interviewee says,

But more than this, I have read the book of Fr. Sivalon. If you read Fr. Sivalon's book . . ., it becomes clear that Mwalimu said openly that his intention was to make Tanzania a Christian country. And the one who is saying this is a priest and not a Muslim.

Concluding on the issue of Nyerere's fear for Islam and his attempt to block Muslims' development projects, the interviewee says:

for us what we see, he [Nyerere] never had any positive perception of the Muslim community. He did not like the development of Muslims. And for that reason he wanted it [the Muslim community] to be a community of lower class, a class which would always be ruled. This means, its ability was to remain small, a lower class, not a class that is powerful. It should not be a class with economic power. It should not be a class with political power, meaning that it has an own voice in politics.

And he continues:

Only he himself knew the reasons for doing such a thing. But, this is the general view of Mwalimu [Nyerere].

When asked to elaborate on the presidents that succeeded Nyerere, the interviewee answered that they all had the same attitude, even the Muslim presidents among them. When talking about the fourth president, Jakaya Kikwete, the interviewee mentioned terrorism, and the impact of the Anti Terrorism Act. The interviewee says that Kikwete sentenced to jail many leaders of Islam without reason.

All those cases of people who are sent to prison concern leaders of Islam, and until today not one case has been heard.

And, he continues,

I myself was imprisoned for a long time without any reason; I was beaten, injured. This was during the last term. I was beaten by the intelligence. Thus, you see that there is no justice. And those who are still in prison are important leaders of Islam.

The fear for Islam also applies to the current president. As evidence, he gives the imbalance between Muslim and Christian appointments in the government. Therefore, "that is one of the issues that give rise to great doubts." On the other hand, he also sees improvement.

> Among the things that I say are good is his intention to try to bring responsibility to the government institutions.

Analysis of the discourse

In the analysis of the discourse I follow the three stages mentioned earlier. First, I deal with the analysis of discourse as a linguistic practice, or the formal features of the text, in terms of vocabulary and grammar.

Looking at the wording, we notice that the interviewee uses political vocabulary. Out of a total of 13,393 words, he uses the word "right" (in different combinations) 28 times; "politics," 17 times; "development," 14 times; and "citizens," 11 times. He speaks about "lowest class of citizens," "oppression," "violation of human rights," "power," and "class." Furthermore, he repeats words (over-wording) to make his point:

> [Nyerere] wanted it [the Muslim community] to be a community of lower class, a class which would always be ruled. This means, its ability was to remain small, a lower class, not a class that is powerful. It should not be a class with economic power. It should not be a class with political power, meaning, that it has an own voice in politics.

In these three sentences he repeats the word "class" six times. Over-wording is a sign of intense preoccupation pointing to peculiarities in the ideology of the group responsible for it (Fairclough, 1992, p. 193).

Looking at the grammar, by frequently using the passive voice ("a class which would always be ruled," "are being oppressed," "are being denied their rights"), he frames the debate in terms of oppressors and oppressed, urging that the agency lies elsewhere.

Secondly, I deal with the analysis of discourse as a discursive practice, which is the production, distribution, and consumption of text, in terms of intertextuality and mental models.

The interviewee draws on historical instances in the past that are stored in long-term memory, such as the banning of the East Africa Muslim Welfare Society and the banning of its development projects, such as the Muslim University.

To make his point, the interviewee refers to "many authors" who wrote about Nyerere's fear for Islam and rootedness in the Catholic Church. He refers to an (anonymous) author of an article, who draws on Van Bergen's book on religion and development, and quotes Nyerere. By using the word "class" frequently, he implicitly draws on the vocabulary of what is known as the 'Dar es Salaam school,' a group of neo-Marxist economists and political scientists at the University of Dar es Salaam in the early 1970s.

Thirdly, I deal with the analysis of discourse as social practice, or the social conditions and social effects of the texts, in terms of social identities (subject positions), social relations, and social cognitions (mental maps).

The interviewee positions himself as an individual, as a member of the Muslim community, as a secretary of an Islamic organization, and as a citizen of the nation. He frequently shifts between these *I*-positions, or 'selves,' in speaking about injustice done to him personally when he was in prison, and injustice done to him as a member of the Muslim community, but above all, injustice done to him as a citizen of the nation. In terms of dialogical self theory (Hermans, 2018, pp. 65–71), his position as 'citizen' serves as a promoter position, a position that gives direction to the other positions in the position repertoire.

By adding "the supreme leaders of Islam are still in prison" to "after I was released from prison," he shows that he does not consider himself to be one of the "supreme leaders of Islam," although in the mass media he is identified as such. The interviewee positions himself as a social activist rather than a Muslim scholar. There are no references to the Qur'an, the Prophet, or Islamic thought, nor does he use typical Islamic vocabulary. Only once, at the very end of the interview, he uses a common Muslim expression, *Insha'Allah* (micro level of discourse).

He identifies the government leaders and the political institutions (meso level of discourse) as discriminative against Muslims instead of doing justice, and he transforms the general picture of Nyerere as "Mwalimu" (teacher; also referred to as Father of the Nation) to a "Son of the Church," insinuating that he favored one group above other groups.

And he transforms the general picture (mental map) of the Tanzania government from promoting national "unity" to creating religious "divides."

By saying "this is the general view" (of Mwalimu), he naturalizes the debate. Through naturalization, heterogeneous realities become fixed and stable by converting situations and interpretations that are contingent into the one and only one (Fairclough, 1992, p. 75). According to Fairclough (1992, p. 97), such a process of naturalization is essential to establishing new hegemonies in the sphere of discourse.

Conclusion and discussion

When I look at the case analyzed in this chapter, I conclude that the interviewee shifts between various positions. On the one hand, he uses quite a few 'us' (Muslims) versus 'them' (government) classifications. On the other hand, he transcends the 'us' and 'them' classifications in a promoter position, namely '*I* as a citizen.' He also changes his perspective by saying, "Among the things that I say are good is his [President Magufuli's] intention to try to bring responsibility to the government institutions." At least in this interview, sheikh Ponda Issa Ponda does not position himself as radical and extremist as he is portrayed in the mass media. And, he was released from prison twice because judges could not find evidence of any criminal acts.

My question was, why and under what conditions are people no longer capable of shifting from one position to another, according to different, even contradictory, situations? Hermans and Hermans-Konopka (2010, pp. 3, 28, 40) suggest that uncertainty is the main cause of rigidity. In the case that I analyzed in this chapter, it is humiliation; "the government does not listen to Muslims and is not ready to sit down with them to listen to their grievances" (note the repetition of 'listen'). According to the interviewee, Muslims feel that "they are being oppressed" and "denied their rights."

'Us' and 'them' classifications (as conceptualized in social identity theory) are there, but they are overcome by more inclusive classifications under the condition that there are common interests. As the interviewee said, "relations between Muslims and Christians were good" during the struggle for independence in Tanzania, and we know this from other countries as well. Actors are simultaneously collaborators and competitors in different fields (Bourdieu, 1991), and complex theories that combine cognitive and material explanations of inter-group conflicts are needed (Taylor & Moghaddam, 1994, pp. 195–206).

This brings us to a discussion of some of the theoretical issues that were introduced. First, my claim that, better than social identity theory, dialogical self theory can explain that out-group friendship exists; and that dialogical self theory is easier to understand and to explain liquid, hybrid, or multiple identities. Whereas from the perspective of social identity theory it would be possible to conceptualize membership of and identification with various groups, it would be difficult to conceptualize identification with various 'we groups' simultaneously. The underlying logic is exclusive and dualistic, either-or, black or white. The notion of social identity complexity (Roccas & Brewer, 2002) is a step forward in this respect.

Based on my previous findings, I argue that identification is always partial, and that there are degrees of group identification. And, coming back to the relationship between social identity theory and dialogical self theory, I hypothesize that social identity theory conceptualizes mainly dysfunctions, whereas dialogical self theory conceptualizes functions of culture and religion.

Second, (how) can one draw such conclusions from small-scale projects like ours? How can one argue from interviews with individual respondents to societal processes and patterns? Is it legitimate to do so? According to critical discourse analysts, it is, because they study shared knowledge or social cognitions (mental models) that go beyond the individual interviewees. Whereas interviews are always micro-level discourse, there are different layers of discourse. Interviewees speak for themselves, as individuals, as members of institutions, and as citizens of nations, and these levels are interrelated. These discourses are shared and reproduced, or they are not.

Their reproduction can be confirmed by analyzing other discourses, such as social media or policy documents (Fairclough, 1992, p. 238).

In our case, *ujamaa* rhetoric was started by one person, Julius Nyerere. As said before, according to Bourdieu (1991, pp. 107–116), discourse is effective as long as the speaker is considered trustworthy and addresses real-life issues. This was the case with Nyerere. But the effects of his speech continued as long as these conditions were met. In 1985, the *ujamaa* system collapsed, due to another, more powerful rhetoric, neoliberalism. The speaker was no longer believed to be trustworthy, and his speech was no longer considered relevant (Wijsen, 2013, pp. 148–149). Furthermore, he could no longer control the media, which is also an essential element of discourse reproduction.

But, how can discourse have social effects? From the perspective of critical discourse analysis, the answer would be through reproduction. This brings critical discourse analysis close to new institutionalism theory: actors produce institutions; and, if they are reproduced by them, institutions are objectified (Fairclough, 2003, pp. 8, 14, 209). Critical discourse analysis aims at linking a micro-sociological conversation type of analysis to a macro-sociological analysis inspired by critical theory, hence linking humanities and social science. Dialogical self theory notions such as 'the self as a mini society,' or 'the society of mind,' also help to connect micro level and macro-level analysis.

Third, (how) can social identity theory and dialogical self theory be compared? Do they not theorize different things? Whereas social identity theory is basically a social psychology theory about inter-group relations, it theorizes that persons derive their identity from group membership; thus, it is linked to personality psychology. Whereas dialogical self theory originates from personality psychology, it is more interested in the influence of societal processes such as migration and internationalization on individual persons (Hermans & Hermans-Konopka, 2010; Hermans, 2018). So, there is an overlap.

Nevertheless, dialogical self theory remains indebted to clinical psychology. Possibly a cultural psychology perspective, which theorizes that a person and environment co-constitute one another (Kim, 2002, p. 8), would be a way forward, and it is good to note that dialogical self theory is moving into that direction. But, how can one conceptualize this co-constitution? In my work, I suggest linking dialogical self theory and critical discourse analysis. Fairclough (1992, pp. 23–25) is critical about discursive psychology approaches because they lack social orientation. Both traditions nevertheless draw from the same roots (dialogism, constructivism), but there is almost no interaction between them. However, the link between 'subject positions' (critical discourse analysis) and '*I*-positions' (dialogical self theory) is obvious, as is the notion that selves are relational and dialogic, both intra and inter. For critical discourse analysis, the basic question is: whose voice is this?

This also shows the difference between critical discourse analysis and other discourse analytical approaches. Whereas these other approaches are linguistic and cognitive (van Dijk, 2011, 2012), critical discourse analysis is rooted in market mechanisms of production, distribution, and consumption (Bourdieu, 1991). Although, more so than Fairclough, I see not only a mediation between the stages of text analysis and social analysis through discursive practice, but also between the micro and the macro levels of discourse through the institutional (meso) or supra-individual level of discourse.

Fourth, (how) does the contrast between clash of civilizations (social identity theory) and multiple voiced-ness (dialogical self theory) have something to do with the conceptualization and operationalization of civilization and culture, including religion? According to Hofstede et al. (2010), culture is the 'collective mental programming' or 'software of the mind.' This resonates with the concept of culture as a collective meaning system that is shared by the members of a group that unites them and differentiates them from others. But it is not. Culture is not a shared meaning system but the 'organization of diversity' (Hannerz, 1992, pp. 10–15).

Over the past ten years my research assistants and I focused on 'us' and 'them' classifications, or ingroup–out-group polarities in Tanzania (Wijsen & Ndaluka, 2012), Indonesia (Wijsen & Cholil, 2014), and the Netherlands (Wijsen & Vos, 2015). We conducted interviews with some 400 people. We found that most respondents tried to maintain harmony and avoid conflict. Of course, being qualitative in nature, these studies do not pretend to be representative, and 'hard-liners' or 'radicals' were under-represented, though not totally absent in our studies. But our findings are confirmed by large-scale quantitative studies (Esposito & Mogahed, 2007).

I nevertheless hypothesize that large-scale quantitative studies tend to overemphasize exclusion due to the nature of questionnaires. In designing a questionnaire, one needs unambiguous, exclusive, clear-cut categories – dichotomies – such as Hofstede et al. (2010, p. 23) have them. However, there are ambiguities and complexities, multiplicities of meaning that are difficult to grasp in surveys. In a survey conducted by one of my co-authors, Suhadi Cholil, about a quarter of his nearly 300 respondents refused to put themselves in a box and came up with self-identifications he had not thought of before (Wijsen, 2013, p. 188).

This does not mean that large-scale quantitative research is no longer necessary, but that it has limitations, and that quantitative research needs to be complemented by in-depth qualitative research for better understanding. This is not a new insight at all. Hofstede et al. (2010, p. 368) write that analyses of individuals, groups, and societies (the 'Flowers, Bouquets, and Gardens' of the social sciences) must complement each other, but not many studies do this successfully.

Fifth, what about my claim that, better than social identity theory with its 'us' and 'them' dichotomy, dialogical self theory is able to adapt to non-Western culture? All theories are culture-specific (Hofstede et al., 2010,

p. 336), and both social identity theory and dialogical self theory are based in Western culture. I use 'Western' as a historical, not a geographic category. 'Western' stands for the heritage of (European) Enlightenment and the values of (European) modernity, but they are being embraced by people who live in the geographic non-Western World.

Nevertheless, dialogical self theory potentially has a wider application. The 'autonomous self' is a typically 'Western,' modern construct but is paradoxically also criticized in the West (Hermans, 2018, p. 3). According to Descartes, people are independent and distinct from others (Kim, 2002, p. 161). People living in 'non-Western' societies, and who make up 70% of the world's population (Kim, 2002, p. 5) tend to be more community-oriented and 'dialogical.'[2] They are used to adapting themselves to a variety of situations and chose narratives of the self that are appropriate to them (Kim, 2002, p. 181).

Sixth, (how) can these insights be helpful for political and spiritual leaders who try to predict, prevent, and combat radicalism? In my view these insights can help these leaders to transcend narrow-minded group identities and expand closed 'moral circles' (Hofstede et al., 2010, p. 13). Returning to the issue of the conceptualization of culture (including religion), throughout this chapter I have argued that it makes a difference whether cultural identities and moral circles are seen as fixed or fluid.

According to the interviewee, "one of the main violations of rights is the government's refusal to sit down with Muslims, so as to listen to their demands." If this is indeed the case, this is not a wise policy. From the perspective of dialogical leadership, the government must not silence peripheral voices but let them speak. Extremists do not see themselves as 'extremists' but as freedom fighters who want to liberate their fellows from injustices committed against them. Dialogical leadership would require taking a meta-position (Hermans, 2018, pp. 72–75) that allows a helicopter view of other positions, which serves as mediation between them (van Loon & van Dijk, 2015).

Notes

1 See also the reference to David Tracy in K. Gergen, Chapter 1 in this volume.
2 Further evidence for this statement can be found in the *ubuntu* (humankind) philosophy as introduced by ter Avest, Chapter 5 in this volume. *Ubuntu* is close to the notion of *ujamaa* (familyhood) in this chapter.

References

Abbas, T. (2011). *Islamic radicalism and multicultural politics: The British experience*. London and New York, NY: Routledge.

Allport, G. (1958). *The nature of prejudice*. New York, NY: Doubleday.

Assmann, J. (2003). *Die Mosaische Unterscheidung oder der Preis des Monotheismus*. München: Carl Hansen Verlag.

Bakhtin, M. M. (1981). *The dialogical imagination*. (C. Emerson & M. Holquist, Trans.). Austin: University of Texas Press.

Barber, B. (1995). *Jihad vs. McWorld*. New York, NY: Ballantine.

Bauman, Z. (2000). *Liquid modernity*. Cambridge: Polity Press.

Bourdieu, P. (1990). *In other words: Essays towards reflexive sociology*. Stanford, CA: Stanford University Press.

Bourdieu, P. (1991). *Language and symbolic power*. Cambridge: Polity Press.

Burke, P. (2009). *Cultural hybridity*. Cambridge: Polity Press.

Cornille, C. (2008). *The im-possibility of interreligious dialogue*. New York, NY: Cross Road Publishing.

Esposito, J., & Mogahed, D. (2007). *Who speaks for Islam? What a billion Muslims really think*. New York, NY: Gallup Press.

Fairclough, N. (1992). *Discourse and social change*. Cambridge: Polity Press.

Fairclough, N. (2003). *Analysing discourse: Textual analysis for social research*. London and New York, NY: Routledge.

Flood, G. (1999). *Beyond phenomenology: Rethinking the study of religion*. London and New York, NY: Cassell.

Girard, R. (1977). *Violence and the sacred*. Baltimore, MD: John Hopkins University Press.

Hannerz, U. (1992). *Cultural complexity: Studies in the social organization of meaning*. New York, NY: Columbia University Press.

Harrison, L., & Huntington, S. (Eds.). (2000). *Culture matters: How values shape human progress*. New York, NY: Basic Books.

Haynes, J. (2006). Islam and democracy in East Africa. *Democratization, 13*(3), 490–507.

Hermans, H., & Gieser, Th. (2012). Introductory chapter: History, main tenets and core concepts of dialogical self theory. In H. J. M. Hermans & Th. Gieser (Eds.), *Handbook of dialogical self theory* (pp. 1–22). Cambridge: Cambridge University Press.

Hermans, H. J. M. (2018). *Society in the self: A theory of identity in democracy*. New York, NY: Oxford University Press.

Hermans, H. J. M., & Hermans-Konopka, A. (2010). *Dialogical self theory: Positioning and counter-positioning in a globalizing society*. Cambridge: Cambridge University Press.

Hermans, H. J. M., & Kempen, H. J. G. (1992). *The dialogical self: Meaning as movement*. San Diego, CA: Academic Press.

Hofstede, G., Hofstede, G.-J., & Minkov, M. (2010). *Cultures and organisations: Software of the mind*. New York, NY: McGraw Hill.

Huntington, S. P. (1996). *The clash of civilizations and the remaking of the world order*. New York, NY: Simon & Schuster.

Jürgensmeyer, M. (2000). *Terror in the mind of God: The global rise of religious violence*. Berkeley, CA: University of California Press.

Kim, M-S. (2002). *Non-Western perspectives on human communication*. Thousand Oaks, CA: Sage Publications.

Kristeva, J. (1986). Word, dialogue and novel. In T. Moi (Ed.), *The Kristeva reader* (pp. 34–61). Oxford: Wiley Blackwell.

LeSage, A. (2014). *The rising terrorist threat in Tanzania: Domestic Islamist militancy and regional threats*. Strategic Forum No. 288. Institute for National Defense Strategic Studies, National Defense University.

Maalouf, A. (2000). *In the name of identity: Violence and the need to belong*. New York, NY: Arace Publishing.

Mamdani, M. (2004). *Good Muslim, bad Muslim: America, the cold war and the roots of terror*. New York, NY: Pantheon Books.

Marshall, M. (2016). *Major episodes of political violence*. University of Maryland, Center for Systemic Peace. Retrieved May 22, 2017, from www.systemicpeace. org/warlist/warlist.htm

Masuzawa, T. (2005). *The invention of world religions: Or, how European universalism was preserved in the langue of pluralism*. Chicago, IL: University of Chicago Press.

Njozi, H. (2000). *The Mwembechai killings and the political future of Tanzania*. Ottawa: Globalink Communications.

Pinker, S. (2011). *The better angels of our nature: The decline of violence in history and its causes*. New York, NY: Viking.

Robertson, R. (1995). Glocalization: Time-space and homogeneity heterogeneity. In M. Featherstone, S. Lash, & R. Robertson (Eds.), *Global modernities* (pp. 25–44). London: Sage Publications.

Roccas, S., & Brewer, M. (2002). Social identity complexity. *Personality and Social Psychology Review*, 6(2), 88–106.

Scheffer, P. (2011). *Immigrant nations*. Cambridge: Polity Press.

Scott Appleby, R. (2000). *The ambivalence of the sacred: Religion, violence and reconciliation*. Boston, MA: Rowman & Littlefield Publishers, Inc.

Selengut, C. (2003). *Sacred fury: Understanding religious violence*. Walnut Creek, CA: Altamira Press.

Sherif, M. (1966). *Group conflict and cooperation*. London: Routledge & Kegan Paul.

Smith, J. (1982). *Imagining religion, from Babylon to Jonestown*. Chicago, IL: University of Chicago Press.

Smith, W. (1963). *The meaning and end of religion: A new approach to the religious traditions of mankind*. New York, NY: New American Library.

Sumner, W. (1906). *Folkways: A study of the sociological importance of usages, manners, customs and morals*. Boston, MA, and New York, NY: Ginn and Company.

Tajfel, H. (1978). Social categorization, social identity and social comparison. In H. Tajfel (Ed.), *Differentiation between groups* (pp. 61–76). London: Academic Press.

Tajfel, H., & Turner, J. (1986). The social identity theory of intergroup behaviour. In S. Worchel & W. Austin (Eds.), *Psychology of intergroup relations* (pp. 7–24). Chicago, IL: Nelson-Hall Publishers.

Taylor, D., & Moghaddam, F. (1994). *Theories on intergroup relations: International social psychological perspectives*. Westport, CT, and London: Praeger.

Tayob, A. (2017). Religion and life trajectories: Islamists against self and other. In J. Rüpke & C. Uehlinger (Eds.), *Dynamics of religion: Past and present* (pp. 155–170). Berlin and Boston, MA: De Gruyter.

Van Binsbergen, W. (2003). *Intercultural encounters: African and anthropological lessons towards a philosophy of interculturality*. Münster: LIT Verlag.

Van der Leeuw, G. (1973). *Religion in essence and manifestation: A study in phenomenology*. London: George Allen & Unwin, Ltd.

Van Dijk, T. (2011). Discourse, knowledge, power and politics. In C. Hart (Ed.), *Critical discourse studies in context and cognition* (pp. 27–64). Amsterdam and Philadelphia, PA: John Benjamins.

Van Dijk, T. (2012). Knowledge, discourse and domination. In M. Meeuwis & J.-O. Östman (Eds.), *Pragmaticizing understanding: Studies for Jef Verschueren.* Amsterdam and Philadelphia, PA: John Benjamins.

Van Loon, R., & van Dijk, G. (2015). Dialogical leadership: Dialogue as condition zero. *Journal of Leadership, Accountability and Ethics, 12*(3), 62–75.

Von Stuckrad, K. (2013). Discursive study of religion: Approaches, definitions and implications. *Method & Theory in the Study of Religion, 25,* 5–25.

Von Stuckrad, K., & Wijsen, F. (2016). Introduction. In F. Wijsen & K. von Stuckrad (Eds.), *Making religion: Theory and practice of discursive study of religion.* Leiden: Brill.

Widdicombe, S. (1998). Identity as an analysts' and a participants' resource. In C. Antaki & S. Widdicombe (Eds.), *Identities in talk* (pp. 191–206). London and Thousand Oaks, CA: Sage Publications.

Wijsen, F. (2007). *Seeds of conflict in a haven of peace: From religious studies to interreligious studies in Africa.* Amsterdam and New York, NY: Rodopi.

Wijsen, F. (2013). *Religious discourse, social cohesion and conflict: Studying Muslim-Christian relations.* Oxford: Peter Lang Publishing Group.

Wijsen, F., & Cholil, S. (2014). "I come from a Pancasila family." Muslims and Christians in Indonesia. In V. Küster & R. Setio (Eds.), *Muslim Christian relations observed: Comparative studies from Indonesia and the Netherlands* (pp. 29–46). Leipzig: Evangelische Verlagsanstalt.

Wijsen, F., & Mfumbusa, B. (2002). Seeds of conflict: Muslim-Christian relations in Tanzania. In J. Gort, H. Jansen, & H. Vroom (Eds.), *Religion, conflict and reconciliation: Multifaith ideals and realities* (pp. 316–326). Amsterdam and New York, NY: Editions Rodopi.

Wijsen, F., & Ndaluka, T. (2012). "Ujamaa is still alive." A sign of hope for Africa? In A. Bwangatto (Ed.), *Africa is not destined to die: Signs of hope and renewal: The fifth international conference on Africa* (pp. 240–253). Nairobi: Paulines Publications.

Wijsen, F., & Tanner, R. (2002). *"I am just a Sukuma": Globalization and identity construction in Northwest Tanzania.* Amsterdam and New York, NY: Editions Rodopi.

Wijsen, F., & Vos, J. (2015). "Rice and rice with sambal": Indonesians and Moluccans in the Netherlands. In C. Sterkens & P. Vermeer (Eds.), *Religion, migration and conflict* (pp. 53–71). Zürich: LIT Verlag.

4 Plural moralities and the search for meaning

Hans Alma

Introduction

In this chapter, I will address the question of plural moralities from a broad perspective, not just as an ethical question, but as related to what people consider to be good and meaningful in an aesthetical, existential, and spiritual sense as well. People have an urgent need to feel that their life is meaningful and has value. The philosopher Thomas Alexander speaks in this context of the human eros: the urge of the human psyche toward the full, embodied experience of meaning and value in the world (Alexander, 2013, p. 5). I want to stress Alexander's use of the word 'embodiment': the search for meaning is not only, or not even primarily, an intellectual process but involves the whole person in both sensory, embodied, affective, and cognitive ways. Meaning-making is about how I sense the world, how my body relates to it, what feelings are evoked, and the understanding I gain from this general perception. This is why the domain of aesthetics belongs to the human eros (referring to 'aisthēsis' as knowledge of the sensible).

This need for the feeling that one's life is meaningful and fulfilling is not to be thought of lightly; it is rooted in a basic urge to belong to this world. According to the political scientist William Connolly, a secure sense of belonging is lost in the modern world, in which every conception of what is meaningful feels as optional. I come back to his argument in a later section. For now, it is important that he refers to the claim of Gilles Deleuze that today we need to find ways to '*restore* belief in this world' (Connolly, 2011, p. 61). This existential need is at stake in our search for meaning. A core element of the experience of meaning in life is the sense of belonging to something larger than ourselves. On the one hand, we can feel securely related to this larger whole, whether it is our social group, nature, the cosmos, or God. On the other hand, it can evoke our curiosity for exploration and transcending boundaries. The need for security and the need for self-transcendence are closely related but sometimes conflict with one another (cf. Alma, 2005). For a long time in the history of the Western world, religion provided the 'playing field' for their interplay as a key element of meaning-making. It can't be taken for granted anymore that religion or a non-religious world-view plays this role in the life of modern people. It is this change of relevance of (religious) worldviews that I want to address in my reflection on plural moralities. Before I do so, however, one more basic assumption in my approach needs to be made explicit.

Although I sometimes make use of the concept of meaning-making, I don't see this as an activity of an isolated self that has to construct meaning to be able to relate to the world. In my perspective, relationship is most fundamental. People are embedded in relations from the very start of their lives, and it is only through relations that they develop a sense of self. Much in line with the thinking of Kenneth J. Gergen (2009; Chapter 1 in this volume), I see the search for meaning as a relational process in which an embodied person and her/his (social) world participate. It unfolds in a practice of acting upon and reacting to one another, and in this practice, meaning is 'found' or 'received' as much as 'made.' To be able to experience meaning in, for example, nature, we relate to a natural environment with our sensitivities that receive an 'answer' from the natural surroundings. This answer may not be what we had expected; we may be disappointed or overwhelmed. It is exactly because we cannot control the experience of meaning that we can feel joy, or awe, or bliss.

From this relational perspective on human's search for meaning, I build a case for pluralism as a way of coping with today's challenges of moral pluralities in secularized, Western countries. First, I will further explore the role of (religious) worldviews in how people connect to their world and find meaning in it. I will then focus on the diversity of worldviews in modern societies and the claimed neutrality in liberal, secular countries like the Netherlands. I will argue that this neutrality cannot be realized and hinders a public debate about the issues that matter most to people living in these societies. The challenges of our times ask for another way of dealing with plural moralities, and I will defend a form of pluralism that rests on three pillars: justice as evenhandedness (Carens, 2000), building new connections that contribute to a sense of belonging (Connolly, 2011), and moral imagination (Lederach, 2005). Finally, I will argue that this form of pluralism can be realized only by strengthening a relational approach to moral and spiritual leadership.

Worldview and 'big questions'

The cultural anthropologist André Droogers (2014) relates (religious) worldviews to a set of basic and ultimate questions that people have always and everywhere asked themselves out of a deep need to understand, trust, and emotionally connect to the world they live in. We can distinguish several varieties of these ultimate or big questions. I follow the distinction of religious scholars Ann Taves, Egil Asprem, and Elliott Ihm (2018) and come to the following sets of questions (with their related philosophical disciplines):

- What exists? What is the nature of our world? (ontology)
- What is good and bad, beautiful and ugly, valuable and valueless? What is the meaning of life? (axiology)
- What should we do? (praxeology)
- How do we gain knowledge about what is true? (epistemology)
- Where does everything come from, and where are we going to? (cosmology)

Together, answers to these five sets of questions give insight into what people consider to be the good life in both an existential and identity-building way: they touch on the foundations of our existence and orient us towards who we are and where we belong to. Of course, in normal life people don't often explicitly deal with these questions, but a worldview rests on the human capacity to ask and answer big questions, thus contributing in important ways to people's sense of belonging. This holds for both religious and so-called secular worldviews; I use the term worldview as an overarching term for both.

The capacity to ask and answer big questions has both cognitive and affective components. I would like to propose a third component, or rather, a bridge between cognition and affection: credition. This proposal is based on the Credition Research Project developed by the theologian Hans-Ferdinand Angel at the University of Graz (cf. Seitz & Angel, 2012, 2015). A basic assumption of this project is that the process of believing – to be distinguished from belief as a noun that is often associated with religion – is a basic human capacity. In analogy to the terms cognition and emotion, Angel refers to this process of believing as credition, derived from the Latin 'credere.' There is a constant interplay between cognition, credition, and emotion. The process of believing involves cognitive contents and gains emotional charge. Cognitive processes are seldom purely rational but are influenced by emotions that give credibility to cognitions. Due to our emotional involvement in the world around us, we hold some cognitive contents to be more credible than others. This interplay between cognitions, creditions, and emotions helps us to find our balance in coping with our changing circumstances. We are more resilient with regard to the challenges we face when these three processes work together. According to this view, unbelief is not an option. We can find the same thought with Connolly: "Every existential stance is infused with belief, though often operating at several levels and punctuated by doubt" (Connolly, 2011, p. 85).

Central to processes of believing is the human capacity to see things not only as they *are*, but also as they *could be*. We relate to the world not only as it presents itself factually to us, but also in its possibility: the world opens itself to the future in a fundamentally undetermined way. I refer to the human capacity to relate to possibility with the term imagination, and I will argue that the imagination plays a pivotal role in every worldview. To do so, I distinguish imagination from free-floating fantasy, which disconnects us from the reality we share with others. In contrast, the imagination is rooted in an attentive perception of the actual situation, resulting in the discovery of new possibilities in that situation. Thomas Alexander defines imagination as the ability to see the actual in light of the possible. Every situation carries potentials that we can either neglect or pay attention to. Artists are talented in discovering and articulating these potentials. But we all use our imagination in daily matters, e.g., in preparing for a meeting we will have tomorrow. We imagine what the other participants will say and how we will react to that. In this 'mental rehearsal' we explore several possibilities, and this helps us to come to adequate reactions in the real meeting.

The philosopher John Dewey distinguishes between two closely related forms of imagination: (a) taking the perspective of others (empathy), and (b) creatively tapping a situation's possibilities (cf. Fesmire, 2003). Both empathy and creativity depend on attentive perception of what is actually taking place (listening to the other, opening oneself to everything the present situation has to offer), but also on the knowledge and experience we carry with us to understand the situation. We can take the perspective of another person, because we have ample experience in communicating with other people. We can discover the potentials of a situation, because we have experienced something like this before or have read about it. A good example of this latter form of imagination comes from the paintings of Vincent van Gogh. Although he painted mostly in open air, his work is never an exact representation of the landscape. He painted his surroundings in a surprising way. From the letters to his brother Theo, we learn that he was inspired by paintings he had seen before, or by books he had read. He trusted the (art) tradition he participated in to be innovative in his paintings.

In this chapter, I am mainly interested in how the imagination can help us to answer the five sets of ultimate questions that build the core of a worldview. In these answers, cognition, credition, and emotion come together: worldviews offer contents that are credible because of the emotions they evoke in us. The answers to the ultimate questions (what exists, what is beautiful and good, what should we do, what is true, what is our purpose) orient us in our convictions regarding the good life. Convictions come with imaginaries of the good life that imbue them with moral power. The imagination enables us to really aspire to what we consider to be good. This is not without risks, especially when imagination is confounded with fantasy or even delusions. In history, we find many examples of imaginaries of the good life that were realized in disastrous ways, both on individual and collective levels. On an individual level, one's ideals may be self-destructive; on a collective level, the social imaginaries of people can be manipulated in dictatorial ways. A famous example is the movie *Triumph des Willens* by Leni Riefenstahl, in which art and Nazi propaganda blur. The imaginaries that come with ideologies and worldviews ask for critical reflection to realize what I will later present as moral imagination. First, however, I explore the role of worldviews in the context of our late-modern societies.

Worldview in the context of a late-modern society

My point of departure is that people have a deep-rooted, embodied longing for a meaningful life that has value. This longing inspires them to imagine the good life. The imagination that enables them to do so has a social basis: it develops from an early-acquired capacity to take the perspective of others and from imaginaries of what is meaningful and valuable in their social environment. These social imaginaries of the good life have an existential and identity-building value, and they usually work in implicit ways. However, they are the building blocks of more explicit worldviews.

For a long time in history, worldviews and their institutions have had a huge influence on how societies were organized. Processes of modernization in the Western world have changed the dominant societal role of Christianity tremendously. According to the philosopher Charles Taylor (2007), each form of (religious) belief has become a matter of choice in the age of the secular. Due to processes like migration and the power of the mass media, 'repertoires of belief' meet, disturb, and challenge one another (cf. Connolly, 2011, p. 59). Connolly argues that a 'minoritization of the world' is taking place at a very fast rate. Minoritization involves, on the one hand, the rapid introduction of minorities of multiple types (e.g. religious, spiritual, ethnic) and, on the other hand, "intense pressures to counteract or avoid this result through extreme action, such as building walls between countries, ethnic cleansing, fundamentalization of religious faith, or legal repression of gays" (Connolly, 2011, p. 60). One result of minoritization is that every belief feels optional. Diverse creeds are engaged in close encounters, engagements, negotiation, and rivalry. This can lead to feelings of resentment that are sometimes translated into tactics of revenge against groups that are felt as a threat. Another result is that worldviews lose their power to provide people with a basic sense of belonging and a convincing belief in this world.

At the same time, modernization processes have led to a fundamental change of interest. Modern rationality is not interested in 'final questions' that ask for the purpose and meaning of reality, but in the causes and functions of concrete objects (Vanheeswijck, 2008). Under the influence of this modern rationality, existential themes are relegated to the private sphere, while penultimate questions about problems that have to be solved dominate in the public domain. This is a radical transformation that not only pushes worldview issues out of the public sphere, but also corrodes the credibility of existing traditions. Until recently, social scientists assumed that religion would not survive secularization processes. Indeed, in the West, institutional Christianity has lost considerable magnitude and influence. However, due to migration and new religious movements, the landscape of worldviews diversifies without the disappearance of religion. Yet, cultural philosophers like Zygmunt Bauman warn for atrophy: the situation in which people increasingly depend on themselves in their moral and spiritual quest, and this may result in embarrassment, loss of articulation, and even loss of moral and existential sensitivity (Bauman & Donskis, 2013). What can't be expressed disappears from people's consciousness. For this reason, worldview issues are not only pushed to the private sphere – denying them 'voice' in the public debate – but they never become articulate because people can no longer relate their personal experiences to what they consider to be the archaic language and rituals of a religious tradition. I refer to this situation as 'worldview deficiency.'

An institutional worldview with moral, existential, and spiritual expressiveness is no longer part of the lifeworld of many people in Western countries. This does not mean that their deep-rooted longing for a meaningful life with value has disappeared, but the way this longing is fulfilled takes highly individualized forms. For many, a language to share this longing with others is missing, and social life does not encourage them to express their longing. Belief and religious convictions are not popular topics of conversation, although young people display curiosity in these matters. The classroom appears to be the only place to discuss these issues (REDCo research; see Weisse, 2010). According to authors such as Bauman and Donskis (2013), Heijne (2017), and Sandel (2005), the neglect of ultimate questions in our society is a problem. It prevents us from exchanging our views on the good life and to reflect together on social imaginaries that can give guidance to our practices. In the meantime, the way our society is organized is far from neutral, but is dominated by a neoliberal belief in the market that manifests itself in all areas of our life, including healthcare and education. This undermines the sense of belonging to a community with shared goals. A vital democracy that people can engage with, cannot afford 'worldview deficiency.' It depends on a moral imagination that can make use of diverse articulations of the good life that are vividly discussed in public debate.

This view is in sharp contrast to political choices in secular societies, which prefer to see the public space as neutral in order to allow people a freedom of religious choice in their private lives. Neutrality is seen as a condition for a peaceful way of coping with religious diversity, but one of its consequences is that political choices are not evaluated in terms of their worldview-based moral commitments. The (neo)liberal emphasis on economic growth and market forces is definitely rooted in an image of man and world, but it is usually taken for granted without articulating the worldview stance that is taken.

The political philosopher Michael Sandel (2005) points out two causes why a public debate about our deepest values fails to happen. In the first place, the widely shared belief in the market prevents us from reflecting on our society in moral terms. Consensus about moral values is not necessary when the common good is defined in terms of market forces. In the second place, people fear not to agree about questions of the good life, and disagreement would infest the public debate with tension and enmity. It feels more secure to leave our ethical and spiritual convictions behind us in the political arena. Important modern thinkers in the tradition of liberalism, like Rawls and Habermas, advocate that the state is neutral with regard to moral, spiritual, and metaphysical convictions. According to them, only neutrality allows for pluralism and individual rights: every moral perspective has the same right to exist, but public space is organized according to neutral legal rules. This way of thinking is fundamental to many secular societies.

According to Sandel, however, the proposed neutrality is neither possible nor desirable. All choices to organize society are rooted in moral assumptions related to worldview traditions, which cannot go without evaluation. Sandel thinks it is possible for politics to draw explicitly upon moral and spiritual ideals and to still further pluralism. A pluralistic society can open discussions on moral and religious convictions that citizens bring with them in the public sphere. The idea that a government should only provide for a neutral framework of rights, within which people can choose their own values and purposes, does not inspire a sense of community and societal commitment. This idea easily leads to disappointment, because it takes away the moral dimension from political discourse. It does not do justice to people's longing for a societal life that has meaning and value, a longing that may come to expression in moralism or fundamentalism, for example. According to Sandel, the hesitance to have public discussions in moral terms is one of the causes of intolerance. Modern societies are characterized by very diverse and sometimes conflicting moral and spiritual ideals. Without public debate about these matters, people withdraw into their own groups and their own sense of righteousness. Tolerance may then take the shape of indifference to the position of others, or change into intolerance.

Pluralism

What would a pluralism look like that does not evade moral discussion in the public sphere and that allows for an organization of society that is inspired by moral and spiritual ideals? In this section, I will argue that such a pluralism rests on three pillars: justice as evenhandedness (Carens, 2000, p. 2), building new connections that contribute to a sense of belonging (Connolly, 2011), and moral imagination (Lederach 2005). Both justice as evenhandedness and connection-building depend on the imagination understood as the ability to see the actual in light of the possible. Thomas Alexander stresses the social importance of the imaginative capacity, allowing for a community of social imagination that experiences the world as meaningful and valuable through a common endeavor to realize new ways of relating to the world. When this endeavor is enriched by critical reflection on basic values and their consequences for people that are directly or indirectly involved, conditions are met to speak of moral imagination.

Justice as evenhandedness

In his book *Culture, Citizenship, and Community*, political theorist Joseph Carens argues convincingly that the conventional liberal conception of justice as neutrality is not enough to understand the actual ways in which communities deal with diverse claims about culture and identity. He advocates a contextual approach that shows the need for a conception of justice as evenhandedness and an understanding of citizenship that is open to multiplicity. His approach fits in well with the relational perspective on plural moralities chosen in this volume, and with my criticism on 'worldview deficiency' – while Carens shows why neutrality still can be important in some respects. Although Carens does not use the concept worldview, his pluralistic, evolving, open-ended view on culture and identity, related to conceptions of the good, comes close to the way I understand worldview in this chapter.

Carens critically analyzes the view that the liberal state ought to be neutral between competing conceptions of the good, and that "justice requires a hands off approach to culture and identity, out of respect for the equality and freedom of individuals" (Carens, 2000, p. 8). Although a hands off approach can be wise and advisable in particular situations, Carens advocates another view on justice, "which is derived from the assumption that to treat people fairly we must regard them concretely, with as much knowledge as we can obtain about who they are and what they care about" (p. 8). In this approach, 'hands off' is replaced by, or rather supplemented with, 'evenhandedness' in responding to the claims that arise from different conceptions of the good. It means immersion rather than abstraction, embracing particularity instead of abstracting from it, and sometimes choosing practices of differentiated citizenship rather than insisting on identical formal rights.

In the same way as Michael Sandel, Carens argues that a liberal democratic political culture is not neutral, because it fits better with some ways of life and conceptions of the good than with others. It can't make an objective abstraction from competing claims for recognition and support in matters of culture and identity. Sensitive balancing of these claims to come to justice as evenhandedness does not mean that they will all be given equal weight, "but rather that each will be given appropriate weight under the circumstances within the framework of a commitment to equal respect for all" (Carens, 2000, p. 12). Justice as evenhandedness is clearly not compatible with a relativistic approach. It allows for a strong commitment to basic values and criticism of those of others, but always based on self-reflection, immersion in the details of a case, openness to others' justifications of their practices, and contextually sensitive, respectful judgments. Under these conditions, Carens argues that it is justifiable to criticize, for example, forms of social organization that restrict women's life chances or in which the consent of the people does not count. "We should try to understand, we should listen respectfully, but we should not abandon our own commitments for the sake of respecting those of others" (Carens, 2000, p. 42).

Pluralism based on evenhandedness takes careful notion of cultural differences between groups, without necessarily entailing or legitimizing inequality. According to Carens, pluralism and equality are usually compatible and often mutually reinforcing. Learning about the qualities of a specific group may heighten the chance of equal treatment. This is one of the arguments in the plea for more women in leading positions. To evaluate the relationship between pluralism and equality, we need to take into account that power may have shaped cultural differences and that actual group inequalities are rather the result of differences in power than of differences in culture. "When considering the legitimacy of inequalities between groups, we cannot simply assume that interactions among groups are benign" (Carens, 2000, p. 97). This is an important point when it comes to the encounter between worldviews. In many countries, we witness tensions with regard to religious expressions in the public sphere that arise out of a polarized political climate, especially with regard to Islam, and that tend to accentuate religious differences. When it comes to Islam, these differences are seen as a threat to liberal democratic institutions of the West, and for this reason Islamic beliefs and practices are treated with greater distrust than those of Christians and Buddhists. Carens is very explicit with regard to this issue. "A commitment to the idea of justice as evenhandedness requires us to consider whether there are relevant similarities between Western cultural and religious practices that are generally regarded as morally permissible and Islamic practices that are widely seen as morally problematic. I will argue that these similarities are greater than is commonly thought" (Carens, 2000, p. 141). Without losing sight of the view that liberal democratic commitments can justify the non-tolerance of certain cultural differences, Carens warns us not to create unwarranted forms of inequality for political reasons.

Another issue with relevance for pluralism is that culture and identity are often not as unitary and clear-cut as is often assumed. Carens refers to Charles Taylor, who uses the term 'mosaic' identity, and we can also turn to dialogical self theory (DST) to understand that multiple 'voices' may inform one's identity and cultural or religious commitments (cf. Hermans, Chapter 2 in this volume). This has important implications for pluralism, because it asks for a more nuanced understanding of similarities and differences between cultural and religious views. Justice as evenhandedness does not treat groups as if they were clearly definable, but allows for a multiplicity of convictions and practices within groups that may facilitate inter-group exchange and dialogue.

In his case studies, Carens (2000) argues "for more flexible and open-minded readings of cultural practices and more appreciation for the ways in which liberal commitments themselves should open space for pluralism" (p. 258). When we take his plea for justice as evenhandedness seriously, we face the challenge of opening our societies to a diversity of conceptions of the good, without losing basic commitments to equality, freedom, and democracy. Under these conditions, how can we prevent fragmentation of our society or minoritization in terms of Connolly? How can we build communities on which people can rely for a sense of belonging? Carens seems to be optimistic in this regard. In one of his case studies, he argues that "paradoxically, greater respect for difference is more likely to generate more genuine unity than any attempt to manufacture that unity directly" (Carens, 2000, p. 194). That may be true, but I think further reflection is needed on the issue of building connections to come to a convincing pluralism with regard to conceptions of the good (a relational ethic in terms of K. J. Gergen, Chapter 1 in this volume).

Connection-building

Carens realizes that his contextual approach "necessarily entails a great deal of indeterminacy in generalizing about what ought to be done" (Carens, 2000, p. 59). In psychological terms, this raises uncertainty. How can a pluralistic, evolving, open-ended view on culture and identity, and a concomitant focus on what a culture can *become*, still contribute to a society in which people can experience a sense of belonging? I will explore this question with the help of the book *A World of Becoming* of William Connolly. In this book, Connolly discusses the need for existential attachment and the need to restore belief in this world, a world that often stretches and disrupts a sense of belonging. One of his questions is "whether it is possible to forge a new pluralist assemblage composed of minorities of various types who diverge on belief and creed while sharing positive affinities of spirituality across those differences" (Connolly, 2011, p. 13). This does not mean that he takes a religious perspective. His 'philosophy of immanence in a world of becoming' stresses the importance of existential spiritualities infused into different beliefs, and is open to a specific sense of transcendence. He relates spirituality to transcendence "as an intensification of everyday experience so as to amplify sensitivities, open the self or constituency to experimentation, or augment experimental ties across lines of difference" (Connolly, 2011, p. 39). In this conception, spirituality is an important contributor to a pluralism that exceeds justice as evenhandedness.

When it comes to a restoration of belief in this world, Connolly distinguishes between belief and faith. *Belief* permeates our engagement with the world in implicit ways that are hard to access. *Faith* consists of those elements of belief that we can articulate and that can be contested. Articulation can open a faith to engagement with modes of inspiration and argument from others' faith, and allows for exploration of what to cultivate, what to adjust, and what to reject. Articulation helps in developing new lines of political alliance across multiple modes of difference in faith. This is highly necessary against the backdrop of minoritization as described by Connolly. "The minoritization of the world, the awareness that you could 'choose' another faith, the challenges to self-confidence in your own faith, the temptation to amplify existential resentment, and the drive to blame specific constituencies for this general condition, resonate with one another" (Connolly, 2011, p. 61). The link between man and the world is broken, and we need reasons to find faith in this world. Thinking of the world in terms of 'becoming' might be a way to realize this.

Connolly's approach to a world of becoming relates complexity theory as it is developed in natural science to the concerns of cultural theory. Against the idea of a linear, deterministic science (or the image of an omnipotent God), complexity theory makes space for real creativity in the trajectory of natural and cultural processes. The new does not come into being through mechanical causation, but emerges in unpredictable ways. In an immanent world of becoming, the future is not entirely implicit in the past. This has implications for how we think of agency. Connolly links it to the formation of novel modes of behavior that were not extant before – and this form of agency is not an exclusive quality of human beings, but can be found at different levels in reality. I won't elaborate on this theme in his work, but it is important to realize that he sees agency and creativity throughout our heterogeneous world. This has implications for how we think of cultural change: we have to make space for surprise, for the new that diverges from past regularities. We certainly have to leave behind the idea of subjects with agency that act upon objects without agency, in favor of the idea of connection between multiple modes and levels of agency, feeling, experience, and responding. "Connectionism presents a world in the making in an evolving universe that is open to an uncertain degree" (Connolly, 2011, p. 35).

As humans, we participate in a world of real creativity that also finds expression at other levels of existence. We can connect to creative processes extending beyond us as part of "the radical task [. . .] to find ways to strengthen the connection between the fundamental terms of late-modern existence and positive attachment to life as such" (Connolly, 2011, p. 63). Positive attachment and affirmation do not exclude negative experiences, for example, in confrontation with events that challenge one's agency, or with others that disagree with one's vision of the world. Jumps, interruptions, and dissonance in experience that can give rise to negativity and resentment can be seen as intrinsic to our participation in a world of becoming, and can be translated into positive possibilities. This does not mean that exploitation and suffering, for example, should be embraced; they can be challenged out of new ideas for and energy to come to action and creative invention. We can learn in this respect from movies, theological accounts, philosophical explorations, novels, and visual arts that render our own participation in 'bumpy processes' more vivid. These cultural sources help us to come to terms with the enduring modern fact of dissonance and minoritization, and to accept the contestability of our belief without profound resentment. Productive conjunctions between disparate traditions of faith may engender what Connolly calls a positive intensification of life. "It is precisely at this juncture that generous devotees of both traditions can foster positive political assemblages" (Connolly, 2011, p. 75). It is also here that a deep, multidimensional pluralism can develop.

> By deep pluralism, I mean the readiness to defend your creed in public while acknowledging that it so far lacks the power to confirm itself so authoritatively that all reasonable people should embrace it. By multi-dimensional pluralism, I mean a political culture in which differences of creed, ethnicity, age, first language, gender practice, and sensual affiliation find expression in a productive ethos of political engagement between participants.
>
> (Connolly, 2011, p. 83)

Connolly advocates an 'ethic of cultivation,' anchored in care for the diversity of life and the fecundity of the earth. Such an ethic brings this care to bear on new and unexpected situations, and it stimulates critical reflection on a new situation in order to revise or adjust old norms and fixed conceptions whose mode of operation is now up for reconsideration. Both affirming one's belief and being open towards change are of critical importance in a world in which connections risk becoming lost. Constituencies who diverge along lines of faith, ethnic identification, sexual affiliation, etc., have to work together to counteract resentment. "This involves affirming a world in which the faith you embrace regularly brushes up against living alternatives that challenge, disturb, and disrupt its claim to universality." (Connolly, 2011, p. 91) Connolly speaks of an ethico-political need to amplify modes of generosity with respect to several creeds, and to forge new assemblages to foster deep pluralism, egalitarianism, and care for future generations.

Moral imagination

As we have seen, Connolly advocates a positive ethos of engagement between diverse modes of belief that both affirm their own faith and open themselves to reflection and change. As we have seen, the capacity to believe and to critically reflect on our imaginaries of the good is related to the imagination. I will now return to this theme and discuss it with the help of the book *Moral Imagination* by John Paul Lederach, an expert on peace building and reconciliation. Lederach (2005) defines 'moral imagination' as "the capacity to imagine something rooted in the challenges of the real world yet capable of giving birth to that which does not yet exist" (p. ix). It is deeply rooted in the reality of what exists and seeks ways to move beyond the grips of inhibiting patterns. It is a crucial force in what Lederach calls 'transcending violence.'

One of the requirements to engage in moral imagination is paradoxical curiosity that allows one to embrace complexity without reliance on dualistic polarity, that simplifies reality in a reductionist way. Paradoxical curiosity stimulates attentiveness and careful inquiry reaching beyond accepted meaning. One also needs a fundamental belief in and pursuit of creativity. Although he confines himself to the level of interhuman relationships, Lederach seems to advocate a world of becoming just as much as Connolly does. He uses the metaphor of the artistic process, which leaves room for serendipity, discovery, and unpredictable responses. He advocates a constructive approach to complexity "for from complexity emerges untold new angles, opportunities, and unexpected potentialities that surpass, replace, and break the shackles of historic and current relational patterns of repeated violence" (Lederach, 2005, p. 37). Moral imagination is about creating connections between different groups, exploring and discovering how these groups can mutually enrich each other. It depends on the sensitivity and attentiveness of the artist, rather than on technical problem solving.

Lederach explores the practice of haiku as a metaphor for the core practice of peace building. A haiku is a poem of three lines of five, seven, and five syllables, respectively. In these 17 syllables, a haiku must capture the complex fullness of a moment or experience. The practice of haiku is a metaphor for embracing complexity through non-reductionist simplicity. The 'Haiku moment' presents itself when something resonates deeply. It depends on a quality of sensuous sharpness out of which the clarity of great insight may emerge in the form of an image or an artistic way of describing something. The practice of haiku may inform peace building as an art of giving birth to a process and keeping it creatively alive; it may inform listening to attend to poetry in conversation, to the images people talk in to give expression to their experience of living in the world. It may invite us to draw images of relationships and processes of change in order to understand them better. Lederach gives examples of his own drawings that helped him to come to terms with complexity and conflict. According to him, the sensitivity of the artist opens us to the playfulness of mind and the creative act that underpins the birth and growth of personal and social change.

How can Lederach's conception of moral imagination help us to build connections between plural moralities, and to realize deep, multidimensional pluralism? In my opinion, it allows us to assess what is needed to build political assemblages that go beyond dissonance and minoritization. Moral imagination instills in participants of social processes an attentiveness to more than what is immediately visible (power of perception), a capacity to give birth to something new that, through its emerging, changes our world (creativity), and to rise toward something beyond the particularities of our belief (transcendence). It enables them to imagine themselves in relationship instead of enmity and to risk venturing on unknown paths. Departing from a contextual approach like that of Carens, Lederach (2005) argues that "turning points and a journey toward a new horizon are possible, though based on perplexing paradoxes" (p. 29). It is the love of paradox and complexity, which is characteristic of the moral imagination. It grasps what is at stake in a specific context and articulates it in such a way that it resonates with those involved and stimulates transformation.

The lessons Lederach draws from his long experience in situations of violence are important for the challenges of plural moralities secular countries face in late modernity. According to him, the moral imagination "is built on a capacity to imagine that it is possible to hold multiple realities and worldviews simultaneously as parts of a greater whole without losing one's identity and viewpoint and without needing to impose or force one's view on the other" (Lederach, 2005, p. 62). Its place is the accessible public sphere. A central question is whether a permanent dialogue can be realized that invites all relevant modes of belief and cultural practices to contribute to community building. Is it possible to enter into meaningful conversation that gives voice to all participants and that really makes a difference? Is it possible to stimulate a moral imagination that gives birth to something new in the midst of difference and polarization? Lederach stresses that political leaders can encourage and promote moral imagination, but that communities have their own responsibility in this regard. This brings us to the question of moral and spiritual leadership: where is it located, and what can it achieve?

Moral and spiritual leadership

Both Connolly and Lederach point out that we live in a creative space that is pregnant with the unexpected. This brings potentiality, but also risk and uncertainty. Rather than focusing on a politics of security and protection, pluralism involves explicitly addressing that uncertainty and the diverging ways people try to secure their sense of belonging in this world. One of the pillars of such a pluralism is justice as evenhandedness, which allows for commitment to our own culture and identity while opening our societies to a diversity of conceptions of the good. According to Connolly, this asks for new ways of connection that restore our belief in this world. Affirmation of one's own belief can go together with the emergence of new political assemblages in which people of different faiths work together towards a common good. From Lederach we can learn that this depends on skills we can learn from artists and the practice of haiku, working with paradox and complexity in ways that give birth to something new and unexpected.

It is clear that these views on pluralism and moral imagination are hardly compatible with conceptions of leadership in a top-down model or with techniques of social engineering. With its sensitivity to multiplicity, open-endedness, emergence, and unpredictability, pluralism as it is advocated in the previous section can't be controlled or implemented according to a blueprint. Yet, violence and polarization in our conflict-ridden world clearly show that pluralism will not emerge out of the blue, either. All of the authors discussed make clear that a politics of technical problem solving will not suffice to bring people together in ways conducive to social change. There is need for an ethos of political engagement among not like-minded people, who strive for ways of connecting that inspire both existential affirmation and existential openness. Pluralism asks for fundamentally relational ways of moral and spiritual guidance. These need to be developed along lines discussed in Chapters 5–7 of this volume. In anticipation of these conceptions of dialogical leadership, I want to point out some elements that have to be taken into account.

A pluralism that has as its pillars evenhandedness, connection-building, and moral imagination depends on a social structure that allows for the dynamics of change. Lederach discusses this in terms of web making. A web is a structure that is never permanent, fixed, or rigid. It allows for reconstructing and reshaping in response to the circumstances in a given space. The web can be seen as a 'process structure' of connections that allows for strain and stretch. Social webs are both vulnerable and strong. Relationship and engagement need to be sustained in the presence of continued conflict, existing differences, experienced pain, and perceptions of injustice. To realize change under these circumstances requires "the art of strategically and imaginatively weaving relational webs across social spaces" (Lederach, 2005, p. 84). Social change relies on the 'smart flexible' ability to take advantage of emerging and context-based challenges. Leading a process of social change is not about providing solutions, but about generating creative responses in relational spaces that keep not like-minded people in change-oriented interaction.

The metaphor of the web seems to imply that we need a 'spider' to provide the structure that allows for social change. Yet, we have seen with Connolly that agency can emerge at different levels and in different forms. It seems fruitful to think of moral and spiritual leadership not in terms of a leading individual, but in terms of an imaginative mediative capacity that works throughout the web without being located within one person. "*Mediative* suggests a quality of relational interaction rather than the specificity of a role. The term underscores attitudes, skills, and disciplines that include engagement of the diverse perspectives about a conflict and a capacity to watch for and build opportunities that increase creative and responsive processes and solutions around conflicts" (Lederach, 2005, pp. 95–96). It takes both the personal responsibility of participants and a learning environment to develop the skills necessary for this mediative capacity. Again, these skills are rather those of an artist than those of a social engineer. They depend on the powers of perception, creativity, and transcending the given with an eye to the possible. They allow for a relational moral and spiritual leadership that builds laboratories of shared learning and creating, in which failures are accepted as part of an ongoing process of transformation. In these laboratories, the arts will play a decisive role, both through collaborating with artists and through introducing artistic skills into the methods used. Participants will have to explore and liberate their creativity, to benefit from the multiplicity of talents that can be found in a group.

Next to skills, however, imaginaries of the good and articulations of answers to ultimate questions are needed to inspire social change. Uncomfortable though it may feel to bring our faiths to the so-called neutral public sphere, the moral imagination has to work with what the participants care for and value most deeply. Disagreements and dissonances are painful, but they may be translated imaginatively into the emergence of something new, resulting in a positive intensification of life. Productive conjunctions between different traditions of faith may bring about 'haiku moments' that resonate deeply with the participants. As we have seen, the practice of haiku is a powerful metaphor of giving birth to deep insights by the attentive perception of concrete situations showing paradox and complexity. The metaphor of haiku may inform ways of moral and spiritual leadership that don't steer clear of diverging imaginaries of the good, even if they conflict, but that work with them creatively to come to novel ways of relating to our world that were not implicit in the existing imaginaries.

Yet, as Carens insists, not every conception of the good can be accepted. He clearly draws a line where conceptions challenge commitments to equality, freedom, and democracy. Pluralism is an art of sensitive balancing, but also of making clear choices. Within the framework of a commitment to equal respect for all, it chooses for affirmation instead of resentment, for care instead of oppression, for cultivation instead of coercion, and for a playfulness of mind instead of rigid dogma. Lederach points out that we do not need masses of people who make these choices to bring about social change. People can find one another around issues of concern to them, such as ecological questions or situations of social injustice. This may result in processes of web making in which people with diverging faiths are involved. Moral and spiritual leadership in those situations means a shared commitment to keeping these processes creatively alive. Even if one person takes the lead, that person cannot expect to be the spider in the web; the web of pluralism emerges out of relations and connections that always involve the agency and creativity of more than one participant.

Conclusion

I have related the question of plural moralities to people's search for meaning: what do they consider to be good and meaningful in an aesthetical, existential, and spiritual sense? The search for meaning is rooted in a basic urge to belong to this world. In a late-modern world, however, the sense of belonging is challenged because every existential stance is felt as an option and an individual choice out of competing possibilities. The relevance of (religious) worldviews has changed dramatically due to processes of modernization and secularization. This is discussed in terms of minoritization, meaning on the one hand that minorities of multiple types encounter and confront one another, and on the other hand that there are intense pressures to counteract or avoid this situation. These are the dynamics of plural moralities in many societies.

Against this backdrop, I advocate a form of pluralism that rests on three pillars: justice as evenhandedness (Carens, 2000), building new connections that contribute to a sense of belonging (Connolly, 2011), and moral imagination (Lederach, 2005). This form of pluralism can be realized by strengthening a relational approach to moral and spiritual leadership. In this conclusion, I want to collect the insights gained that are relevant to such a form of leadership.

Relational moral and spiritual leadership has to take into account divergent conceptions of the good. I have discussed this in terms of the capacity to ask and answer ultimate questions that address what people consider to be the good life in both an existential and identity-building way. These conceptions of the good need to be part of public debate on how we want to organize our societies. Recognition that there is no neutral public sphere, and that political choices always rest on worldview commitments, is important.

Central to these worldview commitments is the human ability to see things not only as they *are*, but also as they *could be*. The moral imagination allows us to develop images of the good that rely on social processes. The resulting social imaginaries give moral power to our convictions and guidance to our practices. Relational moral and spiritual leadership is about reflection and evaluation of these imaginaries, in the light of justice as evenhandedness.

Relational moral and spiritual leadership will have to counteract feelings of resentment and acts of revenge that come with minoritization. This asks for attentive perception of and immersion into what people care for in their lives. It may be necessary to embrace particularity and choose practices of differentiated citizenship rather than insisting on identical formal rights. It also means paying attention to a multiplicity of convictions and practices within groups that may facilitate inter-group exchange and dialogue.

Relational moral and spiritual leadership focuses on connection-building around themes of common interest and concern. Divergent conceptions of the good may find each other around situations that are problematic to all groups involved, such as regarding climate change or violent attacks. These situations ask for dialogue and the building of counterforces across differences of faith. The resulting initiatives need not attract masses of people. A small number of well-placed, not like-minded people may form 'social yeast' with impact that exceeds their numbers.

Relational moral and spiritual leadership recognizes and acknowledges both people's need for existential attachment and their agency and creativity. It creates 'laboratories' that provide both security and room for experimentation, and it stimulates paradoxical curiosity with its love of complexity and aversion to dualistic polarity. In situations that are conducive to social experimentation, something new may emerge, and devotees of divergent faith traditions can foster positive political assemblages that commit themselves to a deep, multidimensional pluralism.

Relational moral and spiritual leadership creates connections not only between different groups but also between, for example, the personal biography of participants and the shaping of responsive social structures that allow for the dynamics of change. This is discussed in terms of web making. It depends on an imaginative mediative capacity that works throughout the web without being located within one person.

The imaginative mediative capacity that strengthens the social web can be fostered by the arts in many ways. A guiding metaphor may be the practice of haiku, which informs us about translating complexity into a simple but illuminating articulation. The metaphor helps us to realize that playing close attention to what is at hand may result in something new that was not implicit in our existing imaginaries.

Finally, I want to repeat that pluralism is an art of sensitive balancing, but also of making clear choices: for affirmation instead of resentment, for care instead of oppression, for cultivation instead of coercion, and for a playfulness of mind instead of rigid dogma. Pluralism asks for critical reflection both on one's own worldview and on that of another, and for the willingness to enter into respectful conflict.

References

Alexander, T. M. (2013). *The human eros: Eco-ontology and the aesthetics of existence*. New York, NY: Fordham University Press.

Alma, H. A. (2005). *De parabel van de blinden: Psychologie en het verlangen naar zin*. Amsterdam: Humanistics University Press.

Bauman, Z., & Donskis, L. (2013). *Moral blindness: The loss of sensitivity in liquid modernity*. Cambridge: Polity Press.

Carens, J. H. (2000). *Culture, citizenship, and community: A contextual exploration of justice as evenhandedness*. Oxford: Oxford University Press.

Connolly, W. E. (2011). *A world of becoming*. Durham, NC, and London: Duke University Press.

Droogers, A. (2014). The world of worldviews. In A. Droogers & A. van Harskamp (Eds.), *Methods for the study of religious change: From religious studies to worldview studies* (pp. 17–42). Sheffield: Equinox.

Fesmire, S. (2003). *John Dewey and moral imagination: Pragmatism in ethics*. Bloomington, IN: Indiana University Press.

Gergen, K. J. (2009). *Relational being: Beyond self and community*. New York, NY: Oxford University Press.

Heijne, B. (2017). *Staat van Nederland*. Amsterdam: Prometheus.

Lederach, J. P. (2005). *The moral imagination: The art and soul of building peace*. Oxford: Oxford University Press.

Sandel, M. J. (2005). *Public philosophy: Essays on morality in politics*. Cambridge, MA: Harvard University Press.

Seitz, R. J., & Angel, H.-F. (2012). Processes of believing: A review and conceptual account. *Reviews in the Neurosciences, 23*(3), 303–309.

Seitz, R. J., & Angel, H.-F. (2015). Psychology of religion and spirituality: Meaning-making and processes of believing. *Religion, Brain & Behavior, 5*(2), 139–147.

Taves, A., Asprem, E., & Ihm, E. (2018). Psychology, meaning making and the study of worldviews: Beyond religion and non-religion. *Religion & Spirituality*. Retrieved from www.biteslide.org

Taylor, C. (2007). *A secular age*. Cambridge, MA: Belknap Press of Harvard University Press.

Vanheeswijck, G. (2008). *Tolerantie en actief pluralisme: De afgewezen erfenis van Erasmus, More en Gillis*. Kapellen and Kampen: Pelckmans, Klement.

Weisse, W. (2010). RedCo: A European research project on religion in education. *Religion & Education, 37*(3), 187–202.

Part II

Developing theory and practice in dialogue

Leadership in an age of plural moralities

5 Provocative guidance

A practice of narrative leadership

Ina ter Avest

Introduction

The year was 1415, a decisive year in the Hundred Years' War (1337–1453).

King Henry V of England crosses the Channel with his troops and sails to France. The English are not convinced that they will achieve victory over the French. The French soldiers far outnumber them. The night before the great battle, Henry walks back and forth in the camp, past the fires where his men warm themselves. Cloaked by the darkness, he listens to their debates, their worries, their questions, their fears. Back in his own tent, he asks himself the same questions that went back and forth among his soldiers. How should he respond to this situation, which is so worrying? How to be a good leader to these men? Then, on the morning of the Battle of Agincourt, Henry gives an impassioned speech[1] to his soldiers. He urges his men to remember the defeats the English troops had previously inflicted on the French, the previous victories they had won.

> . . . *That he which hath no stomach to this fight,*
> *Let him depart; his passport shall be made*
> *And crowns for convoy put into his purse:*
> *We would not die in that man's company*
> *That fears his fellowship to die with us.*
> . . .
> *From this day to the ending of the world,*
> *But we in it shall be remember'd;*
> *We few, we happy few, we band of brothers;*
> *For he to-day that sheds his blood with me*
> *Shall be my brother; be he ne'er so vile,*
> *This day shall gentle his condition . . .*

On October 5, 1415, the English troops led by Henry V won the battle, even though they were vastly outnumbered by the French.

What was characteristic of Henry V's leadership? Why is he seen as a good leader? How did he get done what he wanted to be done: his troops throwing himself in battle and victory for the English? What does 'fight and win' mean in this context, and what can we learn from this speech – a speech that has been staged in theaters around the globe and is referred to in many situations where leadership is at stake?

In this chapter, the concept of 'good leadership' is first explored from the theoretical perspectives of dialogical self theory (DST) (Wijsbek, 2009; van Loon & van Dijk, 2015) and organizational psychology (Heres, 2014). In their publication on DST, van Loon and van Dijk focus on the questions a leader should ask herself/himself ("Why are *you* the leader at this specific time and place?" "Why are *you* the leader capable of understanding the professional world?") (see also van Loon and Buster, Chapter 6 in this volume). These questions place leaders who are involved in their reflections *outside* the group. The context in which this approach to 'good leadership' is situated is that of a crisis caused by diagnosed tame or wicked problems, and this evokes a certain leadership style. Accordingly, the authors distinguish between different styles of leadership and coin 'dialogical leadership' as a solution for leadership that knows itself to be confronted with wicked problems.

Van Loon and van Dijk's focus on the leader as a person contrasts with the approach of the organizational psychologist Heres (2016), who focuses on the context. The focus of Heres is on employees' perceptions of leadership. However, in both approaches, the leader has a central place and is viewed as not included in the group of employees for whom s/he has to be the leader. This brings us to a different approach to 'good leadership' – an approach according to which the leader is interconnected with the employees s/he directs. Leadership in this approach is not viewed as the isolated quality of a single person – very often accompanied by power – but leadership includes being led – in a flexible balance – on both a personal and a group level. Leadership is therefore a quality of the group as a whole (see Ardon, 2009).

In order to take the discussion on 'good leadership' a step further, the concept of 'moresprudence' is introduced, with the concept of 'provocative guidance' associated with it. With these concepts we point to a leadership style that evokes employees' moral and spiritual positionality with regard to the situation to be confronted. In such a process in which a plurality of internal and external moral voices can be heard – including so-called dissonant voices – a safe space is preconditional. To cross boundaries of comfort zones ("This is how we've always done it") and to establish flexible, temporary new spaces ("This is how we could do it this time"), a model of narrative moral consultations (NMC) is presented as an 'example of good practice'; an NMC constituting 'moresprudence.' With a description of the model of NMC that leads to moresprudence, we conclude our contribution to the debate on moral and spiritual leadership in an age of plural moralities.

In search of good leadership

In the publication *'Leiden of lijden?'* ('Leading or Suffering?'; Moen et al., 2000), the concept of transformational leadership was introduced to meet the need for new leadership styles in a world transitioning from clear hierarchical vertical top-down structures to democratic structures of responsibilities. Individuals meeting the criteria of this transformative leadership style, who had developed a vision of the organization's future development, were expected to possess a probing communication style, to profile themselves as role models for their subordinates, to be capable of communicating their ideas and arousing the curiosity of employees, and to pay personal attention to their subordinates. Transformative leadership aims to change or improve the motivation of employees (Moen et al., 2000, p. 13). The transformative leader has a clear focus on getting things done that need to be done. The question is, "How do we get our employees into the right mode" to get done what needs to be done? While Moen et al. seem to cling to the hierarchical position of leaders towards their subordinates, Ardon explores the potential of leaders to place themselves in an equal position with their employees. Based on a literature review, Ardon (2009) comes to the conclusion that most leaders work according to principles of unilateral control in their leadership practice (p. 24),[2] which is these leaders' theory-in-use. Ardon quotes Argyris (1990), who states that such a theory-in-use "instructs individuals to seek to be in unilateral control, to win, and not to upset people. It recommends action strategies that are primarily selling and persuading and, when necessary, strategies that save their own and other's face" (p. 13). Such a theory-in-use gives the leader an experience of control. According to Argyris, however, the result of unilateral control is a paradox. If one person exercises unilateral control over another, this results in a feeling for the first person that s/he is "keeping things under control." However, this person with leadership authority thereby reduces the decision-making freedom of the other, which will result in a submissive, passive, and dependent attitude on behalf of the other (Argyris, 1990, in Ardon, 2009, p. 27). A leader with a strong unilateral authoritative attitude therefore leads to passive employees.

From unilateral control to dialogical leadership

In order to overcome the situation that a leader with a strong unilateral authoritative attitude leads to passive employees, the philosopher and consultant Joep Wijsbek (2009) introduced the concepts of 'dialogical organization' and 'dialogical leadership.' Wijsbek's analysis of a series of dialogical conversations with eight interviewees enabled him to create a profile of the dialogical leader. In line with the criteria of Moen et al. (2000) for transformative leadership, Wijsbek states that a leader must first of all have a vision of future developments within the organization in which s/he works. He adds that a leader should investigate how employees can be involved in these developments. In addition, Wijsbek's dialogical leader has a view on social and societal developments, in the context in which the organization is operating. The dialogical leader reflects on the relation between organization and context. The commitment of the employees has her/his attention. Such a dialogical leader, who is oriented towards the future of the organization, knows how to inspire employees with her/his views. Wijsbek points to the precondition of the 'horizontal orientation' of dialogical leaders. A vertical orientation is based on hierarchy and focuses on rules and regulations that prescribe how the work needs to be done. According to Wijsbek, a horizontal orientation emphasizes the interrelatedness and interconnectedness of all the employees' work processes. For example, when staff members want to change things in the organization, they will enter into conversations, interact, and feel connected to each other and to the organization, in line with the horizontal orientation of the leader. They will share their visions, values, and insights and acquire new knowledge 'as an outcome of relational processes' (see also Gergen, 2009, p. 204; K. J. Gergen, Chapter 1 in this volume). This horizontal space can be seen (and organized) as a free and safe space in which people leave their functional position behind and reflect on everyday organizational problems from a meta-position; a first step towards meaning construction and meaning-giving in the context of a diversity of answers to questions like "What is the right thing to do?" and "Do we act in a fair way?" Such conversations are referred to as 'contemplative reflection' (Wijsbek, 2009, p. 112) – a concept that evokes associations with spirituality as described by Roothaan (2007, p. 43). According to Roothaan, the practice of reflection on who I am and what moves me results in a point of reference for the ongoing evaluation of my actions. Reflection and action meet in an interpretation of spirituality as a practice-based life orientation (2007, p. 50). The 'contemplative reflection' of Wijsbek, understood as the reflection on what is put forward for consideration in relation to the issues at stake, is dialogical by nature, including for internal and external dialogues.

The internal dialogue is what Hannah Arendt calls thinking. Arendt views thinking "as an internal conversation assuming that I am not just myself, but that I am with my self" (1999, p. 131). In order to express my opinions, I have to agree with myself. I have to defend 'as one' what I want to say. That is possible only if I have reflected thoroughly. Reflection can never be performed 'as one,' however. Reflection urges me to open myself up to 'twoness' and to enter into a dialogue with 'us' – me and my self – which results in an authentic position among a diversity of interpretations of morality (see, for example, Arendt in De Kesel, 2008, p. 50). The authenticity of the leader in the spaces of 'contemplative reflection' is a prerequisite for the acceptance of her/his leadership by the colleagues. An authentic leader lives what inspires her/him and shows the strengths and vulnerabilities of her/his way of life and her/his style of leadership. As a living 'example of good practice,' the leader is, according to Wijsbek, a role model for the employees (see also: relational leading in Gergen, 2009, p. 334ff.; see also K. J. Gergen, Chapter 1 in this volume).

The dialogical aspect of leadership was extensively studied by the psychologist and philosopher Rens van Loon (2006), in collaboration with Gerda van Dijk (2015), and with Tessa van den Berg as co-authors (2016). In *Het geheim van de leider* ('The Secret of the Leader'), van Loon's focus is on leadership styles, the sources of influence, and the roles of the leader. Under leadership styles, van Loon distinguishes between a result-oriented style (push factor) and an inspiration-oriented style (pull factor). With regard to the sources of influence, van Loon points to non-verbal communication, knowledge and cognitions, and intuitive knowing (knowing 'by heart'). At the end of his account, van Loon comes to the concept of 'situational leadership,' which he describes as a flexible way of implementing specific leadership styles that are needed in a particular context. Situational leadership also figures in the ability of the leader to steer, coach, help, or delegate where necessary, in response to the situation (van Loon, 2006, pp. 62–63).

The focus of van Loon and van Dijk (2015) is on the questions a leader should ask her/himself ("Why are *you* the leader at this specific time and place?" "Why are *you* the leader, capable of understanding the professional world?"). The authors pay attention to the context in the sense that they situate leadership in a context of crisis, which is caused by tame or wicked problems. 'Tame' problems can be easily solved by following existing procedures; 'wicked' problems, however, are problems for which there is no single solution but many possible approaches and solution options. For example, the deep complexity of post-modernity and of global interconnectedness, and the continuous changes generated by these, cause wicked problems. In *Dialogical Leadership* (2016), van Loon and van den Berg elaborated further on the role of context. This publication was informed by dialogical self theory (Hermans & Hermans-Konopka, 2010). The context is now seen as a partner in a dialogue. "A Dialogical Leader is able to facilitate a dialogue where new meaning emerges in the interaction between two or more people. Dialogical Leadership implies being able to create the conditions for new meaning to emerge in the interaction" (van Loon & van den Berg, 2016, p. 78). The authors make a clear distinction between dialogue and debate: "While debate is about defending your assumptions, opposing, and winning, dialogue is about questioning your assumptions, working together in a mutual space and trying to find common ground" (van Loon & van den Berg, 2016, p. 78). The aim of dialogue is to find a solution to problematic issues, which can be tame or wicked. Both types of problems require an adequate leadership style. Tame issues can be solved by following well-known norms and regulations, while there is no standardized solution for wicked issues, "the solution is still shrouded in mystery" (van Loon & van den Berg, 2016, p. 79). "For wicked, complex issues leaders cannot assume to have the answers. They must empower people/their team to deliver solutions, and should accept the recurrent review and refinement of 'clumsy' solutions as a valid way of tackling wicked issues" (van Loon & van den Berg, 2016, p. 79). Preconditional for a dialogical leader to create and enter the space of dialogue is familiarity with dialogical self theory that underlies this leadership style, and possession of a set of dialogical competencies, namely listening, respecting, suspending judgment, and voicing (van Loon & van den Berg, 2016, p. 92).

Relational leadership

Our comparison so far has focused on the way the authors mentioned earlier have conceptualized dialogue and therefore recommended a specific leadership style. In the two approaches previously discussed, the leader takes the initiative for the dialogical encounter but does not see her/himself as included in the group of employees for whom s/he has to lead. What is lacking in these approaches is what this dialogical leadership evokes in the employees.

These approaches focus on the leader, with her/his vision of the organization in context, and her/his communication style among a plurality of opinions. In the research of the organizational psychologist Heres (2014, 2016), the subordinate employees are central. "The leader-centred focus of research limits our understanding of how leaders can effectively build a reputation for ethical leadership" (Heres, 2014, p. 17).[3] According to Heres, it is important to know what the expectations of the 'followers' are (as she calls the staff that is 'controlled' by the leader or manager) so that the leader can use this information as a starting point for the development and praxis of an adequate leadership style. " 'Followers' expectations of leadership affect their subsequent perception and acceptance of the characteristics and behaviors they observe in their leaders" (Heres, 2014, p. 18). With her PhD study *One Size Fits All? The Content, Origins and Effect of Follower Expectations of Ethical Leadership* (2014), Heres wanted to contribute to a better understanding of the role of followers in the construction and further development of ethical leadership. She explores the organizational context, in particular the employees' expectations regarding ethical leadership, and the relationship of these with actual leadership styles. The initial definitions of 'leadership' and 'follower' in her research give way to a relational approach of employment. According to Heres, leadership is "the process of influencing others to understand and agree about what needs to be done and how to do it, and the process of facilitating individual and collective efforts to accomplish shared objectives" (Heres, 2014, p. 32, based on Yukl, 2006, p. 8). Followership is characterized by Heres (2014) as "the acceptance of influence from another person or persons without feeling coerced and towards what is perceived to be a common purpose" (p. 33, based on Stech, 2008, pp. 48–49). For her research, Heres conducted semi-structured interviews with 18 managers and a quasi-qualitative Q-study among 59 adult employees. In addition, a cross-sectional survey was carried out with 1,263 professionals. Heres concluded that the employees' expectations regarding ethical and moral aspects of leadership consisted of a set of five ideal-typical views, summarized under the labels 'safe heaven creator,' 'the practicing preacher,' 'the moral motivator,' 'the social builder,' and 'the boundaries setter' (Heres, 2014, pp. 99–117). A 'safe heaven creator' is seen as "someone who above all creates a safe environment for employees, leaves room to make and learn from mistakes, and helps employees to understand the morality in decisions – but without talking about ethics too much" (Heres, 2014, p. 100). 'Practicing preachers' take an explicit and proactive approach to fostering ethics among followers. For the followers, the emphasis is on the role of leaders in modeling ethical behavior. The leader is expected to communicate regularly about ethics in order to stimulate autonomous ethical decision making among followers (Heres, 2014, p. 102). For the followers of the 'moral motivator,' it is all about the personal integrity of their leader: their authenticity, charisma, and ability to inspire others with their moral character. Within this view, the ethical leader is more a moral person than a moral manager (Heres, 2014, pp. 105–106). For 'social builders,' social interactions and societal interests play a central role in their efforts to foster ethical behavior. Within the perspective of the 'social builder,' ethical leaders focus on building open, respectful, and caring relationships with others, promoting shared goals and values, and standing up for the greater good (Heres, 2014, p. 108). 'Boundary setters' are fair and loyal towards followers but also 'tell it like it is' and set clear boundaries for behavior. Within this view, norms for behavior must be clearly set and clarified primarily by ethical leaders themselves, and must be enforced in a very strict and consistent manner (Heres, 2014, p. 111). According to Heres, in most cases one or two of these views dominate in a composition of expectations. Each of these expectations regarding leadership indicates a "variety of interpretations of what 'ideal' ethical leaders look like, what they should do, and how they should do it. Insight into these differences in people's ethical leadership expectations can assist managers/leaders to more systematically reflect on and perhaps adjust their own practices to become more effective ethical leaders" (2014, p. 125). In addition to Heres's conclusions regarding the characteristics of employees' expectations, Heres's research reveals a relation between morality and the hierarchical position of employees (see also Heres, 2015, 2016). Expectations regarding moral leadership are awakened when followers increasingly experience severe dilemmas in their work. When this occurs, they expect a more explicit style of moral leadership. Employees who experience moral dilemmas, and employees who experience their work as less morally ambiguous, have the same expectations regarding a safe space in which they are given room to make mistakes. Both types of employees expect moral leaders to have a strong moral character and to use affirmation to strengthen the motivation of employees.

Inclusive leadership

Heres's conclusion about the relational aspect of followers' expectations, and the connection of these with moral leadership, brings us to the line of thought on how 'the other' figures in the thinking of the leader who aims to develop an adequate leadership style. Important indications can already be found in the Rules of Benedict, i.e., his rules for living in peace and harmony with strangers who arrive in the cloister. These rules were written in the sixth century and are still studied daily in every Benedictine monastery around the world. These Rules begin with the word 'Listen!' – listening as the art of knowing what the situation requires of the person at the helm, and how to act in accordance with the needs of the situation and of other people involved (Nieuwenhuis, 2012, p. 20). The three pillars on which the Rules of Benedict are built are action, reflection, and inspiration: action as the way to contribute to living together in peace and harmony; reflection to guide consideration of the question "Did I do the right thing, and did I do it in a just and fair manner?" and to guide the effort of improving one's actions, if necessary; and inspiration, motivation to cultivate an attitude of openness at all times in order for something 'surprisingly new' to develop. This motivation is stimulated by the study of inspiring texts – in the case of the Rules of Benedict, these are texts from the Bible. 'The other,' whether it be a fellow brother or a stranger who arrives at the gate of the monastery, receives special attention in the Rules of Benedict. The relationship with the other is there from the beginning, because the gospel says: "For I was hungry and you gave me something to eat, I was thirsty and you gave me something to drink, I was a stranger and you invited me in, I was naked and you gave me clothing, I was sick and you took care of me, I was in prison and you came to visit me" (Matthew 25: 35, 36). This text connects the inhabitant of the monastery and the stranger as relational beings.

Hospitality according to the Rules of Benedict, and hospitality as a result of an attitude of openness and genuine curiosity, means creating space for the stranger: space for them to open up and to show their own calling and life orientation, space that is created because the other deserves your attention and might offer a new perspective on life in the monastery. A characteristic feature of this space is its openness, albeit limited by the boundaries set by the Rules of Benedict (Nieuwenhuis, 2012, p. 138). The stranger does not arrive in an empty house, in a place without boundaries. By practicing the Benedictine life orientation comprised of action, reflection, and inspiration, the newcomer is offered a point of orientation, a point to relate in solidarity. We conclude that a leadership style in line with the Rules of Benedict is characterized by knowledge of the situation and knowledge of the needs of the people involved. But above all, the authentic feeling of interrelatedness with the other prevails, the experience of being 'brothers in arms.'

Ubuntu leadership

It is not only in the Benedictine monasteries that the interrelatedness of people comes to the fore. Let us consider the views on interconnectedness that Antjie Krog unfolded in 2006, in the 24th *Van Der Leeuw Lezing* ('Van Der Leeuw Lecture'). In this lecture, Krog referred to the words of Mrs. Cynthia Ngewu, whose son, Christopher Piet, was killed by the South African Security Police in 1986. Mrs. Cynthia spoke these words during the time of the Truth and Reconciliation Commission. In response to the plea for forgiveness from the man who had killed her son, she said:

> This thing called reconciliation . . . if I am
> understanding it correctly . . . if it means this
> perpetrator, this man who has killed
> Christopher Piet, if it means he becomes
> human again, this man, so that I, so that all
> of us, get our humanity back . . . then I agree,
> then I support it all.
> (Krog, 1998, p. 22, translated from
> Xhosa in Krog, 2006, pp. 8–9)

"Of all the definitions," Krog states, "by important and learned people, this must count as one of the most perfect formulations of how African interconnectedness, based on the idiom *umuntu ngumuntu ngabantu* (a person is a person through other persons) is practically lived by ordinary people" (2006, p. 9).

According to Krog, Mrs. Cynthia's statement showed that she was aware of the moral implications of the murder, because of her reasoning that the killer must have lost his humanity – being no longer human was what enabled him to kill her son. Mrs. Cynthia understood and accepted that if she could forgive the murderer, this would open up the possibility for him to regain his humanity. The most important thing, according to Krog, is that Mrs. Cynthia implicitly assumed that her son's death touched upon her own humanity; she herself had to live with a damaged humanity from now on. This led her to conclude that her forgiveness could enable the murderer to regain and renew his own humanity (Krog, 2006, p. 9). Mrs. Cynthia was guided by her need to regain her own humanity, and as a consequence, she became a moral leader for her son's murderer.

Leadership includes being led – in a flexible balance – on both a personal level and a group level (see also König's reference to dance, in Chapter 7 in this volume). Leadership is therefore a quality of the group as a whole (see also Ardon, 2009. Krog does not deny that there is an 'I,' nor does she deny the need to be involved in mind-changing dialogues. In line with the Ubuntu concept of leadership, the dialogue that creates a moral stance does not only take place within the self, but it requires a mind-changing conversation.

The conversation that will create the moral entity is not merely a dialogue with the self, but also a conversation with the people around you, with your community. The fundamentally different starting point for an African and Western worldview, according to Krog, lies in the perspective of where and how the moral compass is formed. For Arendt, it is formed in the self through conversations with the self.[4] For the African awareness, it is formed not in the self, but through conversations with others. According to Krog, the departure point for Arendt is "inside the individual towards the self. The departure point for African awareness is also inside the individual, but towards the community" (2006, p. 6).

In our conception, informed by research and inspired by the spirituality of the Rules of Benedict and the writings on Ubuntu philosophy (Krog, 2006; Gergen, 2009; Ramose, 2017), leadership cannot be perceived as the isolated quality of a single person, very often accompanied by power. The leader should not be seen as an outsider, but as an insider, as one brother in 'the band of brothers,' who knows what is occupying her/his subordinates, who is aware of the plurality of expectations regarding moral leadership in employees' minds. In order to develop a leadership style that includes cognitive and experiential knowledge about what is happening in a professional world of plural moralities, the concept of 'moresprudence' and the concept of 'provocative leadership' associated with it will be explored in the next section.

Innovative leadership

In liquid times, when leaders are invited to leave their comfort zone and initiate 'surprisingly new' and innovative actions, a safe space is required. To cross the boundaries of comfort zones ("This is how we've always done it"), the establishment of flexible *Tijdelijk Werkbare Overeenkomsten* (TWOs, 'Temporarily Workable Agreements'; Wierdsma, 2003, p. 135ff.) can be helpful. TWOs ensure a bearable lightness in complex situations – a provisional decision is taken just for now. The feature of temporality in a TWO introduces flexibility and the possibility of change in the near or further future. Frequent reflection in narrative moral consultation (NMC), on complex situations and surprisingly new solutions, will lead to what we coin as 'moresprudence' (Kanne & Grootoonk, 2013, p. 75). Just as jurisprudence in jurisdiction consists of ongoing stories about the integrity of and considerations regarding the application of the law, moresprudence consists of proceedings regarding (possibly surprisingly new) applications of organizational values in complex situations (Wierdsma, 2013, p. 21). During the process of discussing concrete dilemmas in the workplace – a process that must be well documented – the participants learn about a frequent return of values that dominate the respective final decisions about the solutions to dilemmas. Decisions on the way out of a dilemma in NMC always include care for the possible negative effects. The steady recurrence of specific values ultimately results in the constitution of the value orientation of the organization, a reference point for innovative leadership in a context of diversity.

The development of NMC is inspired by the work of the scholar in business administration Eelco van den Dool. Van den Dool researched leadership styles in the context of innovative organizations, with a focus on leadership spirituality. In his PhD study *Spiritual Dynamics in Social Innovation: An Organizational Context, Lived Spirituality and a School of Spirituality* (2017), van den Dool first analyzed the practical spirituality of the German theologian Dorothee Sölle. Based on this analysis and on in-depth interviews with eight participants (four males and four females, aged between 30 and early 60s), van den Dool developed a model of and for the development of leaders in innovative organizations; in other words, for leaders in liquid times.

We elaborate on this model, in particular on the first phase of the model, which in our view should be brought in line with the self confrontation method (SCM; Hermans & Hermans-Jansen, 1995) and dialogical self theory (DST; Hermans & Hermans-Konopka, 2010). Van den Dool's model first of all is helpful for the individual who is perceived as and expected to be the formal leader, and after that – because of the interconnectedness of leadership expectations and leadership styles – with all people involved. 'Provocative guidance' is a competency needed by the interviewer/facilitator in the process of SCM, resulting in provocative guidance as a leadership style in a context of plural moralities.

Narrative moral consultation

Narrative moral consultation (NMC)[5] begins by making an inventory of issues associated with the professional life of the leader in question (step 1). For this inventory, van den Dool developed a semi-structured interviewing method. For the implementation of this phase we recommend the self confrontation method (SCM). SCM, as developed by Hermans and Hermans-Jansen (1995), starts with an interview. The individual is invited by the interviewer (in SCM terminology, the facilitator) to tell about her/his life, and about 'critical incidents' that took place in the course of that life. This narrative is triggered by so-called *'ontlokkers'* (questions or statements with an 'eliciting' function). *Ontlokkers* direct the storytelling activity by specifically asking the interviewees about situations or persons that were important for them in the past (yesterday marks the beginning of that past), or are important for them today, or that – according to the expectations of the interviewees – will be important for them in the future. The focus is on situations related to the professional context.

With the help of the interviewer, the interviewees' reactions to the *ontlokkers* are summarized in so-called *valuations*: short statements that represent the core of the response. In general, the outcome of such an interview is a list of 20–30 valuations. In the next phase (step 2), the individual is invited to relate each valuation to a list of validated affects (such as tenderness, loneliness, care, and anger). The strength of the affect in a particular valuation is represented by a number between zero and five. Zero means that the valuation has no relation with this particular affect, five means that the affect is very strong in the situation described in the valuation. Any valuation can give rise to a mix of feelings. The scoring of all the valuations shows a pattern that, through the correlations, gives insight into a theme that connects a number of concrete issues that occupy the interviewee – either in a positive or in a negative way, either revolving around the interviewee her/himself (S-motive) or around the role of 'the other' (O-motive) (see also König, Chapter 7, and van der Zande & Bakker, Chapter 9 in this volume). This results in a feeling, "Things can't go on like this!" followed by a realization, "I can't go on like this!"

The next phase (step 3) consists of re-examining the valuations, with an emphasis on the potential of taking a risk and a significant step towards changing an unwanted situation. The focus in this step is on the empowerment of the individual by vividly bringing to mind 'moving moments,' situations in which the individual in question showed her/his strength to change an unwanted situation, in relation to the theme that occupies her/him.

In step 4, one of these powerful situations (in SCM terminology, one of these *valuations*) is selected as an object of deep reflection, because "we assume that this occasion, action or experience has taken the participant to some degree beyond the borders of human existence, as if he has gotten a glimpse from another side; from a 'beyond' to some degree" (van den Dool, 2017, p. 141). This reflection is deepened in step 5 by means of a mirroring text, which is placed next to the selected valuation from step 4. Both the facilitator and the interviewee select such a mirroring text, one of which is then selected for further exploration in dialogue with the facilitator (van den Dool, 2017, p. 143). The mirroring text can be chosen from one of the sacred scriptures (the Bible or the Qur'an, for example).[6] It is important that the context of the individual (as expressed in the valuation) is brought into dialogue with the context of the historical figure or character portrayed in the mirroring text. For life in a secular age – besides stories from the Bible or the Qur'an – poems, episodes from novels, or movie fragments have even greater potency as a 'mirroring text.' The interviewee is familiar with the mirroring text because the interviewee has chosen the text, or the text was jointly decided in consultation. At the same time, the text should challenge the interviewee to leave her/his comfort zone. With regard to this twofold objective of the mirroring text, the facilitator must bring the competence of 'provocative guidance' into the dialogue: i.e., challenging the interviewee and caring for this person at the same time. Contrasting the selected valuation and the mirroring text forges hope and courage for a renewed professional praxis.[7]

This is where the van den Dool model ends. So far the role of the facilitator has been to assist in the process of reflection, mirroring, and finding solutions to complex problems and moral dilemmas. However, in order for the new insights to be put into practice, allies must be found – colleagues who are prepared to become followers of innovative actions to improve the situation experienced as "Things can't go on like this!" In our view, the self confrontation method in its organizational version (Van de Loo, 2016) is a promising way to evolve from a personal innovative motivation to a broadly supported change in the organization. Repetition of these kinds of reflective processes – on both an individual and a group level – during recurring moments over the year, results in a set of insights into potential actions that can put innovations into practice in situations characterized as "Things can't go on like this!" This 'set of insights' is coined as 'moresprudence.'

For this 'moresprudence,' a coaching style of invitation is required, or even a challenging one, as well as care, all of which I bring together in the concept of 'provocative guidance.' The concept 'provocative' can be read as a hyphenated concept, consisting of the Latin '*provocare*,' which means 'challenging,' and '*care*,' which points at 'love'; or, in a professional context, at 'being concerned.' Provocative guidance requires the competence to invite people to express their concerns; it insists on the possibility of different truths and moralities. Provocative guidance challenges the solutions that people take for granted, while at the same time people need to be taken care of in this process of leaving their comfort zone and entering the free space of exploring solutions to wicked problems that have never been thought of. Provocative guidance points to a coaching style that challenges the moral and spiritual positionality of leaders with respect to situations they have to confront, which are experienced as "Things can't go on like this!" or even "I can't go on like this!" Provocative guidance in structural moral consultation with the leader and her/his team invites storytelling – the own individual story and/or the group story and their relationship to the mirroring text. A story is told, and a history is created of recognizable but flexible ways to respond to complex situations. This creates a theme that can function as a point of reference for future difficult and entangled situations. The narrative that is developed in an individual structural moral consultation, about who I was and what I did, constructs the identity of the leader and determines what s/he is capable of doing and will do. Through moresprudence, provocative guidance becomes an integrated aspect of a leadership style in liquid times. The narrative that is developed by the employees in structural moral consultation contributes to a culture of collectivity. Being part of that shared narrative, combined with the power of imagination, contributes to the commitment of employees, followers, and colleagues to the concrete and innovative actions needed.

In search of good leadership – an ongoing story

We started this chapter with the narrative of King Henry V's speech to what he called – in a relational way – his 'band of brothers.' We asked ourselves the questions: What was characteristic of Henry's leadership? Why is he seen as a good leader? How did he get done what he wanted to be done – and what can we learn from his speech? Using the knowledge constructed so far, standing on the shoulders of our predecessors and colleagues, we might answer this question as follows. Henry had taken the trouble to find out what was going on in the minds of his soldiers. He knew about the plural moralities among his troops. He attended to the vulnerability of their position and gave his troops what they needed: reminding them of their shared history, their common dreams, confirming their need for belonging as relational beings. He positioned himself next to his soldiers by using the metaphor 'brothers.' They were all 'brothers' – Henry included. The king's speech acknowledged the qualities of his troops and stimulated the growth of their power rooted in their shared history. In response to the situation at hand, the English opted for a temporary workable agreement – and they won the battle, despite being vastly outnumbered by the French. With his speech, Henry met the expectation of his followers that, in the situation in which the French far outnumbered them, someone had to take the lead – and so he did.

In search of good leadership in a context of plural moralities, action and reflection go hand in hand. The action of getting to know your people, their expectations, their anxieties in a world of uncertainties, their need as relational beings in a 'band of brothers.' The action of developing a leadership style rooted in a shared narrative, a shared imagined future, in line with the actual needs of your followers. The action of showing courage and behaving accordingly. This cannot be done without reflecting on each and every temporary workable agreement, resulting in a shared history, an ongoing story: moresprudence – an emerging point of orientation for narrative leadership in liquid times.

Notes

1 This speech was chronicled as the 'St. Crispin's Day Speech' in Shakespeare's play *Henry V*. St Crispin's Day falls on October 25 and is the feast day of the Christian saints Crispin and Crispinian. The day became synonymous with the English victory at Agincourt during the Hundred Years' War. Since then, the 'St. Crispin's Day Speech' has inspired many leaders. See, for example, the eve-of-battle speech Col. Tim Collins held in Iraq in 2003, for the First Battalion of the Royal Irish Regiment.

2 Ardon refers to Argyris, who coins principles of a unilateral Model I approach. In Argyris's line of thought, a Model II approach is characterized by mutual learning and the encouraging of employee inquiry. In both models, the focus is on the leader; the leader takes the lead. In his PhD thesis, Ardon concludes that the best leadership style is developed through reflection on what he calls 'moving moments.'

3 To avoid conceptual confusion with existing and contested constructs, Heres interprets 'ethics' and 'morality' and their adjectives 'ethical' and 'moral' as synonyms that designate the group of normative judgments which appeal to generally

accepted ideas about what is 'right,' 'good,' and 'just.' These normative judgments provide a frame of reference for evaluations, appraisal, and action (Heres, 2014, pp. 34–35).

4 Earlier we referred to Arendt's view on thinking "as an internal conversation assuming that I am not just myself, but that I am with my self" (Arendt, 1999, p. 131).

5 The concept of 'narrative moral consultation' evolved among others from an over ten years' practice of 'structural identity consultation' (SIC) in primary schools in the Netherlands. See ter Avest and Bakker (2009).

6 In his model, van den Dool (2017) explicitly refers to biblical texts for the spiritual development of leaders in innovative organizations. We see this as an interesting and promising excursion into 'the sacred potential of relational being' as described by Kenneth J. Gergen in the final part of his extensive study *Relational Being* (2009) (see also K. Gergen, Chapter 1 in this volume).

7 In *Macht en Verbeelding* ('Power and Imagination'), the criminologist Femke Halsema (2018) refers to Rebecca Solnit's *Hope in the Dark* (2004). Solnit states that hope is not the same as believing that everything will be okay at the end of the day. She compares 'hope' to an axe: to be used in emergencies, to open a door by force.

References

Ardon, A. (2009). *Moving moments: Leadership and interventions in dynamically complex change processes* (PhD thesis). VU University, Amsterdam.

Arendt, H. (1999). *Politiek in donkere tijden: Essays over vrijheid en vriendschap*. Amsterdam: Uitgeverij Boom.

Argyris, C. (1990). Inappropriate Defenses against the Monitoring of Organization Development Practice. *The Journal of Applied Behavioral Sciences, 26*(3), 299–312.

Avest, I. ter, & Bakker, C. (2009). Structural identity consultation: Story telling as a culture of faith transformation. *Religious Education, 105*(3), 257–271.

De Kesel, M. (2008). *"Een tempel voor de Chariten": Over politiek en vriendschap bij Hannah Arendt*. Damon: Hannah Arend Cahier, Radboud University Nijmegen.

Gergen, K. J. (2009). *Relational being: Beyond self and community*. Oxford: Oxford University Press.

Halsema, F. (2018). *Macht en Verbeelding*. Diemen, Netherlands: Stichting Maand van de Filosofie.

Heres, L. (2014). *One style fits all? The content, origins and effect of follower expectations of ethical leadership* (PhD thesis). VU University, Amsterdam.

Heres, L. (2015). Van amoreel naar ethisch leiderschap. In *Jaarboek Integriteit* (pp. 22–29). Den Haag: Bureau Integriteitsbevordering Openbare Sector.

Heres, L. (2016). Moreel leiderschap; Het belang van impliciete verwachtingen. *De Psycholoog*, maart nummer, 10–20.

Hermans, H. J. M. & E. Hermans-Jansen (1995). *Self-Narratives. The Construction of Meaning in Psychotherapie*. New York/London: The Guilford Press.

Hermans, H. J. M., & Hermans-Konopka, A. (2010). *Dialogical self theory: Positioning and counter-positioning in a globalizing society*. Cambridge: Cambridge University Press.

Kanne, M. E., & Grootoonk, E. (2013). Het moresprudentieproject: werkplaats voor normatieve professionalisering. In H. van Ewijk & H. Kunneman (Eds.),

Praktijken van normatieve professionalisering (pp. 75–96). Amsterdam: Uitgeverij SWP.

Krog, A. (1998). The Truth and Reconciliation Commission: a national ritual? *Missionalia: Southern African Journal of Mission Studies, 26*(1), 5–16.

Krog, A. (2006). *"I speak, holding up your heart": Cosmopolitanism, forgiveness and leaning towards Africa*. 24th Van Der Leeuw Lecture. Groningen: Stichting Van Der Leeuw Lezing.

Moen, J. J., Ansems, P., Hanse, J., & Vintges, M. (2000). *Leiden of lijden? Het handelingsrepertoire van de manager*. Assen: Van Gorcum.

Nieuwenhuis, (2012). *Benedictijns Leiderschap. De Regel van Benedfictus als inspiratiebron* [Benedict Leadership. The Rule of Benedic as source of inspiration]. Utrecht: Uitgeverij Ten Have.

Ramose, M. (2017). *Ubuntu: Stroom van het bestaan als levensfilosofie*. Utrecht: Ten Have.

Roothaan, A. (2007). *Spiritualiteit begrijpen: Een filosofische inleiding*. Amsterdam: Boom.

Solnit, R. (2004). *Hope in the Dark. Untold Histories, Wild Possibilities*. Edinburgh: Canongate.

Stech, E. L. (2008). A new leadership-followership paradigm. In R. E. Riggio, I. Chaleff, & J. Lipman-Blumen (eds.), *The Art of Followership*. San Francisco, CA: Jossey-Bass.

Van de Loo, R. J. P. (2016). SCM-organization: A method for assessing and facilitating organizational dialogue and development. In H. Hermans (Ed.), *Assessing and stimulating a dialogical self in groups, teams, cultures, and organizations* (pp. 153–172). New York, NY: Springer.

Van den Dool, E. (2017). *Spiritual dynamics in social innovation: An organizational context, lived spirituality and a school of spirituality* (PhD thesis). Radboud University, Nijmegen.

Van Loon, R. J. P. (2006). *Het geheim van de leider: Zoektocht naar essentie*. Assen: Van Gorcum.

Van Loon, R. J. P., & Van den Berg, T. (2016). Dialogical leadership. In H. Hermans (Ed.), *Assessing and stimulating a dialogical self in groups, teams, cultures, and organizations* (pp. 75–95). New York, NY: Springer.

Van Loon, R. J. P., & van Dijk, G. (2015). Dialogical leadership: Dialogue as condition zero. *Journal for Leadership Accountability and Ethics, 12*(3), 62–75.

Wierdsma, A. (2003). *Co-creatie van verandering*. Delft: Eburon.

Wierdsma, A. (2013). Remedie voor morele eenzaamheid van managers. *Organisatie en Ontwikkeling, 2*, 18–22.

Wijsbek, J. (2009). *De dialogische organisatie*. Assen: Van Gorcum.

Yukl, G. A. (2006). *Leadership in Organizations* (6th edition). Upper Saddle River, NJ: Prentice Hall.

6 Dialogical leadership

Leading yourself across boundaries of self and culture

Rens van Loon and Angel S. Buster

Introduction

What makes us human?

Learning how to live with diversity might be the greatest challenge for each of us; it requires openness and humility, an acceptance that our view is one of thousands, and that, at any one moment, I can never know something with absolute certainty. Yet, within this mindset, I can still be firm in my being human. In Plato's dialogues, Socrates begins with *ignorance* (Plato, 1969). How can you join with one another in the inquiry? How can we open our minds for diversity of our own thought – so that we may free space for the different voices across boundaries of self and culture?

When we ask the question, 'What makes us human?' we are inherently asking what connects us as human beings, what we share as a whole rather than what separates us individually. It is our ability as human beings to make choices (Dennett, 2017, pp. 367–369), including the choice to deviate from a system to which we have a strong, nearly biological connection, and to take personal leadership, especially in difficult circumstances. An existing path does not need to become a destiny when we fully employ all aspects of our selves.

Contributing to a book on the *contemporary challenges of plural moralities*, of what it means to live in a world with blurring boundaries, we will explore perspectives using dialogical self theory, which includes different identities and cultures. We want to listen to what people around the world tell us, if we invite them to reflect on questions of morality, love, war, religion, and family.

This chapter presents fragments of stories from Yann Arthus-Bertrand's movie *Human*,[1] which helps illustrate the binds that we encounter as products of our own cultural history. These serve as a foundation to explore how we might move from fixed and rigid positions to places where we are freer to take responsibility for our own lives, where we may begin to recognize that the boundaries we place are one small part of a cultural heritage, a single view, a short story, and that the battles we fight with each other can be reconciled within our minds. When we use our humanness to its fullest capacity, we find our strength not in arms but within the power of our minds, and the human spirit which connects us. Incorporating concepts from Dennett, Harari, Evans, and the Amman Message, along with the authors' own experiences, this chapter uses dialogical self theory to consider how we might move across the boundaries of self and culture in order to become better leaders of ourselves and others. A dynamic and relational view on the self is articulated in this theory (Hermans & Hermans-Konopka, 2010; Hermans & Gieser, 2012; Hermans, 2015). In Hermans's view, the autonomy of the self is not constituted in an internal intra-individual negotiation made by one *I*-position with respect to another, but it is intensely interwoven with external dialogical relationships with actual others. Leaders who have developed the capabilities to flexibly enter into and reflect on these dialogical relationships can consciously take greater ownership of the impact they have across internal and external boundaries of self.

Moments of insight into your self and your actions are relational to others, nurtured or discouraged by them. A relational *self* can be positioned at the intersection of time and space, in the present between past and future; in the relation between self and other, 'I' is positioned in an internal and external spatial relation (van Loon, 2017). The core of dialogical self theory is constituted by permanently changing relations, internally and externally. At the heart is a self as a continuously changing process of relational co-creating and relational positioning in space and time. We will explore several examples of polarities and complementarities in self as a society of mind, which we may encounter as we navigate and negotiate through our own life circumstances, such as experiencing and narrating, controlling and losing control, tolerance and intolerance, and self-responsibility and revenge.

Looking in man himself

We had a meeting with students at Tilburg University, where we watched and had conversations about Yann Arthus-Bertrand's movie *Human*. The movie is a collection of stories and images of our world, offering an immersion to the core of what it means to be human. Arthus-Bertrand and his team had long conversations with each of their subjects and asked them questions, such as "What is the toughest trial you have faced? What did you learn from it?" "When was the last time you said 'I love you' to your parents?" "What does love mean to you?" "What are your thoughts on homosexuality, the destruction of the environment, and the cost of war?" "What was it like growing up in your country?" "Why is humanity making the same mistakes?" "What is the meaning of life?" "Are humans born with a view on a conflict, a standpoint that they want to defend with their own lives and for which ideal they want to kill?" These questions, and the responses to these questions, are examples of the contemporary challenges of plural moralities. The challenge of plural moralities becomes visible by the way of responding to the question "*What makes us human?*" Arthus-Bertrand looked for an answer in man himself, not in statistics or scientific analysis. This is conceptually similar to the dialogical self theory view, which takes the individual, the unique person as a collection of *I*-positions, as the starting point. Unique interactive relations between individuals and within individuals are used, rather than questionnaires or personality tests. Taking fragments of this movie for our analysis enables us to reflect on what is meant by *you leading your self* across boundaries of self and culture as well as to zoom out to a higher and more generic level of shared humanity.

Through these stories that are full of love and happiness, as well as hatred and violence, *Human* brings us face to face with the other, making us reflect on our lives. From stories of everyday experiences to accounts of the most unbelievable lives, these poignant encounters share a rare sincerity and underline who we are – our darker side, but also what is most noble ·in us, and what is universal. Our earth is shown at its most sublime through never-before-seen aerial images accompanied by soaring music, resulting in an ode to the beauty of the world, providing a moment for introspection. It is a politically engaging work that allows us to embrace the human condition and to reflect on the meaning of our existence. After having watched part I of the movie, one of the students reflected: "It is slapping my face." She was visibly touched, as many others were. The movie was a kind of self confrontation. The portraits can make us reflect on our behavior, in the past at home, now in how we consume and defend a view, and how we might change our world and the lives of many on earth into a better one. All the narratives of the movie are expressions of explicit or more implicit moralities. Some examples given are focused on plurality (opposing and reconciling), in the self, in cultures, in moralities. In our view, this illustrates the importance of personal leadership in dealing with the challenges of plural moralities.

From coincidence to constraint

Watching this movie with the students, having dialogues and reflections, made us more aware of our own perspectives on this chapter, as did reading Daniel Dennett's *From Bacteria to Bach and Back: The Evolution of Minds* (2017). He explains that a crucial shift in human cultural development occurred when humans developed the ability to share '*memes*,'[2] ways of doing things not based on genetic instinct. Language is composed of memes, which gave humans the power to produce thinking tools to design new memes (e.g., in marketing, art, business, technology, etc.). In Dennett's view, this cultural evolution resulted in a *mind* that perceives, controls, creates, and comprehends. "Nobody is born a priest, a plumber or a prostitute, and how they 'got that way' is not going to be explained by their genes alone or just by the memes that infest them." (Dennett, 2017, p. 242). This illustrates how ideas germinate around the world; dialogue and dialogical self are important vehicles in how concepts and behaviors are formed and distributed in the world.

What is compelling, looking to the process of educating young children, is paradoxically how *open* they are, and simultaneously, how *inflexibly* they can stick to 'habits' that are purely coincidentally formed. The same is true for adults. The book *Creating Organizational Value Through Dialogical Leadership* describes an experience one of the authors had when he was flying from Amsterdam to Montréal.

> The flight attendants asked, "Is there anybody who wants to change their seat because this mother wants to sit with her child?" I'm observing. In this case, I thought, "Why are people resisting, why are they not willing to change their seats? It's not about the space for their legs as they were identical seats. Why is it so difficult for people to give up their seat?" Then I started thinking about what happens in our minds when the airline gives us our seat number. We think that's *our* seat. If somebody is sitting there, we say, "No, no, no, that's *my* seat." Although we to a certain level choose our seats (aisle, windows, etc.), it's coincidental that we have that particular seat as we could have had a different seat with essentially the same value – unless you are traveling in business class or first class. I coined this *Phenomenon 34C* the number of my seat, and I started thinking about what happens in society and organizations, what happens in life. It seems a mechanism because we may get something by chance, but then, once we have it, we say, "No, that's mine." We need to be aware of how this happens in the process of our lives.
>
> (van Loon, 2017, p. 90)[3]

This happens in our own lives. By coincidence, we were born somewhere, our parents raised us in a specific way, and we went to a particular school. We met a mystery Ms. or Mr. X or Y, and we attach meaning to what coincidently happened to us. Now, instead of coincidence, it's, "No, this is how it is, and how it should be. If you deviate from that, that's not good. I don't like that." That's where resistance comes in. Kenneth J. Gergen's *Relational Being* (2009) beautifully describes how our thinking, feeling, and acting are the results of a process of relational co-creating over time that, of course, we cannot fully influence. By assigning meaning, a coincidental circumstance might turn into destiny, freedom to constraint.[4] Here we have illustrated a first polarity that is important for our analysis of moving across boundaries of self and culture: coincidence versus constraint. We will add two more in the following sections, but we will mention them here: opening versus closing, and experiencing versus narrating.

The next section provides a transcript of two interviews in *Human*, with emotional outlooks of a Palestinian father and an Israeli father who both lost a child in the conflict. After each fragment we briefly reflect and comment from a dialogical self theory perspective, and we help the reader with some questions. Our motivation to formulate questions for the reader here is twofold. The first reason is that dialogical self theory is about *dialogue*, about the interplay between *questioning and answering*, both *internally* in the self and *relationally* with other people. The second motive is that, as a reader being injected with content on plural moralities, you have to take time to *reflect* and digest the content of the text. Our intent is not to be condescending, but to make you think and rethink what is offered here in order to further develop your own personal leadership. In this sense, the text can also be experienced as a dialogue.

Moving across boundaries of self and culture

[25:22] The Arab father:

On the 16th of January 2007, an Israeli border policeman shot and killed my 10-year-old daughter Abir in front of her school in Anath where I live. She was with her sister and two friends, 9:30 in the morning. In her head in the back from a distance of 15 to 20 meters by a rubber bullet. Abir wasn't a fighter. She was just a child. She doesn't know anything about the conflict and she is not part of this conflict. Unfortunately she lost her life because she is a Palestinian.

[26:08] The Israeli father:

I am an Israeli who lost his daughter to a suicide bombing on the 4th of September 1997. And I am a product of an education system. These are two societies at war. They socialize the young generation to make them able to sacrifice themselves when the time comes. This is true to Palestinian society and this is also true to Israeli society.

[26:44] The Arab father *continued*:

Because we are human beings sometimes you think 'If I kill the killer, or anyone from the other side, from the Israeli's, or maybe ten, this will give me back my daughter.' No. I'll cause another pain and another victim to the others. I decided to break this circle of violence, and blood and revenge by stopping killing and supporting revenge, by myself.

[27:20] The Israeli father *continued*:

My definition of sides has changed dramatically. Today, on my side are all those who want peace and are willing to pay the price of peace. On the other side are those who do not want peace and are not willing to pay the price of peace.

[27:39] The Arab father *continued:*

Some people say it's not your right to forgive in her name. And the answer: it's also not my right to seek revenge in her name. I hope she's satisfied. I hope she rests in peace.

[28:00] end of this fragment.

Closely reading the stories and reflections of these two fathers from different sides makes us aware of a few things. For example: 'I as deciding to break the circle of violence.' This is a new way of positioning his 'I,' expressing his ability to break with how he is educated and exerting his will (his personal leadership). Are *revenge* and *breaking the circle of revenge* acts of free will? Are both an effect of education? *'I' as not wanting peace* as opposed to *'I' as wanting peace.* This illustrates how, within the individual self and society, the same polarity is active, which we call *I as a society of mind.* Different voices are speaking simultaneously and 'a third I' has to take responsibility to break the cycle. Is this a form of *sacrifice?* In the final excerpt, a new way of positioning self emerges: *'I as forgiving.'* Can an 'act of forgiving' happen unconsciously (as related to forgetting)?

We will now explore the concepts of *coincidence, indoctrination, revenge, and forgiveness* in greater detail, weaving in perspectives from other literature.

The difference between education and indoctrination is that in the second case, only one view/self dominates the entire system of self. So there is no dialogue between the *I*-positions. That is why we use the word indoctrination, as opposed to education, in which you try to teach people how to think and act from other perspectives. We use the word indoctrination several times in the following section. If we have to define radicalization in terms of DST, it would be: one *I*-position dominates the entire system of self (see Hermans on radicalization, Chapter 2 in this volume).

Coincidence and indoctrination

As described in 'phenomenon 34C,' something happens in your life by coincidence. The example of the plane is without great consequences, but the two girls were – by coincidence – in the wrong place. They were not killed on purpose, but because of a situation at hand. Of course, the killing resulted from a conflict that has deeply conditioned the minds of the Israelis and the Palestinians. In Dennett's terms, the Israeli state and the Jihad are spread from person to person by *memes*, which act as units for carrying cultural ideas, symbols, and practices. In the stories of the two fathers in *Human* we discover how they are embedded in a local education system that *indoctrinates* both Palestinian and Israeli people. They make you think that by killing somebody of the other party, you will symbolically get your child back. The misfortune is that when someone is killed, a reaction of hatred and a wish for vengeance are often generated in return. And you get locked into a cycle of violence from which you cannot escape, *unless you decide to*. You can break the cycle only when you inevitably realize, like the person in the movie, that you don't have the right to revenge in the name of the victim.

Revenge or forgiveness?

How can you pay the price for peace if you want revenge? You will get trapped in the cycle of violence. What is required to open the mind of a human being, be it a soldier or a terrorist? Several stories illustrate how individuals took responsibility to break the cycle of violence. We give three examples from literature.

Hannah Arendt argues in her book *The Human Condition* (1998) that forgiveness "is the only reaction which does not merely re-act but acts anew and unexpectedly, unconditioned by the act which provoked it and therefore freeing from its consequences both the one who forgives and the one who is forgiven" (p. 241).

Edith Eva Eger describes how she did this in her book *The Choice: Embrace the Possible* (2017). In this book, a mental health professional braids stories of her patients' epiphanies with her own personal journey through Nazi Germany. Her poignantly crafted memoir is a meditation on two motifs: the internal struggle of psychologically troubled individuals, and the deep shadows cast upon the future of concentration camp survivors. She grew desperate to redress a history scarred by evil: "What happened can never be forgotten and can never be changed. But over time I learned that I can choose how to respond to the past" (Eger, 2017, p. 7). She intriguingly compares her office sessions, and in reflecting upon the roots of pain and victimization, she declares that "suffering is universal . . . but victimhood is optional" (Eger, 2017, p. 9). The distressed fabric of the author's traumatic past becomes a beautiful backdrop for a memoir written with integrity and conviction. "Victimhood comes from inside. No one can make you a victim but you. We become victims not because of what happens to us but when we choose on our victimization. We develop a victim's mind" (Eger, 2017, p. 9). Throughout, Eger is strong in her knowledge of what makes life better for those of us willing to relinquish past regret and unresolved grief and enjoy the full, rich feast of life.[5]

Linda Pallone describes in *Forgiveness: On the Journey to Reconciliation* (2017) a story of a World War II survivor, Hannelore Zack, who was deported as a child and rescued by the British government. Based on an in-depth analysis of the case, Pallone concludes that *forgiveness* as a virtue is formed in the fire of offense; it begins in the mind with an intention to forgive, matures in the heart, and culminates in action, demonstrating forgiveness has taken place. This will be further explored in a later section (sharing experiences of suffering).

We can see in the case of revenge how one voice has become dominant in the decision-making process, thereafter determining certain behaviors. This sedimentation of thought leaves no free space for new choices or possibilities. The 'I as vengeful' or 'I as unwilling to forgive' is a radicalized position; it silences the other possible voices in the society of mind, narrowing the range of alternative outcomes. You can almost imagine that 'I as vengeful' momentarily takes the other *I*-positions energetically hostage, holding them behind a barrier in the mind, where free movement is no longer possible. The radicalized aspect of self barricades the other parts so that they become disconnected; with no free flow of energy, they will struggle to 'make sense' of this hostage situation. In daily life we are sometimes momentarily hijacked by a dominant position – where we exhibit 'beside ourself' behavior.

Although all of these authors come from different philosophical strands, each helps underpin the 'I as forgiving' as a form of re-organizing the self. Not only is forgiveness a conscious choice, it is also an internal and external reconciliation process (Kalayjian & Paloutzian, 2010) where a past '*I*-position' is relinquished to allow space for a promoter one to emerge.

Closing the mind

What makes someone so radically fixed that s/he is willing to kill for it, even to die for it? That is the question we want to understand better. How do you prevent a mind to close for other views and experiences over time? And once a mind is closed (i.e., radicalized), how do you access and re-open it? How do you begin to counter or loosen some of the positions to which people desperately cling? In Arthus-Bertrand's movie we see examples of *closed* minds and examples of *opening* minds: "looking in his eyes (of a bomber) I saw a scared man, begging me for help. It put a face to every one of them." According to Dennett, human consciousness "is a product in large part of cultural evolution, which installs a bounty of words and many other thinking tools in our brains, creating thereby a cognitive architecture unlike the bottom-up minds of animals" (Dennett, 2017, p. 370). Dennett describes a process of the evolution of memes, which might help us to better comprehend the process of radicalization and the possibility of moral plurality. Let us start with an in-depth look into the process of closing and opening the mind, to better understand how 'memes' influence the human mind.

Creating space in your mind and heart

Van Loon describes how he learned from Viktor Frankl (1985), psychiatrist and creator of logotherapy, that accepting where you are and what the situation requires from you in the here and now gives a great sense of inner peace.

> I became aware that I am not fully determined by the past, that I can change my way of living and giving meaning. To realize this positive

message of possible change gave me solid energy to look for new futures, beginning with my own future. By creating 'space,' by meditating and by listening to other people, I can consciously take a decision to do something different, to confirm my freedom.

(van Loon, 2017, p. 270)

Let us describe a case in which someone created space in thinking and feeling. A woman has been in therapy with one of the authors for quite a while. She said, "My mother always asks me whether or not she was a good mom. She says it like: I was not a bad mom, right? Or I was a good mom?" The client used to answer from the position of wanting to please her mother rather than from her own feeling. She would lose a part of herself by trying to please her mother rather than relating from her authentic self. She then switched positions completely and took the counter position. "Whenever my mother asks this I change the subject or try to avoid answering her because I do not think she was a good mother." So the therapist asked her, "What do you think your mother means by 'good mother,' and do you think it might be different from what you mean by it?" She was a bit dumbfounded by this question. The therapist then asked, "Do you think it is possible that your mother actually was a good mother according to how she defines it – but that you are evaluating her based on how you define it?" It is a conflict of meaning, which is getting in the way of putting things aside so that there can be a connection. Here the therapist created space in the client's mind by asking questions from new perspectives and allowing the client to fundamentally rethink and re-evaluate her relationship with her mother.

When worlds of meaning conflict, this collision may lead to alienation and aggression, thus undermining relations and their creative potential. The other person (i.e., the father, mother, the therapist, the coach) has the responsibility to create space for plurality, for other views, by asking questions from different perspectives. This essentially is dialogue (Bohm, 1996; Isaacs, 1999; Gergen, 2009; van Loon, 2017). You might experience that these types of questions increase your awareness to identify with your current position. If there is no physical other, we must access these parts of ourselves, through the process of self-reflection, in order to create space. Practicing self-reflection and taking time to understand our own thinking processes is one way we can lead our self, to move across the inner boundaries. As in the movie *Human*, the sole act of taking the time to sit down and reflect on 40 questions in front of another human being with a camera creates this mental space.

Feeling respected is critical when opening your mind for new perspectives. George Kohlrieser (2006) describes the impact of respect in hostage situations, with physical intimidation, when he was working for the American police as a negotiator in these situations. He applied the principles of dialogue: listening, showing respect, suspending judgment. By being completely in the *present*, destructive energy might be transformed. That's what the story of an American soldier in the next fragment of *Human* illustrates.

> [*Human*, Part 2, 17:29] There is a moment. And the reason his face is always going to be with me. There is a moment when he looked at me. Our eyes kind of met. At that moment, it was like everything else disappeared, there was no sound, and it was just two people. Looking each other in the eyes. For a moment connecting like two human beings in an event that is beyond any of their control. But at that moment he wasn't a terrorist, he wasn't an insurgent, he wasn't an Iraqi. He was a scared man and he was asking me for help. From that moment on the war changed for me. It became a little more scary and it became a little more . . . I started to question decisions a little more, because of that event, it put a face. That scared, crying man peeing himself could be any or all of them.

Here we observe that the soldier was completely *in the present* and stopped acting automatically. He was able to look *beyond*, to see what really was happening. His 'I' was separate from the immediate situation; there was space in his mind. Recently Yuval Harari makes a similar division in *Homo Deus* (2017) as he distinguishes between an *'experiencing self'* and a *'narrating self.'*[6] "The experiencing self is our moment-to-moment consciousness . . . it remembers nothing. It tells no stories and is seldom consulted when it comes to big decisions" (2017, pp. 296–297). In the narrating self memories, construing, and telling stories are dominant. The most striking connection is that, as with DST, there is not one core self, but a distinction between an experiencing and a narrating self.

A similar process is described in the following fragment, where an Israeli soldier describes his experiences.

> [*Human*, Part 2, 15:45] One evening while being in the reserves my unit had to stop a suicide attack by capturing a terrorist in a village near Nablus. I deployed our forces. To flush him out, we shot at the walls as a demonstration of strength. A woman came out of the house, carrying a girl and holding another by the hand. It was 3 AM. The girl panicked and ran toward us. I was afraid she'd blow herself up. I yelled at her in Arabic to stop. She kept coming. I fired above her head. She stopped.
>
> At that moment the time stood still. It was the shortest and the longest moment of my life. The girl remained alive. And so did I. But at the same time, something died in us both. When a child is shot at, it kills something inside. I don't know what. When an adult shoots at a child, it kills something inside. Something dies and something has come to life. I was ashamed of shooting at her. A painful shame. And above all this sensation of my finger pressing the trigger and shooting at the girl. From

this finger pressing the trigger something had come to life (looks away from the camera). [17:25]

The fragment illustrates how an '*experiencing self*' breaks through the '*narrating self*.' The latter construed a story over time about the conflict and how to deal with that. The challenge is *not* to identify with your point of view, with who you have become and what you have been thinking, but to realize that this is just one meaning out of an infinite range of other possible meanings. The experiencing self is the part of us that is still open, still moving in free space, where we have the full freedom to choose the next step. Once we activate our narrating self, we might become attached to the outcomes; we inherit a role, with a part to play, and to step outside of the narrative means that we can no longer control or predict what will happen. In moments like these, if we remain fully present, we can choose from the current context, rather than from an old story, which may no longer be relevant. Here we take full responsibility for the moment by not hiding behind someone else's decision.

In thinking about 'leading your self,' this is important, as we have to accept that whatever is possible and exists, does so by virtue of nature and biology. If we have a moral assumption or statement about biology, it is derived from culture, religion, and ethics. Nature in itself is without morality (amoral); morality comes from human creative power as culture, religion, ethics, and other human creations. In the stories of the Palestinian and the Israeli, this is illustrated as indoctrination, education. As explored previously, education is teaching people to think autonomously and openly; being able to make your own choices based on rationality, intuition, and morality. Indoctrination is closing people's views into one specific direction, that dominates the entire system of self (one radicalized *I*-position, personally and/or culturally). Neither party was born with these views; they were learned over time (although you might oppose that aggression per se is also natural and innate).

We tend to identify with our narrating self, when we say 'I'; we don't refer directly to an immediate stream of experiences, but we primarily mean the story we tell about our experiences, the meaning we give to them (Harari, 2017, p. 301).[7] In this sense the 'self' is not a simple unchangeable *thing*, but a lifelong '*work in progress*.' Our 'self' consists of continually changing layers of experience. "My sense of self is a tiny man, kicking a can down the road." Van Loon uses this expression (2017, pp. 17–18) quoted from the psychologist Baggini (2011), who uses the expression " 'I' is a verb dressed as a noun" (p. 126). So how do we make space for other *I*-positions? How can I detach my 'self' from a fixed position so that I feel freer to move across the boundaries within myself and into relations with (unknown) others? How do we allow ourselves to fully embrace the self as a 'work in progress'? *Experiencing* and *narrating* are located at the junction of internal and external relations of self. Am I an *actor* in the story of my life following the *author's* intentions? When are the two merged? At what times are they extremely separated?

How to 'unself'

In a society where we are constantly plugged in, with expectations, demands, and growing responsibilities surrounding all aspects of our lives, how, and where, might we find freedom? What options do we have to break through the self-created and social rules that limit our possibilities and imprison us in our own mind and culture?

Jules Evans wrote a book with the thought-provoking title *The Art of Losing Control: A Philosopher's Search for Ecstatic Experience* (2017). In this intriguing book, Evans describes several forms of ecstasy, such as music, drugs, religion, sex, and violence. What happens with the self in a state of ecstasy is what Iris Murdoch calls 'unselfing.' "All of us need to find ways to unself. Civilization makes great demands of us: we must control our bodies, inhibit our impulses, manage our emotions, and 'prepare a face to meet the faces that you meet.' We must play our role in the great complex web of globalized capitalism. Our egos have evolved to help us survive and compete. . . . But the self we construct is an exhausting place to be stuck all the time" (Evans, 2017, p. xi). He refers to a book of Harari (2008) in which he collected accounts of 'combat flow': *Violence absorbs the mind and annihilates the ordinary self.* Harari illustrates this in a convincing manner. Ecstasy and violence both appear to be experiences where the self seems to dissolve. As citizens, we are mostly unaware of this risk. Most people think they are able to withstand these kinds of pressures on their minds, but they are not, as has been demonstrated in the Lucifer experiment of Zimbardo (2007).

In *Human*, this is illustrated in a fragment where a man talks about how he gradually became addicted to violence while he was in combat. What Harari describes as the tension between the experiencing self and the narrating self is illustrated by Evans as the need of human beings, living in a social environment, to let go of the cultural constraints once in a while. Could this explain why human beings – with all risks – need to *let go of the rules of human civilization?*

> [Human, Part 2, 21:14] One of the most impactful things that will occur after being in combat is the feeling of killing another human being. Once you've experienced it, you'll see that it is not like anything else that you have experienced before. And unfortunately that feeling your body will want to experience again. It's really difficult to try to explain to somebody what that feeling is like. Right now, I still feel like experiencing that again and it's probably why I keep a loaded weapon in my house. I yearn or desire for someone to try to hurt me, or to break

in, or to give me an excuse to use that violence against somebody else again. [22:22]

Think about this for yourself. Are you able to distinguish between what you experience and how you construct that experience into a narrative? What is the role of your physical experiences, your body, in this case (experiencing self)? What is the risk when you construct your experiences into a narrative? What do you lose? What do you potentially win?

Here the experiencing self is illustrated in a frightening manner. Evans (2017) quotes a hooligan: "I am attracted to the moment when consciousness ceases: the moment of survival, of animal intensity, of violence . . . the present in its absoluteness" (p. 166). What does this observation imply for an *embodied, experiencing, and narrating* human being moving across the boundaries of self and culture?

Is this what happens with a radical terrorist when attacking people? Are we able to consciously counterbalance this phenomenon, once a human being has experienced it, in our selves, in others, in society? How can one create space in his mind? What about the freedom to choose?

Creating freedom and space using participative mode

"Tell me, good Brutus, can you see your face?"
"No, Cassius, for the eye sees not itself
But by reflection, by some other things."
  – Shakespeare, Julius Caesar, Act 1, Scene 2

To reconcile a potential conflict between experiencing and narrating, van Loon uses *'participative mode'* in his book (van Loon, 2017, p. 25), in line with Bohm (1996) and Libbrecht (2007). A participative mode of being resembles experiences with complete here-and-now awareness (cf. mystic or ecstatic experiences). In a process of acculturation, people get used to a specific way of dealing with issues and, after a period of time, claim that this is the *'only* right' approach. Libbrecht considers in his book *Within the Four Seas* 'reason' as a *function* of the human body: "Man is not an animal with added intelligence, but a *specific human body* capable of freeing energy and transforming it into deeds" (Libbrecht, 2007, p. 109). Are you able to lead your life in the tension between *controlling* and *losing control*? Evans (2017) uses the challenging expression: *The Art of Losing Control*. Are we able to live in a culture and follow its rules and regulations, and at the same time be open to crossing the boundaries between self and others, between cultures and countries? as an illustration of the participative mode. In our view, teaching people how to live from a participative mode could bring the cultural tensions in the world to a next stage of possible reconciliation. We describe a *participative mode of being* as a reconciliation between *active* and *passive* between *I as experiencing* and *I as narrating*, between *controlling* and *losing control*. This is what we point out as dialogical leadership: you are able – as an expression of a participative mode of being – to reconcile these polarities. Doing this in an effective and authentic way is designated as personal leadership, the core question of our chapter.

We will now illustrate a participative mode of being and acting with the Amman Message and the intra- and intercultural dialogue (see also König, Chapter 7 in this volume). Hardy, Mughal, and Markiewicz (2017) use the *Amman Message* an initiative from the king of Jordan, Abdullah II, to call for tolerance and openness by clarifying the 'true nature of Islam and the nature of true Islam.'[8] This example helps highlight how a voice from within the system can free space for new ways of thinking, bridging inner and outer tolerance. One of the contributors to this book, Kristin Shamas, provides an introduction to the processes surrounding identity construction, significantly highlighting that identity is both a process of being acted upon (such as in the 'clash' narrative, through which one is described as useless) and one of agency (where subjects take on hybrid, non-static, and multiple identities). This also illustrates Dennett's view of how memes proliferate over the earth in language, symbols, and concepts. Take as examples the messages that are nowadays shared on Twitter (positive and negative), how they build up clash stories between people who have never met face to face; the importance of corporate narratives and symbols, and how these are used in competition (positive and negative). With our modern technologies, the current situation is that memes can propagate all over the world in less than an hour!

At the same time we see connection with the dialogical self theory approach in this chapter as forming a hybrid, non-static (participative) identity (creating promoter- and meta-positions), which is encouraged through dialogue and can be used to undo and deconstruct a passive self-narrative (Shamas, 2017, pp. 13, 220–225). As noted before, we observe the tendency of (narrative) selves to become static. Even with highly educated liberal leaders who are not caught in a traditional religious network, we see their identity radicalized in one position. As was illustrated by Zimbardo in *The Lucifer Effect* (2007), students were randomly divided into groups of prisoners and guards. In less than a few days, people completely identified with their (accidentally) attributed roles. In two weeks, they had to stop the experiment because of unacceptable personal risks. The tough issue here is how people can be moved into a process of more open and realistic self-reflection. This is even more difficult with people caught in a traditional religious static identity, be this Christians, Muslims, or Jews.

When do you recognize that you are acting in a 'participative mode'? Were you aware at the moment itself? Are you able to apply this mode consciously? Do you recognize moments of hybrid, non-static self in your life? Do you know people who represent this form of identity? Do you recognize where you identified with a position or role that was attributed to you accidentally (think about work, sports, or gaming)?

Sharing experiences of suffering

Shamas (2017) concludes with a suggestion to redefine violence: "through processes of narration, victims and witnesses of violence remake themselves from someone who is acted upon to someone who acts. They reshape their world. We should therefore broaden our definition of 'collective empowerment' to include the sharing of experiences of suffering. Such dialogic 'subjectivity' disempowers the forces of violence and emphasizes humans and their interrelations: a necessary first step to (re)constructing society on the basis of justice and collective good." (p. 224). This sounds idealistic and yet happens in reality. The movie *Human* shows conversations where this happened, where victims of violence redefined their identity and were even happier than before. One of the most touching stories is that of a murderer and the family of his victims, the opening scene in the movie.

> [Human, Part 1, 4:05] I remember my stepfather who would beat me with extension cords and hangers, and pieces of wood and all kinds of stuff. After every beating he would tell me 'It hurts me more than you.' 'I only did it because I love you.' It communicated the wrong message to me about what love was. So, for many years, I supposed that was love and I hurt everyone that I loved. And I measured love by how much pain someone would take from me. And it wasn't until I came to prison, in an environment that is devoid of love, that I began to have some understanding about what it actually was and was not. And . . . I met someone . . . and she gave me my first real insight into what love was, because *she saw past my condition* [Italic by the author] and the fact that I was in prison with a life sentence for doing the worst kind of murder that a man can do: murdering a woman and a child. It was Agnes, the mother and grandmother of Patricia and Chris, that I murdered, who gave me my best lesson about love. By all rights she should hate me. But she didn't. Over the course of time, and through the journey that we took, it has been pretty amazing, she gave me love. [Long pause, tears on his face] She taught me what it was. [7:01]

The key fragment here is that the woman was able to look beyond his condition and to forgive him. A remarkable act. The fragment gives us no more information; we don't hear her version of the story. The combination of indoctrination with violence under the name of love, of an experiencing self that is misled by a narrative of a violent stepfather, and – unexpectedly – an opportunity to re-educate and re-experience love by someone who was willing and able to forgive. An atrocious and beautiful story, an example of moving across boundaries of self.

Would you be able to replace a revenging self with a forgiving self? Look for the moments in your life when you have intentionally forgiven. What did this require for you to shift within yourself? It is easy to write about a forgiving self, but how does this work out for your self? Take a moment of reflection, as these questions are the most difficult if we talk about dialogical leadership and leading yourself across the boundaries of self and culture.

The act of forgiving is a courageous act, which we don't often encounter in life. Edith Eger describes that human beings can opt for freedom and still has to carry the burden of pain from the past. She speaks about forgiving because this is *healing*, not because it is morally necessary or appropriate. Mandela (2014) said after many years of captivity: "As I walked out the door toward the gate that would lead to my freedom, I knew if I didn't leave my bitterness and hatred behind, I'd still be in prison" (para. 1).

The ultimate challenge is how to get radicalized human beings, individually and collectively, to become open for relational self-other reflection in a conversation. So far we examined ways in which we can free our *selves* by consciously taking other *I*-positions, by reconciling opposites and looking from new perspectives to our lives. Although not central to our descriptions in this chapter, we mention that in organizations you can see similar patterns. In our practice as boardroom and leadership consultants, we have met leaders who were 'fixed, closed' in their mind, dominant in a single *I*-position. Should we use the same term 'radicalized' for this phenomenon? By being closed in their minds, they negatively impact their own leadership effectiveness. This illustrates 'memes' reproducing in organizations as concepts and language (such as 'agility,' 'KPI,' 'deliverable,' 'corporate values,' 'authenticity,' and many others), as most people never think, 'What exactly is meant here?' We tend to lock up our 'selves' in concepts and language, and we can't see our openness and creativity (inclusively, that of other people around us) anymore. Some leaders are led solely by the language and the concept of the 'spreadsheet' and are not inclined to look around to validate if what is shown is right. Harari's book *Homo Deus* might help to understand how this type of language and the corresponding thoughts deeply impacted our society globally and contributed to a generic process of radicalization of specific ideas (in particular liberalism). While human beings are potentially free to design their own lives, to make their own liberal decisions, there is not *one* self that is able to coordinate and structure this process. That makes the process challenging. Decisions on how to design your life are made relationally, between different aspects of your self internally (between conflicting *I*-positions) and externally, as there are several people and events influencing you permanently. But there is no single, unified self that orchestrates all that happens and takes centrally coordinated decisions.

It is not easy to create conditions for closed minds to re-open. Van Loon (2017) gives examples of how re-opening might work, what the risks are, and which skills a facilitator needs to have to safely guide this process. If we try to give some characteristics based on what we have seen here, it starts with *respect, the basic condition for dialogue*. Human beings need to feel that they are respected, exactly what very often doesn't occur. For these very extreme situations where 'respect' has never been experienced, how do we learn to show it? Where does the responsibility lie for showing (and receiving) respect? At what point does blame end and personal leadership begin? How do I suspend judgment when I've been only judged? How do I listen to others when I've never been heard? How do I voice in a healthy way when I feel silenced at my core? How do I *move* across boundaries rather than remaining frozen and imprisoned?

By unreservedly embracing what has happened, an opening might emerge, although one never knows for sure. Only if an opening is realized can the work be done. Our experience is that human beings who start thinking, feeling, and acting in a mutually accepting open manner after having been radicalized can become strong and sustainable learners. Peter Senge (2006) introduces the concept of *metanoia* in the context of learning organizations which literally means 'a shift of mind,' to emphasize that fundamental change or movement of mind is a necessary part of sustainable change. *The most difficult step is the first step.* Each of us has to take a step like this, in our direct environment, with a colleague, a partner, a neighbor, our children, our boss, the person we meet coincidentally in the street.

Hardy and his colleagues (2017) are optimistic in the sense that the Amman Message provides us with a great strength: "Its ability to facilitate the reader in framing their understanding of Muslim identity through awareness of pluralism, change, modernity, and consensus is a very powerful counter-narrative" (p. 231). It has to start within the small spheres of influence we have – in communities, in schools, and on campuses – to visibly put prejudice to the one side and promote pluralism in our daily lives. It is about re-educating the *closed* mind, which was born *open*. Yuval Harari (2017) describes pessimistic scenarios of the future, where science is the all-encompassing dogma, which says that organisms are algorithms and life is data processing: dataism (pp. 372–402). What about consciousness? Is that less valuable than intelligence? Is life really just data processing? What will happen to society, politics, and daily life when non-conscious but highly intelligent algorithms know us – humans – better than we know ourselves? (Harari, 2017, p. 402). If you ask us for our view on development of humanity and humans in the future, we would underpin the importance for us to learn how to deal with polarities in life, between ourselves and society, with self as different *I*-positions. We would also indicate another aspect – a vertical dimension.

A vertical dimension?

In the final part of this chapter we invite further research and reflection. In our view, Yuval Harari is pessimistic, but he devotes his book to his teacher S.N. Goenka,[9] who lovingly taught him important things. We invite him to also share his personal experiences in how he learned to lead his life in such a passionate way, in writing books, teaching, and practicing meditation. In our experience, meditation can be an important opening to a moment of 'unselfing,' of depositioning (where no one position is dominant, as opposed to radicalization) and becoming less motivated by a static and ego-driven self, teaching you that you are not always in control over your thoughts and your feelings. Much of what we do, we do in an automatic-pilot mode, and we think, feel, and do it because we have learned it that way – not because it is the best, most authentic, and most ethical way to do it. In this sense, 'unselfing' as 'not identifying your *self* with one sole *I*-position' is a positive process. If you can develop a participative mode, this will enable you to flexibly switch between different *I*-positions that you developed over time in different contexts and cultures. But it needs 'awareness' and 'a sense of direction,' which will be considered in the next section.

A tough question you might ask is, *what makes you human?* Is it the longing for meaning in life, for spirituality and religion? In the interviews in the movie *Human*, a vertical dimension of life is often mentioned as a response to explicit questions, and also spontaneously. What can be the meaning of religion as a dimension in the lives of more than 80% of the worldwide population? (Hardy et al., 2017, p. 229). Why do so many people profess a religious affiliation? What is the meaning of human beings reaching for a transcendent dimension in life? Is it our undying curiosity for who we are and why we are here?

Although Western liberal societies don't confess publicly, we know how important Christian and Jewish faiths are in the United States to be successful in politics and business, and probably the same is true of Europe. In line with the psychiatrist Herman van Praag (2010), we would make a plea to recognize that human beings have a *natural* inclination towards a vertical, transcendent dimension in life. This is not religious in the traditional sense as being subjected to the rules of a church, but it is about our human potential to develop multiple, dialogical selves across coincidentally created constraints. If you listen to the conversations in *Human*, many people refer to this vertical dimension in a beautiful, open, and accepting way. When you listen carefully to people in your direct environment, the mystery of life is not illuminated by rational explanations. Human beings are seekers who continuously try to understand who they are and why they are here. Religious experiences might offer us some direction – but we must not stop asking the questions ourselves. In order to remain open, we cannot allow the answers of life to be given to us through a system of rules, or dictated by a church. We must continuously wonder, with childlike curiosity. The miracle and intelligence of the universe cannot be grasped purely rationally; it must be *experienced*. Each 'religion' brings its own interpretation of what this miracle and intelligence is. Leaders of modern organizations visit workshops where they have to find and formulate a purpose and the values of their lives, their organization, and the impact they might make on society. *Leading your self across boundaries of self and culture* seems to start with a 'sense of direction.' This might have a vertical dimension. This dimension (in line with van Praag, 2010) refers to our human potential to develop multiple dialogical selves across coincidentally created constraints. We mentioned examples of people who were able to use this potential (without being complete, examples from the movie *Human*, Eger, Frankl, Mandela, and the Amman Message).

Throughout this chapter we have demonstrated our core message by providing examples of how people have been able to respond to their circumstances in new ways, to move across the boundaries of self and culture in order to become better leaders of themselves and others; each has managed to shift their own mindsets and free space to make new choices. Peter Senge (2006) emphasized that this type of shift requires personal leadership and mastery, "from seeing ourselves as separate from the world to connected to the world, from seeing problems as caused by someone or something 'out there' to seeing how our own actions create the problems we experience" (p. 369). If such a change in mindsets can create positive change in organizations, what could it mean for society as a whole? What would be possible if we could collectively create the space to transcend patterns and make more conscious choices?

In closing, we would like to revisit Frankl, as his experiences were part of such coincidentally created constraints, and yet, his own personal leadership allowed him to transcend the inhuman conditions in which he found himself and move across the boundaries of self. "Between stimulus and response there is a space. In that space is our power to choose our response. In our response lies our growth and our freedom" (Pattakos, 2008, p. viii). In essence, Frankl is talking about our capacity to learn and grow as human beings, and that the space that we create in our own minds allows us to experience ourselves, our relationships, and our circumstances differently. That might be a spark of hope to live in a world with plural moralities.

Notes

1 www.human-themovie.org/
2 A *meme* is an idea, behavior, or style that spreads from person to person within a culture – often with the aim of conveying a particular phenomenon, theme, or meaning represented by the meme. A meme acts as a unit for carrying cultural ideas, symbols, or practices that can be transferred from one mind to another through writing, speech, gestures, rituals, or other imitable phenomena. (Source: *Merriam-Webster Dictionary* and *Wikipedia*.)
3 The *minimal group paradigm* is a methodology employed in social psychology by H. Tajfel (1970). Although it may be used for a variety of purposes, it is most well known as a method for investigating the minimal conditions required for discrimination to occur between groups. Experiments using this approach have revealed that even arbitrary and virtually meaningless distinctions between groups, such as preferences for certain paintings or the color of their shirts, can trigger a tendency to favor one's own group at the expense of others, even when it means sacrificing in-group gain. Although there are some variations, the traditional minimal group study consists of two phases. In the first phase, participants are randomly and anonymously divided into two groups (e.g., 'Group A' and 'Group B'), ostensibly on the basis of trivial criteria (e.g., preference for paintings or the toss of a coin).

Sometimes, these participants are strangers to one another. In the second phase, participants take part in an ostensibly unrelated resource distribution task. During this task, participants distribute a valuable resource (e.g., money or points) between other participants who are only identified by code number and group membership (e.g., 'participant number 34 of Group A'). Participants are told that, after the task is finished, they will receive the total amount of the resource that has been allocated to them by the other participants. (Source: Wikipedia.)

4 Cf. Nietzsche's 'amor fati.'

5 Kirkus reviews.

6 This reminds us of the distinction W. James (1890) made in 'I' and 'me.' In James's view, the 'I' is equal to the 'self-as-knower,' continuously organizing and interpreting experience in an immediate and subjective manner. The 'me' is identified with the 'self-as-known,' a narrative construed by the 'I.' This distinction is a fundamental starting point in the valuation theory and the self confrontation method, as developed by Hermans and Hermans-Jansen (1995), as they operationalize the self as author *and* actor in the narrative a subject 'writes' about her/his life.

7 Cf. 'me' in James, or the 'actor' in Hermans and Hermans-Jansen (1995).

8 The Amman Message (Arabic: رسالة عمّان) is a statement calling for tolerance and unity in the Muslim world that was issued on 9 November 2004 (27th of Ramadan 1425 AH) by King Abdullah II bin Al-Hussein of Jordan. Subsequently, a three-point ruling was issued by 200 Islamic scholars from over 50 countries, focusing on issues of defining who is a Muslim, excommunication from Islam (*takfir*), and principles related to delivering religious edicts. (Source: Wikipedia.)

9 Satya Narayan Goenka (30 January 1924–29 September 2013), commonly known as S.N. Goenka, was a Burmese-Indian teacher of Vipassana Meditation. Born in Burma to a rich Indian family, he moved to India in 1969 and started teaching meditation. His teaching was notable for emphasizing that the Buddha's path to liberation was non-sectarian, universal, and scientific in character. He became an influential teacher and established meditation centers worldwide. Goenka was an invited speaker at the Millennium World Peace Summit of Religious and Spiritual Leaders on 29 August 2000 at the United Nations in New York. (Source: Wikipedia.)

References

Arendt, H. (1998). *The human condition*. Chicago, IL: University of Chicago Press.

Baggini, J. (2011). *The ego trick: What does it mean to be you?* London: Granta Books.

Bohm, D. (1996). *On dialogue*. New York, NY: Routledge.

Dennett, D. (2017). *From bacteria to Bach and back: The evolution of minds*. New York, NY: W.W. Norton & Company.

Eger, E. E. (2017). *The choice: Embrace the possible*. Scribner Book Company.

Evans, J. (2017). *The art of losing control: A philosopher's search for ecstatic experience*. Edinburgh: Canongate Books.

Frankl, V. E. (1985). *Man's search for meaning*. New York, NY: Simon & Schuster.

Gergen, K. J. (2009). *Relational being: Beyond self and community*. New York, NY: Oxford University Press.

Harari, Y. N. (2008). *The ultimate experience: Battlefield revelations and the making of modern war culture, 1450–2000*. New York, NY: Springer.

Harari, Y. N. (2017). *Homo Deus: A brief history of tomorrow*. New York, NY: Harper Collins.

Hardy, M., Mughal, F., & Markiewicz, S. (Eds.). (2017). *Muslim identity in a turbulent age: Islamic extremism and Western islamophobia*. London: Jessica Kingsley Publishers.

Hermans, H. J. M. (2015). Human development in today's globalizing world: Implications for self and identity. In L. A. Jensen (Ed.), *The Oxford handbook of human development and culture*. Oxford: Library of Psychology.

Hermans, H. J. M., & Gieser, Th. (Eds.). (2012). *Handbook of dialogical self theory*. Cambridge: Cambridge University Press.

Hermans, H. J. M., & Hermans-Jansen, E. (1995). *Self-narratives: The construction of meaning in psychotherapy*. New York, NY: Guilford Press.

Hermans, H. J. M., & Hermans-Konopka, A. (2010). *Dialogical self theory: Positioning and counter positioning in a globalizing society*. Cambridge: Cambridge University Press.

Isaacs, W. N. (1999). *Dialogue and the art of thinking together: A pioneering approach to communicating in business and in life*. New York, NY: Doubleday.

James, W. (1890). *The principles of psychology*. New York, NY: Henry Holt.

Kalayjian, A., & Paloutzian, R. F. (2010). *Forgiveness and reconciliation: Psychological pathways to conflict transformation and peace building*. New York, NY: Springer.

Kohlrieser, G. (2006). *Hostage at the table: How leaders can overcome conflict, influence others, and raise performance*. San Francisco, CA: Jossey-Bass.

Libbrecht, U. (2007). *Within the four seas: Introduction to comparative philosophy*. Leuven: Peeters Publishers.

Mandela, K. (2014, May 19). My grandfather taught me forgiveness. *The Huffington Post*.

Pallone, L. (2017). Forgiveness: On the journey to reconciliation. In R. Koonce, P. Robinson, & B. Vogel (Eds.), *Developing leaders for positive organizing: A 21st century repertoire for leading in extraordinary times* (pp. 159–172). Bingley: Emerald Group Publishing.

Pattakos, A. (2008). *Prisoners of our thoughts: Viktor Frankl's principles for discovering meaning in life and work*. San Francisco, CA: Berrett Koehler Publishers Inc.

Plato. (1969). *Parmenides and other dialogues*. (J. Warrington, Eds. and Trans. with an introduction). London: Everyman's Library.

Senge, P. (2006). *The fifth discipline: The art and practice of the learning organization*. New York, NY: Crown Publishing Group.

Shamas, K. (2017). The Amman message "Other": Repositioning identity politics for dialogue and justice. In M. Hardy, F. Mughal, & S. Markiewicz (Eds.), *Muslim identity in a turbulent age: Islamic extremism and Western islamophobia* (pp. 220–226). London: Jessica Kingsley Publishers.

Tajfel, H. (1970). Experiments in intergroup discrimination. *Scientific American, 223*, 96–102.

Van Loon, E. J. P. (2017). *Creating organizational value through dialogical leadership: Boiling rice in still water*. Zurich: Springer.

Van Praag, H. (2010). The seat of the divine: A biological "proof of God's existence?" In P. J. Verhagen, H. M. van Praag, J. J. Lopez Ibor, J. L. Cox, & D. Moussaoui (Eds.), *Psychiatry and religion*. New York, NY: Wiley Blackwell.

Zimbardo, P. (2007). *The Lucifer effect: How good people turn evil*. New York, NY: Random House.

7 Developing intercultural sensitivity in a world of multicultural identities

Jutta König

Introduction

In the early 21st century, the debate about citizenship, migrants, and identity has become strongly polarized in the Netherlands, across Europe, and globally. Fear of cultural differences, the influx of refugees, and terrorism often dominate in public and theoretical debates and are increasingly reflected in the political policies of building walls, selective national entry policies, and the monitoring of 'potentially radicalizing' Muslim youth. The complex, intercultural situation into which societies have progressively moved is part of the background of this polarization and is closely linked to global, social, political, and economic processes.

More than ever before, people, information, ideas, weapons, etc., are 'on the move,' thereby dramatically changing everyday living conditions around the globe. Jobs from Western economies migrated to India, China, and Indonesia, leaving behind small American communities in despair (Vance, 2016). The outcome of the 2016 elections in the United States came as a shock, where the 'strong leader' Donald Trump was voted president to 'save' a majority of Americans from poverty, negligence, and foreigners. A recently published book (Dunbar, 2017) shows a correlation between an increase in hate crimes in the United States and the fear-mongering propaganda that Trump utilized while running for president. It also examines how economic and cultural differences and perceived inequities pushed America away from liberal democratic principles of choice, secularism, freedom of expression, and multiculturalism towards authoritarian, ultranationalistic, and xenophobic social philosophies.

I shall first explore the contemporary challenges of plural moralities from the perspective of individuals with multicultural identities. It is important to develop an understanding of the multiplicity of these identities that transcend traditional ingroup/out-group thinking patterns towards a thinking in multiple belongings and loyalties in liquid modern societies. It is also important to become aware of the tensions public and theoretical debates cause within individuals that have multiple cultural identities, resulting in the tendency to hide or disenfranchise personal voices that may not seem fitting in national contexts. I shall present a case study illustrating the tensions of multiple belongings and how multiplicity and complexity show up in an individual with a multicultural identity. I will also explore relational and dialogical interventions that may be used to help an individual refind focus while shifting from the personal through the social to the global layers of identity.

From an acculturation perspective, the public and theoretical debates could be considered to be a first developmental step in a learning process of intercultural sensitivity, and I will describe knowledge that is often used to prepare expats on their first international posting. It helps them to become aware of their reactions to the change in their environment, and it enhances their self-reflectivity. Perhaps this model could be implemented to help citizens with little intercultural experience to reflect on their reactions to the enhanced diversity of their environments to facilitate their development of global consciousness.

Bauman's (2000) concept of liquid modernity and fluidity finds resonance in the concept of VUCA in the spiritual management literature. VUCA is an acronym used to describe and reflect on the Volatility, Uncertainty, Complexity, and Ambiguity of general conditions of being 'in between' in an increasingly interconnected post-modern world (Johansen, 2009).

I shall conclude with some thoughts about the kind of leadership that is needed in the evolving complexity of closely knitted global countries, which include the enhancement of self awareness and reflectivity, community building and the ability to shape shift depending on different contexts. I shall introduce the metaphor of 'liquid leading processes' to navigate the volatile in-between.

Multicultural identities

According to Berry:

> There is probably no more serious challenge to attaining social stability and cohesion in the contemporary world than the management of intercultural relations within culturally plural societies. These goals are important to achieve in these societies because they underpin mutual acceptance and trust across cultural groups. The successful attainment of these goals depends on many factors, including a research-based understanding of the historical, political, economic, religious and psychological features of the groups that are in contact.
>
> (2017, abstract)

The implications of his recent research for policy and program development are clear:

> provide cultural space for all groups and their members to feel secure in their place in society; provide opportunities for intercultural contact

and engagement; and encourage the maintenance of multiple identities and ways of living together in plural societies.

(Berry, 2017)

Growing up in different cultural environments as children, intermarriage of parents from different cultures, or migration from one cultural environment to another predisposes individuals towards the development of multicultural identities. Refugees, economic migrants, expatriates, international students, children that have grown up as global nomads and third culture kids (Pollock & Van Reken, 2001), second- and third-generation migrants and children of mixed marriages develop multicultural identities, as they are exposed to the implicit norms of different cultural settings and learn to see the world through more than one cultural frame of reference (König & Clarke, 2016).

Today two-thirds of the world's population is either bi- or multilingual, with more individuals speaking English as a second language than English as a first! Within clinical psychology, educational, and organizational settings, however, very little attention is paid to the effect that being bi- and multilingual and/or multicultural has on identity, emotions, and mental health (Jones & Bradwell, 2007). In societies, schools, and many organizations, in coaching and therapeutic settings, it is still largely a politician, manager, or professional with relatively little intercultural experience dealing with an increased population of individuals who are bi- or multilingual and/or have multicultural identities (König, 2012). More often than not, the surplus of vision that individuals with multicultural identities have is ignored in educational contexts and organizations in the Netherlands and other European countries.

In these fluid times, the maintenance of multiple identities has never been easier, facilitated by the connectivity across the globe through internet, Skype, and FaceTime, yet the tendency towards nationalistic identifications of belonging increasingly problematizes multiple identities (see also van Meijl, Chapter 11 in this volume).

In their book *Translating Lives: Living Between Two Cultures*, Mary Besemeres and Anna Wierzbicka (2007) say that in Australia, many native English speakers are unaware of what it means to live in between two different languages and they have gathered a wealth of personal anecdotes in their book. They say:

> There is a world of human experience closed to speakers of only one language unless and until they share something of it through bilinguals' autobiographical testimonies. A person moving between languages can be aware of having a relationship with each of them – a different one in each case – and of being shaped by these relationships. They can also be aware that they make choices, using their languages in different

ways in different contexts, identifying with them to different degrees and responding to them emotionally in different ways.

(Besemeres & Wierzbicka, 2007, p. xv)

Another book for individuals who are interested in understanding the complex process of developing a multicultural identity is the Hofman (1989) book *Lost in Translation*, where she describes how she, as a migrant from Poland, learned to adjust to American values, language, and society. She explains that the cure for her 'space sickness of transcendence' where she felt a yearning for her past and is not quite a part of her present, was to learn to retell the story of her life in her new language, thus transcending the divide and reclaiming the self that was lost in the move between two cultures and two languages. She says that by retelling her story in her new language, disparate voices within her are reconciled with each other, and this facilitates the emergence of a person who judges the voices and tells the stories. She seems to be saying that voicing her old self in her new language facilitates the growth of a position that helps her to maintain the balance between the shifting cultural perspectives of two different cultural selves.

Being confronted by a different culture, an unknown language, and unknown codes of conduct can be an unnerving experience because we suddenly realize how many of our taken-for-granted behaviors are tied to a certain cultural context and relational norms and values (Gergen, 2009), (see also K. J. Gergen, Chapter 1 in this volume). It takes time to learn and understand a different culture's implicit rules of conduct. Being curious, voicing uncertainty, and asking for explanations of things we encounter that we do not understand are valuable skills in navigating this learning process. One of the first steps in learning intercultural codes is to slow down our habitual pace of speech, in order to 'catch' the subtleties hidden between the lines of intercultural communication. There is a need for metacommunication between communicating individuals in safe spaces, greater language tolerance, and a desire to learn from each other. There is a saying amongst intercultural trainers that if you ASSUME something about the other, you are making an ASS out of U and ME.

According to Akhtar (1995) and Bhatia and Ram (2001), who have a background of migration between India and the United States, their process of acculturation is accompanied by a constant internal dialogue of positioning and repositioning between then and there and here and now. In the minds of migrants and individuals with multicultural identities, there seems to be an ongoing active dialogue between the different personal positions created in different cultural contexts. The field of tension, where a person is somewhere between new opportunities and threats and a past identity in a different cultural context, requires a shift from a focus on developmental end states like Berry's 'integration strategy' or La Fromboise, Coleman, & Gerton's 'bicultural competence' towards a more process-oriented notion of acculturation that can account for situated, negotiated, and often contested developmental trajectories (Hermans, 2001; Bhatia & Ram, 2001).

Bennet (1993) sees acculturation as an ongoing process. She distinguishes two potential responses to living on cultural margins, encapsulated marginality and constructive marginality, which she sees as stages in a process of acculturation. The characteristics of the encapsulated marginal are disintegration in shifting cultures, loose boundary control, difficulty in decision making, alienation, self absorption, no recognized reference group, multiplistic, conscious of self, troubled by ambiguity, and never at home. The characteristics of the constructive marginal are self-differentiation, well-developed boundary control, self as choice maker, dynamic in-betweenness, authenticity, a marginal reference group, commitment within relativism, conscious of choice, intrigued by complexity, never not 'at home.' I prefer to use the term 'in-between' as the term 'marginal' has a negative connotation.

Research (König, 2012) based on the theory of the dialogical self shows that individuals with multicultural identities love being asked to elaborate and share their stories about their different cultural identities. When they do so, they often realize that others have similar experiences in spite of having a different culture or religion. Sharing personal stories is a way to get beyond the essentialist categorization into different cultures, as we are all far more than the different cultures we were born or have grown into. Safe spaces of connection are more easily established through the telling of complex personal histories than through simplistic identification with a cultural group.

The PEACE (Personal Emotional Account of Cultural Experience) methodology (König, 2012) was developed as an instrument with which to explore the emotional layers of personal cultural positions as a part of a dialogical culture coaching approach (König & Clarke, 2016) for individuals with multicultural identities. By exploring the dialogical self of global nomads, König (2012) found that a number of global nomads that had firsthand contact with different cultures during their formative years identify different cultural positions within themselves and have developed a global perspective on the world. This methodology provides spiritual and moral guidance for individuals whose identities were formed in liquid times. A dialogue between personal cultural positions, an in-between position, and a meta-position increases wellbeing in migrants and seems to facilitate the process from encapsulated 'in-betweenness' to constructive 'in-betweenness' (König, 2012). By exploring the emotional component of personal cultural positions, the power relationships between personal cultural positions become apparent. Different personal cultural positions are valued differently on an emotional level. The dominant culture was often experienced as ambivalent and at times silenced other cultural voices. This can be related to hate spin in society, that is, stigmatizing or negative towards minority groups (George, 2016). By becoming aware of how these negative media mediated voices manifest in the emotional layers of their personal cultural position repertoire, multicultural individuals may be empowered to develop counter-narrative strategies to influence their personal environments. These strategies reach beyond the limits of our current political systems.

The field of tension between the dominant discourses in society and personal cultural positions of individuals with multicultural identities may cause the shutting down of personal cultural voices that are at odds with the present context, causing energy leaks. A voice that has long been suppressed may suddenly becomes dominant in the system, resulting in a dramatic position shift (Hermans & Hermans-Jansen, 1995) Could this be an explanation for the sudden radicalization of individuals? Obviously, further research is needed to explore this avenue of thinking. It is important to become aware of the tensions in multicultural identities caused by the voices emanating from the environment, which may result in the tendency to hide personal voices that may not seem fitting in national contexts. In the following passage, I shall describe a case study to illustrate the complexity of living in liquid modernity.

A case study of a multicultural identity

I received a call from a young woman (MIRA, 42 years old) who had found my name through the ACCESS website. (ACCESS is a welcoming community for internationals that is spreading to the major cities in the Netherlands. It has an international group of counselors on call for psychological resources.)

She sounded rushed and confused on the phone and said she desperately needed to talk to someone. We arranged a meeting a few days later.

A woman of German-Asian origin appeared. Raised by her Chinese mother in Germany, her German father had passed away when her mother was seven months pregnant. Her parents had met in Hong Kong, where both parents had been working, and moved back to Germany a few years prior to the accident that killed her father. Every year, growing up, she and her mother would visit their relatives in Indonesia and afterwards spend a week in Hong Kong or Singapore.

Her mother had passed away three months prior to our first appointment in Germany, after many years of steady decline. While caring for her ailing mother, she had, for some years, worked as a secretary at an international architects firm in Germany.

Her son (22) lived in the United States and was putting himself through college. She had moved with him to New Zealand, America, China, Germany, and then again to America as he was growing up. As she had been a relatively young mother she had not been able to complete her university education in her twenties. She had now sold the family home, and decided to fulfill a dream to complete her master's degree at Leiden University.

She mentioned a number of issues that were overwhelming her in the present that she felt incapable of making clear and rational choices about and needed to talk them through. Her American green card was due to expire within three months, and she was wondering if she should fly back to America to renew the card. She explained that she had felt very much at home and accepted in the United States as almost everyone was an immigrant there, as opposed to always feeling the odd one out with her Asian appearance, while growing up in southern Germany. She was considering spending the summer touring the West Coast to decide where to find a home and settle. At the same time, she felt drawn towards Asia and was eager to go to Taiwan to learn to speak Chinese.

In accordance with the burial traditions of her mother's native Sumatra, her mother's ashes should be flown to Indonesia by the 100th day after her death (within three to six weeks, at the time we met) to participate in a family burial celebration. Confronted with these existential questions, she felt overwhelmed, wondering how to resolve the current conflicting issues, where she should settle, work, and how to spend the rest of her life. She looked frail, with much energy in her head and little in her body, ungrounded, uprooted.

I listened in growing amazement as she struggled to describe the complexity of her situation. How could I analyze her situation from a relational and dialogical perspective in order to provide her with moral and spiritual guidance in the liquid times she was experiencing?

From a relational perspective, her son in America, her in-laws in Germany, and her mother's remaining Chinese relatives in Indonesia had her relational loyalties spread-eagled around the globe. Too many choices and too many options in her saturated self (Gergen, 1991). She had absolutely no interest in living in Germany, although she did mention that her former employer was wooing her back, and that she had a supportive relationship with the family of her son's father and visited them occasionally in Germany. I realized that she must still be mourning her mother, her sole anchor in life, be it an ambivalent one, as she had always felt over-protected. Raised by a single Chinese mother in a conservative region of southern Germany, she had internalized the message that things that were normal for other children were 'not for her.'

By starting her studies in the Netherlands, she had moved to a new environment that offered her, as yet, little social/relational support. She was struggling with an issue of choice, what to do in the next three months – bring her mother's ashes to Indonesia or secure her green card in America – while at the same time trying to meet the oppressive deadlines of end-of-year papers as well as with longer-term issues on where to settle permanently. She had not yet completed her grieving process and could not focus on her studies. She was cut loose from her moorings by her mother's passing, a critical life incident. From a dialogical perspective, she admitted to lacking someone with whom she could discuss the issues she was grappling with in a calm and collected manner and often stressed the fact that she felt that so few people understood her complex multicultural identity.

A dialogical self is a multivoiced self that transcends the monological character of the self as a self-contained entity. The self is seen as developing in dialogue with its context and is made up out of many independent *I*-positions that when brought into dialogue with each other have the capacity to develop new meanings. The voices of the different cultural positions of MIRA were very manifest in our conversation as she regularly switched between English and German, often saying that she felt it hard to express herself on the spur of the moment, as she was constantly negotiating between different layers of language. This made it difficult for her in public speaking and presentation exercises at the university. Also, the voice of her mother was ventrilocated (Bakhtin, 1973) and very manifest in saying "this is not for you."

This case illustrates the fields of tension between her different cultural positions and options in America, Germany, China, Indonesia, and the Netherlands. She explicitly mentions the charm that living on the West Coast of America holds for her with the many Asian immigrants that live and work there.

Using a time line method devised by Alan Seale (2011), I invited her to choose a position in the room where she felt she was right now, and to experience how she felt there. She described her feelings of restlessness, hopelessness, impatience, and exhaustion.

I then invited her to choose another position in about a years' time and describe how she felt there. She described a sunny home with a garden where she would be doing tea ceremonies. She felt calm, serene, and in control at that point.

I invited her to move back to her first position, taking some of the future's energy with her. She returned to her first position and immediately felt the agitation returning. It was difficult for her to retain the calming energy. She felt again overwhelmed by the choices confronting her.

I invited her to take a first step, in the direction of the second position and asked her what that step symbolized.

She immediately took three or four rushed steps, and realized that she was thinking about too many issues at the same time. She also realized how difficult it was for her to feel. Thoughts were racing through her head, and she could hardly feel her body and make use of her other knowledge centers, her heart and her stomach. She reminded herself how valuable her early morning meditation sessions were to help her feel more grounded, but somehow she did not get around to doing them. She realized she was spending too much time on her own in her room, unproductive time, that she could well be spending socializing with other people, doing research for her master's thesis, etc. Realizing this, she became calm.

I asked her to return to her original position, and take just one step. What would that first step be? With tremendous clarity, she said "Finish my studies," with a bright smile.

I asked her to take a second step, and she did so. She would take her mother's ashes to Indonesia in the summer, to finish her grieving process with members of her family. I asked her to write me a short note reflecting on the meaning of our session.

She responded to the session with the following email message, which was written in German, but which I have translated into English:

> *Thank you for the contact. You asked me what I thought of the session, but I was unsure of how to quickly respond, only that I knew that I wanted to continue, if possible. To articulate my feelings I needed to be alone, to become clear on what it had meant for me.*
>
> *I have so many stories to tell that the session was far too short. I had found your profile at Christmas and thought oh wow, perfect, a psychologist with cross cultural experience, global nomad and career coach. You could perhaps understand me, and you have experience in the world of business.*
>
> *When I finally called you I may have projected onto you that you would be able to help me to answer all my questions. I believe that as the hour drew to a close I felt disappointment that this was not and could not be the case! But I also noticed how you led me to answer my own questions and how I doubt my own intuition (that in the past has always been right).*
>
> *The value of the exercise that you did with me only became clear to me in the evening, when I returned home and what it meant to me. And I continually felt this over the past days. Intellectually I knew this, but now I feel the contrast. Out of my head and spread out in my body, then hopefully I will know at some point in the future where to spread myself out on the planet and how things will evolve.*
>
> *This image of 'something that spreads and melts,' or the movement, which you said would do me good hits the nail on the head. And I also sense why it was so difficult for me to take the first step. . . . You first had me take the last and middle steps in order to be able to feel the first, and to walk instead of to run. . . . The first step is to find some calm, to 'spread out' my new word. I notice that this does not come quickly (or perhaps it does) and I feel a need to talk with you. My conditioning is strong, but I want to become free of them. Thank you for helping me on my way.*
>
> *Thanks again and see you soon . . .*

A few sessions later, her personal cultural positions were explored on an emotional level using the PEACE methodology (König, 2012). The different cultural positions that she identifies are related to encounters with different cultures during her formative years. We bring them all into the virtual arena of her personal cultural position repertoire as if the self were a society of cultural voices. She is invited to conduct a dialogue between two personal cultural positions and chooses the German and Chinese position. She is also invited to voice an in-between position and a meta-position. The in-between and the meta-position are important positions with which to bridge conflicting positions and navigate the complexities of our dialogical selves. She is asked to rate the amount of conflict between her two positions that are conducting the dialogue, and to conclude, she is asked how she usually feels, and how she would ideally like to feel (König & Clarke, 2016).

Then the client is invited to score each statement on a five-point scale using a standard set of 24 affects, as described in Table 7.1. The rationale underlying this procedure is that when a person values something, he or she always feels something about the valued object. In order to do this quickly and efficiently a computer program has been developed.

The PEACE methodology, as does the self confrontation method (SCM), appeals to the self-organizing capacity of the person. Both methods invite the person to organize and articulate their world into a differentiated meaningful whole. The client as knower is invited to investigate, in cooperation with the interviewer, the self as known. The difference between the SCM and the PEACE methodology is that the latter focuses on stories voiced from an individual's cultural perspectives and explores an individual's cultural complexity.

In valuation theory (Hermans, Hermans-Jansen, & Van Gilst, 1985), the statements with their affective connotation are called 'valuations.' This procedure ultimately enables the measurement of the psychological concepts of self-enhancement (S) and contact and unity with the other (O) and helps to investigate and clarify the valuation system of cultural voices and its organization into a complex whole at a certain moment in time in a certain contextual environment. Figure 7.1 illustrates the general types of valuations that can be generated depending on their particular affective profile.

Valuations are organized by combining the sum scores for feelings grouped under S, O, P, and N into eight different affective types (+S, –S, ±S, +O, –O, ±O, +SO, –LL), which provide information about the affective quality of each valuation as seen in Figure 7.1.

The valuation of Strength and Unity (+SO) is one of the eight different types of valuation shown in Figure 7.1. Valuations are computed following

Table 7.1 Standard list of 24 affect terms

1. joy (P)	7. shame (N)	13. guilt (N)	19. safety (P)
2. powerlessness (N)	8. enjoyment (P)	14. self-confidence (S)	20. anger (N)
3. self-esteem (S)	9. caring (O)	15. loneliness (N)	21. pride (S)
4. anxiety (N)	10. love (O)	16. trust (P)	22. energy (P)
5. satisfaction (P)	11. self-alienation (N)	17. inferiority (N)	23. inner calm (P)
6. strength (S)	12. tenderness (O)	18. intimacy (O)	24. freedom (P)

Note: S is affect referring to self-enhancement; O is affect referring to contact and union with the other; P is positive affect; and N is negative affect.

(Source: Hermans & Hermans-Jansen, 1995, p. 277.)

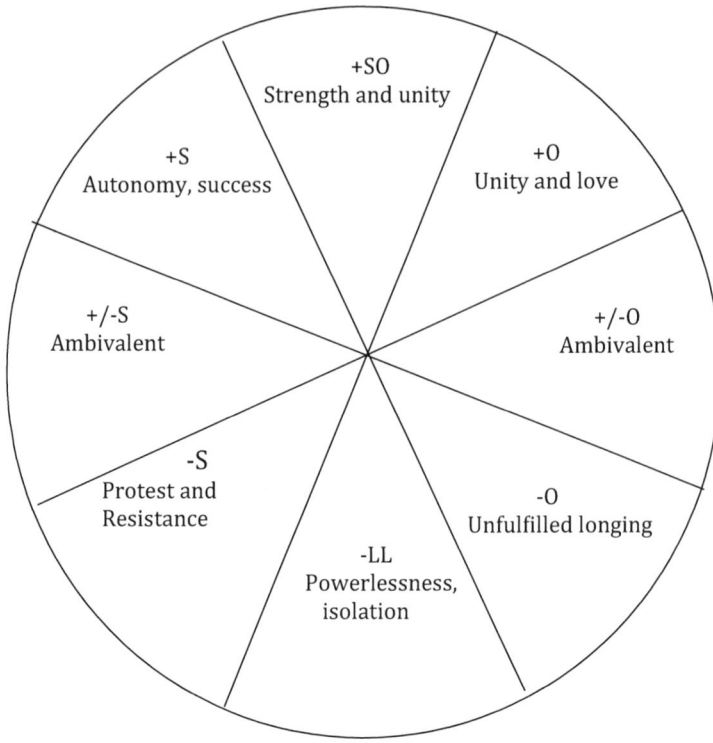

Figure 7.1 A variation of Hermans & Hermans-Jansen's (1995) original figure with
   types of valuations

the methodology devised by Hermans and Hermans-Jansen (1995, p. 42).
For example:

Strength and Unity Valuation	S	O	P	N	
I as Chinese like refinement	20	19	36	1	+SO

1   Index S is the sum score of the four affects expressing self-enhancement
    (self-esteem, strength, self-confidence, pride). In this valuation, a maxi-
    mum of 5 points for each affect was scored, resulting in a score of 20.
2   Index O is the sum score of four affects expressing contact and union
    with the other (caring, love, tenderness, and intimacy). A maximum of
    5 points was scored for each affect except one, resulting in a score of 19.
3   Index P is the sum score of eight positive (pleasant) affects (joy, satisfac-
    tion, enjoyment, trust, safety, energy, inner calm and freedom). A maxi-
    mum of five points was scored for four affects and four for the other
    four affects, resulting in a score of 36.

4   Index N is the sum score of eight negative (unpleasant) affects (powerlessness, anxiety, shame, self-alienation, guilt, loneliness, inferiority, anger). A minimum number of points for each affect was scored, resulting in a score of 1. Note that the sum scores of the S and O indices range from 0 to 20, the P and N from 0 to 40. For each valuation, the P:N ratio can be studied. This indicates the wellbeing that an individual experiences in relation to the specific valuation.

If P – N > 10, then + Wellbeing is positive
If N – P > 10, then – Wellbeing is negative
If P = N, then ± Wellbeing is ambivalent
The positive and negative feelings determine if one feels positively, negatively, or ambivalently about a certain specific valuation.

MIRA identified the following personal cultural positions (Table 7.2), Chinese, Hong Kong, New Zealand, USA, Germany, Singapore, and values

Table 7.2 Cultural valuations MIRA

Valuations MIRA	S	O	P	N	
I as Chinese	16	16	28	11	+SO
I as Hong Kong	18	19	35	0	+SO
I as New Zealand	13	14	27	4	+SO
I as USA	13	12	27	2	+SO
I as German	4	1	4	23	–LL
I as Singapore	15	17	34	2	+SO
I as a Chinese am polite	16	17	31	11	+SO
I as German am honest	11	5	19	8	+S
I as Chinese like refinement	20	19	36	1	+SO
I as a German like security	4	4	4	29	–LL
I as an "in between" love internationality	18	15	37	3	+SO
As an 'in between' I am precise	16	14	27	8	+SO
I really feel drawn to Singapore, Hong Kong, New Zealand (meta-position)	18	18	32	4	+SO
I feel aversion against the German side (meta-position)	9	5	16	15	+/–
Was ich nicht spüre wenn ich zu Besuch bin: zum Beispiel spreche ich beim Einkaufen in Deutschland, English (meta-position). (I do not feel this when I am visiting, for example when shopping in Germany I speak English).	16	11	32	6	+S
I as an Anglo Saxon don't like the Engstirnigkeit (narrow-mindedness) I experienced from 'them' (meta-position)	17	14	30	12	+SO
But I appreciate the German love for quality (meta-position)	16	12	30	0	+SO
I experience a 5 in conflict between German and Chinese positions	12	17	15	27	–O
In general I feel	15	13	23	30	+/–SO
Ideally I would like to feel	18	13	38	0	+SO

almost all of her personal cultural positions with Strength and Unity (+SO), with the exception of her German position, which is valued with powerlessness and isolation (−LL). She experiences a conflict of five between her German and her Chinese position, and this is valued with a feeling of unfulfilled longing (O-). In general she feels an ambivalent sense of strength and unity (+/−SO), and ideally she would like to feel a positive sense of strength and unity (+SO).

In the dialogue between her Chinese and her German positions, MIRA says she is polite (+SO) and likes refinement (+SO) as a Chinese, and as a German she is honest (+S) and likes security (−LL), which again is valued with feeling of powerlessness and isolation. From her 'in-between' position she mentions that she loves internationality (+SO) and is precise (+SO).

From her meta-position, she says that she feels drawn to Hong Kong, Singapore, and New Zealand (+SO), and that she feels aversion to her German side, which is valued with ambivalence (+/−). She mentions that she does not feel the ambivalence when visiting Germany and while shopping there she speaks English, which she values with (+SO). The Anglo Saxon voice offers a meta-position saying that she doesn't like the *Engstirnigkeit* (narrow-mindedness) she experienced from 'them' (the Germans) (SO+).

It is apparent that there are no Unity and Love (+O) and Protest and Resistance (S-) valuations in her cultural position repertoire.

I wondered what causes the aversion and ambivalence towards her German position. In conversation with the client, these scores were evaluated, and she offered the following explanations:

> She says that she felt frustrated and annoyed/depressed by criticism and judgment growing up in Germany. "I always felt the odd one out, different, unwelcome and lonely. My mother told me that because of my black hair and HER different appearance the kids in kindergarten bullied me. I became so scared and shy that I refused to go there. My new kindergarten was more 'safe,' but I still felt 'scared' to be myself. That's all I remember and that one boy even kicked my mom in the butt when she was tying my shoes. This anxiety feeling (shame) continued throughout school and appears as performance anxiety nowadays. What I constantly felt and internalized was the constant contrast between how I really felt and what people expected me to feel – what I thought I have to BE in order to be accepted (from both the German AND Chinese side), rather than feeling my true feelings."
>
> She recalls a teacher in Germany saying that she could not study, and should become a 'Hausfrau.' Her unfulfilled longing was to belong. This was the reason that once she was old enough to leave Germany, she moved to New Zealand, and later to America, both countries with considerably more cultural diversity than southern Germany, felt more welcoming to her. She seemed to have fled an oppressive situation in Germany as a child and now as an adult resents the German part of

herself. She does however mention that she appreciates the German love for quality, in what seems to be a moment of reconciliation in her final meta-position statement.

After reading this chapter, she offered some additional comments:

Nowadays I say I am a 'citizen of the world' when some stranger asks where I am from or what I do. It's easiest and makes me feel comfortable because I don't feel German or truly Chinese, but the contrasting feeling described above still exists here because many people look surprised when I say this.

I am very happy, even proud to be a 'mixed blood.' I am not half-half though, I'm 'double'! It seems that the older I got I learned to adjust and switch mentalities depending on with whom I am in order to be heard correctly. I like this asset of mine, but for a change I would like to be reciprocated sometimes. It would be nice if I felt I can live out of both mentalities at the same time, instead of switching (and suppressing) one side to be heard or fit in.

Neither so called 'pure' society (German or Chinese) consider the 'other,' they only consider their own truth and what they think is 'right.' Moreover, neither understands generally spoken that one can have both worlds at the same time.

I think 'to be heard' is essential, people don't have to agree, but recognize the 'other.' It is quite normal, even within the same cultural position, that there are different 'points of view' when looking at the same thing. If people could understand that from each point of view one has a different perspective in a multidimensional world, understanding would become easier. The good thing about having internalized different cultural positions and being adaptive is that I learned in my relationships with others to accept where they are coming from, and to understand their point of view.

E.g. the architect firm I worked for was German but Muslim, and they were mainly building religious structures in Mekka and Medina. I had to deal with people from over 20 different countries who I think I accommodated very well to while pulling strings between the different departments from the CEO's office. My Pakistani co-worker (who had lived in Pakistan and Saudi Arabia before) had more difficulties in his interrelationships because he only considered his 'viewpoint' and the result was a power struggle between two or more people trying to communicate their 'truths' about how things are or what is necessary or what they want. In the end, this creates a win-lose situation, which stiffens each viewpoint to create more separatedness, rather than coming closer to create a win-win situation. Moreover, understanding the 'other' (being heard) makes the other more willing to see and consider one's own 'truth' and vice versa.

I wish that people in general would at least try to understand the intentions of others without assuming that they have the same angle when looking at things (I-am-right-and-you-are-wrong attitude). I say this from my personal experience interculturally as well as when taking the same 'cultural position.' This requires not only openmindedness and tolerance but that people assume the 'good' intention of others and not let prejudice or opinionatedness rule their viewpoint of others. And it requires curiosity and reflection.

How boring would the world be if we all are the same, rather than exploring each other? That's just my 50 cents to the present hostile and conflicting issues in view of politics and especially migration. Besides, there is no 'pure culture' since humans migrated/traded since the beginning of time. . . . People have to relax.

On a sideline, I am wondering why I was writing all this, but reading your chapter and dealing with my 'case' stirred something up in me in the light of my difficulties in transforming the 'dialogical workings of cultural positions in the self' to an authentic self that does not switch positions but embraces/includes them all, which would eliminate the constant feeling of 'contrast' that is rooted, in my case at least, in 'shame.' (Do you know Brene Brown, a sociologist? She says that 'vulnerability' is the key to 'connection.') Afterall, the dynamics of inter-relationships with people and things occupy my mind a lot because in the end this is all there is in this world, I mean of the important things, because we ('self') only exist (can be seen) in relation to 'others.' I feel I have a good grasp to recognize the subtlety of these 'things' like seeing through a curtain, because of my ambivalent history. I also think that's why I am drawn to philosophical Daoism and Zen, where the goal is to return to 'no-self' and emptiness while alive in world of duality.

This case illustrates the dialogical workings of cultural positions in the self.

As a child in Germany, she experienced the power structures of not being accepted, always feeling the odd one out, as well as being exposed to the limiting beliefs of a parent and teachers. This case shows how the power structures to which she was exposed as a child have become deeply ingrained in the emotional layers of the self. In the self-reflective process in a safe dialogical space they can be examined, made conscious, and transformed. The client enjoyed exploring her personal cultural positions in this way, and enthusiastically started up dialogues between her other personal cultural positions.

Citizens in the 21st century are expected to be capable of functioning in socio-political environments that are characterized by substantial cultural and religious diversity. Living in such social contexts requires of citizens the capability to articulate their own views in debates about values and also consider and integrate new insights and skills.

Developing global consciousness

Drawing from dialogical self theory and cosmopolitanism, Liu and Mac-Donald (2016) speak of a need to develop global consciousness to respond adequately to the ethical and identity challenges presented by globalization. They state that "Global Consciousness requires a knowledge of both the interconnectedness and difference of humankind, and a will to take moral actions in a reflexive manner on its behalf" (p. 82). They argue

> that in summary, global consciousness is a complex state of mind involving identity, awareness, knowledge, emotion, and moral responsibility all existing in a complex interaction. . . . Global Consciousness is a project in the making, and a journey for our times. The wedding of empirical science with more prescriptive elements of moral interdependence proposed here is an invitation to go beyond the monological roots of social science and towards a global dialogue of possibilities.
>
> (Liu and MacDonald, 2016, p. 93)

Liu and MacDonald also say that

> a defensive reaction to globalization is an emphasis on group centrism which sometimes intensifies conflict and contradiction between cultural perspectives (Mustakova-Possardt, 2006; Kruglanski, Pierro, Manetti, & De Grada, 2006). This is most evident in the case of fiercely-nationalist or religiously-fundamentalist identities; identities which involve a retreat to 'sacred values,' sets of religious, nationalistic or ethnic preferences that are highly resistant to dialogue or compromise (Atran & Axelrod, 2008). In contrast to secular values, which are typically flexible in intercultural negotiation (Tanner & Hanselmann, 2008), situations in which material incentives are perceived as attempts to 'buy off' sacred values tend to evoke intense resistance (Dehghani, Iliev, Sachdeva, & Atran, 2009), amplified by perceptions of external threat to the ingroup (Sheikh, Ginges, Coman, & Atran, 2012).
>
> (Liu & MacDonald, 2016, p. 83)

Where on the one hand these authors point towards a need for the development of global consciousness, they also signal a defensive reaction to globalization in an emphasis on group centrism amplified by perceptions of external threat to the ingroup. They speak of individuals that retreat to sacred values, sets of religious, nationalistic or ethnic preferences. Is the building of walls and selective national entry policies of the Trump administration not a similar reaction?

According to Bennet (1993, p. 29), groups and individuals open and close themselves, depending on the stage in their developmental process of intercultural learning and sensitivity. The basic learning goals of intercultural communication are generally agreed upon, encompassing self awareness, other culture awareness, and various skills in intercultural perception and communication (Gudykunst & Hammer, 1983; Paige & Martin, 1983 – referred to by Bennet, 1993, p. 22). He sees isolation, separation, denigration, superiority, and minimalization of cultural differences as a natural first reaction when individuals are confronted with the increased complexity of a different culture. These reactions are seen as the ethnocentric stages in a developmental model of intercultural sensitivity. These stages of ethnocentrism, or closing, are followed by ethno-relative stages where respect for behavioral and value differences, empathy, pluralism, contextual evaluation, and constructive marginality prevail. Ethno-relativity implies an opening towards and an appreciation of difference as individuals and societies learn to navigate the increased complexity with which they were originally confronted. This knowledge is generally used to prepare expats for the culture shock of a first cross-cultural experience. Perhaps now it is time to teach it to individuals with little cultural experience to enhance understanding about the acculturation process to the enhanced diversity in many social environments in Europe and globally due to the increased migration flows, caused by war and famine.

This brings me to the following questions: What are the challenges and pitfalls in this learning process of intercultural sensitivity? What enhances the ability to open up, and what causes the self to close down? Are these processes relevant to radicalization? The gradual shift from closing to opening is facilitated by interpersonal exchange, a welcoming glance, a meal, a developing friendship to help a newcomer to gradually start to feel at home.

Finding work in the new environment is an ideal way to learn new cultural codes firsthand (König, 2012).

The dialogical process through which multicultural identities develop ideally leads to the valuing of a different culture. Understanding and learning the new invisible cultural codes requires explanation and metacommunication about unwritten rules of which locals are generally unaware because it is simply their routine of living life. When these routines are questioned by newcomers, new inspiration may arise. If the dialogical selves of migrants become engaged in dialogue in safe spaces, it could enhance creativity in international businesses and understanding of cultural differences in the workplace and/or bring about innovative personal solutions to identity issues in coaching and therapy sessions (König, 2012). As multicultural individuals become empowered to speak their own minds, they have the potential to innovate society at the same time. This, together with maintenance of personal cultural identity, language, and ties to family, creates multicultural identities that are versatile and can shape shift depending on the context at hand.

Individuals with multicultural identities could be considered to be on their way to developing global consciousness but are often considered to be outsiders in many national contexts as they are often identified only by the 'foreign' part of their multicultural identity. They experience fields of tension between personal cultural positions and voices in the environment. In a worst case scenario, individuals may feel excluded, feel shut out, shut down, resist dialogue, and become 'lone wolves,' which may enhance the liability of radicalization.

I have mostly been made welcome in the countries and cultures where I have lived. I am not sure that this can be said of the refugees who have entered our countries in the past 20 years, and I often wonder if this is one of the causes for the dramatic increase in radicalization. From my professional vantage points I have learned how difficult it is for the refugees coming from Syria, Iran, Iraq, and Afghanistan to find suitable work in the Netherlands and how individuals with multicultural identities at times struggle with the field of tension of conflicting cultural norms, and how their selves are influenced by the enhanced negativity of media and voices in the environment.

Fewer than 25% of the refugees that have entered the Netherlands are actively employed. Many find themselves ostracized and isolated in our societies, and this makes them more susceptible to the whispering voices of the internet striving to recruit fighters desperate enough for a suicide bombing. Research has shown that radicalization of young Muslims has a lot to do with a sense of not being seen as belonging to the culture in which they find themselves. ISIS offers them a collective place of belonging (Bakker & Grol, 2017).

According to Hermans et al.:

> For a proper understanding of a democratic self, it is necessary to start from the assumption that the self is part of the society at large. An implication of this view is that relationships of social power that emanate from societal institutions, cultural values, and historical traditions, create both opportunities and obstacles for the development of the self. As part of the society, the self is challenged to respond, together or alone with other selves, to these power structures. If influential enough, this response has an impact on the further development of both society and the self. In this sense, a democratic self is 'work in progress' at the interface of self and society.
>
> (2017, p. 7)

In a democratic society we assume that all voices have equal access to the political arena, but recent publications (George, 2016; Lamont, 2017) show that there are prisms of inequality and hate spin that limit the scope of what dissident voices can say to be heard in the democratic arena. Fake news and technological interference with democratic elections are also undermining democracy as we know it.

According to Gergen (1991), we are relational beings, and I often find myself wondering what treatment generated the hate and violence we are witnessing by the countless random terrorist attacks that have been occurring around the globe in the war against ISIS and al-Quaeda. Have we bothered to listen to and acknowledge their grievances? Are the planted bombs, explosions, and killings of countless innocent individuals a retaliation for the treatment we have inflicted over decades?

Internet and Skype connections make it child's play to interact with individuals around the globe at the touch of a fingertip to a screen. Just as easily,

I suppose if I were a second- or third-generation Muslim migrant living in Brussels or The Hague, and feeling disenfranchised with my life in Belgium or the Netherlands, hearing the constant negativity on the radio or television about Muslims and terror attacks, I may be enticed by radicalizing friends to join ISIS and participate in the building of an Islamic state where I felt I truly belonged – where I would be a hero instead of unwelcome and unemployed. It would also be worth exploring the valuations of their different cultural voices. My hypothesis is that if their dissonant voices are heard, the need for aggressive terror attacks could be reduced (see also Wijsen, Chapter 3 in this volume).

Governments spend huge amounts of money on language training and adaptation courses to acculturalize the migrant to her/his new situation. Future research could explore whether a new culture is learned more easily in a dialogical process of comparison between here and there. If the process were dialogical, both parties, locals and immigrants, stand to learn, and to expand their horizons. Could school curricula, and government officials' knowledge, be enhanced by learning more about multicultural identities and acculturation processes and sharing complex stories of personal development with each other?

Dialogues between personal cultural positions and dialogues between individuals of different cultures in safe spaces facilitate movement from ethnocentric towards ethno-relative stages of the intercultural learning process (König & Clarke, 2016). With increased experience of another culture, and the rebuilding of social networks through working and playing together in diverse organizations and leisure activities, familiarity and appreciation grow.

The experience of living in different cultures ideally results in the development of multiple cultural identities (König, 2012), a sense of belonging to multiple cultural groups, an enhancement of the complexity of personal identity and the ability to cope with shifting cultural contexts, global consciousness in the making. Intercultural learning is enhanced when individuals feel safe, appreciated, and understood. When some positions in the self silence or suppress other positions, when an individual is fearful, and feels insecure or angry, monological relationships prevail. When, in contrast, positions are recognized and accepted in their differences and alterity (both within and between the internal and external domains of the self), dialogical relationships emerge with the possibility to further develop and renew the self and the other as central parts of the society at large (König, 2009; Hermans & Hermans-Konopka, 2010).

Knowing in the in-between

In the complex global dynamics currently evolving, we are all living our lives in the liminal space between cultural contexts, and we become cultural migrants as we are confronted with a world that is increasingly diverse.

Many citizens may not have crossed borders but are confronted with a tremendous variety of individuals that have. Currently in Amsterdam, no fewer than 400 nationalities share the city's space. In that sense there is the potential of constant border crossings in our daily lives. We are engaged in a process of 'becoming' in a new environment that we do not yet know. How can we provide moral and spiritual guidance in liquid times, not only to foster democratic attitudes that reach beyond the limits of our current political systems, but also to nourish a global perspective, more friendliness, and less anxiety and fear towards a different other?

A liminal space, the place of transition, waiting, and not knowing, is

> a unique spiritual position where human beings hate to be but where the biblical God is always leading them. It is when you have left the tried and true, but have not yet been able to replace it with anything else. It is when you are finally out of the way. It is when you are between your old comfort zone and any possible new answer. If you are not trained in how to hold anxiety, how to live with ambiguity, how to entrust and wait, you will run . . . anything to flee this terrible cloud of unknowing.
> (Rohr, 2002)

Rohr describes a liminal space as a unique spiritual position where we are finally out of the way, and the question is, how can we get out of the way, and how can we train to hold anxiety? Is he referring to the chatter of the discursive mind and learning to be more contemplative? Contemplative practices like meditation, yoga, and mindfulness are becoming more commonplace in contemporary society and organizations. Contemplative practice enhances consciousness by making us aware of how we think, feel, and construe the world. It enhances the capacity of the contemplative mind to tap into the universal stream of connection and love without the divisive 'chatter' of the discursive mind. The contemplative state helps one to develop an eye for one's place in the larger picture, the ability to take a bird's-eye view of life.

In this way a meta-position is developed from the perspective of which choices can be made calmly while observing the stream of thoughts and emotions produced by the discursive mind. Mindfulness is well researched and is an excellent technique to hold anxiety, increase compassion, and reduce levels of stress. It is increasingly being put to use by thousands of leadership coaches and practitioners to help their clients reduce stress levels by becoming mindful of their thoughts and inner voices, recognizing that they are just thoughts that will come and pass away again. Reybrouck and D'Ansembourg (2017) argue that just as we have in the past 40 years taught children in schools the importance of personal hygiene such as washing hands and brushing teeth, we should increasingly be focusing on teaching children the tools for psychological hygiene, as tools for tolerance and peace. A schoolteacher recently told me that children responded enthusiastically to her meditation lessons.

As the world becomes more complex, confusing, and interconnected, and the self more saturated (Gergen, 1991), meditative techniques may help to facilitate the exploration of other knowledge centers than the rational, empirical, 'mental' mind providing an entrance to comprehending the world as fundamentally interconnected. In this way, too, perhaps we may start to adjust our patterns of overconsumption to more respectful and preserving modes of functioning.

Harman (1988) identifies three ways of knowing: the rational, emotional, and intuitive. He recognizes that in most Western societies there has been a bias towards exclusively rational ways of knowing. Research has shown that the rational mind can handle only up to seven items at once (Draaisma, 2001). As the complexity in the world increases, the rational mind becomes less efficient. We need to increase, facilitate, and explore the use of our other knowledge capacities in our organizations and as human beings. "Creativity and intuition are terms we use to refer to those occasions when unconscious knowing is made accessible to the conscious mind" (Harman, 1988, p. 76).

Alan Seale talks about quantum space:

> If we accept that our mind is actually a field of energy that encompasses the body and the space surrounding it and that accesses the quantum field, then our conscious awareness can also expand to become one with the quantum field. What we have thought of as psychic powers or mystical experiences are actually the result of our expanded awareness into the quantum field, which has been there for us all along. It is just that we, in the rational-thought paradigm, have forgotten to expand our awareness. Opening to intuitive guidance and understanding is the most real we can get, because then we are tapping into the quantum field.
>
> (Seale, 2011, pp. 144–145)

A fast-paced world of change is an extended liminal space, where we find ourselves in the constant in-between. It is a space out of which creativity and new alternatives may arise if leaders are willing to suspend old notions and explore in safe spaces that which is seeking to emerge (Senge, Scharmer, Jaworski, & Flowers, 2004). Qualities of a liminal space are change, disruption, ambiguity, and not knowing.

Conclusion: leadership in a VUCA world

The Center for Creative Leadership appointed futurologist Bob Johansen as visiting fellow in 2016. Johansen also serves as distinguished fellow at the Institute for the Future, a 48-year-old Palo Alto company that offers leadership workshops for global executives. In his book *Leaders Make the Future: 10 New Leadership Skills for an Uncertain World* (2009), he describes a number of leadership skills that are helpful to survive in an increasingly volatile, uncertain, complex, and ambiguous world, a VUCA world. It requires leadership that is enhanced by self-reflectivity (working with inner skills, developing a vision, staying calm), and community building competencies (smart mob organizing, bringing people together, and sharing knowledge), as well as the ability to be bio-empathetic to perceive events in their context of past, present, and future and self and context as interconnected. It requires the ability to be dialogical within the self and with the context, to negotiate between conflicting inner and outer voices.

> Volatility requires vision, when many variables change quickly. If they are complex and vague, we need to become more visionary and flexible.
> Uncertainty requires understanding of the context of what is happening.
> Complexity requires keeping things simple and taking one step at a time.
> Ambiguity requires the ability to hold anxiety and the agility to react flexibly.

Today, in our interconnected world, even individuals who have never moved are confronted with the increased pace of change and disruption of diversifying societies. Intercultural leaders realize that fear, uncertainty, and denigration could be construed as the ethnocentric stages of a developmental model of learning intercultural sensitivity (Bennet, 1993) that was discussed.

They are able to facilitate the move from ethnocentric to ethnorelative in their employees. The first step towards an ethnorelative mindset and intercultural sensitivity is becoming aware of one's own cultural baggage. The second step is realizing that one's own viewpoint is not central to everyone's reality (König & Clarke, 2016). The pitfalls from an ethnocentric to an ethnorelative mindset are often difficult to recognize in oneself as a manager. This makes intervision sessions so important when working with employees from different cultures in the context of diversity.

Intercultural leaders need to be able to create safe dialogical spaces in society and organizations in which there is room for individuals to express dissonant (with the dominant norm) personal voices, and spaces for silence and meditation in which it is possible to move beyond rational knowledge to access emotional and spiritual meaning-making capacities of human thinking and awareness. Safe and silent dialogical spaces are vital to exploring the complexities of intra- and interpersonal reconstructive and revitalizing dialogues in a society that is mindful of an assertive pluralism (König, 2012, p. 23).

> The project of assertive pluralism demands a clarity of purpose that can compete with hate propagandists' simple myth of us-versus-them. . . . An assertive pluralism can be built on the well founded position that a multicultural, equality protecting order is superior to ways of organising nation states that privilege one religious or cultural identity above all others.
> (George, 2016, p. 217)

For us as a species to survive, we need to help each other to become aware of our cultural conditioning in an intersubjective social relational and socio-culturally bounded space, we need to make this a safe dialogical space. It is important to build communities around us that are based on trust and a willingness to empower those less fortunate than ourselves (Friedman, 2016). Increasingly, multinational companies are looking for multicultural employees to navigate the complexities of different cultural environments. Each individual develops their own 'moving experiences,' be it welcomed into new cultural environments or discriminated against. Emotions, which I see as inner 'moving experiences' always accompany valued experience. Reflecting on these emotions helps individuals to unravel subliminal unconscious meanings, stored in their visceral archives, and address these issues in public spaces to foster the development of an open democratic society.

I was inspired by a video on YouTube called liquid lead dancing (Copp & Fox, 2015), where the two dance partners alternate in the roles of leading and following. I invite you to view the video and keep it in mind after reading this chapter. In diverse teams, depending on the issue at hand, members with specific skill sets may take the lead over others. Leaders need to learn sensitivity about how their own communicative style relates to those of the different members of their teams, and at times learn to be led by others.

I argue that it is becoming increasingly important to learn 'liquid leading' and develop programs on intercultural learning with all citizens, policy makers, and educators to facilitate the transition to more ethnorelative vantage points in our multicultural environments. In this way vitality, resilience, and leadership qualities may be enhanced for all individuals finding their way in a liquid world.

References

Akhtar, S. (1995). A third individuation: Immigration, identity and the psychoanalytic process. *Journal of the American Psychoanalytic Association, 43*: 1051–1084.

Atran, S., & Axelrod, A. (2008). Reframing Sacred Values. *Negotiation Journal, 24*: 221–246.

Bakker, E., & Grol, P. (2017). *Nederlandse Jihadisten: Van naïeve idealisten tot geharde terroristen.* Hollandsdiep: Overamstel Uitgevers.

Bakhtin, M. M. (1973). *Problems of Dostoevski's Poetics* (2nd ed.; R. W. Rotsel, Trans.). Ann Arbor, MI: Ardis. (Original work published in 1929).

Bauman, Z. (2000). *Liquid modernity*. Cambridge: Polity Press.

Beck, U., & Beck-Germersheim, E. (2002). *Individualisation*. London: Sage Publications.

Bennet, M. J. (1993). Towards ethnorelativism: A developmental model of intercultural sensitivity. In R. M. Page (Ed.), *Education for the intercultural experience* (pp. 21–73). Yarmouth, ME: Intercultural Press.

Besemeres, M., & Wierzbicka, A. (2007). *Translating lives: Living with two cultures and languages*. Brisbane, Australia: University of Queensland Press.

Berry, J. W. (Ed.). (2017). *Mutual intercultural relations*. Cambridge: Cambridge University Press.

Bhatia, S. & Ram, A. (2001). Rethinking "acculturation" in realtion to diasporic cultures and postcolonial identities. *Human Development, 44*, 1–18.

Copp, T. and Fox, J. (2015). Liquid Lead Dancing – It takes two to Lead. Montreal: TEDx Talks published December 17, 2015.

Dunbar, E. (2017). *Hate unleashed: America's cataclysmic change*. Westport, CT: Praeger.

Draaisma, D. (2001). *Waarom het leven sneller gaat als je ouder wordt: Over het autobiografische geheugen*. Groningen: Historische Uitgeverij

Dehghani, M. Iliev, R., Sachdeva, S., & Atran, S. (2009). Emerging sacred values: Iran's nuclear program. *Judgement and Decision Making, 4*(7), 930–933.

Friedman, T. (2016). *Thank you for being late: An optimists guide to thriving in the age of accelerations*. New York, NY: Farrar, Straus and Giroux.

George, C. (2016). *Hate spin: The manufacture of religious offense and its threat to democracy*. Cambridge, MA: MIT Press.

Gergen, K. J. (1991). *The saturated self*. New York, NY: Basic Books.

Gergen, K. J. (2009). *Relational being: Beyond self and community*. Oxford: Oxford University Press.

Gudykunst, W. & Hammer, M. R. (1983). Basic training design: Approaches to intercultural training. In Dan Landis and Richard W. Brislin (Eds.), *Handbook of intercultural training 1*. Elmsford, NY: Pergamon.

Harman, W. (1988). *Global mind change: The promise of the 21st century*. San Francisco, CA: Institute of Noetic Sciences.

Hermans, H. J. M., & Hermans-Janssen, E. (1995). *Self narratives: The construction of meaning in psychotherapy*. New York: The Guilford Press.

Hermans, H. J. M., Hermans-Jansen, E., & Van Gilst, W. (1985). *De grondmotieven van het menselijke bestaan: Hun expressie in het persoonlijke waarderingsleven*. (The basic motives of human existence: Their expression in personal valuation). Lisse: Swets & Zeitlinger.

Hermans, H. J. M. (2001). The dialogical self: Towards a theory of personal and cultural positioning. *Culture and Psychology, 7*(3), 243–283.

Hermans, H., Hermans-Konopka, A., Oosterwegel, A., & Zomer, P. (2017). Fields of tension in a boundary crossing world: Towards a democratic organisation of the self. *Integrative and Behavioural Science, 51*(4), 505–535.

Hermans, H. J. M., & Hermans-Konopka, A. (2010). *Dialogical self theory: Positioning and counter-positioning in a globalizing society*. New York, NY: Cambridge University Press.

Hofman, E. (1989). *Lost in translation: A life in a new language*. London: Vintage.

Johansen, B. (2009). *Leaders make the future: Ten new leadership skills for an uncertain world*. San Francisco, CA: Berrett Koehler Publishers Inc.

Jones, S., & Bradwell, P. (2007). *As you like it: Catching up in an age of global English*. London: Demos.

König, J. R. (2009). Moving experience: Dialogues between personal cultural positions. *Culture and Psychology, 15*, 97–119.

König, J. R. (2012). *Moving experience: Complexities of acculturation*. Amsterdam: VU University Press.

König, J. R., & Clarke, K. (2016). Dialogical culture coaching. In H. Hermans (Ed.), *Assessing and stimulating a dialogical self in groups, teams, cultures and organisations*. New York, NY: Springer.

Kruglanski, A., Pierro, A., Manetti, L., & De Grada, E., (2006). Groups as epistemic providers: Need for closure and the unfolding of group centrism. *Psychological Review, 113*, 84–100.

Lamont, M. (2017). *Prisms of inequality: Moral boundaries, exclusion and academic evaluation*. Praemium Erasmianum Essay. Amsterdam: Preamium Erasmianum Foundation.

La Fromboise, T., Coleman, H. L. K. & Gerton, J. (1993). Psychological impact of biculturalism: *Evidence and theory. Psychological Bulletin, 114*(3), 395–412.

Liu, J. H., & MacDonald, M. (2016). Towards a psychology of global consciousness through an ethical conception of self in society. *Journal for the Theory of Social Behaviour, 45*(1), 82–94.

Mustakova-Possardt, E. (2006). Clash or meeting between East and West: An analysis of the post-9/11 challenges. *Peace and Conflict Journal: Journal of Peace Psychology 12*(2), 189–203.

Paige, R. M. & Martin, J. N. (1983). Ethical issues and ethics in cross-cultural training. In Dan Landis and Richard W. Brislin (Eds.), *Handbook of intercultural training 1*. Elmsford, NY: Pergamon.

Pollock, D. C., & Van Reken, R. (2001). *Third culture kids: The experience of growing up among worlds*. London and Boston, MA: Nicholas Brealy Publishing.

Rohr, R. (2002, January–February). Grieving as a sacred space. *Sojourners Magazine*.

Seale, A. (2011). *Create a world that works: Tools for personal and global transformation*. San Francisco, CA: Red Wheel, Weiser.

Senge, P., Scharmer C. O., Jaworski, J., & Flowers, B. (2004). *Presence: An exploration of profound change in people, organisations and society*. London: Nicolas Brealey Publishing

Sheikh, H., Ginges, J., Coman, A., & Atran, S. (2012). Religion, group threat and sacred values. *Judgement and Decision Making, 7*(2), 110–118.

Tanner, C., & Hanselmann, M. (2008). Taboo and conflict in decision making: Sacred values, decision difficulty and emotions. *Judgement and Decision Making, 3*(1), 51–63.

Van Reybrouck, D., & D'Ansembourg, T. (2017). *Vrede kun je leren. Le paix, on s'apprends*. Paris: Actes Sud.

Vance, J. D. (2016). *Hillbilly elegy: A memoir of a family and culture in crisis*. New York, NY: Harper Collins.

Education in an age
of plural moralities

8 Plural British Values

Between generosity and fear

Julia Ipgrave

Introduction

The spring and early summer of 2017 proved an unsettling time for British society. The news media reported several tragic incidents that shattered the lives of many individuals and families and that grabbed the attention and stirred the emotions of the nation. In London there was a terror attack outside Parliament and on Westminster Bridge (March 22), another in Borough Market (June 3), and yet another outside Finsbury Mosque (June 19), all of which saw the death and wounding of innocent members of the public. In Manchester (May 22) a brutal attack on those (including young teenagers) attending a pop concert in Manchester Arena killed 23 and injured 250 more, and on June 14, a horrendous fire swept through the Grenfell Tower apartment block in Kensington, London, causing an estimated 72 deaths and numerous injuries and rendering homeless hundreds more.

Nine days after the fire, on June 23, in a speech at the 2017 Festival of Education, Amanda Spielman, the Chief Inspector of the schools inspectorate (Ofsted), announced the importance of what have come to be termed 'Fundamental British Values,' and her determination to ensure that more was done to promote them within schools. The transcript of her speech on the official GOV.UK website placed this statement under the heading, 'Defending our values':

> one area where there is room to improve is the active promotion of fundamental British values in our schools. Recent attacks in Westminster, London Bridge, Manchester and Finsbury Park have brought into stark relief the threats that we face.
>
> (Spielman, 2017)

Spielman proceeded to talk about the importance of helping the young develop resilience to resist those who seek "to put hatred in their hearts and poison in their minds,"[1] and of her "zeal and passion" for "tackling extremism through inspection." At times of crisis, public statements such as these have much to say about the relationship between values and British society.

The statement was in many ways unremarkable, the rehearsal of a common response to terrorist threat. But, in the context of 'values' and of June 2017, what should be remarkable is that no mention was made of the Grenfell fire that had happened just a few days before, the images of its devastation still filling the screens of TV and online media. The threat of terrorism and extremism continue to shape the discourse even though the Grenfell fire could itself be viewed as an object lesson on the current state of 'British Values.' On the one hand, there were the heartening indicators of generous fellow-feeling as churches, mosques, and community centers, supported by numerous volunteers of all ages, races, and social classes, organized immediate accommodation, care, and counseling for the homeless and bereaved, and donations of food and clothing poured in from the general public. On the other hand, the fate of this tower block, part of a pocket of social-deprivation (home to many recent migrants and refugees) in one of the richest boroughs in the country, had much to say about British society's failure at the most basic level of looking after the poor and putting people's welfare before monetary calculations. At the time of writing, a public inquiry into the disaster was still underway, but it appears that inattention to fire safety and the use of (cheaper) substandard building materials allowed the flames to spread at speed through the whole building with the loss and disruption of so many lives. At the same time, reports of residents' earlier concerns about fire safety going unheeded and experiences of the inadequacy of the local and national authorities' immediate response to the crisis have heightened the sense of social injustice surrounding the incident. As one popular newspaper proclaimed, "Grenfell Tower is a symbol of a dangerous inequality and indifference to the powerless in our nation" (Voice of the Mirror, 2017). Grenfell poses a challenge to the identity claimed for Britain in Spielman's speech as "a beacon of liberation, tolerance and fairness to the world" (Spielman, 2017). The newspaper concludes, "the fire was a terrible wake-up call and a reminder that we can do much better to be a decent, true One Nation." British identity is at stake.

Locating the question of 'British Values' in relation to the terrorist incidents and the Grenfell fire, this chapter sets up a dichotomy between values that defend self and values that reach out to others – the fear and generosity of the title – that will act as a critical axis throughout the chapter. Interest in the pluralization of values relates the chapter to other contributions in this volume and theories of the dialogical self (such as those expounded by Hubert J.M. Hermans) where this theme is prominent (Hermans & Hermans-Konopka, 2010). Differences of moralities over time (diachronic) and simultaneously held by different cultural communities (synchronic) are discussed. The subject is not just values, however. Picking up the 'Britishness' of 'British Values' entails explorations of British identity – Britain is the self being dialogized – which are in turn supported by reference to Kenneth J. Gergen's distinction between 'bounded being' and 'relational being' (Gergen, 2009). By introducing my topic in the context of a particular period in time, I have set up this chapter to pursue a comparative analysis that places the current discourse of 'Fundamental British Values' alongside other moments in the recent history of British society (the end of World War II and the rise of multicultural Britain) that have occasioned renewed interest in, and generated different interpretations of, the value basis and moral foundations of our living together. The points of comparison are all on the far side of that historical watershed, the 2001 attacks on the World Trade Center and their aftermath, that forms the context of the British Values drive. They give some indication of the direction of British society and the development of British identity before that date. The prominent place given to education in this chapter reflects the responsibility frequently placed upon schools for improving the moral health of the nation.

'Fundamental British Values'

The 'British Values' to which Spielman was referring are those Fundamental British Values that, since 2014, schools are required to 'actively promote' within their classrooms (Department for Education, 2014a). The formulation of Fundamental British Values has its origins in the government's 2011 anti-terrorist Prevent Strategy (HM Government, 2011). Here the intention was that they should be used as a yardstick for identifying those individuals and organizations who (in their denial of these values) might pose a serious risk to society. The occasion of the British Values requirement for schools was the so-called 'Trojan Horse' affair when a letter warned of an Islamist plot to take over a number of schools in Birmingham. Although the letter proved to be a forgery and the plot not a plot at all, the affair prompted fears about possible extremist influences in schools, a greater emphasis on British Values was backed up by short-notice Ofsted inspections making judgments against the criteria of these values. The fundamental values to be promoted are "democracy, the rule of law, individual liberty, and mutual respect and tolerance for those with different faiths and beliefs." In addition, schools are to encourage respect for others "with particular regard to the protected characteristics set out in the Equality Act 2010 and accompanying guidance" (Department for Education, 2017). These protected characteristics are: age, disability, gender reassignment, marriage and civil partnership, pregnancy and maternity, race, religion and belief, sex, and sexual orientation.

While this interest in British Values might suggest the quest for a common foundation for shared living, the criticism with which they were received (by journalists, by educationalists, by faith communities) implies that that coherence in outlook is not so easily found. Many were unconvinced by the underlying narrative and criticisms came from several angles (Bolleton & Richardson, 2015). The argument that the values (e.g. 'democracy' or 'the rule of law') are not particularly British given their wide application around the world, makes a fair point but does not invalidate efforts for their promotion. Criticism of the process had more weight, with objections to the top-down imposition of these values and the monitoring and punitive power given to Ofsted and to the Education Secretary in their interpretation and application that seem to undermine the democracy they purport to defend (Genders, 2014). Another objection to the list of values was that they do not in fact constitute values in themselves but are rather practical demonstrations of underlying foundational values (such as justice or equality) in society; that they are not in themselves unassailable but need to be continuously assessed against these fundamental criteria. In relation to the value 'the rule of law,' for example, a Church of England briefing document asked what had happened in these British Values to 'the importance of dissent, (as demonstrated by the campaign for the abolition of slavery, the suffragettes, chartists etc.)' (Genders, 2014).

The values being promoted were also judged to be selective; concerns for equality, for example, are directed towards the protected characteristics in the Equality Act and do not include socio-economic categories or migration status, lines of division and prejudice that (as the Grenfell fire and the tensions around the Brexit referendum bear witness) are currently especially problematic in British society. Inspection of the requirement that pupils respect protected characteristics has given emphasis to knowledge about and attitudes towards homosexuality – in 2014 the Secretary for Education described negative views about homosexuality as extremist (Watt & Wintour, 2015). Another Conservative MP suggested that opposition to gay marriage might also be so viewed (Charmley, 2015). It amounts to rejection of the idea of a plurality of value systems in British society leading to different positions on this question. A cynical commentator might observe that this focus plays to the strength of the Establishment (recent governments are, with some justification, proud of legislative advances made in this area), while it puts some religious communities on the back foot. Questions of socio-economic justice, on the other hand, where the positions of the Establishment and faith communities might be reversed, are noticeable by their absence. Other areas inspected under British Values that might similarly disadvantage some faith communities and their schools are sex equality – especially when interpreted by such questions as 'Do they share the same playground?' and 'Do they sit in mixed groups?' – and respect for those with different beliefs – 'Do they include teaching about a diversity of religions?' 'Is it enough?' (Ipgrave, 2015). This brings us to another criticism of British Values, that they are primarily a device to call out potential terrorists, working from an (unsubstantiated) link made in government policy and public discourse between extremism and terrorism, and the association of 'extremism' with religious conservatism.

The Prevent Strategy of 2011 is very clear that extremism is "the vocal or active opposition to fundamental British Values including democracy, the rule of law, individual liberty and mutual respect and tolerance of different faiths and beliefs" (HM Government, 2011). Educational institutions found to be failing with regard to promotion of British Values can be classified as unsatisfactory or put into 'special measures' and subjected to an intense period of official intervention and close monitoring. Individual pupils identified as at risk of being drawn into terrorism are reported to the police and sent on a re-education program (HM Government, 2015). Current research being carried out among Muslim pupils in London schools is revealing their feelings of being under scrutiny, and their perception that they are coming to be viewed as 'dangerous and frightening' by others (Lockley-Scott, ongoing doctoral research at the University of Warwick). An increase in home-schooling in the Muslim community has been directly linked to the Prevent Strategy and the feeling among parents that schools are being encouraged 'to spy on' their children (Khadri, 2016). In this atmosphere, the Britishness of British Values is in danger of becoming a defensive identity, static, inward-looking, and suspicious.

Moral foundations for British identity

Even if the promotion of Fundamental British Values in schools is interpreted as a rather clumsy instrumentalization of values teaching for a security agenda, it need not discredit the broader project to find a moral basis for society. The Church of England response paper sees "a national conversation on values" as "one way to build confidence and coherence in the wake of changes that have been unsettling for many and remain in many ways unresolved" and remarks on the rapid changes in recent years on "the ways we, as communities and a nation, develop the language and practices of equality, diversity, community, and the individual" (Genders, 2014). With its reference to unsettling effects of change, the need for confidence and coherence, and the possibilities for building and developing, this analysis of current actualities and future possibilities is interesting to compare with analyses of other periods of history, still within living memory, when the identity and moral foundation of British society was the subject of discussion and debate.

1944

I first take the story back to the time of the 1944 Education Act. This act, passed while the country was still at war, constituted a radical overhaul of the British education system, part of the (re)construction of a post-war Britain. For present purposes, its significance is its participation in a drive to re-establish a moral basis for society at a time when the rise of totalitarian regimes had revealed the fragility of democracy and the horrors of war had shaken confidence in the basic morality of human nature. The concepts of a moral basis and basic morality (rather than a moral perspective or vision, for example) contain within it the idea of morality as solid foundation for social and civic living. For the educators and legislators involved in the 1944 legislation, a reaffirmation of Christian morality as a foundation of British society was required, and the act enshrined in law for all schools the requirement to provide regular religious education and a daily act of worship for all pupils. Although the act did not specify, religious education at that time was assumed to be Christian and biblical, and school worship tended to conform to a traditional hymns-prayers-and-homily format. Interpretations of the act in local religious education syllabuses generally supported a Christian morality understanding of the subject's purposes. The 1948 Middlesex RE syllabus stated that "the primary function of Christian religious teaching is to show the way in which Christianity offers the right relationship between God and man" and "the chief task of the school is to train for Christian citizenship." The stated aim of the RE syllabus of Carlisle, Cumberland, and Westmorland (1951) was "to train [the pupils] to live a particular kind of life, which, to the Christian, means nothing less than helping them to become servants of God" (cited in Gillard, 1991).

The year 1944 also brought a series of lectures, published three years later under a title that conveys the anxieties of the times – *Our Culture: Its Christian Roots and Present Crisis* (Demant, 1947). In this volume, the contribution of the editor, V.A. Demant (Canon and Chancellor of St Paul's Cathedral), suggested that a return to a stable Christian moral foundation would not be a straightforward move. He described European culture as an historic growth dependent on certain definite influences. If those influences cease to operate, Demant argued, that pattern of life would continue for a while but eventually, like a plant cut off from its roots, it would wither and die. Changing the metaphor, he likened it to "an artificial superstructure upon crumbling foundations" (Demant, 1947, p. 3). By way of explanation, Demant employed a useful distinction between the aims and assumptions of a society. The aims are there in the superstructure, in society's plans, aspirations, and ideals; while the assumptions are the things taken for granted, and presupposed about the nature of reality, the emotional patterns and habits of life considered normal. As a Christian, he understood the aims of people in the 'democratic communities' to be still largely formed by Christian outlooks but made vulnerable by the loss of the underlying assumption on which they rested – that a human being's significance derives not from identity as "a functioning part of the social order" (Demant, 1947, p. 9), but from her/his unique relation to the Eternal and simultaneous involvement in the process of the earth's life (Demant, 1947, p. 13).

Although not all would follow Demant's logic to its conclusion, what his argument offers of more general application, and what it contributes to the theme of this chapter, is a sense of different layers of morality, a superstructure that may be more visible in its operation, and a deep foundation, an assumption about the essential nature of the human being, on which it ultimately depends. Applied to the so-called Fundamental British Values referenced earlier, we could perceive that 'democracy,' 'rule of law,' 'mutual respect,' 'tolerance,' and so on, are aims but are not the underlying assumptions or foundational values. The sense of a mismatch between aims and assumptions is there in the criticisms of Fundamental British Values. The values themselves seem on the surface to be fairly uncontroversial, but changes in underlying political and public instincts (about religion in society, for example) and suspicions of the government's intentions in the imposition of these values give them a different significance for many. Using Demant's language, they represent for their critics "an artificial superstructure" covering growing inequalities and divisions (Telegraph Reporters, 2016). Looking forward to a discussion later in this chapter, it is also possible to find some parallels (though not an exact correlation) between Demant's bi-partite model and Gergen's distinction between "first-order morality" and "second-order morality" (Gergen, 2009, p. 354).

1985

By the 1980s, the presupposition of a homogenous Christian society implied in the Education Act no longer held. The increasing pluralization of British society, through migration from the Indian subcontinent and the Caribbean in particular, required rethinking not just education but the nature of British society in general. The 1985 Swann Report, *Education for All* signaled the scope of this task by beginning its review and recommendations for the education system with a chapter entitled "The Nature of Society" (Swann, 1985). The report was commissioned by the government of the day, which, in drawing up the terms of reference, set the context for the study as a society that is "both multiracial and culturally diverse" (Swann, 1985, p. 3). In its treatment of this theme, the report is both descriptive and aspirational:

> It is essential . . . to acknowledge the reality of the multi-racial context in which we all now live, to recognise the positive benefits and opportunities which this offers all of us and to seek to build together a society which both values the diversity within it, whilst united by the cohesive force of the common aims, attributes and values which we all share.
>
> (p. 7)

This diverse yet cohesive ideal is what the Swann Report calls a "democratic pluralist society" (Swann, 1985, p. 5). In some respects this ideal could be seen as a new British identity, though it is evident in the report that Swann was reluctant to try to pin down a sense of 'Britishness.' "Being British," the report declared, is dynamic, ever changing, adapting, and absorbing new ideas and influences (Swann, 1985, p. 7), but the popular conceptualization of Britishness often lagged behind the reality and could hinder the construction of the new society to which Swann aspired. The starting point was very different from that of the present-day Fundamental British Values and its narrative of Britishness far removed from the narrative of "beacon of liberation, tolerance and fairness" that underlies them (Spielman, 2017).

Rather than Britishness serving as a validating stamp on a set of values, Swann acknowledged its historically rooted problems that needed to be overcome if British people were to align their attitudes and behaviors with the universal principles of justice and equality identified in the document. It recognized how the legacy of empire had infected British attitudes towards others with prejudice, patronizing "unintentional racism" and "the view of other nations and peoples as in some sense 'inferior'" (Swann, 1985, p. 16). What the report objected to was a bounded British identity, "an ill-defined and nebulous concept of 'true Britishness'" (Swann, 1985, p. 7) that othered and excluded those deemed to be beyond its bounds, viewing them as "outsiders" or "immigrants," or else expected them to "adapt their lifestyles to conform to the traditional British way of life" (Swann, 1985, p. 6). The transformation that Swann advocates is major. The report speaks of the need for "a fundamental reorientation of the attitudes" that underlie teaching and learning, educational practices and procedures (Swann, 1985, p. 324), in society; "a fundamental shift in attitude" that "will involve expenditure in 'psychological terms'" (Swann, 1985, p. 37). It was a question changing the underlying assumptions in society so prejudice and racism might be replaced with "belief in justice and equality" (Swann, 1985, p. 4). The boldness of the attack on comfortable narratives and bounded identity is explained and justified by the origins of the Swann Report in an investigation of the underachievement of children of ethnic minorities in Britain and its findings that linked this underachievement to discrimination and (sometimes subconscious) prejudice in society and educational institutions. The report set out "to combat racism, to attack inherited myths and stereotypes, and the way in which they are embodied in institutional practices" (Swann, 1985, p. 767). The solution offered was the championing of a multicultural education that expanded the existing curriculum to incorporate reference to and systematic teaching about the plurality of cultures and religions present in British society. The ambition was to bring about "a fundamental reorientation of the attitudes which condition the selection of curriculum materials and subject matter and which underlie teaching and learning process and practice" (Swann, 1985, p. 343). Multi-faith religious education was in many ways the flagship of this project. The approach had a dual purpose: that the self-esteem of children of minorities should be enhanced by seeing their cultures valued in school; that by learning about these cultures, children of the majority community should gain a greater understanding and respect for their neighbors and "appreciation of the diversity of lifestyles, cultural, religious and linguistic backgrounds which make up our society and the wider world" (Swann, 1985, p. 315). With the plurality of lifestyles, a plurality of value systems was recognized within a broad framework of "commonly accepted values" (Swann, 1985, p. 5). Significantly, the project did not stop there, as the report says:

> *Education for All* should involve more than learning about the cultures and lifestyles of various ethnic groups, it should also seek to develop in

all pupils, both ethnic majority and minority, a flexibility of mind and an ability to analyse critically and rationally the nature of British society today within a global context.

(p. 324)

The phrase "flexibility of the mind" resonates with the emphasis in dialogical self theory on flexibility of the person to move between *I*-positions (Hermans, 2014). If British society is viewed as a corporate self, then the 'various ethnic groups' afford a number of positions from which self-examination can take place. This concept of a society answerable to its (diverse) members contrasts with the approach signaled in the June 2014 Department of Education Press Release about the new obligation to teach 'Fundamental British Values' in schools; "Actively promoting also means challenging pupils, staff or parents expressing opinions contrary to fundamental British values" (Department for Education, 2014b). It is the difference between an open and a closed system.

Although its recommendations were building on existing developments in some progressive institutions, the Swann Report has the strongest claim to be the founding document of the multicultural education that became a characteristic feature of British education in the later part of the 20th century and had an influence which persists today. In a trend similar to that documented in van Meijl (Chapter 11 in this volume), it has become fashionable in Britain in recent years to find fault with multiculturalism. Some of the criticism is well founded. We could talk of the reification of culture, cite the simplistic approach to a complex tangle of interlocking identities, argue that it drew attention away from some deeper-rooted causes of racism in society, identify discrepancies between ideal and practice, or lament the neglect in multicultural discourse and strategy of the identities of indigenous white working classes at a time of destabilizing decline in Britain's traditional manufacturing and extraction industries (Kitson & Michie, 2014), and the lack of attention given to their educational underachievement (House of Commons Education Committee, 2014). One could say that the spirit of the Swann Report makes it open to critique, its principles are responsiveness and adaptation to evidence (the research that shaped it) and to change. The multiculturalism that it advocated, and the democratic pluralism, were not values at the level of Demant's assumptions; rather, they were aims which had no validity in themselves unless firmly rooted in the two values that Swann cites as "fundamental," justice and equality (Swann, 1985, p. 4). If, when assessed against the criteria of justice and equality, they are found wanting, then the critical spirit of Swann allows for a rethink in the conceptualization and application of multiculturalism and democratic pluralism.

Most important of all, whatever the practical and conceptual limitations of Swann, there is an underlying generosity of spirit lacking in more recent constructions of 'Britishness' and manifested in a desire to include (the report speaks of British society extending its self-understanding "to embrace ethnic minority communities"; Swann, 1985, p. 7), responsiveness to people's needs, respect for others in their difference, preparedness to open up self (established structures of acting and thinking) to criticism, and optimistic commitment to change. The contrast between the openness being promoted and the fear the new approach intended to dispel is explicit in this stated aim:

> The aim of education should be to ensure that from their earliest years children learn to accept the normality and justice of a variety of points of view without feeling *threatened*, and are indeed encouraged to find this variety of outlook stimulating in itself.
>
> (Swann, 1985, p. 324)

2000

Fifteen years on from Swann, inequalities in ethnic achievement were still a factor in British schools (Amin et al., 1997) and, despite progress made in this direction, the concept of Britain as "a confident and vibrant multicultural diversity at ease with its rich diversity" was still an aspiration rather than an established reality (Parekh, 2000). The Parekh Report of 2000 presented findings of the Commission on the Future of Multi-Ethnic Britain set up by the Runnymede Trust, an independent think-tank with particular interest in racial equality. The date of the report is significant, for it makes it a snapshot of a country just before the watershed event of the attack on the World Trade Center and its impact on public attitudes and political policy. At this moment in history, the Parekh Report engaged with the concept of British identity stressing its complexity, its state of flux subject to multitudinal, interacting, sometimes conflicting, forces, and the alternative national narratives that try to give it meaning. It summarized seven main sources of social and cultural change that it claimed had increased the sense of fluidity and uncertainty in British society: globalization; long-term decline in Britain's position as a world power; relationship with Europe; devolution; the end of empire; the rapid advance of social pluralism and post-war migration. If such a list were compiled today, some of these would be given different weightings and more sources of change would be added, but there is evident persistence in influencing factors and continuity in trends. Parekh's description of the fluidity, uncertainty, and pluralization of British society, where citizens belong to a variety of moral traditions and live by a range of values, raises once more the question of how we relate to this moral relativism (what Gergen prefers to call "moral pluralism"; Gergen, 2009, p. 363) and still find a common set of values around which we as a nation can cohere. Parekh responded to this challenge by distinguishing three sets of values. Two of these sets, he suggested, all can be expected to share:

Procedural values are the basic preconditions for democratic dialogue, willingness to give reasons for views, to listen and be influenced by others' arguments, tolerance, mutual respect, aspiration to peaceful resolution of differences, and willingness to abide by collectively binding decisions. *Substantive values* underpin defensible conceptions of the good life, freedom to plan one's own actions, equal moral worth of all human beings, equal opportunities to lead fulfilling lives and contribute to collective wellbeing. These values abide by human rights standards and are part of a global moral dialogue. The report also offered a third category of values particular to individuals or groups, freely chosen or originating in culture or religion, but not of general application to society:

> Subject to constraints of [procedural and substantive] values, different individuals and communities should be free to lead their self-chosen lives – they may disagree profoundly on how to structure their families, order intergenerational and intergender relations, or about truth of religious doctrines.
>
> (Parekh, 2000, pp. 53–54)

The third category is crucial for Parekh's vision of a confident multicultural Britain. It addresses the problem of "virtuous evil" raised by Gergen (2009, p. 358). Gergen (2009) argues that the moral problems of modern societies are not so much the deficit of morality but a multiplication of moralities, too many competing, sometimes conflicting ideas about what constitutes virtuous action, so that "in a universe of plural goods, *any* virtuous action is subject to the antipathy of a multiplicity of competing traditions" (p. 358). We could observe an antipathy of competing traditions between Fundamental British Values and the values and customs of some British Muslims today. By Parekh's model, this antipathy might be overcome and negative responses eliminated if they are assessed through the application of universal substantive and procedural values. The clash of different moralities, of different cultural value systems, in relation to gender can regularly be found in media stories and occasionally in legal cases that find their way to court. The conflictual issue of wearing the niqab, for example, while viewed by some as an unacceptable imposition and limitation on a woman's freedom, may not be considered in the same light in cases where it is evident that the woman in question adopted it willingly of her own free choice. If the separation of girls and boys in the classroom does not impinge upon the students' sense of self-worth or opportunities for fulfillment, or contravene any other of the substantive values, then there may not be a moral reason for disallowing this practice. There is a marked difference between the assessment of cultural values against the standards of substantive values and their assessment through the perspective of security by which, because they are different from majority culture interpretations of what is 'good,' they might be viewed as indicators of extremism and cause for alarm. Rather than close down the debate by assuming one person's value represents 'good' and another's 'bad,' such cases could be the occasion for open cross-cultural discussion, for example, around issues of women's freedoms and concerns about the hypersexualization of Western society and teenage culture.

Parekh's distinction between procedural and substantive values is also of interest. While substantive values rest on an essentialized concept of the human self (who-am-I?) and that human self's flourishing, procedural values seem closer to attitudes and the way we relate to others: willingness to listen, openness to changing views, desire for peaceful resolution, mutual respect. Attitudes were given prominence, too, in the report's engagement with British identity. Parekh argued that Britain had reached a crucial juncture in the construction of 'Britishness.' There were, the report suggested, a series of alternatives for the future of this 'Britain at the crossroads': static/dynamic; intolerant/cosmopolitan; insular/internationalist; authoritarian/democratic; introspective/outward-looking; punitive/inclusive; myopic/farsighted; and, the alternatives employed in the title of this article, fearful/generous (Parekh, 2000, pp. 3–4). The report clearly advocated the latter in each of these pairings, although, post 2001, it would be fair to say, there has been some erring towards the former, a trend which if continued could lead to suppression of the external self-positions that, according to Hermans's dialogical self theory, allow for the further development and renewal of self through dialogical relationships with 'the other' (Hermans & Hermans-Konopka, 2010). By contrast, taking all the latter alternatives in Parekh's list, we find they are attitudes of openness to the other ('inclusive,' 'generous') or to possibilities and change ('dynamic,' 'far-sighted'). This is a porous identity welcoming in and reaching out. On the other hand, the first placed alternatives suggest a closed attitude, inward-looking ('insular,' 'introspective'), controlling ('authoritarian'), resistant to change ('static,' 'myopic') and negative ('punitive,' 'intolerant,' 'fearful') towards those who are outside or who unsettle from within this bounded identity. The models produced by these dichotomous pairings seem to fit neatly with the respective approaches of the Swann Report and Fundamental British Values. Relational responsibility and relational being

Two themes have come to prominence in this brief consideration of different attempts to find a moral foundation for British society. One is the categorization of values into different levels, raising questions about the relationship between foundational and surface values, universal and particular values, aims, and assumptions. Another is the distinction between closed, defensive identities and open, generous identities, put forward as alternatives for British society in the Parekh Report and illustrated by the contrasting approaches to values in the education system of the current Fundamental British Values agenda and the recommendations of the 1985 Swann Report. The divergent characteristics of these two approaches enable the assignment to the British identities they assume (or aspire to) of Gergen's concepts of bounded and relational self, respectively (Gergen, 2009). The provenance of one model (Fundamental British Values) in a Home Office anti-terrorism strategy, and of the other (Swann) in research into the educational underachievement of minority children, may account for significant differences in these identity constructs. Indeed, they could be viewed as representing conflicting 'goods'; keeping our community safe and welcoming into our community. The approach adopted by the Swann Report and presented as a model for British society bears the hallmarks of a dialogical self that fuses external and internal positions, of a relational self, defined by its interconnections with others. It models a society that is inclusive in its embrace, sensitive to the needs of others, that accepts responsibility for others' misfortunes or wellbeing, a society that is not a collection of bounded individuals but an overlapping and interdependent network of relationships. Swann viewed society in terms of systems, in this case systems in need of reform. Uncomfortable evidence of the low academic achievement of minority children occasioned the scrutiny and critique of underlying assumptions in institutions (about the ability and potential of ethnic minority students) and deficiencies in curriculum (where within it, can children recognize themselves and learn to understand others?). The lives of these children would, Swann hoped, be transformed by the reform of institutions and of the system and by changes in the attitudes of society as a whole. Essential to Swann's vision of society was openness to critique and preparedness to change.

The second case is quite different. The bounded British identity inherent in the Fundamental British Values agenda is structured into the project through terminology and through procedure. Firstly, these defining values are imposed, not negotiated or open to challenge. Secondly, by calling the values 'British,' by defining 'extremism' as opposition to those values, by making a link between 'extremism' and terrorism, and, on this basis, policing through punitive measures, the project was binding Britishness within a closed circle and excluding individuals or views that this logic made suspect. Among the negative characteristics of bounded being, Gergen includes distrust and artifice (Gergen, 2009, pp. 14, 27). Thirdly, then, the Fundamental British Values agenda owes its existence to fears of the threat posed to British society by the radicalization of young people, and fourthly, the concept of Britishness contained within the formulation of these values is being instrumentalized to identify those deemed to present a risk. It is not so much the values as the processes that ensure the bounded character of the identity they define. This helps explain why values that on the surface seem 'unexceptionable' (democracy, equality, tolerance, etc.) have prompted so much criticism or unease.

Gergen's theory of first- and second-order morality provides a point at which relational being and process converge. It also relates to the emerging theme of value levels. In *Relational Being*, Gergen (2009) puts down a critical challenge to those who are "striving to establish moral foundations or fundamental ethical principles to guide human conduct" (p. 354). Such an undertaking, he suggests, is particularly problematic in this complex age and so, side-stepping the question of universals, he moves straight to the moral implications of relational being. First-order morality is the process by which any relationship or association establishes moral principles ("moral goods") to regulate that relationship. They become, to use Gergen's phrase, "the way we do things here" (2009, p. 358). Some of the efforts reported in this chapter, such as the principles of Swann's multiculturalism, have been attempts to establish moral goods to regulate relationships between individuals and between communities on a national scale. Parekh's substantive values signal this process at a wider, international level when he writes of human rights standards that are part of a global moral dialogue (2000, p. 54). The pluralization of society results in multiple traditions of the good. As Swann puts it: "the reality of British society now and in the future is that a variety of ethnic groups with their own distinctive, lifestyles and value systems, will be living together" (1985, p. 322). Parekh respects this diversity of positions with the stipulation that, provided they do not contradict substantive or procedural values, groups, and individuals, should be allowed to live their lives in the light of their own values (2000, pp. 53–54). As has already been indicated, the multiplication of goods can set up tensions where the acceptance of one set of goods results in the rejection as 'mistaken,' 'false,' or 'evil' the moral goods of another group in society. "As we generate enclaves of the good, we also tend to create an exterior, the less than good. In more extreme form, in establishing the good, evil is under production" (Gergen, 2009, p. 363).

With these more extreme forms, the conflict of moralities may lead to a severing of communication and the end of co-action (Gergen, 2009, p. 364). The increase in numbers of Muslim parents home-schooling their children is just one example of reduction in co-action (between state and Muslim community; between school and family; between Muslim children and non-Muslim peers) (Khadri, 2016). It is at this point that second-order morality comes in. In Gergen's scheme, second-order morality rests entirely on relationship; it is about the exercise of "relational responsibility," which is a collective responsibility for sustaining potential for coordinated action and co-created meaning (2009, p. 364). The importance given to relational responsibility has an echo in the Church of England's response to Fundamental British Values, which both decries the limited consultation, "closing down the broader public debate across communities and schools themselves" (Genders, 2014, p. 11), around their introduction and suggests as a responsible way forward "an important national conversation about the shared values which should form the basis of our education system" (Genders, 2014, p. 17). This would enable collaborative activity and creative meaning-making between different first-order moralities, the Home Office concern for security and the Church's commitment to "love your neighbour" (Genders, 2014, p. 10) being just two of the "realms of good" (Gergen, 2009, p. 370) thus brought into dialogue with each other. The players taking part in this process would now be in a position to generate new first-order morality. For the successful completion of the exercise, they would do well to apply the procedural values "willingness to give reasons for views, to listen and be influenced by others' arguments, tolerance, mutual respect etc." advertised in the Parekh Report. The Grenfell Tower disaster is one tragic consequence of the want of this willingness.

Is, then, as Gergen (2009) suggests, the ideal of second-order morality to be the "non-foundational foundation" for values in society (p. 365)? His emphasis on "relational responsibility" has clear links with what Swann classes as the "fundamental values" of "belief in justice and equality," for justice and equality are about how humans relate to (or how they stand in relation to) each other. It has links with the divine commands of "love for neighbour" and "being prepared to receive from an outsider" drawn from the parable of the Good Samaritan and viewed, in the Church of England's response paper, as lacking in the official formula of Fundamental British Values (Genders, 2014). Gergen, however, presents second-order morality as an invitation for mutual exploration and rejects any idea that he might be attempting to reinstate universal hierarchy. Instead, he describes the process as a "move towards a foundational ethic for going on together, but without declaring this ethic as absolute, true, or ultimately grounded" (Gergen, 2009, p. 365; see also K. Gergen, Chapter 1 in this volume). But is this a strong enough base on which to build the moral values of a society, to support the superstructure of society's aims and ideals? Although not stated at this point, Gergen's *Relational Being* does in fact supply a foundation for second-order morality in his concept of the human as an essentially relational being. The first chapters of his book provide an argument against the idea of the human as an atomized individual and instead see the essential elements of humanity (experience, memory, creativity, reason, action, emotion, pleasure, pain) as relationally constituted (Gergen, 2009). Relationships are constitutive of the self, and so relational being is not just an ethical but an ontological category, just as is Demant's human being, understood in terms of relationship with the Eternal and Creation. Philosophically, psychologically, theologically, spiritually, and ethically recognized, then, the relational self is a shared moral foundation for living in society that each party can further strengthen by interpreting it along the particular lines of their deepest understanding of the human being. Those who incline towards a defensive bounded identity (of individual, group, institution or nation) are challenged to consider how their view of the moral good might be expanded, and their generosity unlocked, by recognition of the relational side of human nature. And those with an open identity are also faced with a challenge – to be alert to the needs of persons with a bounded identity, while at the same time guiding them into an open and safe space of encounter.

Note

1 Here Spielman was quoting former prime minister David Cameron.

References

Amin, K., Drew, D., Fosam, B., & Gillborn, D. (1997). *Black and ethnic minority young people and educational disadvantage.* London: The Runnymede Trust.

Bolleton, B., & Richardson, R. (2015). *The Great British values disaster: Education, security and vitriolic hate.* Institute of Race Relations. Retrieved from www.irr.org. uk/news/the-great-british-values-disaster-education-security-and-vitriolic-hate/

Charmley, J. (2015, August 13). David Cameron's "British Values Agenda" is Anti-Christian. *The Catholic Herald.* Retrieved from http://catholicherald.co.uk/issues/ august-14th-2015/david-camerons-british-values-agenda-is-anti-christian/

Demant, V. A. (Ed.). (1947). *Our culture: It's Christian roots and present crisis.* Edward Alleyn Lectures 1944. London: SPCK.

Department for Education. (2014a). Consultation on promoting British values in schools. *GOV.UK.* Retrieved from www.gov.uk/government/news/consultation-on-promoting-british-values-in-school

Department for Education. (2014b). *Guidance on promoting British values in schools.* London: HMSO. Retrieved from www.gov.uk/government/news/guidance-on-promoting-british-values-in-schools-published

Department for Education. (2017). *Governance handbook for academies, multi-academy trusts and maintained schools.* London: HMSO. Section 2 para. 6. Retrieved from www.gov.uk/government/uploads/system/uploads/attachment_data/file/582868/Governance_Handbook_-_January_2017.pdf

Genders, N. (2014). *National society (Church of England) consultation submission July 2014: Proposed new independent schools standards.* Church of England Archbishop's Council Education Division. Retrieved from https://staging.churchof england.org/media/2112859/140730independentschoolsbritishvaluesconsultation cofe.pdf

Gergen, K. J. (2009). *Relational being: Beyond self and community.* New York, NY: Oxford University Press.

Gillard, D. (1991). *Agreed syllabuses 1944–1988: Changing aims – changing content?* Retrieved from www.educationengland.org.uk/articles/10agreed.html

Hermans, H. J. M. (2014). Self as a society of I-positions: A dialogical approach to counseling. *The Journal of Humanistic Counseling, 53*: 134–159. doi:10.1002/ j.2161-1939.2014.00054.x

Hermans, H. J. M., & Hermans-Konopka, A. (2010). *Dialogical self theory: Positioning and counter-positioning in a globalizing society.* New York, NY: Cambridge University Press.

HM Government. (2011). *Prevent strategy.* London: HMSO. Retrieved from www. gov.uk/government/publications/prevent-strategy-2011

HM Government. (2015). *Channel duty guidance: Protecting vulnerable people from being drawn into terrorism.* HMSO. Retrieved from www.gov.uk/govern ment/uploads/system/uploads/attachment_data/file/425189/Channel_Duty_Guid ance_April_2015.pdf

House of Commons Education Committee. (2014). *Underachievement in education by white working class children.* London: The Stationery Office Ltd.

Ipgrave, J. (2015). "Trojan Horse," "British values" and education for modern Britain. *REtoday, 32*(3): 57–60.

Khadri, A. (2016, March 18). Why some Muslim parents homeschool. *BBC News.* Retrieved from www.bbc.co.uk/news/av/education-35823876/why-some-muslim-parents-home-school

Kitson, M., & Michie, J. (2014). *The deindustrial revolution: The rise and fall of UK manufacturing, 1870–2010*. Centre for Business Research, University of Cambridge Working Paper No. 459.

Parekh, B. (2000). *The future of multi-ethnic Britain (The Parekh Report)*. London: Profile.

Spielman, A. (2017). Amanda Spielman's speech at the festival of education. *GOV. UK*. Retrieved from www.gov.uk/government/speeches/amanda-spielmans-speech-at-the-festival-of-education

Swann, L. (1985). *Education for all: Report of the committee of enquiry into the education of children from ethnic minority groups*. London: HMSO. Retrieved from www.educationengland.org.uk/documents/swann/swann1985.html

Telegraph Reporters. (2016, December 19). Oath of allegiance to British values "would make migrants play a positive role in Britain." *The Telegraph*. Retrieved from www.telegraph.co.uk/news/2016/12/18/communities-secretary-sajid-javid drawn-british-values-loyalty/

Voice of the Mirror. (2017, June 16). Scandal of Grenfell tower is a symbol of inequality. *Mirror*. Retrieved from www.mirror.co.uk/news/uk-news/voice-mirror-scandal-grenfell-tower-10631703

Watt, N., & Wintour, P. (2015, June 30 Tuesday). Morgan: Existing procedures adequate for teachers in fighting extremism. *The Guardian*. Retrieved from www.theguardian.com/politics/2015/jun/30/nicky-morgan-existing-procedures-adequate-teachers-fight-extremism

9 Life orientation as part of professional development

Moral leadership of professionals from a DST perspective

Edwin van der Zande and Cok Bakker

Introduction

In the Netherlands, teacher training programs show a growing interest in the moral and subjective dimension of professionalization. Despite the dominant presence of monitoring and controlling instruments in the field of education, the growing awareness that subjectivity is a constitutive and integral aspect of professionalization, in our view, calls for a nuanced and multi-layered perspective on teacher leadership. Or, at least, that the 'professional free space' and 'professional autonomy' of the teacher are recognized in leadership strategies. This view is attuned to the complexity of teaching practices, with their multitude of elements that influence decision making. In addition to societal and organizational contextual factors, the professional's beliefs, including her/his personal life orientation, need to be taken seriously in the professional's reflections and processes of professionalization. In this chapter, the focus is on the life orientation of professionals, because of our research interest in the underlying, often unarticulated meaning-making narrative of the professional's beliefs and values.

Firstly, we describe the consequences of taking a so-called 'distributed' perspective on leadership, both in general and for teacher leadership in particular. This perspective was coined by Spillane (2006), with the intent to justify the interdependencies between people's actions in a specific situation. Snoek (2014) specifies a development "from a mandated leadership to a strategically distributed leadership, which should be the first step . . . toward more culturally embedded leadership forms in which self-steering teacher teams take the lead in adapting to the dynamic circumstances that they constantly face in providing the best possible education for their pupils" (p. 179).

Secondly, we argue that teacher leadership includes professional attention for the personal, or subjective dimension of professionalization (Bakker & Montesano Montessori, 2016). This conceptual broadening of leadership means that every teacher could occasionally take on a leading role depending on the situation, which asks for the development of leadership and the taking of ownership in professionality. The development of this type of leadership on a personal level affects the interpersonal dialogue at a meso or team level. In this contribution, we mainly focus on the personal level of teacher leadership, which takes place at the micro level – in a classroom, or in contact with parents – and also at the meso level – i.e., the team level.

Thirdly, we introduce our research on the relationship between normative professionalization and the articulation of a personal life orientation. The concept of life orientation as a part of professional education addresses the students' moral and existential learning processes which are aimed at developing their capacity to articulate their position in a moral space (Taylor, 1989).

The fourth step includes the presentation of a study program in life orientation, at a University of Applied Sciences (in Dutch, *Hoger Beroepsonderwijs*; HBO). Within this program, the students' articulation of their life orientation is an educational strategy to foster their normative professionalization. Fifthly, we introduce our recently developed narrative-dialogical analysis instrument, which we derived from dialogical self theory (DST). This instrument makes it possible to gain insight into the relationship between (1) the developmental processes in the students' life orientation and (2) their normative professionalization. This relationship is investigated for two time periods: the students' attendance of a structured, initial curriculum in worldview education, and the students' post-initial professional experience. Finally, we present illustrative quotes from one of the analyzed documents.

The interesting link between our chapter and the overarching theme of this book is the changing understanding of the relationship between leadership and the plural context in which this leadership is performed. We are dealing here with the shift from a given and pre-defined orientation of the leadership horizon, namely the directive to control pluralism, with the inclusion of plural moralities, to a relationship between leadership and the plural context where leadership itself constructively incorporates plurality. In the paradigm of so-called distributed leadership, it is already assumed that plurality is an unavoidable part of how an organization is led by its leaders. Within this change, attention is unavoidably paid to the role of 'moral plurality' in concrete leadership performances. Correspondingly, as an essential part of professionalization, a student is expected to explore and articulate her/his own life orientation, moral framework, and her/his attitude toward the other, and otherness.

Distributed perspective on leadership

In 2006, Spillane introduced the concept of distributed leadership, which has since become an influential part of school leadership discourse (Diamond & Spillane, 2016). Since the introduction of the concept, several interpretations have been proposed, under names such as "shared" or "democratic leadership," which has led to conceptual misunderstandings (Diamond &

Spillane, 2016, p. 147). The main reason for Spillane and fellow researchers to develop the construct of distributed leadership was to facilitate research into the interaction between individual professionals and their roles; in Spillane's interpretation, the activities of leadership in its context receive more attention than the individual leaders themselves. The focus of the research is on leadership practices.

> A practice orientation focuses on how leadership actually gets done on the ground, what people actually do together (and with what resources), how they do it, and why they do it. A distributed perspective frames leadership practice as a product of the interactions of leaders, followers, and their situation, acknowledging that people can move in and out of leadership roles regardless of position.
>
> (Diamond & Spillane, 2016, p. 148)

Here, the focus is on the interaction between the different actors who exercise influence on each other. Moreover, the situation itself represents an influence, which could encompass, for example, legislation, protocols, and other formal rules in the educational context.

The distributed leadership perspective focuses on the interrelatedness of a collective professional performance, paving the way for a dialogical approach. This interrelatedness of individuals with the surrounding societal context is the essence of dialogical self theory (DST) (Hermans & Hermans-Konopka, 2012). DST describes a permeable boundary between the self and society, which reflects a mutually influencing relationship. Diamond and Spillane oppose an isolated focus on, for example, the characteristics of official leaders, at the expense of research attention for social interaction (cf. Diamond & Spillane, 2016, p. 148). However, there could be an intermediate step that justifies micro-level research, namely focusing on the dialogical self rather than on the meso level (that represents the interaction). The DST approach is employed to describe a dialogical interaction within the self, i.e., among different selves and between the self and society. In DST, there is no contradiction between the self and society. "The composite concept 'dialogical self' goes beyond this dichotomy by bringing the external to the internal and, in reverse, by infusing the internal into the external" (Hermans & Hermans-Konopka, 2012, p. 1). On a micro level, this dialogical approach can shed light on what Diamond and Spillane qualify as the "resources" that influence leadership practice. Moreover, this dialogical perspective can deliver on Diamond and Spillane's request for further research on their construct of "educational infrastructure." This educational infrastructure encompasses the components that influence teaching practice, also including norms and cultural-cognitive beliefs (cf. Hermans & Hermans-Konopka, 2012, p. 151). In DST, these norms and beliefs, which have personal and societal dimensions, are perceived as *I*-positions within the dialogical self of teachers-leaders, influencing the way and contents of how their leadership is about to be performed.

Snoek (2014) investigated how post-initial learning arrangements, which focus on teacher leadership, can contribute to teacher development and school development. He presents three case studies on different forms of teacher leadership learning arrangements. "Teachers who were engaged in the learning arrangements of the three case studies reported strong personal and professional growth, as they could relate their practical experience as teachers to new, wider theoretical notions and a change of identity" (p. 177). The respondents in this sample were pioneers in leadership research, because the concept of "educational leadership" was rather new in many schools at the time (cf. Snoek, 2014, p. 176). The main objective of the participants was to develop competencies that helped them to innovate education and support colleagues. Snoek situates the development of teacher leadership within a broader context of professionalization and cultural change within schools. For this reason, he recommends to strengthen strategically distributed leadership, with the intention of growing a culturally embedded leadership in the long run, which extends to all teachers in a team. He states that his study "demonstrated that there is little opportunity to develop this type of leadership within a context where no tradition of teacher leadership exists" (Snoek, 2014, p. 178). The opportunities for developing a culturally embedded leadership, distributed to all teachers, will increase when mandated leadership improves. According to Snoek, teacher leadership needs to be strengthened in a variety of forms, while it takes time to change school culture, a development that should finally lead to self-steering teacher teams. Regarding this development, he cautions against power-related issues and alienating managerial power (cf. Snoek, 2014, p. 179). "School leaders must be aware of these issues of autonomy, power, control, and facilitation in developing and sustaining teacher leadership" (Snoek, 2014, p. 179). The values of autonomy, power, and control are important in a broader discourse on professionalism, which demands flexibility from professionals in a complex society. Schön states that an "awareness of uncertainty, complexity, instability, uniqueness, and value conflict has led to the emergence of professional pluralism" (Schön 1983, p. 17). He means that professionals should develop an attitude of flexible adaptation to an ever-changing societal context. In this context, professionals cooperate with experts, managers, and other stakeholders. Professionalization refers to a continuous process of becoming a professional, instead of being a professional (cf. Bakker, 2016, p. 12).

In conclusion, teacher leadership as a process of professionalization is geared toward the development of self-steering teachers, who take responsibility for the development and quality of teaching and learning in their schools, as a contribution to the best possible education for all pupils and students. Important questions to be answered in this respect are 'What do we consider as the best possible education?' 'What is good education?' and 'What is the higher goal in education?' These normative questions require personal and professional consideration, which interrupts the hands-on reality and mentality in education. A focus on the normativity in professional action justifies the important and relevant role of autonomy and subjectivity in teachers' choices and interpretations.

Teacher leadership encompasses professional attention for subjectivity

The discourse on teacher leadership shows a concern for school improvement and care for quality in teaching and learning (cf. Harris et al., 2003). Every teacher bears responsibility for the quality of education provided to pupils and students. To raise the question of quality is to consider what good education encompasses. Answering this question is both a matter for the individual teacher and the collectivity of the teaching team. In both cases, the teacher has to take a position and to articulate the characteristics of good education. As a team, teachers can describe the general characteristics of what they collectively consider good education to be; but the complexity of everyday practice requires each teacher to interpret specific cases and to make decisions, which are inevitably subjective actions. In addition to the informal but influential 'team narrative' on the characteristics of good education, teachers also interpret relevant legislation, protocols, knowledge bases, and other official documents (which can be referred to as "the educational system"; Bakker, 2016, p. 13) from their own perspectives. Not only being the instrument of the system, the teacher has access to all kinds of pedagogical and didactical instruments (methods, interventions, teaching materials, etc.), which have to comply with a professional quality standard. As in other occupational fields, such as medicine and nursing, teachers are constantly confronted with the demand to ensure quality, relating themselves to collectively agreed standards in their own ways. This process is professional development at its core, and is a necessary process to earn the trust of society and of the people who are entrusted to the professionals (cf. Cruess et al., 2004, p. 75). A danger with describing teachers only as instruments of a system, or as professionals who only dispose of technical instruments, is that the inevitable normative dimension in teacher practice is lost sight of. As Biesta (2010, p. 128) puts it:

> Given that the question of good education is a normative question that requires values judgements, it can never be answered by the outcomes of measurement, by research evidence or through managerial forms of accountability – even though . . . such developments have contributed and are contributing to the displacement of the question of good education and try to present themselves as being able to set the direction for education.

This critical quote of Biesta ties in with the research tradition on normative professionalization, which started out as a critique of the dominant economic paradigm in the discourse on professionalism. The economic values of accountability, profitability, and efficiency are legitimate but should not downgrade or even exclude the pedagogical values in education. In this respect, it is good to understand that the concept of 'normative professionalization' is a pleonasm, because *every* professionalism is normative. As a figure of speech, we want to use this pleonasm to emphasize the necessity to consider the deeper meaning of professionalism and the underlying assumptions and ultimate goals of specific professional behavior. Kunneman (2009) designates this product of moral consideration as mode-3 knowledge, which differs from scientific and applied scientific knowledge. This mode-3 knowledge requires a moral and existential learning process. At this point, normativity and subjectivity move to the forefront. In line with this, Van den Berg (2002, p. 18) argues that educational innovation and improvement require the identification of existential experiences, and a hermeneutical approach to the professional's own teaching practice.

A moral and existential learning process provides room for ultimate questions about purpose and meaning. The discourse on normative professionalization seeks to safeguard human dignity in the techno-economic development of our world (cf. Kunneman 2009, p. 85). In this development, humans are at risk of losing their autonomy and losing control of their professional performance and over their lives in general (cf. Van den Berg, 2002). For this reason, normative professionalization, as a development process, encompasses the meaningful interaction between three interrelated aspects: the personal wellbeing of the professional, the content of work, and the broader social and societal context (Kunneman, 1996). The interaction between these three aspects should have an orientation toward the good, and more specifically, toward what the individual professional considers to be the good. For example, a small change in a professional's personal wellbeing affects the whole interaction between the aspects, which may lead to another appreciation of professionalism, as experienced by the persons receiving the professional service. These three aspects each have normative and subjective connotations, because the orientation towards the good differs from person to person. Every orientation begins with self-knowledge about one's personal position, where one stands, which is constitutive of identity (cf. Taylor, 1989). To gain this knowledge is to become acquainted with a variety of possible other positions. These positions represent different values, which show an orientation toward the good. From a DST perspective, normative professionalization should improve the awareness of guiding values, which have their roots in an experienced life story. These values, embedded in a narrative, are connected to positive or negative affections (cf. Hermans & Hermans-Jansen, 1995). As meaning-making units in an ongoing life narrative, values have an affective modality. In the theoretical framework of

DST, the personal and the professional represent a unity-in-multiplicity and constitute a 'multivoiced' identity.

A DST perspective on professionalization opposes a dichotomy between a personal and a professional identity, an issue that is also addressed in educational research, such as Akkerman and Meijer (2011), who investigate the concept of 'teacher identity.' But this is not always the case in educational research, and quite often the subjective, personal dimension of professional performance is left out. In a DST theoretical framework, a strict distinction would be impossible. The self, metaphorically characterized as a society of mind, consists of various *I*-positions. The construct of *I*-positions represents continuity and discontinuity in the formation of identity. The *I* in this construct safeguards a continuity in time, while every situation is an invitation to take another position. "The *I* in the one position, moreover, can agree, disagree, understand, misunderstand, oppose, contradict, question, challenge, and even ridicule the *I* in another position" (Hermans & Hermans-Jansen, 2001, p. 249). In this sense, identity is constantly (re)constructed, with no clear boundary between a personal and a professional life. Akkerman and Meijer (2011) define teacher identity "as an ongoing process of negotiating and interrelating multiple *I*-positions in such a way that a more or less coherent and consistent sense of self is maintained throughout various participations and self-investments in one's (working) life" (p. 315). This process of multiple *I*-positions incorporates the personal and professional positions, which means that a teacher is "not merely a professional regardless of all that he or she is otherwise; personal histories, patterned behavior, future concerns may all inform the position(s) of the teacher as professional" (Akkerman & Meijer, 2011, p. 316). This last remark explains how subjectivity and normativity continue to play a role in professionalization, in spite of strictly directive, unifying protocols and other safety regulations. If subjectivity is an integral part of professionalism, and as such of teacher leadership, it is better to educate teachers in the content of their often unarticulated subjective moral positions. Moreover, the assumption is that articulation will contribute to an awareness of other possible moral positions, which can benefit the self-steering teacher and teaching teams in their orientation towards good education. In the next section, we will elaborate on our general research into normative professionalization, and in particular the relationship between the articulation of a personal life orientation and professional training and development.

Research on the relationship between professionalization and life orientation

In our research group, 20 researchers investigate the normativity pertaining to professionalization in various disciplines, including education, social work, the paramedical sector, and financial disciplines. The research group is a joint project of the Utrecht University and the HU University of Applied

Sciences Utrecht, set up with the aim to relate the academic discourse on religious and worldview education to normative professionalization. In general, this combined research group takes the perspective of the humanities to research various professional practices, in order to describe the subjective and normative dimension of professionalization. The assumption is that normative professionalization consists of a moral and existential learning process, which traditionally falls within the domain of worldview education.

In our approach to normative professionalization, we distinguish three research perspectives. In the first place, we 'merely' intend to describe the normative and subjective dimension of professionalism, professionalization, and professional behavior on an empirical level. The aim is to understand the process of subjective interpretation, regardless of the (sometimes implicit) alleged objectivity of unambiguous protocols. Secondly, we aim to develop educational interventions and instruments, which would enable students and professionals to detect and articulate the normativity of their professional acting. These instruments improve their reflection on morality and ethics, thereby increasing their awareness of personal and professional values, and their understanding of how these values influence their decision making (and vice versa). Such awareness is necessary to answer the ultimate teleological question, 'What is the higher goal of education?' Our third research perspective touches upon the researcher's and teacher's own normative framework. What is the researcher's and teacher's moral position regarding 'good education'? (Bakker & Wassink, 2015). Developing your own 'philosophy of education' is in itself a normative act, but there is also the normativity of every single question you ask (and do not ask) in one of the many interviews you conduct as a researcher.

In this chapter, one of these studies is presented, which practices the second research perspective – i.e., it was launched with the intention to develop educational interventions. The general question of this particular research project is what the articulation of a personal life orientation means for professionalization. The research context is a minor program in philosophy, world religions, and spirituality that is specifically designed to foster the normative professionalization of the students. We will elaborate on this in the next section. The project started with a clarification of the conceptual relationship between religious or worldview education and normative professionalization. The first step in this conceptual study was to position ourselves in the academic discourse on religious education. Recently, a vivid discussion broke out about the name of the educational subject. Some scholars – for good reasons – are in favor of using the more inclusive concept 'worldview education,' instead of the more traditional concept 'religious education' (cf. Valk, 2007, 2009; Miedema, 2014; van der Kooij, 2016). The primary purpose of this renaming is the inclusion of secular, non-religious worldviews. In this discourse, van der Kooij makes a useful distinction between organized and personal worldviews. Some people have a personal worldview without being affiliated with an organized religious or secular worldview.

In our research, we take an additional conceptual step and propose the concept of 'life orientation.' Taylor's publication *The Sources of the Self* (1989) describes how every human being has an orientation towards the good within a metaphorical space of inescapable questions. These inescapable questions are ultimate questions about the meaning of life, and other sense-giving topics, which are inextricably linked to human life. These questions constitute a moral space in which people must orientate themselves and take a position. Taking a position in this pre-existing moral space of questions is constitutive of identity construction. Taylor states that this personal orientation is a crucial feature of the human agency to define ourselves in regard to inescapable questions. These questions are about 'hypergoods,' which involve 'strong evaluations,' meaning "the fact that these ends or goods stand independent of our own desires, inclinations, or choices, that they represent standards by which these desires and choices are judged" (Taylor, 1989, p. 20). Taylor's concept of identity, rooted in the process of orientation, reflects a dynamic in space and time. The spatial dimension reflects the context people live in: their culture, their nation, and the place in which they currently live. The temporal dimension refers to the interrelatedness of past, present, and future. The spatio-temporal orientation is an ongoing process in which human beings adjust and re-evaluate the position they have taken in regard to inescapable questions, within an ever-changing and complex society.

Describing the complex society we live in, Hermans and Hermans-Konopka (2012, p. 3) speak of a globalizing society. From a DST perspective, the dialogical self is not an entity in itself, but has permeable boundaries with society (cf. Hermans & Hermans-Konopka, 2012, p. 1). In other words, the self and the globalizing society are closely interwoven. Hermans and Hermans-Konopka state that for many people, globalization implies an experience of uncertainty. One of the psycho-educational objectives of DST is to support people in coping with different levels of uncertainty and ambiguity.

These theoretical frameworks develop a dynamic perspective on the self by using the concepts of 'orientation' and 'positioning,' which are spatio-temporal concepts. In addition, a theological perspective can offer a framework to structure meaning-making and orientation within the discourse of religious and worldview education. Even if space and time are without boundaries, a few landmarks might help with the orientation and positioning process. These theological landmarks are the view on the human being, the view on the world, the view on the meta-empirical, and the view on the good life (Anbeek, 2013; Daelemans, 2014). For reasons of limited space, we confine ourselves to our definition of life orientation, which is the product of a fairly extensive conceptual study (van der Zande, 2018): "an existential positioning process pertaining to the meaning of the human being, the world and the meta-empirical, directed towards the horizon of the good life."

This existential and meaning-making process could take place without further articulation. However, according to Taylor, the orientation toward the good is inescapable. "[I]n order to have an identity, we need an orientation to the good, which means some sense of qualitative discrimination, of the incomparable higher" (Taylor, 1989, p. 47). Besides our inescapable orientation toward the good, Taylor (1989) designates another basic human condition, which is that we make sense of ourselves, and "that we grasp our lives in a *narrative*" (p. 47). From a DST perspective, this orientation of the self is a dialogical process between different *I*-positions, which configure in a changing repertoire of positions depending on the situation. Taylor states that 'having an identity' means taking a position, which entails some sense of qualitative distinction and/or discrimination (cf. Hermans & Hermans-Konopka, 2012, p. 105). The next step would be the articulation of this position among other people, which is desirable in professional life but not necessarily required in private life. The condition of articulating a life orientation touches upon the phenomenon of 'worldview deficiency' (see Alma, Chapter 5 of this volume, about this phenomenon). Such an articulation offers the possibility to construe a conceptual relationship between normative professionalization and life orientation. In the moral space of pre-existent questions, professionals have to develop a capacity for critical reflection, a capacity for expressing and articulating their position in an interpersonal dialogue. In conjunction with this, Hermans & Hermans-Konopka construe the concept of the dialogical self as a multiplicity of *I*-positions within a society of mind, leaving room for the concept of an intrapersonal dialogue. However, this intrapersonal dialogue could remain unaware, or 'beneath the surface.' In DST terms, it is necessary for professionals to voice these *I*-positions, which are part of their intrapersonal dialogue. They need to be aware of their *I*-positions and to develop flexibility and a capacity for adaptations of the self in an increasingly complex society (see Wijsen, Chapter 4 of this volume, about flexibility in *I*-positions). Professionals should know each other's position, to understand otherness, and to eventually bear collective responsibility for a decision that they know some colleagues do not entirely agree with. Articulating a personal life orientation goes beyond moral indifference (see K. J. Gergen, Chapter 1 of this volume, about this theme). Professionals have to be aware of, and be able to articulate the multiplicity of positions as voiced in their society of mind – and by other people. Positions, in DST terms, are dialogical partners in their life orientation. In light of the project to articulate these life orientation positions in favor of a normative professionalization process, we developed an educational program as a context for further research. This program is the subject of the next section.

Educational program in life orientation

In Dutch higher professional education (*Hoger Beroepsonderwijs*; HBO), students can choose a so-called minor at the end of their four-year study.

These half-year, full-time educational programs enable students to special-ize in a specific subject of their field of study, or to deepen their personal and professional development. At the HU University of Applied Sciences Utrecht, students can choose from 140 minor programs. One of these is the minor *Philosophy, World Religions, Spirituality*. The general objective of this program is a normative professionalization from a life orientation perspective. The name of the minor covers three subjects, which represent a holistic view on the human being, a being with different knowledge acquisi-tion capacities: cognition, intuition, imagination, and experience. Roughly, the three subjects address all the capacities, although the philosophy courses tend to be more cognitive and the spirituality tutorials predominantly – but not exclusively – address the experiential learning of students. If wisdom is an embodied kind of knowledge, which is experienced in life, then educa-tion should not be limited to purely cognitive learning.

In this educational program, students take courses in Western and Eastern philosophy and attend philosophical tutorials such as moral considerations, Socratic dialogue, art reading, and debating. Students get acquainted with various philosophical domains like ethics, anthropology, aesthetics, cultural philosophy, and philosophy of science. The study track in religion and world-views consists of a presentation of a selection of world religions. In addi-tion to religious and spiritual denominations, traditions like humanism and atheism are presented. In these courses, attention is minimally paid to views on humankind, the world, the meta-empirical, and conceptions of the good life, as held by these traditions. In addition, students also learn about books, prophets, rituals, and other characteristics. In this study track, the students become acquainted with two different perspectives. The first perspective is phenomenological, consisting of an academic approach intended to describe and explain a specific religion from a relatively objective point of view. The second angle is the insider perspective, usually presented by guest teachers, who tell about their lived experience in one of the traditions. Students learn that different perspectives yield different answers, and they experience the wisdom that every individual has an individual interpretation of the tradition s/he adheres to. *The* Christian tradition, for example, does not exist; nor does *the* Islamic tradition, nor any other tradition. The study track in spirituality offers students the possibility to experience a variety of tutorials, in differ-ent forms of meditation, yoga, music experience, bibliodrama, haptonomy, theatre sports, and visual arts. These lessons are designed to draw students out of their comfort zone, make them cross their convenience limit, in order to stimulate reflection. They are not forced to participate. If they do not wish to participate, they are kindly requested to take notes and reflect on the situation and their feelings, behavior, and insights, for which we developed a particular instrument. In conclusion, the minor program as a whole, and the spirituality tutorials in particular, function as a pedagogical interruption.

The pedagogical interruption is meant to enable students to reflect on their own position (cf. Biesta, 2010). The obviousness, the self-evidence of life is put between brackets. Students cross borders of which they were previously unaware. For Gert Biesta, this kind of pedagogical interruption is essential to create the possibility of subjectification, which is an emancipation process, a process of learning to speak with one's own voice (cf. Biesta, 2013, p. 84). Another significant pedagogical interruption consists of three inspirational days spent in a monastery. All students participate in this excursion, where most of them experience an entirely different life orientation. They speak with the monks, but they also visit a mosque, a mandir, and a gurdwara. Over the course of the three days, they encounter different cultures and various views, and during the walks to different holy places, they tell each other about their new insights and questions.

The pedagogical interruption also includes a newly developed instrument, which helps students to articulate their life orientation. This instrument consists of a list of facilitating questions, which address issues of life orientation and normative professionalization. The first question covers the definition of life orientation provided earlier in this chapter, and invites students to describe their view on the human being, the world, the meta-empirical, and the good life. The second question includes the instruction that students hold an interview with their (grand)parents about their life orientation. Thirdly, students describe the most influential moments, experiences, and persons in their lives. The fourth issue encompasses their answers to ultimate questions about the meaning of life, death, evil, and disease. In addition to answering these teleological questions, students also articulate their views on work and on their profession. Fifthly, students delineate their sources of inspiration. The sixth issue encompasses their answers to facilitating questions about dreams and ideals (see Table 9.1).

During the first four weeks of the minor, the students write the first articulation of their views and insights in black (T-0, initial phase). They are not obliged to answer all the questions; after all, the questions are facilitators. The teachers instruct the students to spread this exercise over the four weeks, and in case they find they cannot articulate their views in words, then this is what they write down. After these weeks, they visit the monastery in The Hague, where they discuss their articulations with a peer student. When the lessons start again, they have six weeks to re-read their preliminary articulations. The instruction they receive is that this exercise does not stem from the assumption that their original articulations need to be updated; it is possible that their experiences over the past weeks have led to changes in their views, but not necessarily so. The teachers/ supervisors ask the students to reflect, during this re-reading process, on the meetings, conversations, and dialogues of the past few weeks. During this reflective re-reading, they can add new insights, different terms, or a more nuanced vision, or they might discuss an opposing or different view that they disagree with. In educational terms, the teachers/supervisors ask them to practice their hermeneutic competency. All these new ideas and insights have to be added in a different color, which enables the student and the

Table 9.1 Facilitating questions for the articulation of life orientation and normative professionalization

1. Personal worldviews	What are your personal views on humankind, the world, the meta-empirical (or God), and the good life?
2. Worldview roots	(a) Describe your (grand)parents' views on human being, the world, the meta-empirical (or God), and the good life. Interview your (grand)parents about their personal views (see question 1).
	(b) Describe the dominant societal perspective on these views.
	(c) Describe your socio-economic and cultural background.
3. Biography	Describe life-changing events, critical moments, and significant people.
4. Meaning of life	(a) What is the meaning of life, your life, death, evil, sickness?
	(b) What is the quality of your life in relation to what you have described as the good life?
	(c) What is the meaning of work, of your profession?
	(d) How do you see yourself as part of a larger whole (humanity, society, and the cosmos)?
5. Inspirational sources	(a) What are your sources of inspiration? Think of books, persons, movies, etc.
	(b) Which sources would you like to explore?
	(c) What significance do spiritual and religious sources hold for you?
6. Dreams and ideals	(a) Describe your personal dreams and ideals.
	(b) Describe your professional dreams and ideals.
	(c) Describe your picture of the ideal society.
	(d) Describe your view of 'the good citizen.'
	(e) Describe your professional contribution to a good society.
	(f) How are these dreams and ideals rooted in your worldview?

teacher/supervisor (and later in the educational project, the researcher) to reflect on the hermeneutical development during successive time periods (T0, T1, T2, T3, T4, and T-J). This methodology provides an insight in the hermeneutical effects of the pedagogical interruptions. The next section shows how the theoretical framework of DST provides a structure for analyzing these student-produced documents.

DST used as a heuristic-analytical instrument in narrative inquiry

In this section, we first briefly describe a part of the analysis procedure for our narrative inquiry into the student-produced documents on life orientation. The next step is the description of some DST concepts, which we used for the development of a narrative-dialogical analysis instrument. We discern basic, dynamic, and developmental DST positions, which are helpful for the narrative inquiry.

In this research project, the documents written by the students on their life orientation became the data for narrative inquiry. The first procedure in narrative research consists of collecting the field notes, or narratives, which in our case were the documents on life orientation, written by the students during the minor program (cf. Clandinin & Connelly, 2000; Czarniaw-ska, 2005). After receiving the students' consent, the articulations became data for our narrative inquiry. Through this consent, the students officially became co-researchers because their articulated narratives resulted from their personal narrative research. We consciously opted for self-written texts without intervention of the researcher, to keep the participants' narrative inquiries free from interrupting research instructions. For this reason, the request to participate in the research project was formulated only after the educational program had concluded. The project researcher subsequently took on the role of a second-level narrative researcher.

The second procedure in narrative research is the *restoring* or *retelling* of the story. Firstly, the students composed, as first-level narrative inquir-ers, the restoring of their narrative. As described earlier, a significant meth-odological step was to ask the students to re-read their documents, to add new words, insights, or whatever else they deemed appropriate. In the sec-ond step of the restoring, three or four years after their graduation, we asked them to reiterate the re-reading process once again as 'young profes-sionals.' Our reason for giving this research a semi-longitudinal character was to enable a description of how the students' life orientation evolved in professional life, outside of a structured educational program. In addi-tion, we expected that with a longitudinal study, new insights could be gained about the post-initial period of young professionals; this is useful for a better understanding of the reasons for dropout during the first five years of employment, which occurs in some professional domains, such as the education sector. Secondly, the project researcher re-read all the student documents for narrative analysis. With a view to analysis, eight topics were selected to describe the relationship between personal life orientation and normative professionalization (see Table 9.2). For this stage of the narrative research process, we developed a narrative-dialogical analysis instrument that encompasses various DST concepts. The analysis was performed for each of the eight topics in every narrative, beginning with a reading of the full narrative, in order to take notes about the narrative context in which each topic occurred. In line with the directives of Clandinin and Connelly (2000), interim texts were written during the re-reading process at this stage of the narrative research process (cf. p. 134). The narrative-dialogical analy-sis instrument was applied to each topic, which for every student narrative resulted in a set of eight analyses.

In a third step, the interim texts were compared for similarities and dif-ferences, and after re-reading the narrative once more, a final description of the relationship between life orientation and professionalization was formulated.

Table 9.2 Eight topics derived from the students' documents on life orientation as used in the narrative analysis

Topics in life orientation (personal dimension of NP)				
View on meaning of personal profession (professional dimension of NP)	View on the good life	View on the meta-empirical	View on humankind	Picture of the ideal society (societal dimension of NP)
	Experience of personal quality of life in relation to description of the good life	*View on the meaning of life*	*View on the world*	

Before we take a closer look at one of the analyzed documents, we first describe our narrative-dialogical analysis instrument. This tool consists of a preliminary inventory of some basic elements of DST, which are the *I*-position, the counter-position, the outside position, and the external position (cf. Raggatt, 2012; Zock, 2013; see also Hermans, Chapter 2 of this volume, for an elaborate description). The first concept is the *I*-position, which encapsulates the multiplicity and unity within the self. The description starts with an initial *I*-position, which is, in fact, embedded in the first articulation. If relevant, or detectable, it is possible to discern an S(self)-motive or an O(other)-motive. These are underlying psychological motives that roughly represent the striving for self-enhancement (S) and the longing for contact with others (O) (cf. Hermans & Hermans-Jansen, 1995, p. 16). The detecting of these motives can help to describe patterns or themes in the evolving life orientation narrative. The other basic elements that can be described are the counter-position, the outer position, and the external position. A counter position is an *I*-position that develops in the narrative as an opposite, or conflicting *I*-position. An external position refers to an 'other-in-the-self,' which could be the voiced position of another person or a particular group within the society of mind. An outside position is a position voiced by a physical other person, who participated in a dialogue (cf. Hermans & Hermans-Konopka, 2012, p. 31). The choice for this specific set of 'positions' was made to describe the relationship between the provisionally articulated *I*-position and other kinds of positions, which could shed light on the intrapersonal dialogue of the students. The analysis of these basic DST elements allows a quick overview of the *I*-positions as they occur in the documents over time, from T0 to the juniorship stage (T-J), which is the post-initial period.

The next category of DST elements, distinguished by Raggatt (2012), is the so-called dynamic elements, which include the core position, the meta-position, the promoter position, and the third position. A core position determines the functioning of other positions. A meta-position is a super-ordinate position, the product of two or more positions. Such a position "refers to 'extra-positionality,' the self-moving above itself and taking a 'helicopter view'" (Hermans & Gieser, 2012, p. 15). Meta-positions are not to be confused with a control center. "In order to avoid this confusion, it should be remembered that a meta-position is typically influenced by one or more internal or external positions that are actualized at the moment of self-examination" (Hermans & Hermans-Konopka, 2012, p. 148). Hermans and Hermans-Konopka discern three functions of meta-positions: unifying, executive, and liberating. In their unifying function, meta-positions can even bring together opposed positions. "In its *executive* function, [a meta-position] creates a basis for decision making and directions in life that lead to actions that profit from its support from a broader array of specific positions" (Hermans & Hermans-Konopka, 2012, p. 151). Meta-positions can be liberating in signaling behavior that should be stopped. A promoter position is an accelerator for possible change, and "gives order and direction in the development of the position repertoire" (Hermans & Gieser, 2013, p. 31). Finally, a third position has "the potential of unifying the two original ones without denying or removing their differences (unity-in-multiplicity)" (Hermans & Hermans-Konopka, 2012, p. 10). Such a developmental position is the result of a dialogue between two opposing or conflicting positions. A third position is one of the ways to improve flexibility within the self, which was initially a therapeutic goal in DST but which could be relevant for education as well. A new term, launched in our research project, is that of a 'silent' or 'silenced' position, which refers to an *I*-position that had no voice in the initial articulation. In DST terms, the corresponding *I*-position exists in the society of mind, but with a soft or even silent voice. Sometimes an *I*-position becomes softer or silenced in the intrapersonal dialogue; this does not mean that the position has disappeared, which is quite impossible. Table 9.3 shows this part of our instrument, which consists of dynamic elements drawn from DST.

The last category of DST concepts is the developmental processes, which Raggatt describes as the decentering and centering processes. These

Table 9.3 Dynamic elements as used in narrative-dialogical analysis instrument during the minor program (T0–T4) and juniorship period (T-J)

Core position	T0– Juniorship	Silent (silenced) position	T0–T4 T-J
		Meta-position	T0–T4 T-J
		Promoter position	T0–T4 T-J
		Third position	T0–T4 T-J

(Source: Van der Zande, 2018.)

constructs help to describe whether the articulation process indicates an integration of the position repertoire or a disorganizing effect, which, however, also leaves room for innovation.

An example: the articulation process of Alice

At the time, Alice was a student in occupational therapy. After her graduation, she found work in a hospital. When she enrolled in the minor program, she was in her early 20s. It is important to note that she suffered from rheumatism, a condition that was diagnosed two years earlier.

As discussed earlier, life orientation and normative professionalization are both oriented toward 'the good.' In the list of facilitating questions, 'the good' has been specified in several issues, one of which is the view on 'the good life.' In her first articulation, drafted during the first four weeks of the minor program, Alice wrote:

> A good life is a life in which you're happy. It's a life in which you can be with the people who are dear to you, who make you happy, and whom you can make happy. A good life is different for every human being. For me, a good life is a balance between rest and unrest, a life full of love, to share and to receive. In a good life, you appreciate the other for who he or she is, you respect yourself and your fellow human beings. Enjoying life to the fullest and enjoying in moderation are important aspects of a good life. Being able to let everything go, while still maintaining control.
> (September 2013 – T0)

In this first articulation, the theme of balance is important. Alice describes a balance between rest and unrest, which she articulates in paradoxes at the end. After the three inspirational days in the monastery, she added to this preliminary articulation:

> The good life can have a different meaning for each of us. A good life, as I've learned in the monastery in The Hague, can also be: living for God. Some want to share their life with a partner, others prefer to stay alone, and still others live their lives before God.
> (October 3, 2013 – T1)

In her initial articulation, Alice already acknowledged the existence of differences, but her experience in the monastery resulted in new perspectives. She wrote "to have learned," which she illustrates by using examples in this fragment. A few weeks later, Alice had to re-read her document. Her addition:

> A human being lives a good life when he/she works for a better world, for himself/herself but especially for others.
> (October 22, 2013 – T2)

Remarkably, this addition has a different character. Alice emphasizes a goal in life, which she specifies as a contribution to a better world. This position looks more like a promoter position, which reaches beyond her desire for balance, which predominantly focuses on her own life. In this addition, an emphasis on balance, in the sense of a balance between a better world for others and a better world for herself, is still recognizable. In any case, her orientation on the good life has broadened. As such, her articulations about her view on the world might give greater insight about this picture of a better world. At the end of the minor program, she added:

> A good life means being there for each other, in good times and in bad. You're a good human being when you're there for someone else, when you can put your own grief aside to support someone who suffers more grief than you. In a good life, you appreciate what you have and what you're blessed with.
>
> (January 10, 2014 – T3)

Two days before, her mother-in-law had passed away, an event she recorded under the facilitating question about 'biography.' This context, of course, explains the addition, but it also sheds new light on the theme of balance. Alice states to put her grief aside, in connection with what she describes elsewhere as 'a difficult period.' In this addition, a significant shift from 'the good life' to 'a good human being' is recognizable. This shift shows a resemblance with the articulation on October 22 (earlier in this section). In her earlier articulations, she states that a good life can have different meanings for different people. Now, she takes a position by stating what a good life means, which she connects directly to being a good human being.

Three years later, Alice was willing to continue her narrative inquiry and reiterated the exercise. In the meantime, she had been appointed to her second job, where she felt more comfortable. Another significant event was a trip to Bali, Indonesia. She wrote additionally:

> A good life is a life without selfishness and with love for our environment. In recent years I've learned that I'm allowed to think more of myself. Sometimes I'm maybe too much there for others, which makes me forget about myself. I've learned to draw a line and not always be guided by what others think, believe or want. A good life, I think, is a life in which there is a balance between your own will and the will of the other.
>
> (February 2017 – Juniorship)

The theme of balance is on the forefront again. In DST terms, this seems to be a core position, which influences other positions. During the minor, Alice's view on the good life broadened, which appears to be voiced here in 'love for the environment.' The character of the articulated equilibrium has shifted from rest and unrest to a balance of wills. This new balance has to do with taking a position, because she describes the risk of losing personal space, to forget herself.

The next methodological step is a cross-over analysis between what Alice articulates as the experience of her quality of life, and what she articulates as the good life. In her preliminary articulation, she wrote that she thought she was not (yet) leading a good life, because she had not yet found a balance between rest and unrest. However, she described that she had a good life because of her family and friends. On October 3, her search for balance received another dimension in relation to the topic 'perceived quality of my life':

> I'm very much searching for who I am and what I want with my life. What I've learned is that I 'have to' spend more time with my family and friends, and that I find time for myself very important, by painting, writing, or making music. If I want to lead a good life, I'll have to look more for this kind of relaxation.
>
> (October 3, 2013 – T1)

Here, the search for balance is broadened to a search for who she is, which became a promoter position. The search for balance, her core position, became more articulated and differentiated throughout the minor and her post-initial period. During the inspirational days, she experienced the rest that a painting exercise could bring for her. This pedagogical interruption enabled Alice to concretize her search for a balance between rest and unrest. Moreover, three years later, she wrote to have found balance in her life – in her private family life and in her professional life – which makes it possible for her to be there for another person without losing herself.

> I've grown, I'm aware of what I can and cannot do well. I feel appreciated and realize that I'm allowed to be here. I have people around me who give me a good feeling. I invest in these people and give them the attention and love they need. I've become more self-confident. I've always reflected, even a little too much. I've learned that over-reflecting exhausts me, that I can find peace in who I am and what I do, and that I do that well. All this is special for me to say. For years I thought I was too little, believed that I actually wasn't allowed to be there. I'm still very insecure, about my appearance and sometimes about what I do. But the experiences of the past years have made me grow and give me peace of mind.
>
> (February 2017 – Juniorship)

This balance is also a balance in terms of self-acceptance, and acceptance of how life is. The core position of 'balance' became a promoter position in her narrative: 'becoming aware of who I am, and taking a position.' After three years, the ambiguity and tension that she described between her view on the good life and the experience of her quality of life has at least been silenced. This balance appears to have a deeper existential dimension, which says something about her place in life, among other people, and in the world. A closer look at the development in her view on the world might clarify her position in the world. The initial articulation of her view on the world was:

> A place where we can live, in poverty or in luxury. Where we, as human beings, nature and animals, have to make something beautiful out of it. This can be forgotten sometimes. The world is a place with so many beautiful things to see, which I can enjoy. It offers rest, but it can also cause unrest.
>
> (September 2013 – T0)

The world is beautiful, but she mentions some threats to the coexistence on earth, and to its inhabitants. Again, the tension between rest and unrest comes to the fore. In the minor program, students can choose for an optional study trip to Rome. Alice went to Rome, and she wrote:

> After Rome, I'm more convinced than ever that the world is something beautiful. Because I've seen so many beautiful things. I'm also convinced that we, as human beings, can make something beautiful out of it together. I was lucky enough to experience this in Rome, in the company of special people.
>
> (November 17, 2013 – T2)

Alice enjoyed her trip with her fellow students, which gave her a positive view on the world, and on the possibility to achieve beautiful things together as humans. As human beings, we can 'make' a better world. Her positive view in the former articulation got a boost; she became more convinced. A few months later, things changed.

> During the last days of my mother-in-law, I realized all the more that life and the world are also very unfair. I've always had a lot of trouble with the fact that we have such a good life here in the Netherlands, and others have to suffer. This little piece of powerlessness I feel, is sometimes very difficult for me. After the death of my mother-in-law, I realized that life can be truly unfair. The grief of my father-in-law, because his girlfriend passed away too early, I consider very unfair.
>
> (January 10, 2014 – T3)

The contingency of life brought a sharp ambiguity in Alice's articulation. The experience of powerlessness opposes the earlier belief in the manufacturability and controllability of life. The feeling of joy is replaced by the feeling of unfairness. Significant is Alice's mentioning of a broader perspective. Life is unfair to her mother-in-law and her family, but she broadens this to other parts of the world, and draws attention to another dimension of unfairness. It is understandable that the experience of contingency at that time led to this articulation. What would she have written at the end of the minor program, if her mother-in-law had not died? What we do know, is what she articulated three years later:

> The world is beautiful. There is much to see and experience. I was able to make a tour of America, Java and Bali. Yes, I felt privileged. I worked hard to make it possible, but at the same time, I had the 'luck' to go on these travels. I could experience that the world is different everywhere. That I think with my values and norms, but that there is so much more than that. That there are significant cultural differences that we're not always aware of, and that these cultural differences can make all our lives richer, in different ways. Besides this richness, there is also a lot of poverty. Images on television often caused me grief when I saw that certain groups of people have so much less wealth than I have. In Indonesia, I was able to see that this image is not always correct. That people can be very happy with little. I feel rich in being able to travel, but at the same time I also know that I can be happy with very little. The same applies to these people. We've become so accustomed to certain things, which we take for granted, while we can do with much less. I'm not materialistic, I can manage well with little. At least that's what I think. Because secretly, I'm happy being able to watch television, to have a mobile phone on which I can Facebook, and to have beautiful home furnishings around me.
>
> (February 2017 – Juniorship)

The original core position, 'the world is beautiful,' is back in place. Moreover, her two journeys have silenced an ambiguity caused by a feeling of sorrow for people who live in poverty, due to her awareness that she lives in relative wealth. She experienced the possibility to be happy with almost nothing. A long-existing ambiguity turned into a third position: 'difference in wealth exists, but people can be happy with little.' At the end, she bumps into another tension. Is she really not a materialistic person, or is that just something she likes to tell herself? This last fragment reveals a meta-position, which demonstrates Alice's capacity to look at her positions from a distance. This hermeneutic process that she goes through regarding her view on the world showed a parallel in her articulation about the ideal society. She wishes for a society with peace and rest, and although differences in wealth remain, everybody must have the opportunity to lead a good life. As far as her normative professionalization is concerned, her youngest articulation about the meaning of life is significant. This articulation summarizes the process she has gone through so far.

> I've been working as an occupational therapist in a hospital for more than 2 years now. I notice that in my work, I can mean something to

people with a physical or mental disability. It gives me satisfaction to see that I can do something for these people, help them to give a positive turn to life. I like to be there for others in my work, I don't have to think of myself at those moments, I can focus on my fellow human beings. The appreciation I receive from my patients makes me happy, but makes me feel small as well. People can be so grateful sometimes for the small bits of advice I give them, or the little adjustments I make. I find this valuable and instructive. That fits in nicely with how I view life. We don't need big things to be happy. We are here in the world to make something beautiful out of it, and to ensure that the generations after us can enjoy it as well.

(February 2017 – Juniorship)

Significant is the articulation that her work helps her not to think of herself. With regard to her core position, finding balance, her work seems to function as a third position. In her personal life, she must draw a line and not always allow herself to be guided by what others believe or want, which means caring less about other people. Her job legitimizes her care for other people, which at the same time contributes to her self awareness, because the patients are so grateful. She shows flexibility in her positions regarding personal and professional life. For the sake of completeness, it is helpful to mention that Alice chose a three-day work week, which she had to admit was the best possible balance for her.

Conclusion

The articulation of a personal life orientation contributes to a deeper understanding of the ambiguities of (professional) life, which influence a teacher's professional performance. The DST perspective offers support with describing how different values, represented as *I*-positions, function in an interdependent way. A pedagogy of interruption helps to identify patterns in professional development, and enables students to reflect on their positions. When students experience space and time for reflection, and experience interruptions in their lives, they can develop other perspectives in their life orientation. These other perspectives can lead to promoter and third positions, which enhance the capacity of students to be flexible in shifting positions. First of all, this flexibility is necessary for moral and spiritual leadership, because the contingency in life requires professionals to be aware of their primarily held positions and prejudices. Secondly, the awareness of other possible positions might contribute to greater mutual acceptance among colleagues. This awareness contributes to an increasing development of a distributed leadership, and to the evolution toward a more culturally embedded leadership. Once leadership is no longer understood in terms of a single leader who sets out the directives that team members need to obey, but instead in terms of constantly changing roles and positions, involving complementary (but also opposing) competencies, it is crucial that the professionals who are involved in this leadership are able to reflect thoroughly on its dynamics. The challenge to cultivate distributed leadership self-evidently leads to the articulation of all kinds of differences in a team of professionals, including moral pluralities. Knowing yourself as a professional and being able to relate to your colleagues on this fundamental level, with regard to their competencies and (moral) positions, is a *conditio sine qua non* for contemporary organizations and their leadership. We think that the DST perspective, which we explored narratively and elaborated upon in this chapter, can provide good support in this respect.

References

Akkerman, S. F., & Meijer, P. C. (2011). A dialogical approach to conceptualising teacher identity. *Teaching and Teacher Education, 27*, 308–319.

Anbeek, C. (2013). *Aan de heidenen overgeleverd: Hoe theologie de 21ste eeuw kan overleven.* Utrecht: Ten Have.

Bakker, C. (2016). Professionalization and the quest how to deal with complexity. In C. Bakker & N. Montesano Montessori (Eds.), *Complexity in education: From horror to passion.* Rotterdam, NL: Sense Publishers.

Bakker, C., & Montesano Montessori, N. (Eds.). (2016). *Complexity in education: From horror to passion.* Rotterdam, NL: Sense Publishers.

Bakker, C., & Wassink, H. (2015). *Leraren en het goede leren: Normatieve professionalisering in het onderwijs.* Utrecht: Hogeschool.

Biesta, G. (2010). *Good education in an age of measurement: Ethics, politics, democracy.* Boulder, CO: Paradigm Publishers.

Biesta, G. (2013). *The beautiful risk of education.* Boulder, CO: Paradigm Publishers.

Clandinin, D., & Connelly, F. (2000). *Narrative inquiry: Experience and story in qualitative research.* Hoboken, NJ: John Wiley and Sons Inc.

Cruess, S., Johnston, S., & Cruess, R. (2004). "Profession": A working definition for medical educators. *Teaching and Learning in Medicine, 16*(1), 74–76.

Czarniawska, B. (2005). *Narratives in social science research.* London: Sage Publications.

Daelemans, B., & Brabant, Ch. (Eds.). (2014). *Wijselijk onwetend: De paradox in het christelijk geloof.* Scherpenheuvel-Zichem: Averbode.

Diamond, J., & Spillane, J. (2016). School leadership and management from a distributed perspective: A 2016 retrospective and prospective. *Management in Education, 30*(4), 147–154.

Harris, A., Day, C. H., Hopkins, D., Hadfield, M., Hargreaves, A., & Chapman, C. H. (2003). *Effective leadership for school improvement.* London: Routledge.

Hermans, H. J. M., & Gieser, T. (Eds.). (2012). *Handbook of dialogical self theory.* Cambridge: Cambridge University Press.

Hermans, H. J. M., & Hermans-Jansen, E. (1995). *Self-narratives: The construction of meaning in psychotherapy.* New York, NY: Guilford Press.

Hermans, H. J. M., & Hermans-Jansen, E. (2001). Dialogical processes and the development of the self. In J. Valsiner & K. Connolly (Eds.), *Handbook of developmental psychology.* London: Sage Publications.

Hermans, H. J. M., & Hermans-Konopka, A. (2012). *Dialogical self theory: Positioning and counter-positioning in a globalizing society.* New York, NY: Cambridge University Press.

Kunneman, H. (1996). Normatieve professionaliteit: Een appel. *Tijdschrift Sociale Interventie, 5*(3), 107–112.

Kunneman, H. (2009). *Voorbij het dikke-ik: Bouwstenen voor een kritisch humanisme*. Amsterdam: SWP.

Miedema, S. (2014). From religious education to worldview education and beyond: The strength of a transformative pedagogical paradigm. *Journal for the Study of Religion, 27*(1), 82–103.

Raggatt, P. (2012). Positioning in the dialogical self: Recent advances in theory construction. In H. J. M. Hermans & T. Gieser (Eds.), *Handbook of dialogical self theory*. Cambridge: Cambridge University Press.

Schön, D. (1983). *The reflective practitioner*. New York, NY: Basic Books.

Snoek, M. (2014). *Developing leadership and its impact in schools* (PhD thesis). Amsterdam: Amsterdam University Press.

Spillane, J. (2006). *Distributed leadership*. San Francisco, CA: Jossey-Bass.

Taylor, C. (1989). *Sources of the self: The making of the modern identity*. Cambridge, MA: Harvard University Press.

Valk, J. (2007). Plural public schooling: Religion, worldviews and moral education. *British Journal of Religious Education, 29*(3), 273–285.

Valk, J. (2009). Knowing self and others: Worldview study at Renaissance college. *The Journal of Adult Theological Education, 6*(1), 69–80.

Van den Berg, D. (2002). *Existentiële belevingen van leraren bij hun onderwijs: Een onderwijskundige en psychologische bijdrage*. Nijmegen: KUN.

Van der Kooij, J. (2016). *Worldview and moral education: On conceptual clarity and consistency use*. Ede: GVO Drukkers & Vormgevers.

Van der Zande, E. (2018). *Life orientation for professionals: A narrative inquiry into morality and dialogical competency*. Almere: Parthenon.

Zock, H. (2013). Religious voices in the dialogical self: Towards a conceptual-analytical framework on the basis of Hubert J.M. Hermans's dialogical self theory. In G. Benavides, M. Buitelaar, & H. Zock (Eds.), *Religious voices in self-narratives: Making sense of life in times of transition* (pp. 1–35). Berlin and Boston, MA: De Gruyter.

10 Moral commitment and existential issues in religious and worldview education

Geir Skeie

Introduction

Education is from the start an inherently moral enterprise in the sense that it aims to equip the young generation with knowledge, skills, and attitudes that are necessary for life in a future society. Since the future is yet to come, and society is under construction, we base our ideas about education largely on what we know today, drawing on experience and knowledge produced in the past. Neither the past nor the present is something we agree upon, and human beings have different visions of the future. "Countless 'aims of education' are therefore possible, depending upon what features of a worthwhile form of life any educator thinks is most important to foster." (Peters, 1987, p. 17)

Peters here argues, rightly, that both education as a system and the individual educator is dependent on visions of a good life when aims of education are presented and practiced. I see this 'dependence' to be of an ethical character, because it is value-based and can be accounted for. It is possible to discuss and disagree upon, but it may still rest on deeply held convictions that are not easy to change. Education is also a moral enterprise, because it promotes certain ways of acting and being together, but the ethical foundation and the moral rules are not identical; they are different levels of preferences and arguments. If we differ in morals, we may address this on the level of ethics; and if we agree in ethics, we may still differ in morals.

At a system level, the aims formulated by educational policies in a democratic society can be expected to express what kind of education is believed to be in the public interest, taking account of our diverse visions of life and society while still trying to achieve the common good. The value of the common good can be understood as a regulative idea, in line with Kant, Mead, and Habermas. We may disagree about what is the common good, but we can agree that the best way to discuss this is to assume that our different visions "embody a general interest and that the unity of the collective is at stake in protecting this interest" (Habermas, 1989, p. 93). In educational systems, the visions of the common good that education strives for can be expressed in laws and curricula, as in this example from the beginning of the recently replaced Norwegian core curriculum:

> The aim of education is to furnish children, young people and adults with the tools they need to face the tasks of life and surmount its challenges together with others. Education shall provide learners with the capability to take charge of themselves and their lives, as well as with the vigor and will to stand by others. Education shall qualify people for productive participation in today's labor force, and supply the basis for later shifts to occupations as yet not envisaged. It should develop the skills needed for specialized tasks, and provide a general level of competence broad enough for re-specialization later in life. Education must ensure both admission to present-day working and community life, and the versatility to meet the vicissitudes of life and the demands of an unknown future. Hence, it must impart attitudes and learning to last a lifetime, and build the foundation for the new skills required in a rapidly changing society. It must teach the young to look ahead and train their ability to make sound choices. It must accustom them to taking responsibility – to assess the effects of their actions on others and evaluate them in terms of ethical principles.
>
> (The Royal Ministry of Education, 1997, p. 5)[1]

This particular example from Norway, in my view, mirrors the typically 'modern' vision of education described earlier, where curricula are seen as a product of politics understood as rational deliberation of societal challenges performed through the rule of the better argument. A closer look at the same curriculum shows that it presents an understanding of modernity as a still 'unfulfilled' success, in line with the type of corporative welfare state policies that have been prominent in Scandinavia. In the late 1990s, this was already challenged by ideas about post-modernity, liquid modernity, and diverse modernities and by processes of globalization, socio-cultural pluralization, and right-wing extremism, and even more so today. Nevertheless, there is a kind of balancing between the somewhat disruptive forces of diversity and the former 'sameness.' The crisis unleashed by the right-wing terrorist attack in Oslo and Utøya in 2011 showed this by displaying a strong collective support for both democracy and diversity, and the political leadership at the time also underlined these values.

On the classroom level, similar processes are going on, and teachers try to implement general curriculum aims while at the same time dealing with the attainment targets of different school subjects. An action research project some years ago showed that religious education teachers found it challenging to negotiate between their commitment to general aims of education and to the daily struggle to help their students meet learning outcomes (Skeie, 2011). While Norwegian religious education includes religions, worldviews, ethics, and philosophy as part of the curriculum, this is by no means the case in many countries. I will argue, that irrespective of the national curriculum structure and content, there are good reasons to have these elements in the same subject, and that issues of moral guidance, ethical reasoning, religious commitment, and existential questions represent curriculum content that open a window to exploring basic issues of education as a moral enterprise. I will start by placing this in a wider educational context.

Problems in educational policy aims

Today, we can trace supranational influences as dominating trends in educational policy both in European countries and globally. One strong institutional actor influencing national governments' policies, is the Organization for Economic Co-operation and Development (OECD). Here, education is seen as a critical factor in the development of modern societies. The yearly publication *Education at a Glance* of 2016, is anchored in the 17 Sustainable Development Goals agreed upon by the United Nations in 2015.[2] Goal number 4 seeks to ensure "inclusive and equitable quality education and promote lifelong learning opportunities for all."[3] The aim of *Education at a Glance* is to document and analyze the structure, finances, and performance of education systems in the 35 OECD countries and a number of partner countries. This is done by "developing and analyzing the quantitative, internationally comparable indicators that it publishes annually in *Education at a Glance*. Together with OECD country policy reviews, these indicators can be used to assist governments in building more effective and equitable education systems."[4] Nevertheless, the editorial of the 2016 edition underlines that such measurement does not cover all the aims of education:

> What matters for people and for our economies are the skills acquired through education. It is the competence and character qualities that are developed through schooling, rather than the qualifications and credentials gained, that make people successful and resilient in their professional and private lives. They are also key in determining individual well-being and the prosperity of societies.[5]

OECD has, together with international bodies like UNESCO, for decades emphasized the importance of 'lifelong learning' as a key part of future strategies for global development. This refers to a "holistic and integrated, inter-sectoral and cross-sectoral approach."[6] In the strategy of the UNESCO Institute for Lifelong Learning, this is operationalized by foregrounding the social and economic dimensions, with references to 'transversal skills' (such as social, communicative, collaborative, and intercultural competences), and 'values,' but with no references to religions, worldviews, identity, or existential and ethical questions. UNESCO sees education as a crucial factor in development out of poverty and establishing more sustainable and democratic nation-states and local communities around the world. Also, OECD acknowledges that socio-economic inequality and lack of democratic institutions is detrimental to the development of good societies. In this way, these bodies can be said to launch certain moral values, but they are not really addressing ethics, understood as the justification and anchoring of moral values. While the social and economic ambitions mentioned are widely shared, there are also some questions that can be raised regarding this view of education.

The first issue regards the tendency to exclude those aspects of life that have to do with religions, worldviews, and ethics. I am not implying that the educational policies of OECD and UNESCO do not allow for education about issues like religions, worldviews, and ethics, and many of their member states have such education. It seems, however, that there is an implicit 'privatization' of this as a field of life, and these results in limitations on the contributions of these fields to the curricula of publicly funded schools. Competence in religions, worldviews, and ethics is perhaps allowed in the form of knowledge about religious, worldview, and ethical positions, but these positions are not seen as contributing to a diverse 'we.' Instead, the perspective on issues of human diversity seems to be addressed mainly through 'intercultural education', which clearly has become mainstream policy. The reason given is that this competence is critical in order to work efficiently in heterogeneous groups.

It is not self-evident that the specifics of religions and worldviews are sufficiently represented by being included in 'culture.' While many definitions of 'culture' certainly include 'religion' as one of several aspects, there is also a danger of reductionism. Treating religions and worldviews mainly as either private opinions or as certain collective practices, but still outside the public domain, excludes the active role of religions and worldviews in politics and societal change. This has consequences for the field of ethics and morality, beacause for many people, the motivation for being morally responsible is built on religion and/or worldview.

In spite of the claim that '9/11' was a wake-up call for a new view on religion in the public sphere (Jackson, 2014b, p. 15), it is not easy to detect this change in the educational policies of UNESCO and OECD. Here, another international organization, the Council of Europe (CoE), has taken a different path. Based on a Committee of Ministers' recommendation from 2008, CoE opened the possibility for a 'religious dimension' of intercultural education (CoE, 2008). A follow-up process during the next six years finally led to the publication of *Signposts – Policy and Practice for Teaching about Religions and Non-Religious Worldviews in Intercultural Education* (Jackson, 2014b).

Signposts since then has been translated into at least 14 languages, which seems to suggest interest, if not increasing influence, in many countries. So far, the strongest critique has come from the English context, where there are allegations that the kind of 'contextual' approaches *Signposts* belongs to are influenced by 'securitization' and by a lack of interest in distinct religious traditions and their dogmas. It is claimed that these are post-modern views on religions and distort what religion really is about (Gearon, 2017; Jackson, 2017; Lewin, 2017). *Signposts* is based on recent research and suggests a series of strategies and practical ideas in order to improve the way education deals with both the religious dimension and non-religious worldviews. A key element, is the recognition that religions and worldviews are complex and changing phenomena, which children and young people experience in their everyday world in different ways. In order to represent this diverse reality, education should look for ways of teaching and learning that are creative and secure that different voices are heard in the classroom.

Children do not only encounter religions and worldviews in their neighborhood, but also through different media, and it is therefore argued by *Signposts* that education needs to address critically the representation of religions and worldviews. It differentiates between the level of tradition, group, and individual. This involves an acknowledgment of the difference between organized religion and personal religiosity, which raises issues not only for primary and secondary education, but for teacher education as well. Following this, the personal and existential dimension of religions and worldviews needs to be given attention in school. In order to facilitate personal engagement, dialogical approaches are helpful, but this raises issues about the classroom as a safe space for interpersonal communication. Establishing such a safe space is not a straightforward issue; it does not imply that controversial issues should be avoided, nor does it mean avoiding challenging students (Osbeck et al., 2017).

While both the OECD and the Council of Europe argue for the necessity to improve and develop public education, OECD puts its main emphasis on self-governed learning, flexibility, and intercultural competences, while traditional transmission of an established knowledge content is less emphasized. The CoE also accepts the fact that diverse and changing societies demand change in educational systems, but here the main concern is towards human rights and citizenship, thereby combining knowledge about religions and worldviews with questions about moral action and ethical values. This leaves more space for exploring knowledge about religions and worldviews, including issues of existential meaning, and puts these questions at the core of the big challenge: how to live together with diversity, rather than trying to overcome it. For CoE, 9/11 was a wake-up call, and since then, other incidents have continued to remind people of the importance of addressing the question of how to live together with diversity. So, why does this receive so little attention in mainstream educational policy?

Critique of educational policy

One possible answer can be drawn from the work of the educational philosopher Gert Biesta. He has for several years characterized the demands that the World Bank and OECD put on education as "strong, secure, predictable and risk-free" (Biesta, 2014, p. 3). He has criticized the UNESCO policies on lifelong learning by arguing that they treat learning as something intrinsically good and that this overlooks the tensions in the concept of learning. According to Biesta, a particular understanding of learning, namely as focused on objectives and targets, has led to an instrumentalization of education. This threatens to reduce the challenges of teaching to finding the best method for achieving learning outcomes. Biesta claims that this way of thinking implies a lack of interest in what he calls 'subjectification,' while the other two key dimensions of education, 'qualification' and 'socialization,' sometimes have been overemphasized (Biesta, 2006). Paradoxically, this does not mean that the dominant trends in educational policy ignore the individual. On the contrary, he finds that there is a tendency to individualize the concept of learning, making it a never-ending demand on the individual to adjust and adapt to the demands of the surroundings. The result is an "increasing tendency to turn politic problems into learning problems, thus shifting the responsibility for addressing such problems from the state and the collective to the level of the individuals" (Biesta, 2006, p. 67). This places much too heavy a burden on the individuals, and it is contrary to the legitimate concern for the individual in education. What Biesta refers to as "subjectification" has to do with how individuals "can be independent – or as some would say, autonomous – subjects of action and responsibility" (Biesta, 2014, p. 64). In Biesta's view, subjectification is both an ethical and a political process that education should facilitate. It does not happen as an automatic consequence of human development, nor is it a result of finding proper educational methods. Instead, it has to be deliberated democratically. Therefore, Biesta underlines the necessity to discuss what education is for (Biesta, 2015).

In Biesta's terminology, the aim of education can be seen as a continuous deliberation about the balance between subjectification, socialization, and qualification. While sometimes 'Western' education is seen as individualistic, Biesta, with Miedema, argues that moral education is sometimes used in order "to secure the cohesion and integration of society, [based on] the idea that there is a basic lack of (social) morality, and sometimes even simply a nationalistic or patriotic agenda" (Biesta & Miedema, 2002, p. 174). The political developments in Europe over the last decades suggest that such an agenda is on the offensive, and in a paradoxical way, they mirror the closed and collective hierarchy of values and the social control that they criticize migrant communities and non-Christian religions for supporting.

Based on a criticism of the 'learning paradigm,' Biesta argues for a more relational, emancipatory, and virtuous education, and he even suggests that education should include learning to live with the risk. Like Hattie and other educational researchers, Biesta emphasizes the importance of the teacher, but he does this in a completely different way. His argument is that we should restore the importance of teaching, by emphasizing that this act is something more than facilitating learning processes. It "must be understood as something that comes from the *outside* and brings something *radically new*" and that this is risky (Biesta, 2014, p. 52; italics in the original). Following this, Biesta claims that teaching is asymmetrical and existential, dealing with truth, or rather with "*how* the individual relates to the truth" (2014, p. 54). In order to do this, Biesta favors a teacher education that focuses on the formation of the whole person. The aim should be a professional formation of the ability to make informed and creative judgments, and to do all this in a personal way, through exemplification (2014, pp. 134–137).

The type of educational policies that Biesta argues against is not conservative in the sense that they focus on stability, tradition, and transmission of established knowledge. Rather, they tend to embrace and address the constant changes that characterize late-modern societies. In doing this, they draw on educational theory that emphasizes individual character building and transferable skills and abilities, rather than formal credentials and rote learning. One problem with such aims of education is that they try to deliver precisely the type of flexible human beings that are needed from the perspective of modern capitalism. They also fail to offer ways of questioning the aims. Other educational researchers with quite different positions from Biesta have criticized the same development by pointing towards the failure to address issues of social class and inequality (Young & Muller, 2010). This shows that the problems involved transcend the educational sector and have to do with society at large. They also transcend the traditional demarcation lines between conservative and radical politics and make it necessary to address issues that go deeper.

This resonates with Zygmunt Bauman, who argues that the 'liquid modernity' of our times has contributed to an uncertainty that is not only political, social, and economic, but even existential (Bauman, 2007, p. 92). Further, Richard Sennett argues that this changes the work ethic by pushing the individual sense of duty on the defensive, while flexible individuals, working in groups, is the preferred ideal (Sennett, 2001, p. 122). The result may be both corrosion of (individual) character and undermining of (collective) community. Referring to both Levinas and Ricoeur, Sennett (2001) claims that the flexibility demanded in late-modern societies implies that we leave behind the moral insight that somebody needs us and that we are dependent on one another (p. 181). This suggests that moral as well as existential issues need to be addressed by education in new ways.

In spite of the critical and somewhat dystopian perspectives offered on the present social order, these thinkers are not giving up resistance; rather, they argue for a preoccupation with the human condition and the relations between human beings. In this way they are able to address the 'big' issues of politics and economics, but also to allow the 'small' issues related to oneself, neighborhood, and workplace to exemplify the 'big' ones. Most of us live our lives in the small world of family, work, and neighborhood.

Drawing on these reflections, I will, in the following, exemplify some of the questions about aims of education by pointing towards a particular local context in order to discuss how questions related to moral commitment and existential issues can be played out in practice.

Teaching and learning about religions and worldviews in public education

The liquid modernity of Bauman resembles other descriptions of what can be termed 'modern plurality,' referring to the shifting and multi-layered under-standings of the self and society that have become part of the post-modern or late-modern era (Skeie, 2006). 'Modern plurality' can be differentiated from 'traditional plurality,' which refers to the diversity of traditions and groups living together in society (the term 'multicultural' is sometimes used in relation to traditional plurality. While traditional plurality has been around for centuries, modern plurality is different and still something to which we try to adjust. The critical remarks raised about present educational policy trends imply not that they ignore socio-cultural diversity and issues of moral insecurity, but that these issues are treated mainly as a potential threat to social cohesion and individual qualifications for work life. Therefore, policies usually support intercultural education, but the interest in education about religions and worldviews is lacking. Therefore, the introduction of a religious dimension to intercultural education by the Council of Europe was controversial (Jackson, 2014a, 2016). One possible reason for this controversy is the lack of recognition that religions and worldviews can have a significant role in the ways people find meaning in life and how they understand morality.

While modern education tends to emphasize individual flexibility and diversity management from an economic perspective, this does not necessarily fit with the dynamics of collective and individual identity processes. Today, we see people's identities not as bounded and stable constructions, but this does not mean that they should be shaped only according to the needs of employers and public bureaucracy. Among those factors that are important to identification processes, are commitments to collective religious and worldview positions. This can limit the individual's flexibility by the rules and values of the tradition in question, but the individual commitment to distinct values and beliefs of a tradition can also make it possible to stand up against the pressure from surroundings. Instead of seeing existential and ethical issues as entirely 'private' ones, belonging to the family sphere, they should be recognized as part of how children and youth find their way in life. The issues of meaning and action in relationship with others and the world should therefore be taken seriously in education.

In order to achieve this, it seems necessary to include an introduction to religions and worldviews in education on different levels; as historic and collective traditions, as different practices and beliefs by groups in changing socio-cultural contexts, and as individual commitments and interpretations. These levels interact, influence each other in complex ways, and intersect with other identifications, like ethnicity, gender, national background, etc. (Baumann, 1999). The local, public school, where students with different backgrounds meet, is a well-placed arena for exploring and discussing if and how religions and worldviews have importance for meaning and action. By doing this, students learn to know one another and to form a community, even if this may be a community of disagreement (Iversen, 2018). This is largely in line with an official European understanding of public education, where students are seen as social and political beings and actors, encouraged through citizenship education (Higgs, Sheehan, Currens, & SpringerLink, 2012). Religious education, therefore, overlaps with citizenship education and with education about, for, and through human rights (Vesterdal, 2016).

There is, however, a plethora of models for religious education, suggesting that this subject area does not 'fit' easily into modern educational systems (Davis & Miroshnikova, 2013; Rothgangel, Jackson, & Jäggle, 2014; Rothgangel, Skeie, & Jäggle, 2014; Rothgangel, Jäggle, & Schlag, 2016). As already mentioned, the collective level of religion has raised tensions regarding the influence and representation of different religious communities in religious education, bringing about different solutions (Meer, Pala, Modood, & Simon, 2009). In particular, the individual level of religion seems to raise issues about legality and human rights (Fancourt, 2014, Relaño, 2010). Hardly any other school subject is politically in such a vulnerable and volatile situation and volatile situation politically. I believe this to be the case not only for historical reasons, but it is also an indication that the kind of issues raised by this type of subject 'disturbs' the order of education. This can be productive. First, it introduces issues that are particularly difficult to operationalize into learning outcomes and transferable skills; secondly, it suggests that education should address 'issues of moral and spiritual guidance.' This disturbing issue is relevant not only for religious education, but also for other school subjects, particularly within humanities and social studies, where existential and moral issues are central (Skeie, 2012, 2015). One great achievement of *Signposts* is that it provides a rationale for religious education across Europe, irrespective of the many shapes that religious education may take.

The following section provides an example of how teachers and researchers worked together to implement some type of constructive 'disturbance' in religious education and in history and philosophy teaching and learning, along the lines discussed in this section. The rationale was to learn about diversity of religion and belief among students and beyond school, inspired by elements of *Signposts*. In particular, we therefore focused on engaging individual students with one another across the everyday division lines among peer groups, and linking school with the wider community. The key term was 'dialogue,' initially thought mainly in terms of a conversation between individuals and groups, but also prompting an inner dialogue among students.

Dialogue in religious education – an empirical example

The background for the research project presented here is a local case study placed within a wider study of interreligious dialogue under the leadership of the University of Hamburg (Aminpur, Knauth, Roloff, & Weisse, 2016; Ipgrave et al., 2018). The project reported here was set in a city in western Norway, where teachers of religion, history, and philosophy in upper secondary school co-operated with university-based researchers. The aim was to investigate whether and how dialogical approaches could contribute to knowledge about religions and worldviews, existential issues, and moral reasoning. It was based on ideas about dialogical teaching, coming from the practitioners as well as researchers. The teachers also wanted to explore the educational potential of relating to interreligious practice inside and outside the school, and they wanted to investigate together the role of religions and worldviews in the public sphere. The researchers were particularly interested in what dialogue could mean in an educational context, what competencies teachers need to have in order to lead such processes, and how the students received this. The specific design of the project was negotiated in a community of practice, where teachers and researchers decided together how to proceed, based on action research principles. In short, the ambition was to engage the students, in a more personally involving and relational way, with existential and moral issues related to religious and worldview diversity.

The collaborative group of teachers and researchers formulated the project aims within the framework of the subject area curriculum as these were expressed in the relevant syllabi. The concept of 'dialogue' was understood as focusing on the participation and involvement of students with different 'voices.' They were encouraged from the outset to show tolerance for others' views, willingness to explain one's own position, and readiness to engage in an exchange about personally important issues in life. In both religious education and history and philosophy education, the dialogue activities focused on existential and moral issues where the teachers thought that religion or worldview would be particularly relevant. This was initially justified by referring to earlier dialogue activities that took place after the terrorist attacks in Norway on July 22, 2011. After this incident, religions and worldviews took a more prominent place in public discourse. The different interventions or exercises in the case study were developed jointly by teachers and researchers and evaluated and adjusted during the project in line with action research principles (Zuber-Skerritt, 2002; Altrichter, Feldman, Posch, & Somekh, 2008).

The school where the case study took place, had mainly students from a Norwegian-majority background, most of them with a relatively high level of school achievement. An initial e-based questionnaire to the students confirmed this and showed that they had different experiences with religious education from before and that the majority described themselves as non-religious or atheist. The first intervention was to expose them to a well-known scholar/practitioner in the field of dialogue activities, who introduced them to basic elements of dialogical practice, including a list of 13 very practical and process-orientated points. These were used as guidelines in the project both by teachers and students:

- include participants in the planning;
- get to know each other as persons;
- create equality;
- start with simple issues;
- use active listening;
- try to pose good, open questions;
- do not force others to think as you do, and be prepared for mutual adjustments;
- do not force certain opinions on others;
- compare own ideals with the ones of the dialogue partner and compare own practice with the other person's practice;
- do not accept others' arguments uncritically;
- be open and honest, but draw your own limits regarding what you want to talk about;
- accept and give space for emotions;
- the dialogue can always continue.

The first exercise in which the students engaged involved dialogues where they talked together in groups of three, on their own, following the guidelines above. The framework was as follows: first, each student would present a personal story about values and beliefs that were important to him/ herself. When this first round was over, the three would ask open questions to one another for a certain amount of time and answer them. No particular result was expected, apart from the effect of getting to know more about one another. The reason for this intervention was to expose the students to diversity in order to have this as a backdrop for the following interventions. A follow-up anonymous e-survey was distributed to all students immediately after each intervention. This showed that the experience was somewhat new and disturbing for many students. Previously, they had hardly talked to peers outside their usual ingroup, and certainly not about important issues in life. They discovered that they were more different than they had thought, but also that they were able to understand the difference better when they knew the personal story of the narrator. As they got to know one another better, they discovered the self-reflection that was part of any position, and this had been hidden from them initially. In their responses, they underlined the importance of following guidelines when conducting the dialogue and argued that this increased mutual understanding.

In the second exercise, each individual student was asked to engage in a dialogue with someone outside the school who was willing to be a representative of some kind of religious or worldview community. In addition, the students were asked to observe some kind of gathering or ritual. The students chose from a wide range of groups and formal representatives, mainly by identifying groups themselves. In some cases, they were helped out by a volunteering family member or friend. After the dialogues were over, the students shared experiences and observations with their full class and teacher. The teachers asked them to present a paper discussing and reflecting on particular challenges related to the dialogue with representatives. Some quotations from e-surveys show how challenging this was:

I had to work hard not to engage in a discussion, keeping my questions to myself.

It was really new to me to sit down with a Muslim in his Mosque to talk with each other.

The natural dialogue was disturbed when somebody started to make notes and obviously asked questions they had formulated in advance.

I could recognize my own feelings (unpleasantness, nervousness, excitement, being outsider).

I became acquainted with myself and my own view of life (learned more about myself than about anybody else in the room).

It was very special to listen to how religious peoples themselves experienced religion.

The third and final intervention of the project was a 'dialogue-café,' organized by the teachers. It was set in an informal atmosphere, but with a tight program. First, a pastor in the local Church of Norway and a local imam together introduced their respective religious traditions. They knew each other well and were experienced participants in interreligious settings. The students had the opportunity to ask questions they had prepared beforehand and the representatives gave their answers. After this, the students, in groups of about five, were seated around separate tables and were encouraged to talk about issues coming from the previous round of questions and answers. They were also asked to discuss certain themes that were presented on 'menu-cards,' distributed on the tables, with the following themes: homosexuality and religion; religion and science; the problem of evil; collective school worship in church before Christmas; religious clothes and utterances in the public sphere; and the question of whether religion is outdated. Each table had a student moderator who remained, while the other participants changed every 20 minutes. Each change provided all students with a completely new group. The entire class level of students at the school participated in this, and the large hall buzzed with the activity of 200 students for about two hours. The researchers recorded conversations around five tables throughout the sessions, collected the paper tablecloths that were offered for taking notes or drawing on, and also observed the general interaction in the room. The following is taken from the observation notes:

This setting was quite different from the more calm dialogues of the earlier interventions, and it even brought forward discussions and reactions on the project as a whole. The communication was rather open and considerate, in many cases referring to the experiences from dialogues earlier in the project or to the guidelines for dialogue activities. The moderators intervened several times in order to structure the conversation, secure the possibility for all to contribute, or to comment on certain utterances that were considered out of order. Observations of the young students' behavior in this setting showed that many seemed rather self-conscious and positioned themselves distinctly. Regarding the practice of dialogue ideals, many were rather optimistic on behalf of themselves, but seemed more pessimistic on behalf of the group. While acting with a degree of autonomy and criticism towards one another, asking questions about rationale and motivation for positions on the issues of the menu-cards, they also expressed a wish to share and act more like a community. They declared themselves to be inclusive and to be interested in one another's views. In many ways, the café exposed in public many of the different reactions and experiences from earlier phases of the project. Afterwards, the researchers asked the students, in a new e-survey, to present their reactions, and some examples may convey the varying opinions: 'I have experienced that I am just as stubborn as religious people are.'

Some felt that it was difficult to present themselves as Christian in a majority of atheists/agnostics. If the chair had asked everyone to present their background first, they would have known who was present and behaved differently: 'It was OK to disagree (I have earlier not enjoyed settings where I disagreed with people), and it is no problem having a good conversation in spite of disagreements.'

After finishing the project, the students seemed positive about engaging in dialogue and saw the potential to learn from and through dialogue. While learning about distinct religions and worldviews, they also discovered the value of deeper conversation with peers about existential issues, across religions and worldviews. They even discovered that a type of strong-headed secularist positioning was almost hegemonic in several classrooms. This was confirmed by the teachers, referring to their impression from many classroom conversations. The occasional experiences of students attacking the views of others, or a majority dominating in a way that silenced others, pointed towards a lack of 'safe space' in the classroom. When this came into the open through dialogues, the religious students told of how they experienced this silencing.

In the elective history and philosophy subject, conducted with a smaller group of students, the case study was designed with greater focus on moral reasoning and ethical issues. They started off with the study of two different theoretical positions, one group focusing on Jürgen Habermas and the other on Michel Foucault. Then they were asked to apply the theory to a media debate, where the issue of religious headscarves was discussed. The idea was to investigate what the theoretical approaches contributed to the analytical abilities of the students. The two groups were able to use their respective theoretical starting points constructively, and with a degree of sophistication, and could identify examples of how the media debate rather covered up than revealed the 'real' moral issues at stake. This learning experience was followed by another assignment, where the students were asked to form 'committees' where they would discuss how to solve a controversial issue in the school and try to reach consensus. The issue at stake was the controversial arrangement of a common church service in the cathedral near the school before Christmas holidays. Analyzing this, the researchers found that the students were not able to utilize their theoretical instruments, but instead entered into heated discussions based on their individual positions. Evaluating the experience afterwards, they commented on the change from an engaging, but decontextualized, 'school assignment' to a sensitive and context-bound issue that was much closer to their daily (school) life. The 'committees' therefore had much difficulty in reaching consensus.

One feature that could be observed in both case studies was the dominant tendency to harmonize differences, if possible. This created a community of agreement through silencing or keeping silent about differing views and by enforcing aspects of the conversation that seemed to cover the differences. Regarding the content of the dialogues, a strong wish for greater knowledge about religions and worldviews appeared; in particular, the students wanted to learn about how different people understood their positions from the inside. In relating to this, the skill of asking good and open questions was much appreciated.

At the practical level, the students' advice to teachers was the following: It is important and fruitful to use the opportunity to get out of the physical classroom context. The use of small groups is vital to ensure that dialogue works properly, preferably with fewer than five persons in each group, in order to deal with the type of questions that were raised. In terms of timing, it was regarded as necessary to respect the students' need to proceed at an easy pace from the beginning in order to adjust to new ways of working with the content. In addition, a theoretical framework is necessary; students need to know that the teachers know what they are doing and why. In terms of organization, the students preferred a composition of dialogue groups that always secured difference. Their experience was that, if this was not the case, they tended to echo one another. Finally, the students would prefer this type of work to be integrated with the 'normal' teaching, and not regarded only as a specific project or experiment.

The teachers planned the project together with the researchers but had the full responsibility for the teaching and learning activities. They argued that the project had given the opportunity to address a series of issues related to morality (the 'menu-cards') and spirituality (personal story) that engaged the students emotionally and to combine this with different forms of meta-reflection on what had happened. This was done through classroom conversation about each intervention, through questions in the regular e-surveys and through the feedback from researchers about findings towards the end of the project. Some of the teaching instruments succeeded in creating a situation of equality and 'safeness' that facilitated both learning about others and learning about oneself.

In the following section, I will use this project to discuss some of the issues raised in the first part of the present chapter. The focus is on the role of education in the wider context of public deliberation about existential and moral issues.

The potential of dialogue in education

A strong motivation behind the project referred to in the previous section, was that the teachers wanted to include the personal dimension more in teaching and learning about religious and worldview traditions. The personal dimension meant that individual students were encouraged to share views, both regarding distinct religions and beliefs, but also about issues of life. These are addressed by and interpreted by religious and worldview traditions as well as by the persons who identify with them. Moral issues are placed at the interface of individual and collective identities and, in the case studies on dialogue in education, such issues were central. While the students tried to come to terms with their differing religious and worldview positions, they also struggled with different moral positions. In the last case, they could not solve the entire problem by showing 'tolerance' towards the other. In deliberating moral issues, they had to reach some kind of agreement or to account for disagreements.

The personal and existential openness required by the dialogical approaches that were used influenced many of the students also in their deliberation about moral issues. To some extent, they discovered that other students had their reasons for taking a different stand on certain issues. These stances were, for some, anchored in strong collective commitments; however, a strong current across positions was arguments based on individualism. So, both the respect for difference and the defense of the legitimacy of collectively binding positions of a religious character was grounded in the right of the individual to choose her/his own way. Further, the findings from the case study of the history and philosophy subject suggest that the increased skills in reasoning on a level of principle or theory (ethical level) did not really make it easier for the students to discuss practical issues (moral level).

Since the case studies did not follow individual students through the project, it is difficult to know what happened with regard to their self-reflection. Nevertheless, several utterances reveal that individual students entered into dialogues with themselves about their own behavior, the interpretation of their life story, and positions, prompted by the encounter with other students who told about their behavior, life story, and positions. The social sharing of plural positions contributed to the personal reflection on plural self-understandings, not unlike the meta-perspective that Hermans describes in Chapter 2 of this volume. This suggests that relations with others may feed the inner dialogue with oneself and that such processes can be facilitated in education. At a more general level, one could argue that the plurality of positions and self-understandings, combined with individualism, does not necessarily lead towards moral or existential indifference. There is a possibility of a 'morality of pluralism' based on the recognition that no position can have an undisputed authority (Kekes, 1993). This resonates with many of the practical consequences drawn by Hermans and Hermans-Konopka (2010), arguing the importance of the 'leader' to ensure that people are helped to make a position shift in order to see from a different perspective (p. 327). If we see the teacher as such a leader, however, our case studies did not confirm Hermans's view that the leader needs to participate in the perspective shifts her/himself. Nevertheless, as a result of employing a dialogical approach, different levels of sharing were observed as taking place among the students. There was the sharing of collective positions (the positions of religions and worldviews), a sharing of personal positions (self-positioning), and a sharing of how an individual experiences and narrates her/his individual life (identification). When several levels of sharing become visible like this, it may lead to meta-reflection about sharing, in this particular case about 'dialogue' and its effects.

The different levels of sharing also raise questions about the presence of different understandings of life and of different moralities. To what extent do they exist apart from the way they are made relevant in conversation and practice? This resonates with a critique of using essentialist definitions of religion in religious education, for at least two reasons. Firstly, some definitions are based on assumptions about shared human experience or some kind of religious *a priori*, underlying the different religious traditions (Hylén, 2014). Secondly, teaching about religions and worldviews often tends to take 'world religions' or similar notions as the starting point, without problematizing the existence of such phenomena (Owen, 2011). This does not imply that the teaching and learning process needs to start with a focus on different definitions. In the project outlined earlier, the starting point was more inductive, asking students to share narratives about their relationship to religious and worldview positions or traditions. The narrative approach tended to generate diversity by its own dynamic. According to many students, this opened up their minds, because they had never experienced listening to what may be termed the 'spiritual story' or 'life story' of another student or young person. We do not know to what extent the students included moral issues and ethics in these conversations, and it certainly would be interesting, in a future project, to shift the attention from 'existential' to 'moral' life story in the assignment. What we do know, is that the students discovered the relational character of both their ethical and spiritual learning, the way they were dependent on one another in gaining moral insight. This resonates with the relational ethics of Kenneth J. Gergen. More particularly, it relates to his educational reflections about the advantage of "replacing traditional assessment with practices of evaluation built into dialogic and collaborative processes" (see K. J. Gergen, Chapter 1 in this volume).

The project seemed to indicate that interpersonal sharing of significant knowledge about one another's lives is not particularly frequent, at least among the researched student group. This may lead to reflections about the social relations between young people in particular or even between people in general in late-modern societies. In Zygmunt Bauman's words:

> The roots of microphobia are banal, not at all difficult to locate, easy to understand though not necessarily easy to forgive. As Richard Sennett suggests, "the 'we' feeling, which expresses a desire to be similar, is a way for men and women to avoid the necessity of looking deeper into each other" [. . .] The drive towards a 'community of similarity' is a sign of withdrawal not just from the otherness *outside*, but also from commitment to the lively yet turbulent, invigorating yet cumbersome interaction *inside*.
>
> (2007, p. 87)

If this is a correct observation about the cultural climate of today, the teachers did not start with what may seem to be 'known,' but rather with the 'unknown.' They put the students in a situation where they saw one another from a different perspective than they were used to. By getting closer to the experiences of one another, the students were put in a position to question the 'community of similarity' or 'sameness.' The students in this particular school did not appear from the outset to be particularly diverse in terms of religions, lifestyle, or national or ethnic background. In many ways they communicated sameness, and they even tended to gravitate towards consensus in many situations where controversy might have been expected. Their early encounter with the life stories of fellow students challenged them to acknowledge significant differences in beliefs, way of life, and values that were not visible to them beforehand, and this influenced their discussions about moral issues in the following interventions.

It was only after they had discovered and reflected on the internal differences in the student group through the dialogue activities that many of them were able to uncover the discursive hegemony exercised in the classroom. They could see that secular worldviews dominated and religious ones tended to be silenced, and that they were part of this dynamic themselves. This paved the way for envisaging a possible different kind of community, not based on silencing, but also not based on agreement. Instead, it may be what Lars Laird Iversen has termed a "community of disagreement" (2012, p. 62; 2014). By sharing what is considered personal and therefore different, the students established a community that did not depend on the other persons sharing similar experiences or views. My point in terms of educational philosophy, is that meeting the unknown does not exclude the possibility that this may be of high relevance for the persons involved.

Existential issues in (religious) education

The dialogue between students had the personal narrative as a key element. The idea was that this would make it easier to practice the dialogue guidelines, because the individual story would be respected as belonging to the person speaking and not something that could easily be questioned from an argumentative position. I think it is important to recognize that what the students were asked to tell was their own story, not just any story that was important to them or could reveal something about themselves. This gave the story the possibility to raise existential questions. The reason for using this terminology is that 'existential' is open towards both secular and religious worldviews but, at the same time, keeps the personal dimension intact. In addition, 'existential' may include the moral dimension.

Kirsten Grönlien Zetterqvist, has argued on a philosophical basis, drawing on Heidegger and others, that an existential question can be defined by having both a substantial and a functional aspect. This means that the existential question includes a particular person raising an issue of significant importance in a particular situation (Zetterqvist, 2009, p. 133). These three elements all need to be in place: a person asking, a question that is asked, and a phenomenon towards which the question is directed. The person is unique but, by raising an issue, he or she is entering into a dialogue with oneself. The issue is the 'substance,' but it is not the question or issues alone that makes it significant and important. The importance is a function of the person's relationship with oneself and the world. The source of the question can be religious, or it can be directed towards a religion, but if it has to do with religion; this is not what makes it existential in itself. The existential character of the question is also functional. It has to be important for the person. Similarly, a moral issue can be existential, but it does not have to be. It all depends on the urgency it has to the person. Finally, the person, the content and the urgency are all placed in a particular context; the question is not asked on behalf of all humans in all times and places. Existential questions are therefore not necessarily what are called 'big questions'; they become big for the person involved.

This way of thinking about existential questions corresponds to the way Paul Ricoeur understands and discusses (individual) identity (1992). There is always somebody 'having' an identity; this is the person telling the story. At the same time, the story itself is the content of the identity. One cannot have the one without the other, but they are also not the same. In this way, identity is dialogical, it is the person telling a story about oneself; 'oneself as another.' The dialogical character of identity corresponds to the dialogical character of narratives, which always contain several possible meanings, depending on time and place, and on who is telling and who is listening (Ricoeur, 1990).

This interpretation of the dialogical processes found in the practice development project presented in this chapter is hard to fit into the kind of educational thinking that focuses mainly on learning outcomes. Rather, it takes the starting point of people doing things together, which is closer to the perspective of teaching than that of learning. While learning needs impulses from outside, it tends to focus mainly on the receiving person. Teaching is always a relational practice, since there is no teaching without students. Of course, this does not imply that all teaching considers students' needs or interests, but the relation is always possible to investigate. In the project, the teachers initially established an unfamiliar (learning) situation; but, soon after, the students themselves were set in a position where they took over the responsibility. This not only concerned the educational content, but also had ethical implications. The students were treated as responsible actors, capable of managing their own learning outside the classroom and therefore out of teacher control. Further, they were encouraged to reflect on their own action and thinking and to communicate this to others. In this way, the educational activity itself had to carry the educational value; it was, in Biesta's terms, 'risky.' However, the personal encounter with other fellow students and non-students in the local community infused the educational activity with an authenticity that would be hard to establish within the classroom framework. This interpersonal and authentic dimension made the ethical aspect of the learning process more pronounced. The teachers were not themselves part of the dialogue activities, but facilitated the students' dialogue among themselves, offering a possibility for 'self-guidance' which, according to the students, contributed to an increased self-reflection.

Conclusion

The example presented supports the argument that moral and spiritual self-guidance can be an important element of public education, and this can be (partly) achieved through religious education. The discussion in this chapter has shown that 'guidance' is not a 'master' guiding the 'apprentice,' but rather a teacher facilitating dialogical processes to be set in motion. These processes can include sharing on several levels and for the individual to reflect on existential questions, understood as important questions, including moral ones, raised by a person in a particular context.

Notes

1 This curriculum has been recently replaced after 20 years, and the new text does not have an official translation. Here is a similar section from the new core curriculum (translated by the present author): 'School shall both contribute to general

education ['Bildung'] and education (as qualification). These are interconnected and interdependent. The principles for working with learning, development, and general education ['Bildung'] shall help the schools to accomplish this double assignment. The basic education is a vital part of a life-long process of education that has the aim to achieve freedom of the individual, independence, responsibility and compassion for others. Education shall give the students a good basis for understanding themselves, others and the world, and to make good choices in life. Education shall also give the starting point for participation in all fields of education, work life, societal life. At the same time children and youth live here and now and school shall recognize the inherent value of childhood and young life' (Regjeringen, 2017, p. 10).

2 Retrieved June 30, 2017, from www.un.org/sustainabledevelopment/sustainable-development-goals/

3 OECD. (2016). *Education at a glance 2016: OECD indicators* (p. 13). Paris: OECD Publishing. Retrieved from http://dx.doi.org/10.187/eag-2016-en

4 OECD. (2016). *Education at a glance 2016: OECD indicators* (p. 3). Paris: OECD Publishing. Retrieved from http://dx.doi.org/10.187/eag-2016-en

5 OECD. (2016). *Education at a glance 2016: OECD indicators* (p. 13). Paris: OECD Publishing. Retrieved from http://dx.doi.org/10.187/eag-2016-en

6 Retrieved June 30, 2017, from http://uil.unesco.org/unesco-institute/mandate

References

Altrichter, H., Feldman, A., Posch, P., & Somekh, B. (2008). *Teachers investigate their work: An introduction to action research across the professions* (2nd ed.). London: Routledge.

Aminpur, K., Knauth, T., Roloff, C., & Weisse, W. (Eds.). (2016). *Perspektiven Dialogischer Theologie: Offenheit in der Religionen und eine Hermeneutik des interreligiösen Dialog*. Münster: Waxmann Verlag.

Baumann, G. (1999). *The multicultural riddle: Rethinking national, ethnic, and religious identities*. New York, NY: Routledge.

Bauman, Z. (2007). *Liquid times: Living in the age of uncertainty*. Cambridge: Polity Press.

Biesta, G. J. J. (2006). *Beyond learning: Democratic education for a human future*. Boulder, CO: Paradigm Publishers.

Biesta, G. J. J. (2014). *The beautiful risk of education*. Boulder, CO: Paradigm Publishers.

Biesta, G. J. J. (2015). What is education for? On good education, teacher judgement, and educational professionalism. *European Journal of Education, 50*(1), 75–87. doi:10.1111/ejed.12109

Biesta, G. J. J., & Miedema, S. (2002). Instruction or pedagogy? The need for a transformative conception of education. *Teaching and Teacher Education, 18*(2), 173–181.

CoE. (2008). *Recommendation CM/Rec(2008)12 of the committee of ministers to member states on the dimension of religions and non-religious convictions within intercultural education*. Retrieved from https://wcd.coe.int/ViewDoc.jsp?Ref=CM/Rec(2008)12&Language=lanEnglish&Site=CMBackColorInternet=DBDCF2&BackColorIntranet=FDC864&BackColorLogged=FDC864

Davis, D., & Miroshnikova, E. (Eds.). (2013). *The Routledge international handbook of religious education*. London: Routledge.

Fancourt, N. P. M. (2014). Re-defining "learning about religion" and "learning from religion": A study of policy change. *British Journal of Religious Education*, 1–16. doi:10.1080/01416200.2014.923377

Gearon, L. (2017). Secularisation and the securitisation of the sacred: A response to Lewin's framing of the Gearon-Jackson debate. *British Journal of Educational Studies*, 65(4), 469–480.

Habermas, J. (1989). *The theory of communicative action. Vol. 2: Lifeworld and system: A critique of functionalist reason*. Boston, MA: Beacon Press.

Hermans, H. J. M., & Hermans-Konopka, A. (2010). *Dialogical self theory: Positioning and counter-positioning in a globalizing society*. Cambridge: Cambridge University Press.

Higgs, J., Sheehan, D., Currens, J. B., & SpringerLink. (2012). *Schools, curriculum and civic education for building democratic citizens* (Vol. 2). Rotterdam, NL: Sense Publishers.

Hylén, T. (2014). Closed and open concepts of religion: The problem of essentialism in teaching about religion. In B. O. Andreassen & J. R. Lewis (Eds.), *Textbook gods: Genre, text and teaching religious studies* (pp. 16–42). Sheffield: Equinox Publishing.

Ipgrave, J., Knauth, Th., Körs, A., Vieregge, D., & Lippe, M. V. D. (2018). *Religion and dialogue in the city: Case studies on interreligious encounter in Urgan community and education*. Münster: Waxmann Verlag.

Iversen, L. L. (2012). *Learning to be Norwegian: A case study of identity management in religious education in Norway* (Vol. 21). Münster: Waxmann Verlag.

Iversen, L. L. (2018). From safe spaces to communities of disagreement. *British Journal of Religious Education*. Published online, February 28, 2018. doi:10.1080/01416200.2018

Jackson, R. (2014a). The development and dissemination of Council of Europe policy on education about religions and non-religious convictions. *Journal of Beliefs and Values*, 35(2), 133–143. doi:10.1080/13617672.2014.953295

Jackson, R. (2014b). *Signposts – policy and practice for teaching about religions and non religious world views in intercultural education*. Strasbourg: Council of Europe Publishing.

Jackson, R. (2016). Inclusive study of religions and world views in schools: Signposts from the Council of Europe. *Social Inclusion*, 4(2), 14–25. doi:10.17645/si.v4i2.493

Jackson, R. (2017). Who's afraid of secularisation? A response to David Lewin. *British Journal of Educational Studies*, 65(4), 463–468. doi:10.1080/00071005.2017.1358804

Kekes, J. (1993). *The morality of pluralism*. Princeton, NJ: Princeton University Press.

Lewin, D. (2017). Who's afraid of secularisation? Reframing the debate between Gearon and Jackson. *British Journal of Educational Studies*, 65(4), 445–461. doi:10.1080/00071005.2017.1305182

Meer, N., Pala, V. S., Modood, T., & Simon, P. (2009). Cultural diversity, Muslims and education in France and England: Two contrasting models in Western Europe. In J. A. Banks (Ed.), *The Routledge international companion to multicultural education* (pp. 413–424). New York, NY: Routledge.

Osbeck, C., Sporre, K., & Skeie, G. (2017). The RE classroom as a safe public space: Critical perspectives in dialogue, demands for respect and nuanced religious education. In M. Rothgangel, K. V. Brömssen, H.-G. Heimbrock, & G. Skeie (Eds.), *Location, space and place in religious education* (pp. 49–66). Münster: Waxmann Verlag.

Owen, S. (2011). The world religions paradigm: Time for a change. *Arts and Humanities in Higher Education, 10*(3), 253–268.

Peters, R. S. (1987). Aims of education: A conceptual inquiry. In R.S. Peters (Ed.), *Philosophy of education* (pp. 11–29). Oxford: Oxford University Press. (Originally published 1973)

Regjeringen. (2017). *Overordnet del – verdier og prinsipper for grunnopplæringen.* Oslo: Utdanningsdirektoratet. Retrieved from www.regjeringen.no/contentassets/37f2f7e1850046a0a3f676fd45851384/overordnetdel–verdier-og-prinsipper-for-grunnopplaringen.pdf.

Relaño, E. (2010). Educational pluralism and freedom of religion: Recent decisions of the European court of human rights. *British Journal of Religious Education, 32*(1), 19–30.

Ricoeur, P. (1990). The narrative function. In J. B. Thompson (Ed.), *Paul Ricoeur: Hermeneutics & the human sciences* (pp. 274–296). Cambridge: Cambridge University Press. (Originally published 1979)

Ricoeur, P. (1992). *Oneself as another.* Chicago, IL: University of Chicago Press.

Rothgangel, M., Jackson, R., & Jäggle, M. (Eds.). (2014). *Religious education at schools in Europe. Part 2: Western Europe.* Göttingen: V&R Unipress, Vienna University Press.

Rothgangel, M., Jäggle, M., & Schlag, T. (Eds.). (2016). *Religious education at schools in Europe. Part 1: Central Europe.* Göttingen: V&R Unipress, Vienna University Press.

Rothgangel, M., Skeie, G., & Jäggle, M. (Eds.). (2014). *Religious education at schools in Europe. Part 3: Northern Europe.* Göttingen: V&R Unipress, Vienna University Press.

The Royal Ministry of Education, R. A. C. A. (1997). *Core curriculum for primary, secondary and adult education in Norway.* Retrieved from www.udir.no/upload/larerplaner/generell_del/Core_Curriculum_English.pdf

Sennett, R. (2001). *Det fleksible mennesket: Personlige konsekvenser av å arbeide i den nye kapitalismen.* Bergen: Fagbokforlaget. (Originally published as *The corrosion of character: The personal consequences of work in the new capitalism,* 1998).

Skeie, G. (2006). Plurality and pluralism in religious education. In M. de Souza, G. Durka, K. Engebretson, R. Jackson, & A. McGrady (Eds.), *International handbook of the religious, moral and spiritual dimensions in education* (Vol. 1, pp. 307–320). Dordrecht: Springer.

Skeie, G. (2011). Teachers and researchers cooperating to develop new knowledge for religious education. *PANORAMA International Journal of Comparative Religious Education and Values, 23,* 92–105.

Skeie, G. (2012). Education between formation and knowledge: A discussion based on recent English and Nordic research in religious education. *Utbildning och lärande, 6*(2), 80–97.

Skeie, G. (2015). Memory and heritage in history education and in religious education: A cross-disciplinary investigation into social sciences and humanities education. In S. G. Parker, R. Freathy, & L. C. Francis (Eds.), *History, remembrance and religious education* (pp. 305–320). Oxford: Peter Lang Publishing Group.

Vesterdal, K. (2016). *The roles of human rights education in Norway: A qualitative study of purposes and approaches in policy and in upper secondary schools* (PhD thesis). Norwegian University of Science and Technology, Trondheim.

Young, M., & Muller, J. (2010). Three educational scenarios for the future: Lessons from the sociology of knowledge. *European Journal of Education, 45*(1), 11–27. doi:10.1111/j.14653435.2009.01413.x

Zetterqvist, K. G. (2009). En vidlyftig begreppsflora? Närläsning av en sjuttiotalsdialog. In K. G. Zetterqvist, G. J. Gunnarsson, & S. G. Hartman (Eds.), *Livet tillfrågas – teoretiska förutsättningar för en livsfrågeorienterad religionsundervisning [Life being questioned – theoretical foundations for a life-questions oriented approach to religious education]* (pp. 7–36). Stockholm: Stockholms Universitet.

Zuber-Skerritt, O. (2002). *Action learning, actions research and process management*. Bradford: Emerald Group Publishing.

Citizenship in an age
of plural moralities

11 The culturalization of citizenship in the Netherlands

Towards cosmopolitan sociabilities in a neoliberal epoch

Toon van Meijl

Introduction

Anxiety about the future characterizes contemporary politics in the Western world. In the wake of the credit crunch that hit the stock markets in October 2008 and triggered a long-lasting global recession, expectations of the future seem to have reached an all-time low around the world. Popular concern generally revolves around the unintended consequences of three long-term processes that are mainly beyond the control of politicians and policy makers. First, globalization as an economic ideology has intensified interconnectedness around the world, which simultaneously implies that governments of nation-states are no longer on top of their country's finances (Inda & Rosaldo, 2002). The saying goes that when Wall Street sneezes, the rest of the world might catch a cold, illustrating interdependency on transnational networks that are not managed from a single office but depend on multiple unforeseeable influences. This process, in turn, is intertwined with global policies of neoliberalization, which have introduced the market as a metaphor for society and social relations, nationally and internationally (Springer, Birch, & MacLeavy, 2016). At its heart, however, this economic ideology is based on a simple, utterly amoral idea, namely that of the cost-benefit-calculating individual. Life is understood as a competitive struggle among individuals, each of whom seeks to minimize her or his costs and maximize the benefits. One of the champions of neoliberalism was Margaret Thatcher, who even propounded that there is no such thing as society. This philosophy therefore also strikes at the heart of trust and integrity in public life. After all, if life is understood as a struggle among cost-benefit-maximizing individuals, the idea of a fair and harmonious society evaporates.

Both globalization and neoliberalization result relentlessly in increasing inequality, but their impact is even exacerbated by a third process: postcolonialism (Huggan & Law, 2009). The end of the colonial era leaves many societies with unresolved issues of recognition, redistribution, and reconciliation between peoples who used to be colonized and their former colonizers. Postcolonial relations are especially challenging in countries that are hosting large numbers of migrants and refugees, a phenomenon that is also mainly caused by globalization and neoliberalization. Anxiety about increasing immigration in Western countries emerged gradually over the past three decades, but it has definitely come to dominate debates in recent years. Some people even fear a so-called domino effect of Brexit in Britain, with a majority voting to leave the European Union at a time when it was struggling to deal with an unprecedented influx of refugees. Subsequently, the 2016 presidential election in the United States also focused on immigration, with an unexpected success of Trump's campaign to put America First. As a corollary, commentators expected Brexit and the election of Trump to set in motion a series of electoral victories by populist parties in the Netherlands, France, Germany, and Italy. In the polls in those countries, far-right parties without exception did very well, so they were supposed to grow exponentially with their campaign that focused on rescuing the nation-state from non-European immigrants. This has generated a debate about questions of belonging and how to cope with cultural diversity in nation-states, especially in Europe. Indeed, anxious politics in Europe revolve around one major issue: anti-immigration, especially anti-Muslim sentiments (Modest & De Koning, 2016; De Koning & Modest, 2017).

In this chapter, I will unpack the debate about the impact of migration on the nation-state, in particular with regard to the notion of citizenship. Not only is the relationship between states and citizens being recalibrated and reshaped in light of neoliberal reforms, but as a result of increasing cultural diversity, the notion of citizenship is also being reconsidered. Thus, migrants are not only made responsible for their own integration, but at the same time they have to meet much stricter criteria in order to qualify as full-fledged citizens. Over the years, the conditions for citizenship have been extended from political and economic criteria to cultural criteria. Citizens are increasingly expected to embrace cultural values that are deemed characteristic of liberal democratic nation-states, mainly revolving around the right to freedom of the individual irrespective of gender, religion, or sexuality. As a consequence, it may be argued that a distinction is made between different categories of citizens, between the original members of nation-states who are automatically assumed to support the principles of liberal democracy and those with a migration background who supposedly have not yet internalized its key values. Accordingly, mechanisms of inclusion and exclusion become operative, grounded in a fundamental distinction between 'us' and 'them,' between autochthonous inhabitants of the nation-state and allochthonous newcomers. Not infrequently, natives are considered to be morally superior in relation to migrants and their descendants, especially when their roots are located in non-Western countries. In fact, people with a migration background are virtually prevented from qualifying as full-fledged citizens and thus from belonging to the nation-state.

In this context, I argue that the shifting focus on culture in the debate about the integration of migrants is counterproductive. Alternatively, a new approach will be explored, one that does not aim at assimilating cultural differences, but that instead focuses on recognizing and appreciating human commonalities between different categories of people. Indeed, postcolonial societies in contemporary Europe are facing the challenge to rethink the outdated assumption of homogeneity in the nation-state and to design more inclusive models of society in which a diversity of values, traditions, and ways of life are recognized with a commitment to securing the flourishing of that diversity. In this chapter, the principles of such a model are found in dialogical self theory that helps to build bridges between partial but potent human commonalities.

I begin with a short overview of migration to the Netherlands in order to provide a sketch of the rise of cultural diversity. Subsequently, I describe and analyze the culturalization of citizenship in recent years, to be followed by a discussion of a number of critical analyses and alternative approaches, including Will Kymlicka's (2015) way out of the so-called progressive's dilemma, Nina Glick Schiller's (2016) proposition of focusing on cosmopolitan sociabilities, and Magdalena Nowicka and Steven Vertovec's (2014) conception of conviviality. In view of these discussions, it will be argued that dialogical self theory (Hermans & Hermans-Konopka, 2010) offers an encompassing perspective on all alternatives mentioned by providing the necessary bridges between the multidimensional self of individuals and their multicultural surroundings.

The demise of multiculturalism in the Netherlands

Although debates about diversity and citizenship are taking place in many countries, multiculturalism has probably come under fire nowhere nearly as much as in the Netherlands. This is intertwined with the recent reputation of the country as a so-called guiding country, a small nation-state that was supposed to be leading by example since the 1960s. The Netherlands was known as a laboratory for social and cultural change, boldly pioneering the legalization of prostitution, soft drugs, euthanasia, and gay marriage, while also proudly advocating tolerance of cultural diversity. Some 40 years later, however, immigration has become very controversial and highly politicized. The increasing number of refugees and other migrants is not only thought to be unsustainable, but many also fear that the national identity of the country is under threat. Against this background, some even contend that the Netherlands has turned racist and Islamophobic. The radical transformation of migration and integration policies in the Netherlands over the past few decades illustrates international processes of change throughout postcolonial Europe and elsewhere (Scheffer, 2007, 2011). For that reason, too, it is appropriate to take a closer look at the history of migration and integration policies in that small country on the North Sea.

Although the Netherlands has a history of welcoming refugees dating back several centuries, immigration into the country only started to increase steadily after World War II (Nicolaas & Sprangers, 2006). It started with the independence of Indonesia in 1945, after which many Indonesians who had collaborated with the colonial government of the Dutch decided to move to the Netherlands. In the early 1950s, when the economy was still in dire straits, many young people decided to emigrate to countries such as Canada, Australia, and New Zealand; but when the economy began growing again in the early 1960s, a shortage of laborers manifested itself on the labor market. It was decided to recruit workers abroad, first in southern European countries such as Spain, Portugal, and Italy, soon followed by Greece and Yugoslavia. Not much later, Morocco and Turkey were added as countries from where laborers were hired. Initially, foreign employees were labeled 'guest workers' since they were expected to return to their country of origin when the demand for labor would ease, and perhaps when they were thought to have made enough money to build up a decent life in their own countries. This assumption proved to be correct with regard to the majority of workers from European countries, where the economy was booming in the 1960s and 1970s as well. Many workers from Morocco and Turkey, however, decided to stay. Subsequently, they brought over their families, a process that expanded when their children, for cultural and historical reasons, continued to search for a partner in their home countries. Family reunion and family formation practices caused the emergence of sizeable communities of non-Western immigrants for the first time.

Immigration was intensified after 1975 when another Dutch colony became independent and the population of Surinam was granted the right to enter the Netherlands until five years after independence began. In the course of the 1980s, the Netherlands also began hosting increasing numbers of refugees from countries that were plagued by violent conflict or even war, such as Iran and Somalia. In the 1990s, many asylum seekers arrived from former Yugoslavia, Afghanistan, and Iraq (Gijsberts & Dagevos, 2009). At the same time, the expansion of the European Union with countries from Eastern Europe caused significant numbers of migrants from Poland and later also from Romania and Bulgaria to visit the Netherlands in order to work, a process that has continued to grow over the years. Finally, in recent years, an increasing number of refugees has also arrived from Eritrea, Afghanistan, and Iraq, but especially from Syria. As a consequence, the number of people settling in the Netherlands has been higher than the number of people departing for most years since the mid-1960s (see also Entzinger, 2003, p. 59). In 2017, the population totaled 17 million, with 9.9% of the population having a background in some other Western country, and 12.7% with a migration background in non-Western countries, especially Turkey (2.3%), Morocco (2.3%), Surinam (2.1%), and the Netherlands Antilles (0.9%) (CBS – Statistics Netherlands; www.cbs.nl/en-gb).

The steady influx of immigrants over the past 50 or more years has not only transformed the composition of the population, but it has also induced a change in government policies with regard to immigrants as members of the nation-state. The first shift occurred in the early 1980s when the Netherlands government recognized for the first time that most migrants would stay permanently rather than return home, which was argued to require a concerted policy effort to facilitate their integration in society. In the 1970s, *ad hoc* measures were still the rule, and facilities for migrants were short-term-oriented and scarce, but in 1983 a so-called Ethnic Minorities' policy was introduced. It aimed to achieve the equality of ethnic minorities in the socio-economic domain, inclusion, and participation in the political domain, and equity in the domain of culture and religion within constitutional conditions (Bruquetas-Callejo, Garcés-Mascareñas, Penninx, & Scholten, 2007, p. 15). The main drive behind this policy was the emancipation of ethnic groups, which were encouraged to participate in all spheres of society, including the political. An important assumption was that recognition of their distinct identities would stimulate the emancipation of ethnic minorities within local communities, while it was also expected to have a positive influence on their integration in the wider society.

By the early 1990s, however, several major changes had taken place. Ethnic minorities had almost doubled in size, and they were not only coming from the traditional countries such as Turkey, Morocco, and Surinam, but new flows also began to develop. In addition, a second generation was emerging within established migrant communities, one that was born and raised in their country of residence, speaking the language and being fully educated. These developments challenged the foundation of the Ethnic Minorities' policy, which became more difficult to implement as minorities were becoming larger, more numerous, and more heterogeneous (Entzinger, 2003, p. 70). It also turned out that it was not improving the social and economic situation of minorities, among which unemployment was extremely high. More importantly, however, criticism was increasingly also leveled against the focus on cultural rights and facilities in the Ethnic Minorities' policy, which were feared to harm rather than enhance participation in the labor market. Other aspects of criticism were soon added by the influential leader of the Liberal Party and head of the opposition in Parliament, Frits Bolkestein, who suggested in a public speech in 1991 that Islam was incompatible with liberal democracy and therefore a barrier to the integration of large numbers of immigrants with an Islamic background (Bolkestein, 1991).

These developments triggered the government to introduce a new approach in which less emphasis was placed on cultural emancipation, while the need for socio-economic integration was underlined more strongly. In 1994, the Ethnic Minorities' policy was abandoned and replaced with what was described as Integration policy. Integration as a political concept was considered as a process leading to the full and equal participation of individuals and groups in society (Entzinger, 2003, p. 72). Individuals were mentioned explicitly for the first time, which involved a gradual shift away from target groups to individuals who are in a disadvantaged position. Furthermore, a stronger focus was placed on the socio-economic incorporation through labor market and education measures while, finally, it also involved a shift away from cultural policies in collaboration with immigrant organizations (Bruquetas-Callejo et al., 2007, p. 17).

In the course of the 1990s, the position of so-called 'allochthones,' those of non-Dutch birth or ancestry (Yanow & Van der Haar, 2012), continued to be discussed in light of increasing arrivals of new immigrants and even more refugees. In response to growing concerns about the lack of integration of allochthones, many new initiatives were taken to improve the situation of ethnic minorities, one of which was a compulsory integration program for newcomers from outside the European Union. At the same time, a series of events around the turn of the millennium triggered a new shift in the public and political discourse on immigration and integration issues, which would later cause a revision of policy towards assimilationism.

One of the initial catalysts in this development was the new national debate that was provoked by publication of a newspaper article by Paul Scheffer (2000), a prominent member of the Labor Party. He expressed concern about the failure of integration policies that in his view had resulted in increasing segregation of an ethnic underclass of mainly Muslims. He argued that they do not feel attached to Netherlands' society and appear to be unable and even unwilling to integrate. Scheffer suggested that this long-term process would undermine social cohesion in society as well as the functioning of the liberal democratic state, especially because Muslims were alleged to hold illiberal views. To address the alarming situation, he advocated a 'civilization offensive,' not only to overcome deprivation of immigrants, but also to teach them Dutch culture and history and to make them accept the principles of liberal democracy.

Similar to the debates about minorities that took place in the early 1990s, Islam and the integration of Muslim immigrants were identified as being highly problematic. International developments, such as the 9/11 attacks in 2001 in the United States, reinvigorated such beliefs. In the Netherlands, these views gained popularity, especially following the rise of the populist politician Pim Fortuyn, who was rather outspoken about migration and integration issues, advocating 'zero migration' as in his opinion the country was 'full,' and calling for a 'cold war against Islam' (Bruquetas-Callejo et al., 2007, p. 19; de Koning, 2016a). Fortuyn's campaign was incredibly successful, winning many seats in the municipal council of the second-largest city in the Netherlands, but he himself was assassinated shortly before the national elections took place in May 2002. Still, his party won a landslide victory and entered Parliament as the second-largest party. This success changed the political discourse about immigration and integration radically. Subsequently, most political parties, including the Labor Party, adopted central aspects of this discourse that was described as 'new realism' (Prins, 2002). It revolved around the premise that the left political elite had reinforced the failure of integration policies by neglecting the 'real problems' behind a smokescreen of politically correct speech. This viewpoint was complemented with the contention that ordinary Dutch citizens were victims of it all.

This discourse of new realism brought a radical shift in integration policy, which was increasingly expressed in terms of a so-called 'clash of civilizations' (cf. Huntington, 1996). A series of proposals and measures followed to significantly diminish immigration figures, while mandatory forms of integration for newcomers and oldcomers alike were introduced. In these measures, the emphasis was more on the cultural adaptation of immigrants to Dutch society, on their duty to learn Dutch, to embrace Dutch values, and to assimilate into Dutch culture, in spite of widespread confusion and discussion about its contents. The concept of integration was thus narrowed considerably by effectively rephrasing it in terms of complete assimilation. In her zeal to force migrants to learn Dutch, one Minister of Integration, Ms. Rita Verdonk, even considered outlawing conversations in foreign languages in the public domain. In relation to the goal of integration, the focus shifted from searching for compatibilities between different categories of people, towards abandoning cultural differences (Entzinger, 2003). National norms and values were believed to be under threat, so policies had to be developed to secure their preservation and to prevent an anarchistic practice of plural moralities. A key feature of these new policies was the obligation to pass a civic integration exam before even entering the Netherlands to demonstrate language skills and knowledge about the country's cultural values and practices. The granting of renewals of temporary and permanent permits is subject to successfully passing these courses.

This new phase in integration policy continues today, although a range of minor amendments have been implemented. It is beyond the scope of this chapter to discuss detailed changes in integration policy that have taken place since its introduction in 2002, as its main basis has remained unchanged. Over the past decade, citizenship has become increasingly conditional upon embracing Dutch cultural values and practices as well as the principles of the (neo)liberal and democratic nation-state. The culturalization of citizenship is certainly not unique to the Netherlands (Duyvendak, Geschiere, & Tonkens, 2016). It has been analyzed by some as a form of neo-assimilationism (cf. Bruquetas-Callejo et al., 2007, p. 12), whereas others have scrutinized it as a culturalized form of racism (Schinkel, 2010, p. 269). In the next section, the implications of the radical shift in migration and integration policies for citizenship in postcolonial Europe will be discussed in greater detail.

The cultural politics of citizenship

Toward the end of the 20th century, public discourses on immigration have gradually become riddled with explicit references to 'culture' (Stolcke, 1995). The perceived problem of immigration is constructed as a political threat to national culture and identity because immigrants, in particular those coming from the Global South, bring along different cultural values, views, and practices. And European countries have become anxious about cultural diversity and plural moralities within their boundaries, since it is believed to affect social cohesion. This is related to an essentialized conception of culture that dominates contemporary political discourses about immigration, in which culture is understood as static, fixed, objective, consensual, and uniformly shared by all members of a group (Wikan, 2002). As a consequence, the nation-state is also conceived as founded on a bounded and distinct community, with a shared sense of belonging and loyalty predicated on a common language, cultural beliefs, norms, values, and traditions.

The new prominence of a narrow conception of culture and cultural difference in relation to notions of the nation has been elaborated by Steven Vertovec (2011). He argued that imagining the nation in terms of a cultural dichotomy between 'us' and 'them' is not unique to nationalist thinking, but that it is more and more present in ordinary thought and practice. It has become part of a so-called form of 'banal nationalism,' implying that cultural notions of nation are ingrained in forms of common sense (Billig, 1995). In this debate, Marianne Gullestad (2002) drew attention to the 'imaginary' dimension of this taken-for-granted kind of 'sameness' that is usually based on rather vague and ambiguous content. A significant supposition of this type of thinking is that we know who we are and what constitutes our sameness, because we also think that we know who we are not and what constitutes our difference from others (Gullestad, 2006).

A key device for constructing a national imaginary is, according to Vertovec (2011), the conceptual triad consisting of identities, borders, and political orders. Not only is some sense of cultural identity presumed to characterize a people, but this identity is believed to be contiguous with a territory, demarcated by a border, within which laws and a moral economy underpin a specific social and political order (Vertovec, 2011, p. 245). This order, which is conceived to be different from other orders outside the border, is built on a sense of collective identity that is constructed and reproduced through an arrangement of representations that are expressed in the form of narratives, public ceremonies, and written and unwritten regulations as well as expectations of civil behavior. Public debates about national culture and identity often condense around specific representations that serve as emblems of larger political categories, national models, and cultural sets of meaning, such as the head scarf in France or the murder of the filmmaker Theo van Gogh by a Muslim activist in the Netherlands (Vertovec, 2011, p. 248). Such emblems and events become key symbols which reflect assumptions about 'us' versus 'them.'

In contemporary Europe, these nationalist, if not racist (Schinkel, 2010; de Koning, 2016b) versions of culture increasingly dominate popular imaginaries of the nation. Conjunctural processes such as neoliberalization, globalization, and transnationalism are perceived as threatening established ways of life and pose challenging questions regarding national culture and identity (Grillo, 2003, p. 167). People tend to think they are deprived of their 'own' culture, and as a result, a form of cultural conservationism has emerged that aims at protecting cultural authenticity (Grillo, 2003, p. 160). Thus, nation, race, culture, and identity are woven together in complex ways in a range of national traditions and give rise to different anxieties about so-called 'strangers' who in this type of thinking are categorically excluded from standard constructions of the nation-state. Indeed, these processes on which nation-states are constructed and reproduced also shape the ways that immigration and immigrants are perceived and received. Wimmer and Glick Schiller (2002) have described this type of thinking as methodological nationalism, which is based on the assumption that the nation/state/society is the natural social and political order of the modern world. The adjective 'methodological' refers to the approach of shaping the nation by representing immigrants as alien disturbers of a natural order.

In nationalist discourses that are based on bounded models of society and state, immigrants are regarded as adverse elements of an orderly working of the state. Wimmer and Glick Schiller (2002, pp. 309–311) outline four reasons why migrants become the subject of political controversy and subsequently also the object of policy making. Immigrants are perceived as foreigners to the community that shares loyalty towards the state, because they are assumed to remain loyal to their state of origin, thus destroying the isomorphism between people, sovereign, and citizenry. Immigrants are also believed to destroy the isomorphism between people and nation, which has never been imagined as plural or diverse, not even in immigrant societies. In addition, immigrants are believed to break the natural connection between people and the solidarity group since they are not meant to be part of the system of social security that the national community developed, because they come 'from outside' into the national space of solidarity. Finally, each move across national frontiers becomes an exception to the rule of sedentariness within the boundaries of the nation-state, which is ultimately also based on a nationalist imaginary of territory that contains the nation. Cross-border migration is always an anomaly when migration is analyzed from the viewpoint of methodological nationalism, which departs from the assumption that normally people stay where they are supposed to 'belong,' that is, to their nation-state. In migration studies, belonging has thus been naturalized in the context of modern nation-states (Wimmer & Glick-Schiller, 2002, p. 311).

An upshot of methodological nationalism is that in times of globalization when migration increases, the nation and the state no longer automatically overlap, with due implications for notions of citizenship. When society and nation still coincided, citizenship routinely involved inclusion in society. When societies become ethnically, culturally, and ethically more heterogeneous as a result of migration, however, citizenship of immigrants is immediately problematized. The nation is no longer considered to be overlapping with society, which causes the state to reorient itself regarding society and its various categories of citizens: autochthonous versus allochthonous citizens, those who were born elsewhere, or who descend from people born elsewhere, and who are thought not to belong naturally to the nation-state because they have crossed borders. As a corollary, citizenship becomes a political instrument to distinguish between natural members of the nation-state and unnatural members of the nation-state who have to be resocialized in order to become integrated. In plural societies, citizenship is used as an instrument of exclusion because it is founded upon a methodological nationalist conception in which the nation is naturally closed in view of a differentiation between autochthonous citizens and aliens. In this context, Schinkel (2010) has argued that citizenship becomes virtualized since immigrants may become citizens in the formal sense, but they are generally construed as insufficiently integrated so that their citizenship is reduced from actuality to virtuality. Accordingly, citizenship has increasingly become a virtue, which enables a distinction between formal citizenship and moral citizenship (Schinkel, 2010, p. 271).

Formal citizenship refers to legal rights and duties of citizens as members of states. Formal citizenship, however, has reference not only to the legal status of members of a legal-political order, but also to social rights and obligations as member of a society. Social citizenship is, in order words, part of formal citizenship. Moral citizenship, on the other hand, entails an extralegal dimension of normativity, as a formal citizen is not necessarily also a good citizen. The conception of moral citizenship is not only factual and descriptive, but it is also counterfactual and prescriptive, demanding people who are considered to be culturally and morally anomalous to adjust to mainstream thought and action and to embrace individual rights to freedom regardless of gender, religion, and sexuality (Schinkel, 2010, p. 268; see also Schinkel & van Houdt, 2010). Not only are cultural differences to be assimilated, but plural moralities are to be abandoned as well. Thus, the distinction between formal and moral citizenship is not simply a theoretical issue, but it has far-reaching implications for practices and policies. The moralization of citizenship has in recent years been given substance in national and local policies of immigrant integration, especially since the turn of the millennium when integration discourses made a decisively assimilationist turn and citizenship became increasingly culturalized.

Although the scope of this contention reaches far beyond the Netherlands, I will briefly revisit the case study of this country to illustrate the shift in emphasis from formal citizenship to moral citizenship with a few examples derived from Dutch discourses of integration. In recent years, they focus increasingly on notions of culture, norms, and values and proper definitions of Dutchness and of Dutch society. At the same time, plans to find out and reach agreement about what is actually understood by Dutch culture were implemented, resulting, for example, in a Dutch Historical Canon. The government that was installed in 2017 has made lessons in the national anthem mandatory at all schools, that are also obliged to take all children to the

Rijksmuseum (National Museum) and Parliament at least once in the course of their school career.

A moral shift has also taken place in civic integration processes that most recently were set out in the Charter Responsible Citizenship of 2010. This document departs from a so-called shared responsibility between government and citizen for integration, but the liberal values of freedom and individual responsibility have become non-negotiable. Non-Western immigrants especially are assumed to be lacking liberal values such as tolerance, respect, and participation in society, which are consequently made into the heart of integration policies. These values have also been turned into a central component of civic integration exams, which are increasingly also set up in moral terms. Formerly, formal citizenship through naturalization was the end of the integration process. Granting citizens equal rights was considered to be the key principle of integration. Currently, however, formal citizenship is regarded only as the beginning of integration, which still has to be consummated through a moral conversion (Schinkel & van Houdt, 2010). This specific change in policy is intertwined with a widespread belief that second-generation migrants are insufficiently 'integrated' by still being culturally different and, accordingly, morally alien. The priority that is now given to moral citizenship enables the state to address those belonging to the second generation of migrants as people who are still lacking citizenship in cultural or moral terms. As a consequence, citizenship has been transformed from a right to be different to a duty to be similar, that is 'assimilated,' both culturally and morally (Schinkel & van Houdt, 2010, p. 204).

Between diversity and solidarity: the progressive's dilemma

The neo-assimilationist integration policy is built not only around anxieties about the suspected dilution of national identity and morality, but also around the dwindling sustainability of the welfare state. In welfare states, governments take responsibility for education and healthcare, for example; but in the 1970s, these had become largely unsustainable in view of declining birth rates. As a consequence, neoliberal reforms were introduced to restructure the welfare state, with due consequences for the relationship between government and citizens, with citizens becoming responsible for their own welfare. This policy move also implied that immigrants have gradually been made responsible for their own integration, as outlined earlier. This change followed from the dilemma that emerged around the fear that there is a trade-off between facilitating immigrants and maintaining the welfare state. Large-scale immigration, bringing about cultural diversity and plural moralities, may make it more difficult to build or sustain the feelings of shared belonging and solidarity required to maintain a robust welfare state. Extending justice to newcomers may weaken justice for the less-well-off members of the autochthonous working class.

The Canadian political scientist Will Kymlicka (2015) has described this predicament as the progressive's dilemma: a choice between neoliberal multiculturalism (inclusion without solidarity) or welfare chauvinism (solidarity without inclusion). He offers a way out of this dilemma by constructing a third option: inclusive solidarity through a multicultural welfare state. This argument extends from his liberal theory of multiculturalism, in which he argues that policies of multicultural recognition and social redistribution are not necessarily in conflict with each other (Kymlicka, 1995). Partly in view of his far-reaching influence as the first person, along with his fellow countryman Charles Taylor (1992), to radically rethink the status of ethnic minorities in multicultural nation-states, it is interesting to unpack his reflections on the political and cultural impasse, and to consider the alternative that he offers.

Kymlicka (2015) argues that we should first recognize that the categories on which constructions of cultural diversity are based are arbitrary at best, and meaningless at worst. 'Others' are defined in many different ways: some researchers look only at those immigrants who have not been naturalized, others include anyone who was foreign-born regardless of their legal status; some look only at the first generation of foreign-born people, others assume that the native-born second generation also should count; some researchers include immigrants from all foreign countries, others count only people from outside the European Union, on the assumption that fellow Europeans are not really 'others'; and so on. For the purposes of testing whether cultural diversity erodes a feeling of national belonging, should a Surinamese child born in Amsterdam, for example, be counted among the national 'we' that is being challenged by immigration, or amongst the immigrant 'they' who are believed to pose a challenge?

Once we recognize the contingency of arbitrary perceptions of otherness, it might seem that the very idea of a progressive's dilemma relating to immigration is misguided. There is no reason to assume in advance that immigrants form a 'they,' or indeed that the native-born form a 'we': the lines of identification are likely to be infinitely more complex and variable (Vertovec, 2007). To assume otherwise is to commit the sin of methodological nationalism (Wimmer & Glick Schiller, 2002): naturalizing and reifying the nation-state, exaggerating its internal cohesion, and assuming that it defines the natural boundaries of the nation, the state, and society. As pointed out earlier, much of the existing literature on the progressive's dilemma does indeed suffer from this sort of methodological nationalism, thereby implicitly and uncritically justifying an essentialist form of nationalism.

The progressive's dilemma, however, cannot be dismissed so easily because nationalism, with its inevitable constructions of an imaginary 'we' versus a strange 'they,' is an omnipresent feature of the contemporary world and immigration is widely considered an abnormal contamination of naturalized nationalism. Furthermore, the progressive project of defending immigration and multiculturalism also leads into different directions from that of the progressive project of defending national solidarity in the context of the welfare state. Neither is more or less natural: they are both projects for making the world more decent and humane. And the challenge is to think about how to reconcile them, and how to minimize any negative effects each might have on the other.

So the progressive's dilemma may be summarized as follows: if national solidarity is important as a progressive political resource, how can it be reconciled with support for immigration and multiculturalism? Kymlicka's (2015, p. 12) alternative suggests the development of a form of multiculturalism that is tied to an ethic of social membership, i.e., a form of multiculturalism that enables immigrants to express their cultural identities as modes of belonging to, participating in, and contributing to a nation-state. This type of multiculturalism would simultaneously promote a form of solidarity in the nation-state that is based on the premise that one way to express pride in citizenship is to be a proud Moroccan-Dutchman or Iranian-Dutch woman, and that social and cultural activities of one group are understood as forms of belonging and of investing in society, not primarily in an economic sense, but also in a social and even moral sense. Not surprisingly, Kymlicka (2015, p. 13) refers to Canada and Australia as examples of nation-states in which multiculturalism and national solidarity are intrinsically linked, which has led to promising examples of inclusive solidarity – or, if you like, a liberal multicultural form of nationalism.

Cosmopolitan sociabilities and conviviality

Kymlicka's article and argument was discussed at great length on the pages of the journal in which it appeared, *Comparative Migration Studies* (2016), with contributions by Adrian Flavell, Nina Glick Schiller, Nasar Meer, Godfried Engbersen, and Rainer Bauböck. Most of the responses to Kymlicka's essay share his view that the supposed progressive's dilemma needs to be critically re-examined since there is no hard empirical evidence that multicultural policies are responsible for, or reinforce, welfare state retrenchment. Furthermore, they all discuss the potential political trade-offs between, on the one hand, openness for new immigration and multicultural recognition of diversity and, on the other hand, social solidarity within the welfare state.

Although in his rejoinder, Kymlicka (2016) regards the discussion as friendly, some aspects in this conversation trigger quite some controversy. One of these is Kymlicka's liberal view of nationalism in combination with multiculturalism. Glick Schiller (2016), for example, contends that while Kymlicka addresses in his article the critique of methodological nationalism (Wimmer & Glick Schiller, 2002), he does not adequately respond to it. Starting from a historical conjunctural analysis, Glick Schiller (2016, p. 2) warns that most European welfare states evolved in a context where nationalism served to justify the extraction of value from colonies, rather than as a source of inclusive solidarity with migrants and minorities. In light of a historical perspective on the colonial past of European nation-states, she therefore argues that Kymlicka lacks sufficient reflexivity which she deems necessary in order to acknowledge inextricable links between past nation-state building in Europe and North America, massive extraction of wealth, and associated struggles for justice of which the effects continue to linger in the contemporary era of migration.

Glick Schiller (2016) also points out compellingly that Kymlicka's argument that the nation-state is necessary for the preservation of welfare regimes is flawed, not only because he obscures the sources of national wealth, but mainly because he unquestioningly conflates the concepts of nation-state and society. Since migration and innovations in communication technology enable people to maintain transnational connections, nation-state and society are, after all, no longer automatically congruent. Boundaries between societies have become more fluid and dynamic, with migrants and many others living in more than one society simultaneously. Indeed, the idea that nation-state and society are linked is old-fashioned, going back to Durkheim and Tönnies. Nowadays, increasing numbers of people have a multiplicity of identities and move in between societies with due consequences for the boundaries of the nation-state becoming ever more fuzzy.

The critique of Glick Schiller revolves essentially around Kymlicka's view being rooted in an ethnic lens that is founded on cultural difference. As a consequence, he inevitably maintains a binary logic that makes a distinction between those who belong to the nation and those who do not. The latter are defined as 'strangers' to whom we respond with a different dimension of affect, namely that of humanitarianism rather than solidarity. In Kymlicka's words, all forms of justice to strangers is humanitarian rather than solidaristic, which implies that he does not manage to abandon the sin of methodological nationalism. Instead, he revives archaic conceptions of alterity that conceive of strangers as a challenge to the age-old constitution of society as a stable nation-state.

In view of the ethnic foundation of Kymlicka's perspective, Glick Schiller (2016) proposes the notion of 'sociabilities' as an alternative to the ties of nationhood. It refers to how people in their everyday lives build all sorts of social relations based on shared interests, emotions, and aspirations within a range of networks and settings. Everyday sociabilities are, in her view, based not on tolerance of ethnic or cultural differences, but instead on recognition of partial but potent human commonalities, on common domains of affect, mutual respect, and shared aspirations. She refers back to the German sociologist Georg Simmel (Glick Schiller, 2016, p. 7), who noted that sociability consists of relations in which one 'acts' as though all were equal, precisely because everyday interactions are not about difference, but about human domains of commonality that emerge from some of those interactions. Accordingly, Glick Schiller (2016, pp. 6–7) argues that a focus on cosmopolitan sociabilities might lead to more inclusive solidarity, with cosmopolitanism also being understood as built on domains of commonality rather than tolerance of difference.

Glick Schiller is not the only one who has made a plea for shifting the focus from ethnic differences to domains of commonality that she described as cosmopolitan sociabilities. Magdalena Nowicka and Steven Vertovec (2014) have made a similar point by suggesting that the concept of conviviality might equally serve the purpose of exploring conditions of living together in multicultural societies. In their joint introduction to a special issue entitled *Comparing Convivialities: Dreams and Realities of Living-with-Difference*, they show some of the ways conviviality may be used as an analytical tool to explore and analyze human modes of togetherness in multicultural spaces.

Nowicka and Vertovec (2014, p. 344) focus on the need to negotiate shared meanings in the contemporary world and to offer the concept of conviviality as an alternative to multiculturalism, which they argue, following Paul Gilroy, is positioned in a world of 'racial hierarchy.' The advantage of the concept of conviviality is that it renders racial and ethnic differences unremarkable, since they become ordinary instead. Based on the Latin roots for 'with' and 'living,' the term conviviality has long been associated with friendly and festive traits, but Nowicka and Vertovec demonstrate that it can also be used for understanding human relations in a sense of interdependency at the root of human existence. The advantage of conviviality above a range of other notions, including cosmopolitanism and multiculturalism, is that it is not political. It offers a new vocabulary to discuss a collective without referring to fixed categories of ethnicity or cultural otherness, even though it does have a normative dimension that conveys an optimal social setting for conditions of cultural diversity and moral plurality. Instead of focusing on difference, it highlights mutually respectful relationships among neighbors in common spaces. As such, it shifts the focus toward others in the context of everyday life, thus making multicultural spaces more positively interactive, or, conversely, by making multicultural spaces more convivial through everyday practices and routines of people inhabiting them (Nowicka & Vertovec, 2014, p. 350).

Dialogue in everyday multiculturalism

The concepts of cosmopolitan sociability and conviviality resonate with many scholars who have conducted research in multicultural neighborhoods (e.g. Wise & Velayutham, 2009; Vollebergh, 2016), and who have drawn attention to everyday lived reality of cultural difference in super-diverse cities and spaces (see also M. Gergen, Chapter 12 in this volume). Wise and Velayutham (2009) especially have collected numerous narratives about interminglings and encounters present in multicultural situations around the world, where people rub along most peacefully; where in spite of cross-cultural discomforts, inter-ethnic exchanges take place and people live positively with cultural difference. If indeed one looks closely at the question of how various social actors negotiate cultural difference on the ground, it appears that there is a widespread lack of insight into experiences of positive recognition by diverse people in everyday situations. In this context, Greg Noble (2009) has argued that youngsters with a migration background who are growing up in and between different cultures prefer to neglect their ethnicity, which they frequently feel is not the most significant aspect of their identity. A focus on ethnic aspects of identity, however, is usually embedded in the 'politics of recognition,' which, from the viewpoint of young people themselves, fails to capture the complex nature of social being for second-generation migrants. Highlighting, if not objectifying, ethnicity is experienced as a kind of 'boxing in,' excluding other identifications that they value much more, including age, gender, and subcultural features such as food, clothing, music, etc. Noble (2009) therefore argues that everyday recognition involves recognizing others in their full humanity, rather than as representatives of a particular category or group. In such an approach, the situated sociability of young people's identities is foregrounded: multiple and fluid attachments, the temporality of being, and the situated and provisional nature of subjectivity (see also Wise & Velayutham, 2009).

This approach, in turn, might be given greater analytical depth by bringing to bear dialogical self theory (van Meijl, 2012, 2013). The cultural complexity of contemporary societies is after all closely related to multiplicity and dialogical interlinkages between different cultural positions in the lives of individuals. For that reason, too, the dialogical self is a useful construct, not only for the analysis of multicultural identifications and for relating plural, competing conceptions of identity to the notion of a person as a composite of multiple, often contradictory self-understandings; but also for analyzing the reflection and implications of plural and dialogical selves at the level of society.

In short, the dialogical self may be described as a dynamic multiplicity of *I*-positions in the landscape of the mind, intertwined as the mind is with the minds of other people (Hermans, Kempen, & Van Loon, 1992; Hermans & Kempen, 1993; see also Hermans, Chapter 2 in this volume). Dialogical self theory is inspired, on the one hand, by Bakhtin's (1984) metaphor of the polyphonic novel, which allows for a multiplicity of positions among which dialogical relationships may be established; and, on the other hand, by William James's (1890) classic distinction between 'I' and 'me.' James described the 'I' as "the self as knower," as the observing agent. The 'me,' on the other hand, was portrayed as "the self as known," as the object of self-observation. On the interface between these traditions, Hermans and Kempen (1993) have argued that the 'I' has the possibility to move from one spatial position to another in accordance with changes in situation and time. The 'I' fluctuates among different and even opposed positions, and has the capacity to endow each position with a voice so that dialogical relationships between positions can be developed.

Thus, it may be argued that migrants in multicultural societies are often involved in a dialogue between different conceptions of their cultural identity, between viewpoints rooted in their home country and viewpoints that are dominant in the country to which they have migrated. The contrasting voices speaking in their self function like interacting characters in a story, involved in a process of agreement and disagreement. Each of them has a story to tell about her/his own experiences. As different voices, these characters exchange information about their respective 'me's,' resulting in a complex, narratively structured self.

Bakhtin (1981, p. 360) especially proves very helpful for the purpose of acknowledging the dialogue in which people in multicultural spaces find themselves. He describes "hybrids" as having two voices, two languages, two consciousnesses, two epochs; being situated at "the collision between differing points of view on the world" but also "profoundly productive historically" and "pregnant with potential for new world views" (Bakhtin, 1981, p. 360). Thus, Bakhtin creates the possibility for the self to be conceived of as a dynamic multiplicity of different and even contrasting positions or voices that allow mutual dialogical relationships.

Hermans (2002, 2018) has also drawn attention to the similarities between self and society, both functioning as a polyphony of consonant and dissonant voices, since there is no essential difference between the positions a person takes as part of the self and the positions people take as members of heterogeneous societies (see also Hermans & Hermans-Konopka, 2010, pp. 31–32). As a consequence, the dialogical self may be considered a "society of the mind" (Hermans, 2002) to the extent that different and contrasting cultures are represented in the diverse repertoire of collective voices playing a part in a multivoiced self. This insight, in turn, raises questions regarding the mixing of cultural positions or voices. Should we conceptualize of different cultural identifications of people living in multicultural societies as two separate cultural positions that are available and between which a person shifts from time to time? Or, alternatively, is a third position emerging that may be a mixture of two original positions? And if a third space emerges for the construction of a new, hybrid self, do the original positions retreat or even vanish, or do they continue to be accessible in their original form depending on changes taking place in spatial positions?

For several reasons, the conception of the self as multivoiced and dialogical has proved a valuable device for the analysis of the dynamic connections between the global and the local at the level of personal identifications (Hermans & Dimaggio, 2007). In a globalizing world, people are no longer living in bounded and relatively isolated societies that are radically different from other societies. Instead, an increasing number of people are living on the interfaces between societies, implying intimate contact with different cultural customs, which also explains why approaches based on methodological nationalism are outdated. The increasing interconnectedness of societies and peoples, however, leads not only to an increasing contact between different cultural groups, but also to an increasing contact between different cultural conceptions within individual persons. This compounds the socio-cultural development of migrants, especially children and adolescents of migrants (van Meijl 2012, 2013; see also König, Chapter 7 in this volume). Intercultural contact leads to the emergence of a multiplicity of cultural positions or voices coming together in the self of single people. And such positions may become engaged in mutual negotiations, agreements, disagreements, tensions, and conflicts between cultural values, views, and practices. The global-local nexus is, in other words, not just a reality outside the individual, but it has penetrated the self of people living in multicultural societies who have no option but to engage into a dialogue between various cultural positions and plural moralities (see also Wijsen, Chapter 3 in this volume).

An additional reason why a dialogical conception of the multicultural self is required to orchestrate the dynamic relationship between local and global institutions, and between pre- and post-migration values and views, is intertwined with the necessity for migrants to interact with people from a different cultural background by recognizing and accepting their alterity. This is unavoidable in a world in which divisions between different cultures can be bridged only by means of dialogical exchange. After all, only dialogue may contribute to making cultural differences meaningful and comprehensible (Hermans & Kempen, 1998). Since other persons and groups with different cultural customs are increasingly part of an extended self in terms of a multiplicity of contradictory voices or positions, a dialogical conception of the self seems therefore also indispensable.

As we have observed in the debate about citizenship in the Netherlands, however, dialogical relationships are frequently riddled with hierarchy. Different cultural positions may not be valued equally, neither in society nor in the self. Hermans and Kempen (1993, p. 73) take the hierarchical ranking of cultural positions into account by highlighting the concept of dominance as an important feature of dialogical relationships between self and other, which they, in turn, exemplify with reference to the relationship between self and community (see also Hermans & Hermans-Konopka, 2010, pp. 38–40). If the self is defined as a multiplicity of different *I*-positions, it may be argued that the community is able not only to address the self in a variety of identifications, but also to let the self know how these identifications, and the way the self functions in them, are approved. In contemporary European societies, for example, where citizenship is primarily understood in cultural and moral terms, migrants are expected to adjust to the cultural values of their new country and to neglect the cultural aspects of their identity derived from their country of origin. Thus, the self of migrants is monitored by the community approving or disapproving their behavior and concomitant construction of a cultural identity. Thus, communities also have the capacity to make some identification more dominant than others. And the dominance of cultural communities in the identification process not only organizes but also restricts the multiplicity of possible identifications in the public arena of multicultural societies.

The implications of this view of the (dialogical) self for rethinking relations between cultural diversity in multicultural societies are fundamental. Contrary to the individualistic conception of the self, the most important implication of the dialogical perspective on the self is that it is not an intra-psychic but a relational phenomenon that transcends the boundaries between the inside and the outside, between self and other (van Meijl, 2012). The constant dialogue between different voices within a self's discourse reflects dialogical relations between different cultural positions in society. The self is, in other words, a society of mind that mirrors dialogical relations at other levels of society. Thus, a dialogical conception of individuals as plural and composite persons is not only significant for understanding how migrants deal with cultural diversity in their daily lives in multicultural societies, but it also opens up the possibility for a dialogical perspective on multicultural relations and plural moralities in contemporary European nation-states.

Concluding remarks

Against a backdrop of globalization and migration, neoliberal reforms and the yet unfinished process of decolonization, European nation-states increasingly think that their future might be at stake. The identity of the nation-state and its cultural heritage is believed to be under threat of an allegedly unceasing influx of foreigners, migrants, and refugees. In response, the boundaries of nation-states are being reinforced, with due implications for all citizens with a migration background. Criteria for citizenship are strengthened and extended with cultural norms and moral principles, partly derived from the right to individual freedom irrespective of gender, religion, and/or sexuality. As a consequence, citizens with a migration background are systematically excluded from the traditional view of the nation-state. In representations of European nation-states, there is no place for those whose roots are located elsewhere. Even second- or third-generation descendants of migrants are refused the right to belong in the country where they were born and raised.

It goes without saying that the view of the nation-state as homogeneous and bounded is not only incorrect, but also completely outdated. All cosmopolitan cities in the western provinces of the Netherlands, for example, have become so-called majority-minority cities where the formerly clearly defined majority group of Dutch people has turned into a minority group like all other ethnic groups. Needless to say, this challenges standard notions of 'mainstream' and 'ethnic majority group' (Crul & Schneider,

2010). Members of migrant minorities are forced to adjust to Dutch society, but in response they increasingly raise the inevitable question of to whom they should adjust. Indeed, changes in the composition of the population of European societies make it necessary to rethink the modernist foundation of nation-states. Essentialist views based on a rigorous dichotomy, between those who are included and those who are not and never will, are to give way to a more open outlook on the fuzzy boundaries of the nation-states that is more in line with contemporary practices.

In this chapter, we have considered some alternative conceptions of post-colonial nation-states in Europe, including Will Kymlicka's suggestion of inclusive solidarity through a multicultural welfare state. The problem with his idea is that, as Nina Glick Schiller argued compellingly, ultimately it is based on an ethnic lens, whereas migrants and particularly their second- and third-generation descendants are weary of being addressed in terms of their ethnic identity or migration background, as Ethnic Others. Instead, they prefer to be identified as cosmopolitan citizens with multiple identifications. Glick Schiller has conceptualized this in terms of cosmopolitan sociabilities, while Nowicka and Vertovec propose to rethink ethnic relations in post-colonial and multicultural states in terms of conviviality. A more suitable and analytically refined alternative, however, may be found in dialogical self theory, which although developed for the analysis of individual selves, may easily be extrapolated to the level of society. After all, the metaphor of dialogical relationships between different cultural positions has been used successfully for the analysis of plural and composite selves of individuals in multicultural societies, which in turn can easily be uplifted for the analysis of dialogical relationships between cosmopolitan sociabilities of multicultural citizens.

References

Bakhtin, M. M. (1981). *The dialogical imagination: Four essays*. Austin, TX: University of Texas Press.

Bakhtin, M. M. (1984). *Problems of Dostoevsky's poetics*. Minneapolis, MN: University of Minnesota Press. (Originally published 1929)

Billig, M. (1995). *Banal nationalism*. London: Sage Publications.

Bolkestein, F. (1991). *The integration of minorities*. Address to the Liberal International Conference, Luzern, September 8, 1991; published on the op-ed page of *De Volkskrant*, September 12, 1991.

Bruquetas-Callejo, M., Garcés-Mascareñas, B., Penninx, R., & Scholten, P. (2007). *Policymaking related to immigration and integration: The Dutch case*. Amsterdam: Institute for Migration and Ethnic Studies (IMES), International Migration, Integration and Social Cohesion Research Network (IMISCOE), Working Paper No. 15.

Crul, M., & Schneider, J. (2010). Comparative integration context theory: Participation and belonging in new diverse European cities. *Ethnic and Racial Studies*, 33(7), 1249–1268.

Duyvendak, J. W., Geschiere, P., & Tonkens, E. (Eds.). (2016). *The culturalization of citizenship: Belonging and polarization in a globalizing world*. London: Palgrave Macmillan.

Entzinger, H. (2003). The rise and fall of multiculturalism: The case of the Netherlands. In C. Joppke & E. Morawska (Eds.), *Toward assimilation and citizenship: Immigrants in liberal nation states* (pp. 59–86). Basingstoke: Palgrave Macmillan.

Gijsberts, M., & Dagevos, J. (Eds.). (2009). *Jaarrapport integratie 2009*. Den Haag: Sociaal en Cultureel Planbureau.

Glick Schiller, N. (2016). The question of solidarity and society: Comment on Will Kymlicka's article: "Solidarity in Diverse Societies." *Comparative Migration Studies*, 4(1), 6.

Grillo, R. (2003). Cultural essentialism and cultural anxiety. *Anthropological Theory*, 3(2), 157–173.

Gullestad, M. (2002). Invisible fences: Egalitarianism, nationalism and racism. *The Journal of the Royal Anthropological Institute*, 8(1), 45–63.

Gullestad, M. (2006). *Plausible prejudice: Everyday experiences and social images of nation, culture and race*. Oslo: Universitetsforlaget.

Hermans, H. J. M. (2002). The dialogical self as a society of mind. *Theory and Psychology*, 12(2), 147–160.

Hermans, H. J. M. (2018). *Society in the self: A theory of identity in democracy*. New York, NY: Oxford University Press.

Hermans, H. J. M., & Dimaggio, G. (2007). Self, identity, and globalization in times of uncertainty: A dialogical analysis. *Review of General Psychology*, 11(1), 31–61.

Hermans, H. J. M., & Hermans-Konopka, A. (2010). *Dialogical self theory: Positioning and counter positioning in a globalizing society*. Cambridge: Cambridge University Press.

Hermans, H. J. M., & Kempen, H. J. G. (1993). *The dialogical self: Meaning as movement*. San Diego, CA: Academic Press.

Hermans, H. J. M., & Kempen, H. J. G. (1998). Moving cultures: The perilous problems of cultural dichotomies in a globalizing society. *American Psychologist*, 53(10), 1111–1120.

Hermans, H. J. M., Kempen, H. J. G., & van Loon, R. J. P. (1992). The dialogical self: Beyond individualism and rationalism. *American Psychologist*, 47(1), 23–33.

Huggan, G., & Law, I. (Eds.). (2009). *Racism postcolonialism Europe*. Liverpool: Liverpool University Press.

Huntington, S. P. (1996). *The clash of civilizations and the remaking of the world order*. London: Simon & Schuster, Touchstone.

Inda, J. X., & Rosaldo, R. (Eds.). (2002). *The anthropology of globalization: A reader*. Malden and Oxford: Wiley Blackwell.

James, W. (1890). *The principles of psychology* (Vol. 1). London: Palgrave Macmillan.

Koning, A. de, & Modest, W. (2017). Anxious politics in postcolonial Europe. *American Anthropologist*, 119(3), 524–526.

Koning, M. de (2016a). *Een ideologische strijd met de islam: Fortuyns gedachtegoed als scharnierpunt in de racialisering van moslims*. Uithoorn: Karakter.

Koning, M. de (2016b). "You need to present a counter-message": The racialisation of Dutch Muslims and anti-Islamophobia initiatives. *Journal of Muslims in Europe*, 5(2), 170–189.

Kymlicka, W. (1995). *Multicultural citizenship: A liberal theory of minority rights*. Oxford: Clarendon Press.

Kymlicka, W. (2015). Solidarity in diverse societies: Beyond neoliberal multiculturalism and welfare chauvinism. *Comparative Migration Studies*, *3*(1), 1–19.

Kymlicka, W. (2016). Rejoinder from sociability to solidarity: Reply to commentators. *Comparative Migration Studies*, *4*(1), 9.

Modest, W., & Koning, A. de (2016). Anxious politics in the European city: An introduction. *Patterns of Prejudice*, *50*(2), 97–108.

Nicolaas, H., & Sprangers, A. (2006). Internationale migratie: Nederland in een Europese context. In F. van Tubergen & I. Maas (Eds.), *Allochtonen in Nederland in internationaal perspectief* (pp. 13–35). Amsterdam: Amsterdam University Press.

Noble, G. (2009). "Countless acts of recognition": Young men, ethnicity and the messiness of identities in everyday life. *Social and Cultural Geography*, *10*(8), 875–891.

Nowicka, M., & Vertovec, S. (2014). Comparing convivialities: Dreams and realities of living with difference. *European Journal of Cultural Studies*, *17*(4), 341–356.

Prins, B. (2002). The nerve to break taboos: New realism in the Dutch discourse on multiculturalism. *Journal of International Migration and Integration*, *3*(3–4), 363–379.

Scheffer, P. (2000, January 29). Het multiculturele drama. *NRC Handelsblad*.

Scheffer, P. (2007). *Het land van aankomst*. Amsterdam: De Bezige Bij.

Scheffer, P. (2011). *Immigrant nations*. Cambridge: Polity Press.

Schinkel, W. (2010). The virtualization of citizenship. *Critical Sociology*, *36*(2), 265–283.

Schinkel, W., & Houdt, F. van (2010). The double helix of cultural assimilationism and neo-liberalism: Citizenship in contemporary governmentality. *The British Journal of Sociology*, *61*(4), 696–715.

Springer, S., Birch, K., & MacLeavy, J. (Eds.). (2016). *The handbook of neoliberalism*. New York, NY: Routledge.

Stolcke, V. (1995). Talking culture: New boundaries, new rhetorics of exclusion in Europe. *Current Anthropology*, *36*(1), 1–14.

Taylor, C. (1992). *Multiculturalism and "the politics of recognition."* Princeton: Princeton University Press.

van Meijl, T. (2012). Multicultural adolescents between tradition and postmodernity: Dialogical self theory and the paradox of localization and globalization. *New Directions for Child and Adolescent Development* (Special Issue "Applications of Dialogical Self Theory," edited by H. J. M. Hermans), *137*, 39–52.

van Meijl, T. (2013). Multiple identifications of multicultural adolescents: Dialogues between tradition and postmodernity in a global context. In B. L. Hewlett (Ed.), *Adolescent identity: Evolutionary, cultural and developmental perspectives* (pp. 203–221). New York, NY: Routledge.

Vertovec, S. (2007). Super-diversity and its implications. *Ethnic and Racial Studies*, *30*(6), 1024–1054.

Vertovec, Steven (2011). The Cultural Politics of Nation and Migration. *Annual Review of Anthropology 40*, 241–56.

Vollebergh, A. (2016). The other neighbour paradox: Fantasies and frustrations of "living together" in Antwerp. *Patterns of Prejudice*, *50*(2), 129–149.

Wikan, U. (2002). *Generous betrayal: Politics of culture in the new Europe*. Chicago, IL: University of Chicago Press.

Wimmer, A., & Glick Schiller, N. (2002). Methodological nationalism and beyond: Nation-state building, migration and the social sciences. *Global Networks*, 2(4), 301–334.

Wise, A., & Velayutham, S. (Eds.). (2009). *Everyday multiculturalism*. Basingstoke: Palgrave Macmillan.

Yanow, D., & Haar, M. van der (2012). People out of place: Allochthony and autochthony in the Netherlands' identity discourse – Metaphors and categories in action. *Journal of International Relations and Development*, 1, 1–35.

12 Beyond the boundaries

Overcoming resentments, resistance, and revulsion

Mary Gergen

It was 4:30 in the morning when I slipped out of bed to turn on the tv. The headlines said, "Trump has won." I wondered if I was having a nightmare, or if this could really be true. This terrible feeling that it might be real reminded me of being in Japan and hearing in a badly spoken English, "Bush won." Yes, it was true. No delaying, only dismaying. Trump was the winner. How did it happen? How could it be? A feeling of sickness pervaded my sense. I went back to bed, hoping things would be different in the morning. But, of course, they were not.

Introduction

The outcome of the 2016 presidential election in the United States led many people who did not support Donald Trump to feel extremes of shock, revulsion, anger, despair, and other negative emotions. One woman, after hearing that Trump had won the election, felt such a tremor in her chest that she went to the hospital emergency room, thinking she was having a heart attack. Students, young immigrants, homosexuals, people with serious medical needs, American Muslims, and many others who voted for Hillary Clinton have also experienced deep concerns about their personal safety and wellbeing, and anger at Trump and his supporters for campaign rhetoric and executive orders designed to be against them. The day after the presidential inauguration, January 20, 2017, the so-called Women's March took place. In Washington, D.C., thousands of people, mostly women, many wearing funny pink pussy cat hats, paraded for a diverse set of issues, but mostly in protest against the election results. The mood of the demonstration was assertive, energetic, and as well, quite jolly. Every person I talked to about going expressed their delight in being a part of a resistance movement to the election of Trump. The joy of disruption was heady. The number of marchers far exceeded the crowd that gathered the day before to witness the inauguration. Similar events took place around the globe, including marches in 63 cities, from Buenos Aires to Budapest.

On the other side, people supporting Trump were feeling triumphant and assertive, and with some degree of aggressive affirmation of their own position. Over 100 days after the election, about one-third of the population expressed support of his presidential activities, and two-thirds did not. The Congress and the country is said to be polarized. This means that many governmental activities cannot be accomplished, not just because there are sharp differences of opinion as to what is the best way forward, but that one side cannot give the other the satisfaction of winning an argument, making a successful policy, or changing something that is not working.

The purpose of this chapter is to address the challenge of cohabiting – perhaps collaborating, cooperating, and even healing – under conditions of mutual loathing. The theoretical overview emphasizes a relational approach to understanding conflictual events and, within this social constructionist perspective, explores the contributions of positioning theory and interpretations dependent upon the metaphor of the rhizome, as well as the limits of attitudinal approaches to this issue. The bulk of the chapter is given over to specific forms of action that can be useful in helping to shift from dissonant to more harmonious outcomes. These outcomes can be achieved without sacrificing facets of difference that result from the existence of plural moralities. These activities are organized into three groups: Relational Engagement, Finding Common Ground, and Engaging in Transformative Potentials. The chapter concludes with a commentary on social constructionism as a helpmate in advancing the cause of civility in a world of different and often conflicting moral positions.

The plethora of protests

After the shock of the election results wore off, many thoughtful people suggested ways to respond to these very distressing emotions and desires for protest or revenge. Yet, in the months since the election, protests have been held whenever there has been a move by the White House that angers opponents: an anti-Muslim ban yielded marches; refusing to sign the Paris Climate Change agreement provoked more gatherings; rescinding the protection for immigrants who came to this country as children brought more protests; and speaking sympathetically about white supremacists in Charlottesville caused violent confrontations, among others. Most practices to lessen the hurt, to help people move on with their lives, and to make steps to counteract the alienation and despair that characterize many of them have been rare; the activity that has helped to energize, even though it often has not been healing, is the protest action. Marches, sit-ins, and confrontations with others have inspired emotional outbursts. Here, the pleasures of intense dislike, even hatred, have been expressed. People have been able to act out in aggressive ways, as an alternative to feeling hopeless and impotent; in some cases, there are also strategic moves to influence those on the other side. For example, occupying the office of an elected official to challenge him/her to change a position or face the distress and anger of constituents has been a frequent form of protest. Of late, in 2018, election results are also beginning to show anti-Trump sentiments, and the possibility of changing the political landscape in the legislative branch inspires his opponents. The dominant position of the Trump supporters is vulnerable, and new options for compromise and agreement are possible.

But there have been few efforts to find positive ways of reducing the distrust, dislike, and distress that marks the country. Although the election of President Trump is a vivid and recent example, there are many places around the world where seemingly intractable differences, conflicts, and outright warfare characterize the nature of the territory. From Afghanistan to Zambia, various cultural, political, and economic groups are fighting one another, and are far from making peace or reaching a reasonable settlement in order to avoid bloodshed. On a smaller scale, neighbors quarrel with each other; families become torn apart by various arguments and disaffections; religious organizations split over dogmatic differences. Friends fall out. Lovers part in bitterness. The nature of conflict is omnipresent, powerful, and disturbing for most of those involved. Clearly, now needed are ways to reduce the hatred and suspicion that separates one from another in many places. Perhaps we cannot start with the most vivid examples of resentments and hate, but we need to start somewhere.

Theorizing the healing process

This chapter is designed to explore the various ways that people might respond to personal and political challenges in a way that is helpful to healing the divides that have defined various individuals and groups as antagonistic enemies. These practices are not addressed to the politics of Washington, D.C., in particular. They can be seen as ways that any individuals or groups who are antagonistic toward one another, in attitudes and/or in actions, can find ways to surmount their enmity and cobble together ways of living and working together so as to minimize their dislikes, even hatreds, and to come closer to a peaceful resolution of their differences. The focus is on relationships and practices that inspire people and tap into their creativity in their search for meaning and to reach beyond the limits of our current political systems, as well as our personal commitments, customs, and conclusions.

Social constructionist and healing practices

Before turning to efforts to reducing conflict and creating healing practices, I wish to introduce social constructionism as the metatheoretical framework of this chapter (Gergen, 2015). The central focus of a social constructionist position is on the relational processes that create the ways in which we understand, interpret, and act in the world. People, together, in words and in actions with other people and things, within particular contexts, over time, have deigned these as such. The world becomes real, facts become true, and things become good or bad because influential groups of people have constructed and sustained these views, and these constructions have been disseminated among the population. These perspectives have power to mold people's entire lives, and yet, at the same time, these constructions are subject to the continual affirmation of those who live with them. If enough people declare that the emperor has no clothes, then he is naked. And the opposite is also true. Because *Reality* is constructed, and not referential, many possibilities for world-making exist. This is the note of hope that a social constructionist perspective lends to the mission of healing the wounds of conflict. The 'world' does not require any particular construction of it. Whatever is, is, but is subject to naming. With a desire to create the conditions for peaceful resolutions, the notion that there is a certain freedom to recreate the events, histories, and ongoing unfolding of actions is an exhilarating prospect (see also K. Gergen, Chapter 1 in this volume).

While there are many possible interpretations of 'reality,' in principle, this is not always easy to produce in practice. Our strong social customs, traditions, and habits shore up our usual constructions of reality, such that we do not question our sense of reality most of the time. When we do recognize the potential for there to be multiple constructions, it may not always be positive. Instead, it may undermine the security with which we hold our sense of the past, what exists in the present, and what may lie ahead. It also puts into question how we should classify objects and events, and what constitutes motivations, actions, and outcomes. In addition, we may not have the power to resignify what is the real. Thus, as Winston Churchill famously said, the "history of war is written by the victors." Losers cannot write that history, at least until the tides of power have turned. Multiple ways of writing history, from many different moral systems complexify this binary-based conclusion.

This is not to say that within various discursive systems there cannot be truths, but they are established on the basis of the system itself. Thus, for example, within organic chemistry, there can be accurate or inaccurate descriptions of a chemical compound. Within every constructed framework, true and false can exist. However, there is no 'last word' about what is truly true or real or valuable beyond the scope of particular system of construction (Gergen & Gergen, 2004; McNamee & Hosking, 2012; Gergen, 2015). From a constructionist position, there is no truth with a capital T.

With a social constructionist perspective on social issues, moral conflicts, and political problems, the prospects of creating new and more promising horizons exist. Nothing is necessarily forever; nothing is required; nothing is fixed. New possibilities may be imagined from this perspective. The flexibility and openness to change that characterize a social constructionist perspective encourage prospects of healing in emotionally charged situations.

Social constructions and positioning theory

People do not generally have equal access to the creation and promulgation of various constructions. Positioning theory addresses these differences

Harré, 2012). In terms of words and actions, some people are positioned in ways that give them more power over what is agreed upon and acted upon than others. Economists working in government agencies declare what the state of the economy is, e.g., the rate of inflation, unemployment rate, percentage of people in poverty. They then have the power to regulate the nature of economic institutions, including setting interest rates for the banking system. Conflicts and controversies often arise when those who have been positioned as without power become determined to take the position from which they have been previously excluded. 'Black Lives Matter,' a protest group that challenges the notion that only white lives matter, came into being as a protest against police brutality and other racial injustices, as seen from their perspective. Challenges may be made to the discourse that has been dominant, the distribution of rights and obligations, and the actors who are capable of engaging in determining the reality of the situation (Hammack, 2011). Moghaddam and Harré suggest that "Positioning has direct moral implications, such that some person or group are considered 'trusted' or 'distrusted,' 'with us' or 'against us,' 'to be saved' or 'to be wiped out'" (2010, p. 2).

Since the late 1990s, positioning theory has been seen to allow "for a very natural expansion of scale, from the analysis of person-to-person encounters to the unfolding of interactions between nation states" (Harré, Moghaddam, Pilkerton Cairnie, Rothbart, & Sabat, 2009, p. 6). Leaders of nations become figureheads that stand for the entire country. An example of this was played out during a NATO event in Brussels in May 2017, when President Trump, representing the powerful United States, literally pushed the prime minister of Montenegro aside as he strode to the front of the group of world leaders for a photo op. It is unlikely he would have dared to so boldly shove aside another world leader, had it been Merkel of Germany or Macron of France.

The flow of events: the denial of individual responsibility

Of special import, the relational processes that construct reality are ongoing; there is no point of origin for the causation of conflicts and no clear laws of cause and effect that specify who did what to whom. Thus, holding particular individuals responsible for outcomes, which is a pillar of the justice system and the social services, as well as much of the social sciences, is an unsatisfactory viewpoint that obscures the blend of relational processes that informs interactions that precede and surround persons, actions, and outcomes. It is not possible to finally know how things happen, despite efforts to discover the cause or causes of events. In any conflict, the actions that occur, either in the unfolding of the conflict or in the efforts to find a way to resolve it, are muddled, and any analysis should be focused on the relational processes that are active, despite the tendency we all have to look at individual actors as responsible for conflicts and their resolutions. This individualistic focus distracts from the more subtle ways in which actions of any particular group or individual have been co-created within a context of other influential elements.

The rhizomatic metaphor, borderlands, and relational processes

Within the relational framework, conflictual activities may be described using the metaphor of the *rhizome*. Taken from horticultural discourse, a rhizome plant grows laterally, moving from one cluster of roots to another. There is no central root, from which smaller roots grow. It is not possible to discern the origins or the endings of the root structure. It is a system of flow that is shaped by encircling roots, spreading outward, from one node to another. Ginger and bamboo plants are examples of rhizomatic structures. As French philosopher Gilles Deleuze and psychiatrist Felix Guattari (2004), who have advanced this metaphor, suggest, old formulations of top-down, hierarchical cause-and-effect models of change, in which there are origins and conclusions of events, is outdated and poorly advised. The rhizomatic perspective sensitizes us to the potential of a conflict to have no clear beginnings nor an obvious ending. Whatever seems to be the story at one point may be restoried at another. A conflict may seem to be ended, and perhaps resolved, only to flare up in another spot a month later. Various conflicts in the Middle East, the former Yugoslavia, in Africa, and also in the United States, as seen in racially affected protests and public displays by white supremacist groups reminiscent of race conflicts of the 1850s, 1900s, and 1960s, come to mind. Taking the view that any conflict and its resolution may be examined with a rhizomatic metaphor reminds us to be humble in the face of success in ending conflict, and optimistic when all possibilities of resolution seem lost. In addition, the rhizomatic perspective encourages peacemakers to regard nodes of activity that may not be the usual focus for describing a problem as having potential for future action. Marginal zones of activity, those at the periphery of a conflict, may be ripe for involvement and a source of healing potentials (Gemignani, 2011). Latina theorist Gloria Anzaldua (1987/2012) describes this ambiguous zone as the *borderland*. According to her, there are no absolute sides in conflict, and adversaries are contingent. Any group can be oppressive in certain circumstances, and victims in others. She speaks of the *mestizo consciousness*, being able to see multiple realities at the same time. In Latin America, for instance, it would be possible for a family to feel victimized by the government, and yet feel proud that their child has managed to go to the national university on a scholarship provided by those who profit from the corruption in the government they despise.

Attitudes as relational markers

Social scientists often are concerned about the attitudes of parties to a conflict, and those who work with such issues may survey participants in order to assess how involved people might be in the conflict and what their attitudes toward various elements to the conflict might be (Albarracin, Johnson, & Zanna, 2005). Yet, those who accept the notion that attitudes are fixed and firm, unchangeable and unitary, and useful for predicting outcomes, may be sadly mistaken. Within the relational perspective, the formation of individual attitudes is dependent upon the social worlds people have grown up in, and what the current context of their involvement in a particular situation might be. This flexibility in the '*I*-position' as posited by Hermans and Hermans-Konopka (2010) is also pertinent here (see also Hermans, Chapter 2 in this volume). From this perspective, it is difficult to fix any definite meaning to what people may express about their attitudes within the context of a conflict. As people engage and shift in their relational contexts, their attitudes also change. If one is a part of a protest march, strongly negative attitudes may well prevail. Later at a family gathering, one's attitudes may mellow, and more nuanced viewpoints might be expressed. Among friends, critical remarks about the protest march and the way it was organized may be the topic of the day. Each of these contexts might shift the nature of one's attitudes toward the supposedly same target. This flexibility in attitudes creates difficulties for those trying to assess the outcomes of processes designed to reduce conflict and encourage peaceful outcomes. The formation and maintenance of positive attitudes toward oppositional others depend on context. One intervention designed to change persistent attitudes will, most likely, be ineffective, if the context remains basically untouched. If the ways reality is constructed in one's social group is constant, the perpetuation of certain norms and values will persist. One weekend retreat with undervalued others cannot change attitudes for long, if social group ties are strong and relatively stable.

Another important aspect of attitudes is that whatever cultural context surrounds you, you will become exposed to the various viewpoints that exist there, some more than others. If you are an older woman, a lesbian, and a Chicano, you may have expressed many attitudes supportive of your own identity. At the same time, you also have within you the capacity to express ageist, homophobic, and racist views. It is hard to argue in favor of an easy stability, a known identity, or a fixed position on any issue. As Zygmunt Bauman has described it, we live in 'liquid modernity' (2011). As people, information, ideas, weapons, etc., are 'on the move,' the meaning of boundaries changes. The meaning of who we are changes as well.

Practices for mitigating conflict and healing wounds

The theoretical orientation of social construction, with its emphasis on relational processes, and the subordinate orientations of positioning theory and rhizomatic analysis provided here are central to the ways in which we approach efforts to resolve, mitigate, and heal conflicts at all levels. The provisions of temporality, partiality, and uncertainty are cautionary moves that may temper all optimism that these are proven practices that may work for any conflict at any time. Yet, there are also optimistic potentials in these efforts, no matter how fragile they may be in terms of efficacy and longevity. The bulk of the chapter is devoted to introducing a series of practices that are designed to heal the divides that characterize the conflicts among people and groups. These practices are divided into three types, along with various approaches associated with each: Relational Engagement; Finding Common Ground; and Transformative Potentials. In the following kinds of practices, Relational Engagement primarily serves ceremonial or trust-building functions (Goffman, 1955). Seeking Common Ground and Transformative Potentials include directionality and action potentials for reducing conflict and producing an environment that encourages resolutions and satisfaction. Finding common ground may be the beginning of a strategy for resolving conflicts. In transformative practices, significant positive changes may be created, often in a sudden shift from one moral orientation to reality to another.

As I peruse the various resources for creating and enacting these practices, from early work in South America to more recent work in the rest of the world, I am overwhelmed with choices for inclusion in this chapter. It is impossible to include all of the significant contributions that practitioners have made. The more I encounter various literatures – peace building, mediation, therapy, counseling, coaching, and arts-based and cultural programs – the more my dilemma of what to include has increased. I must admit that in what follows I have skimmed the surface in terms of breadth, although I try to give a deeper sense of significant trends, with detailed descriptions of some of the major practices. Each of my choices resonates with a social constructionist perspective. There is no end in sight in terms of what may be workable, just, and good enough for the moment. Yet, there is so much to be accomplished in this time of war and strife.

Relational Engagement Practices

Relational engagement practices are those that encourage parties to a conflict to join together in activities that go beyond or avoid the core focus of the conflict. The purpose of this type of approach is to cast outlines of positive connection from one to another, across the separation of the parties' conflicting interests. Several effective practices are illustrative of each approach.

Relational engagement through sharing culture

Many conflicts are outcomes of cultural differences. Magnified negative images of the other may enflame differences, especially where scarce resources are at stake. Often fear of the outsider based on cultural differences increases the difficulty of reaching a peaceful resolution of conflicts.

Becoming more familiar with another culture in a positive context is an important step in bringing less strife to a situation. Two efforts to do this are profiled here.

During the civil war in Somalia, which raged throughout the 1990s, many people fled. Of all Somalis who came to the United States, about one-third of them (25,000) came to live to Minnesota. Voluntary agencies helped to settle those who were refugees. In some ways it was an unlikely place for Africans to live, given the extremes of cold weather that characterize Minnesota, and the fact that most of the local people are from European stock. Yet, as the Somali people stayed, communities with strong ties, economic roots, and educational opportunities were created among them, and, although many Somalis went back to their home country after conditions became more settled, in part to help rebuild it, many others stayed. These Somalis lived primarily in the large Twin Cities of Minneapolis and St. Paul, but there were smaller enclaves in towns located miles away. One of these was St. Cloud, a college town about 75 miles from Minneapolis. Racial and ethnic difficulties became increasingly conflictual, as the Somalis came into contact with other local groups of African Americans, Whites, and tribal Native Americans. In an effort to encourage knowledge of each other and friendlier feelings, the city council, with the help of outside consultants, decided to plan a festival that featured each sub-group's culture, in such a way as to draw others in. Each group made their traditional foods to share with others, showcased their music and dance, as well as modeled their traditional costumes. The Somalis were of special interest, as they were the newcomers. This festival was very helpful in overcoming some of the animosity that had grown up, primarily out of ignorance and fears of the others. Each cultural group partook of the offerings of the other groups. Relationships began as people talked together, ate together, and enjoyed each other's programs. These became the grounds from which more productive interchanges could grow.

Another example of fostering relational engagement through sharing recently took place in Philadelphia, where a program called Breaking Bread, Breaking Barriers was initiated. Begun in the fall of 2016, cooking demonstrations and meals were made by various groups, including Syrians, Mexicans, Koreans, and Cambodians, at the centrally located Reading Terminal Market. This market is famous in Philadelphia for its diversity of food stalls and customers. On an ordinary day people from all walks of life comfortably stroll about, buying groceries and eating foods prepared by chefs from many ethnic backgrounds. The ever popular Amish, who are traditionalist Christians, come in from the countryside with their famous wares to add to the tableau. The sponsors of the special event of Breaking Bread, Breaking Barriers is the Human Relations Commission of the city government, a resettlement agency, and the Penn Project for Civic Engagement. The project was inspired by Elijah Anderson's (2011) *The Cosmopolitan Canopy: Race and Civility in Everyday Life*, and was funded by an $85,000 grant from a local foundation. The concept of 'canopy' was central to Anderson's vision of bringing people together, and the Market was seen as the most appealing location that could shelter all groups under its roof. Without a proper meeting place, these types of encounters would be less likely to succeed. The Reading Terminal Market was central, safe, and, most importantly, unidentified with any one ethnic group.

Relational engagement through sharing symbols

The preceding practices involved sharing food and other culturally significant activities, such as music making and dance, in special activities that were not intended to foster a permanent organization. The United Religions Initiative (URI) was designed to become something more permanent. The idea for this organization came to California Episcopal Bishop William Swing in 1993, after an invitation by the United Nations to host a large interfaith service in San Francisco, marking the 50th anniversary of the signing of the UN Charter. At that time, he asked himself, "If the nations of the world are working together for peace through the UN, then shouldn't the world's religions as well?" Through dozens of meetings with world religious leaders, he recognized that many large religious groups had had little or no contact with other groups since their founding. Their histories were of indifference or even outright hostility. He also discovered competition among them, a focus on expanding individual denominations, and little institutional commitment to building bridges. But from many at the grass roots of the world's religions, he also found a deep desire for cooperation and peace. From this inspiration, the vision for United Religions Initiative (URI) took shape: a supportive network connecting people across religions and cultures in the service of peace and justice. Over many years the United Religions Initiative groups worked together to find a means of pursuing their goals in the world beyond their walls. Finally, in June 2000, the charter for the founding of URI was affirmed (www.uri.org).

Preparing for the initial meeting of hundreds of religious leaders, the organizers recognized that many of the customs that Americans shared for getting together at conferences would not work for this group. They did not necessarily share food preferences, and various restrictions applied to various groups. There would be no cocktail party! Ways of greeting, dress, gestures, personal space, and language were all roadblocks to warm interchange and mutual understanding. Finally, the planners settled on a practice that turned out to be highly successful in beginning this sensitive process. Each representative brought to the gathering an icon that was especially meaningful to them and their group – a cross, a statue of a god, a picture, an artifact. Along with this, the religious leaders were asked to tell stories of why this particular object was meaningful to them. What this practice did was to open the leaders to each other, as the feelings told in relation to the objects were very similar across the various religions. The practice showed how the respect and reverence each had was shared amongst them. They were more similar to each other, and they shared more together than they had anticipated before the meeting. This practice helped them to come together more easily and to work together to achieve their mutual endpoint (Whitney & Trosten-Bloom, 2003; Cooperrider & Whitney, 2005). Today the URI is composed of Cooperation Circles. These are self-organizing groups of at least seven members from at least three religions, spiritual expressions, or indigenous traditions – including atheists and agnostics, which have been formed around the globe. In these circles, people of different backgrounds work together to tackle important community issues in their locales. An excellent example of this effort culminated in *Interfaith Education for All: Theoretical Perspectives and Best Practices for Transformative Action* (Wielzen & ter Avest, 2017), in which the editors brought together theoretical approaches and 'best practices' that would serve as guidelines for the education of teachers.

Relational engagement through aesthetic experiences

Those who work in the area of peace building and conflict resolution are keen to acknowledge that rational argument and logical sense-making are limited in helping people work out ways of settling conflicts. Most conflicts are fraught with emotional turmoil, combined with stories of past injustices, and previous insults and injuries. In order to address these powerful non-rational aspects of a conflict, a prominent form of intervention has been to create artistic projects that are able to address these aspects of the conflict (United States Institute of Peace, 2017). Aesthetic experiences, which emphasize the sensual, engage the emotional and spiritual qualities of a conflict, and they invite embodied activities. Artistic endeavors create opportunities for shared commitment, receptivity, serenity, and playfulness among the participants, regardless of their intellectual differences. These qualities of presence afford unique opportunities for empathy, imagination, and innovation, all of which are central to reducing conflict (see also Alma, Chapter 4 in this volume, on imagination and embodiment).

The arts incorporate many modes of expression: literary forms, musical works, painting, mural productions, photography, video, theater, and dance. Artist-based works emphasize highly talented expressions of an artist or ensemble and, through their virtuosity, invite transformations in those who witness. Community-based works are inclusive and generally focus on transformation of those who engage in creating and performing the art, as well as the community that observes.

The arts, generally, aim to embody a kind of power that rests not on injury or domination, but rather on reciprocity, connectivity, and generativity (Leavy, 2018). Yet, clearly not all artistic works build peace. In fact, in many instances the power of art has served militaristic regimes. Leni Riefenstahl created *The Triumph of the Will*, a blockbuster movie, in order to glamorize the rise of Hitler and the Nazi Party in pre-World War II Germany. ISIS, the contemporary terrorist organization, has lured countless young people to the Middle East to fight for their cause, via compelling propaganda videos. The context in which an arts-based project is produced is crucial in evaluating whether it is enhancing peaceful and ethical outcomes or evil and degenerative ones, as are the perspectives of the actors involved. Contrast the views of a militant ISIS leader with an anti-ISIS group in 2017 as to the purpose of a recruitment video.

A variety of projects around the globe have been created on the basis of engaging in an artistic project. The general view is that the project supersedes consideration of ethnicity, nationality, and other demographic distinctions that could yield conflict. In many cases, the project is a mode of activity designed to overwhelm other existing prejudices and dislikes. A few examples of artistic projects that have helped inspire greater cooperation and goodwill among those who participate and those who witness follow.

Relational engagement: creating music together

Conductor Alan Gilbert, formerly of the New York Philharmonic, is creating an orchestra called Musicians for Unity in partnership with the United Nations. The musical group will be engaged in serving the interests of world peace. It will be a multinational orchestra that will have concerts in strategic places; not only will they make music, but also show in their membership how art crosses borders (Stearns, 2017). Their description says, "Musicians for Unity . . . calls attention to the need for us all to play our part in building a safer and more humane world. Music can bring inspiration, reflection, and love. If Music for Unity can add to those it will have done its job."

Another well-known musical group, the West-Eastern Divan Orchestra, is a youth orchestra based in Seville, Spain; this group consists of musicians from Israel, Egypt, Iran, Jordan, Lebanon, Palestine, Syria, and Spain. It was founded in 1999 by the conductor Daniel Barenboim and academic Edward Said, and named after an anthology of poems by Goethe. They tour throughout the world and show through their cooperation how these often antagonistic groups of people can make beautiful music together, on and off the stage.

Most recently, the 2018 Winter Olympics became the site of a peaceful interchange, as the North Koreans sent a delegation of athletes and fans plus a 140-member orchestra to play at the 'peace games' in Seoul and Pyeongchang, the first time in 16 years that a North Korean arts group has performed in South Korea. It is hoped by both sides that the agreement would bolster broader relations between the two Koreas as well as celebrate their 'cultural homogeneity,' according to South Korea's Unification Ministry, which is in charge of relations with the North (Fifield, 2018).

Relational engagement: creating art together

Many groups internationally form artistic enclaves for producing artistic works, painting, sculpture, and other graphic arts. Peace Building and the Arts, a program of the International Center for Ethics, Justice, and Public Life at Brandeis University, leads to a master's degree developed to enhance the use of artistic methods to reduce conflict. This program is for artists, cultural workers, coexistence practitioners, peace-building scholars, and all who are interested in how the arts and cultural traditions can be crafted to bridge differences, mediate conflicts, and contribute to peace. They collaborate with artists who work in divided communities, supporting them to reflect on, document, and strengthen their practice. The lessons from these collaborations are accessible through publications, trainings, courses, and a virtual resource center. A recent publication that emphasizes the role of theater and ritual in the aftermath of violence is *Acting Together: Performance and Creative Transformation of Conflict* (2011). The two-volume series describes case studies in which diverse groups of people contribute to the growing field of peace-building performances.

Relational engagement: creating theater together

Perhaps the most common form of artistic endeavor in creating relational engagement is theater. From improvisational activities to well-wrought plays, being and observing theater performances has a powerful effect in promoting positive engagement of various parties in a conflict (Shank, 2005).

The Peres Center is Israel's leading non-profit, non-political, non-governmental organization focused on developing and implementing programs in Innovation, Peace Education, Medicine, Business, and Environment, reaching tens of thousands of participants over the last 20 years. Founded in 1996 by the late ninth president of Israel and Nobel Peace Prize laureate, Shimon Peres, the Peres Center for Peace and Innovation aims to realize his vision for a prosperous Israel within a peaceful Middle East. Program participants include Jews and Arabs, Israelis and Palestinians. One of their major programs involves doing theater productions as a means of fostering dialogue among the members of their diverse audiences.

In the Philippines, theater artists tour various islands to emphasize the concept of peaceful coexistence among Christians, Muslims, and indigenous people (Fernandez, 1995).

Many projects are multi-focused, with various arts, music, theater, and meditative practices combined. For example, in Sri Lanka there is the famous Butterfly Peace Garden, where children and adults engage in music, arts, yoga, and theater as ways of recovering from war trauma (War Child International's website: www.warchild.org/projects/WC_Canada/Sri_Lanka/sri_lanka.html).

Seeking common ground

Conflicts are seldom defined such that there are no overlapping interests, values, or understandings. Many times there are great areas of agreement, which become overlooked in the focus on the areas of disagreement. In seeking common ground, mediators, for example, strive to emphasize the commonalities that may become the basis for reaching a more peaceful settlement of the conflict. Peacemaking activities create the possibilities for bringing more attention to the overlapping agreements. The conflictual elements become overshadowed by the similarities that are highlighted through various practices. A focus on the shared elements also tends to enhance the prospects of a settlement, thus bringing optimism and a greater sense of goodwill to the bargaining table. Among the ways of seeking common ground are those that focus on the specifics of language used to interpret the reality of the situation, and the ways that conversations are arranged within a social context, as well as how storytelling provides modes of yielding new versions of a conflict.

Seeking common ground: playing the language game

Generally, conflicts are framed by specific words and phrases exchanged in a conversation. Powerful metaphors capture an image of a dynamic that is primarily antagonistic. During the Cold War, which shaped the relationship between the United States and the Soviet Union in the 1950s and 1960s, the so-called 'domino theory' was the American metaphor that symbolized the conflict. The vision that helped perpetuate the Vietnam War was the game of dominos, in which the fall of one country to communism would force the next country to follow suit. Thus, the view of the government was that communism must be stopped by whatever means in all areas of the globe, or there would be horrible consequences. The choice of words, and the choice of topics, created the pathways along which the conflict developed. If other choices were made, the arguments and conflicts could be reduced, avoided, or resolved. Paying special attention to the nature of language is critical in finding ways to reduce conflicts among combatants. By substituting other linguistic formulations, parties to a conflict can find new ways to communicate and work towards better relations. This may pave the way for later problem solving.

Sensitivity to language use in a conflict between two people in an intimate relationship, a friendship, or a professional relationship can be helpful, especially in circumstances when the actors do not wish to completely separate or have a lengthy clash of opinions. It is helpful if the general attitudes of the partners to a dispute are such that they basically respect each other and believe the other has a right to express opinions that differ from their own. If the positioning of the parties is not balanced, then resolutions may not necessarily be gained via these practices. Their primary purpose is to reduce hostility, but not necessarily to address the specifics of various conflictual states. The basic premise of finding common ground is to reduce negativity towards the other(s), and to find ways in which there can be an identification of similarities across disparate spaces.

Dialogic options in the face of oppositional views can either be directed at the topic at hand, or strategically diverted from the central issue, for example, if Partner A argues for a view that is not shared by Partner B. In each case, the desired outcome is for Partners A and B to come into greater accord and find the common ground that is the basis of the relationship.

Among the range of dialogic options that are designed to mitigate arguments and ill will and find common ground are the following:

A argues in favor of stricter laws regarding X; B does not share this view.

> *B partially agrees.* B finds an aspect of the counterargument that is in accord with A's views. This reduces the anxiety of A, who may have anticipated an attack from B. There is a new platform for creating a better form of conversation. The educational groups in Thrace, Greece, mentioned later in this chapter, rely on this dialogic idea that each party to a conflict may have an important piece to contribute to a synthesis.

> *B opens up a tangential topic,* which is somewhat related to the discord. This topic may be displaced from the present in time or place. (As a child, did you enjoy playing with X?) This approach is designed to shift the content of the discussion and thereby alter the tone of the encounter. A's attitude is modified by positive memories of childhood, such that A and B share a common space historically. Narrative mediation, described in the next section on transformative dialogue, finds this approach a resource in resolving conflicts among competing participants.

> *A and B discuss how each came to have these opinions.* Telling episodes about one's past cannot be argued with. Stories have an integrity of their own. They are in a separate category from argument and do not require counterarguments. One cannot say, "I disagree with your story," unless it is a shared story. The similarity of the stories can create the sense of a common ground. The Essential Partners organization noted below capitalize on this tendency to respect others' stories.

> *A and B look for connections in order to find common ground.* "Can you see how I might have come to this view?" This discursive move encourages the other to be empathic, which counters antagonism. Each may have the same common ground, which increases the sense of unity. Various other forms of common ground are listed later.

> *A and B show their own weakness/vulnerability/uncertainties.* This is the move of the wolf in a losing fight baring his neck. This

action is designed to evoke sympathy, less aggression, more compassion, and the possibility of a more peaceful and potentially powerful dialogue.

A and B recognize that a viewpoint is not a person. They can depersonalize the viewpoint. The argument stands outside the bounds of the relationship between the actors, and in a sense, belongs to the culture at large, and not to one's adversary. This process is often at the core of work in narrative therapy, in which a character external to the person may be created to reduce the sense of shame that comes from having a problem, such as wetting the bed (White & Epston, 1990).

A and B recall that every one has a multiplicity of views, and this is the one being put forth at the moment. But in other moments, other views may be favored. Everyone who participates in a culture imbibes some of the general opinions, even if they are against one's own preferences, social group, or selfhood. This idea is a central tenet of social constructionism and the construct of the multi-being as a framework for understanding personal identity (Gergen, 2009).

A and B remind each other of the desirability of balance and moderation. They emphasize the dangers of extremes, or a single point of view, even if it is one's own. In terms of constructionist ideas, having a single point of view on a topic shuts down potentials for creativity and innovative solutions, as well as creates the possibility for dogmatism and despotic actions.

These practices are primarily dialogic, and language centered.[1] Some are useful for certain situations, but not for others. Some may be expanded to be useful in larger groups.

Creating common ground: sharing points of view despite disagreement

Essential Partners, formerly called the Public Conversation Project and created by a Boston-area counseling service in the 1970s, has developed an approach that has had highly effective outcomes among participants in conflictual situations (Herzig & Chasin, 2005). Their approach combines many of the 'good practices' mentioned earlier. Today, they have changed their mode of organizing, but they continue to facilitate conversations and activities that are designed to help people face difficult questions, which are often conflict laden (https://essentialconversationsproject.com/essential/).

In perhaps their most well-known case, they took on the highly controversial topic of abortion rights, which pitted the so-called Pro Life vs. Pro Choice groups. The animosity was so great that it even led to the murder of one of the doctors who provided abortions. Daily protests and confrontations were common in the Boston area, as were other murders, including two abortion center receptionists in the 1990s.

The process that was used to bring these two groups together involved a specific structure of interactions. To begin, the group had a meal together, with the stipulation that the topic under review was not to be discussed. Instead, the group of 8–12 conversed about ordinary things: weather, neighborhoods, children, sports teams, jobs, and leisure activities. Later, they convened to discuss the topic of concern. The rules of engagement allowed people to speak only from their personal experiences, and not from a dogmatic, doctrinal position. They were not allowed to use crude, inflammatory language, such as 'baby killer.' They spoke about their histories and how they came to their viewpoints. In general, a personal story tends not to be challenged, which allows diverse opinions to be put forth without argument. Speakers also described what was at the heart of the matter for them, as well as any uncertainties they may have had about their own positions. Through these conversational channels, the nature of the encounter remained calm, and there tended to be an open and accepting willingness to listen to one another. Also, often unanticipated overlap occurred between the seemingly two distinctive positions.

The organizers promised the participants that there would be no effort to change their views on the matter. This strategy tended to reduce anxiety about the process they were participating in. Although this was their promise, the result of the encounter was that a high level of tolerance and acceptance of the others pervaded the meeting, and people's general orientations were often changed in positive ways as a result. The willingness to demonize those who disagreed with one's position was greatly diminished. Among one group of participants, a secret pact was made to keep in touch with each other, and to help each other, if there was news of a violent activity being planned. This group of women stayed in communication with each other for over six years. The common ground they found exceeded their disparate views. As one woman who was interviewed by a local newspaper said, after they had revealed their meetings, "This has been a rare opportunity to engage in sustained, candid conversations about serious moral disagreements. . . . We have learned to avoid being overreactive and disparaging to the other side and to focus on affirming our respective causes." As the six concluded: "We hope this account of our experience will encourage people everywhere to consider engaging in dialogues about abortion and other protracted disputes. In this world of polarizing conflicts, we have glimpsed a new possibility: a way in which people can disagree frankly and passionately, become clearer in heart and mind about their activism, and, at the same time, contribute to a more civil and compassionate society" (Fowler et al., 2001).

Finding common ground through artistic endeavors

Although engaging in artistic ventures may be used to reduce tensions among rival groups, to increase knowledge and respect for other cultures, and to create friendly interactions among groups that are in divisive relations, artistic ventures can also be used to discover and expand common ground. An excellent example is the Forum Theatre, invented by Brazilian theater artist Augusto Boal (1995). This project involves a series of interactive theater techniques designed to help communities discuss and problem-solve pervasive community conflict. The Forum Theatre is a process in which an unresolved problem is shown theatrically to an audience, after which the audience is invited to suggest and enact solutions.

Other artistic projects, including those mentioned in the previous section on relational engagement, are also powerful in helping to create a sense of a common ground. The importance of relational engagement is centered on affective content. Seeking common ground has as a focus a recognition of common elements, which may change the logical force of an argument, or shift its structure, as adversaries come to realize that the elements of the differences are not as stark or powerful as they had imagined.

Moving to the transformative: the sky is the limit

> Love the flow. Trust the flow and follow it. No matter if you embark for one destination and you end up at another. Plans, maps, compasses are just tools. They are not a means in themselves. It is the flow that assisted me during this journey. And the journey continues.

These are the words of a young man, a youth worker, at a closing group session of the Creative Youth Workshops, operating within the overall frame of the Project on the Education of Muslim Minority Children (Vassiliou & Dragonas, 2017).

Whether there are ways of reaching a transformative moment or not is impossible to gauge from any moment or context. There is a bit of magic in the sudden turn of events that may shift everything from the way it seemed the moment before. As in the turning of a kaleidoscope, the components of the design shift sufficiently that a whole new vision of what might occur or is possible comes into view. Along with this recognition, which must be of a general nature shared by the participants, comes a sense of renewed optimism, hope, inspiration, and creativity. Suddenly, there are new ways forward, which were not there minutes before. Various components are necessary for this type of transformative change to occur, but it is not clear that all of them are necessary or that any of them are sufficient for sudden, noticeable change to occur. Among the potential change elements are new and novel opportunities, options, and/or objects, which were previously unnoted. Often it is in the language that new forms can be produced. Interpretations and perceptions of reality are altered, and suddenly the dowager becomes the damsel, as in the old Gestalt formulations. Each acquires the capacity to be used to create new outcomes and opportunities. Disappointingly, sometimes the transformative energy is depleted, without a goal being achieved. What seemed transformative failed to produce a successful outcome. To become committed to a transformative option is to risk failure and, as well, to being taken for a fool. The Munich agreement entered into by British prime minister Chamberlain and Hitler, which promised a transformative shift in policy so that there would be "peace for our time," later became known as a moment of treachery, not of transformation, in the eyes of the world.

Given the chanciness of making transformative moves occur, it is important to make rather insubstantial claims of the ways transformative dialogues can occur and be successful in helping to turn around parties to a conflict. Some of the possibilities are described here.

Transforming dialogues: the potentials of the political system and civic organizations

Relying on diplomacy as an alternative to war is a heady and significant choice to make. Diplomacy involves a variety of linguistic moves and action potentials. There are possibilities for silencing, ignoring, discussing, compromising, trading, begging, and re-storying. All of these moves, and more, are possible, as was noted in the previously described forms of 'language games.' But all are not equally significant or helpful in changing the situations of antagonists. One form of transformative dialogue can involve the engagement of political groups. Two examples follow: first, of a political party that takes seriously the relational approach to understanding reality, and that offers potentials for everyday folks to try to manipulate their political system, and through them, confront and reduce conflict; and second, a community newspaper that is organizing an effort to change the nature of discourse and political activity in Tennessee.

An example of transformative dialogue: the Alternative

What kind of political movements will embrace the long-term vision for cultivating a deeper kind of welfare that revolves around looking after the personal development of citizens in an open and democratic way? And what kind of phenomenon is going to emerge in party politics to work in accordance with the framework of co-development, democratization, and deliberation? The answer to this may be seen in the Alternative, a new Danish process-oriented political party – that is, a party that emphasizes how policies are created more than what they are. In order to do this, the members think about how they agree on a topic or issue before talking about how they disagree. Party members must put themselves in a position to be able to agree on something. Each must be willing to listen to one another (Freinacht, 2017). Through this approach, the party members establish that they begin their deliberations from a common ground. Whether such a political party will have a chance to make major changes in a Western European country is open to conjecture, but the means for transformation seem to be present.

An example of transformative dialogue: USA Today Network – Tennessee

The editorial board of the publication USA Today Network – Tennessee decided that they would attempt to transform the civic dialogues in Tennessee by engaging in a variety of activities that might be helpful to the mission of restoring civility. The project, called Civility Tennessee, is a yearlong effort to promote these values among the citizenry:

1 to encourage conversations that are civil and respectful, even if they are hard;
2 to enhance civic participation in important conversations such as the local, state, and federal elections of 2018;
3 to help promote voter registration efforts;
4 to increase news literacy and enhance trust between our consumers and our publications.

In order to achieve these goals of transforming the dialogues in Tennessee, the media group is committed to engaging in several practices:

• offering monthly perspectives on how to practice civil discourse, manage conflict and get to the root of issues in constructive ways;
• writing mini-profiles of 'Champions of Civility';
• presenting virtual and 'live' presentations and experiences for the public.

Transformative dialogue: collaborate with potential partners

In 2017, Moon Jae-in was elected president of South Korea. He took office during an extremely dangerous and dynamic time in which North Korea and the United States are engaged in a raging war of words, in which President Trump has insulted Kim Jong-un, their leader, and the North Koreans have replied in an equally hostile manner, sending missiles over Japan, conducting bomb tests, and threatening to shoot down American planes. Relations between the United States and North Korea were at their worst. If there is a military strike, South Korea cannot be protected from attack, despite the missile defense shield (which is untested against nuclear attack, and only partially effective against conventional missiles, and unappreciated by South Koreans and by China). Contrary to this bellicose strategy, President Moon has emphasized his willingness to talk to Kim Jong-un and urged defense ministers to meet and discuss their issues. He wishes to return to days of "sunshine" when diplomats of the two Koreas engaged in talks, had trade, and arranged exchanges of visits of family members. Other players on the world scene also strongly urge a return to the negotiating table to restart conversations about de-escalation.

Of special interest in this situation is the arrival of new characters on the scene. It is easier to have a rapprochement when there are new faces at the table. There is no need to revisit old disagreements with new partners. More potentials for agreement are open when there is no need to defend old positions. Also of significant was the 2018 Winter Olympics, held in PyeongChang, which allowed teams composed of Koreans from both North and South to compete, under a 'unified Korea' flag that shows an undivided Korean Peninsula. South Korean officials stated that this event created a "thaw" in relations that had been frozen for decades.

Transformative dialogues: focus on shared values and ideas

Returning to the United Religions Initiative (URI), mentioned earlier in this chapter, the growth of the organization has been done in a grassroots manner. Over many years the United Religions groups worked together to find a means of pursuing their goals in the world beyond their walls. The form that was agreed upon is based on 'cooperative circles.' These circles are dedicated to addressing community matters that are important to them, such as conflict resolution and reconciliation, environmental sustainability, education, and human rights. Despite obvious differences in religious designations, the circle members find ways of supporting each other in solving local problems by sharing interpretations of what is important and good for their people.

In some situations, active bystanders may be required to get antagonistic groups to develop shared goals and joint efforts. Bystanders can promote human rights by fighting censorship, intimidation, and control of the media by authorities (Staub, 1999). An example of an international bystander group is the UN peacekeeper organization, identified as a unique and dynamic instrument developed as a way to help countries torn by conflict to create the conditions for lasting peace.

Another common intervention – both of external NGOs and internal peace-building organizations – is the development of joint projects between disputing groups. The general public must also be informed about the benefits of peace and the ways in which officials are trying to bring it about. In Problem Solving Workshops, unofficial representatives of groups or states which have engaged in protracted conflict try to find some basis for reducing the harm that civil wars and guerilla actions create (Kelman, 1992).

Transformative dialogue: Appreciative Inquiry

One of the most popular and widespread organizational programs in the past three decades is Appreciative Inquiry. The core of this program is that those who are involved search for the positive core at the heart of their organization. In order to highlight what this positive core is, the people of the organization, from the top executives to the lowest-paid workers, join together to discover the power for good that is present in the organization. Often the means for this exploration is the sharing of stories that people tell in answer to questions about their organization. For example, consultants may help by asking a question such as: can you tell about a time when you were working with colleagues, and the project was very successful and everyone played a part in its success? Once these stories are collected, the people in small groups begin to find the basis for the successes these stories represent. This base becomes the source from which plans are made to grow and expand these good practices. By enlarging the positive processes in the organization, the poorer practices are pushed out, and the organization becomes stronger and more vital. Unlike problem solving programs, the appreciative inquiry process enhances optimism, solidarity, and good spirits. Through the AI process, transformations occur, in respect for one another, for appreciation, and for a belief in the future transformation of the organization (Cooperrider & Whitney, 2005; Whitney & Trosten-Bloom, 2003). Dozens of projects, created throughout the world, support the viewpoint that an appreciative approach yields very successful outcomes for those who pursue the path with enthusiasm and commitment.

Transformative dialogue and narrative mediation

In 2017, Senator Rand Paul of Kentucky was at home, mowing his lawn on his power mower, wearing his earphones. As he got off his mower, his neighbor, with whom he had a longstanding feud over the grass clippings that his mower blew onto his neighbor's yard, came rushing at him, tackled him, and threw the senator to the ground. Due to his fall, Paul broke six ribs and was taken to the hospital. The neighbor was heard to shout, "I've been trying to sell my house for years, and I can't because of you." Two very different stories of how this conflict led to this outcome occurred. Given the scenario, is there any potential for a transformative dialogue here?

Two mediators, Gerald Monk and John Winslade, have been working with such types of conflicts for many years. In the format that Monk and Winslade (2013) have created, parties to a conflict each tell their stories in private to the mediators. They unfold their grievances without any oppositional comments from their adversaries. The mediators listen closely to the told story, but they are also listening for the untold, partial, hidden stories that may provide clues for a changing story. As they listen to the stories of the two (or more) adversarial parties, they seek to discover shared interests, overlapping concerns, and common values and fears. By bringing these together, and either challenging the told story or inventing a new story or a revised story, the two parties come closer together in important ways. Once the groundwork is established that they are not oppositional in a win-lose situation, they can commence to tell new stories that begin to incorporate the other. New potentials for solutions come about. Agreements can be reached, at least partially. Fires can become controlled or extinguished. For example, in the typical neighbors' disagreements, there are issues of property, ownership, and responsibility for damages. A tree on one side harms the property of the other. When it is found that both parties are very partial to shade from trees, and value trees themselves, and if reminded of mutual interests activated in the past to preserve trees, less distance is found between the formerly warring parties. Economic solutions can be created with less friction and punitive damages. Transformative dialogues can be created that end the conflict.

Transformative dialogues: co-creating new narratives among ancient adversaries

How can new narratives be created among culturally oppositional parties of long standing? What if the history of antagonisms does not go back ten years, but ten generations? The Project on the Education of Muslim Minority Children is an example of a comprehensive intervention inside and outside the classroom since 1997 in the northeastern Greek province of Thrace. The project is an effort to help children who have a Turkish ethnic identity and are Muslims; these children bear the stigma of belonging to a group that has as its history that they are lifelong enemies of Greece.

In Thrace, there exists a system of separate schooling for minority children; at the secondary level, common education is more frequent. The project in question aims at the social inclusion of minority children, who tend to fail at school and to drop out. It is a complex intervention, which involves parents, youth workers who are from both Turkish and Greek backgrounds, and teachers.

The children created a name and a place for themselves called D.E.N., which are 'real,' 'imagined,' or 'symbolic' spaces that host activities for children, adolescents, and young adults across various divides of Thracian society. These venues offer the potential for collaborative learning and the material reality of a workshop with many resources, tools, supplies, and equipment. Youngsters are urged to explore their psychosocial environment, to look inwards towards themselves, to look outwards towards their community, and to express themselves creatively through various artistic means, such as drawing, theatrical games, narration and written text, constructions, clay modeling, collage, photography, video, and computer processing. They are encouraged to exercise collaborative projects and participate actively at every stage; that is, to visualize them from the start, to plan, to implement, to reflect upon the process of creation, and finally to come up with an end product.

Thus the aim was, and still is, to support existing community initiatives, while introducing new methodologies in empowering young people and drawing upon social constructionist and systemic principles. In all phases of the intervention, D.E.N. gradually opened up to the broader context. They developed extensive cooperation with the local community and the local government in order to form a human support network that would contribute to the self-sustained future of this institution.

Dreaming and fantasy have been powerful resources in the dialogic search for meanings and understandings. In the youth workers' own words, while they were looking back at these first experiences of transformative dialogue:

> It was when we started sharing the same space, sharing our concerns, our dreams, our expectations. When we touched each other's soul. When we gradually started looking into each other's eyes, capturing the reflection of our gaze . . . so that a chain was formed, a chain of gazes that was getting stronger and stronger as 'in unity we stand strong,' and this strength acquired shape and smell, such as of a pine tree, . . . Who can tell me that there is no room for dreams?

The success of this work in Greece shares the vision that is also present in the work of Pearce and Littlejohn (2011), who emphasize that strong moral concerns are at the heart of many conflicts. The ability to move across the divides of moral differences depends upon becoming close to the lived experiences of the others. Being exposed to their moral actions unsettles the stories that have been created by others historically, and they begin to feel differently about the ways of the others. This sense of discomfort can lead to transformative actions among the partners.

Reflections on opportunities in a 'liquid modernity' world

If there is some hope for our aging planet and peoples, and the potentials of social constructionist ideas for helping to overcome resentments, resistances, and revulsions among people in various walks of life, what outcomes might we expect? Some possibilities lie herein:

- Accepting the significance of relational processes dulls the propensity to hold individuals responsible for deeds, evil as well as good. Taking a relational perspective allows for the possibility of framing actions as outcomes of complex threads of context, timing, and clashing systems of values and interests. The metaphor of the rhizome helps us to formulate new understandings of conflict in action. The potential then exists to find forms of relating that foster growth for all parties to a conflict, to some degree. Transformative initiatives are encouraged.
- Looking for synergies and overlapping realities, caring for the potentials of all groups to have some moral goods and worthy goals, being appreciative and open to new possibilities, and the transformative power latent in all encounters, no matter how seemingly fraught with difficulties and conflicts. Being sensitive to how marginalized certain parties to a conflict might be, and how to engage with various positioning of parties to a conflict.

- Creating practices that seek to build trust in relationships, encourage curiosity about the other, finding common ground in conflictual situations, and exploring the possibilities for transformative moments.
- Being sensitive to the power of language to build or disrupt connections among adversarial groups; seeking ways of minimizing differences and maximizing common concerns.
- Choosing times, places, and activities that are non-threatening, aesthetically pleasing, and socially engaging so as to reduce anxiety, fear, and hateful expressions.
- Recognizing that all positions are value-laden, and that good and evil are embedded in the constructions that people have made of their lives and their realities. The acceptance of the view that multiple constructions can be created to evaluate others' moral standards, and that there may be several ways that another's moral code within a particular context can be evaluated. Plural moralities require complex, nuanced, and careful inquiry and understandings.

Note

1 These points summarize much of the literature on conflict resolution found in the counseling and therapy literature. This list, developed specifically for this chapter, was created by the author and Kenneth J. Gergen, 2017.

References

Albarracin, D., Johnson, B. T., & Zanna, M. (2005). *The handbook of attitudes.* Mahwah, NJ: Lawrence Erlbaum Associates.

Anderson, E. (2011). *The cosmopolitan canopy: Race and civility in everyday life.* New York, NY: W.W. Norton & Company.

Anzaldua, G. E. (2012). *Borderlands/La Frontera: The new Mestiza* (4th ed.). San Francisco, CA: Aunt Lute Books. (Originally published 1987)

Bauman, Z. (2011). *Culture in a liquid modern world.* Malden, MA: Polity Press.

Boal, A. (1995). *The rainbow of desire: The Boal method of theatre and therapy.* London: Routledge.

Cooperrider, D. L., & Whitney, D. (2005). *A positive revolution in change: Appreciative inquiry.* San Francisco, CA: Berrett Koehler Publishers Inc.

Deleuze, G., & Guattari, F. (2004). *A thousand plateaus: Capitalism and schizophrenia.* (Brian Massumi, Trans. in 1987). London and New York, NY: Continuum. (Originally published in French, 1980)

Fernandez, S. P. C. (1995). Contemporary theatre in Mindanao. *DULAAN: The Filipino Theatre and Arts Magazine.* Retrieved from www.msuiit.edu.ph/ipag/dulaan/mindthea.html

Fifield, A. (2018, January 16). North Korean orchestra to perform at Olympics. *Philadelphia Inquirer,* A7.

Fowler, A., Gamble, N. N., Hogan, F. X., Hogan, M. K., McComish, M., & Thorp, B. (2001, January 28). Talking with the enemy. *Boston Globe,* F1.

Freinacht, H. (2017). *The listening society: A metamodern guide to politics* (Book one). Metamodern ApS.

Gemignani, M. (2011). The past is past: The use of memories and self-healing narratives in immigrants from the former Yugoslavia. *Journal of Refugee Studies, 24,* 132–156.

Gergen, K. J. (2009). *Relational being: Beyond self and community.* New York, NY: Oxford University Press.

Gergen, K. J. (2015). *An invitation to social construction* (3rd ed.). London: Sage Publications.

Gergen, K. J., & Gergen, M. (2004). *Social construction: Entering the dialogue.* Chagrin Falls, OH: Taos Institute Publications.

Goffman, E. (1955). On face work: An analysis of ritual elements in social interaction. *Psychiatry: Interpersonal and Biological Processes, 18,* 213–231.

Hammack, P. (2011). *Narrative and the politics of identity: The cultural psychology of Israeli and Palestinian youth.* New York, NY: Oxford University Press.

Harré, R. (2012). Positioning theory: moral dimensions of social-cultural psychology. In J. Valsiner (Ed.), *The Oxford handbook of culture and psychology* (pp. 191–206). New York, NY: Oxford University Press.

Harré, R., Moghaddam, F., Pilkerton Cairnie, T., Rothbart, D., & Sabat, S. (2009). Recent advances in positioning theory. *Theory and Psychology, 19,* 5–31.

Hermans, H. J. M., & Hermans-Konopka, A. (2010). *Dialogical self theory: Positioning and counter-positioning in a globalizing society.* Cambridge: Cambridge University Press.

Herzig, M., & Chasin, L. (2005). *Fostering dialogue across divides: A nuts and bolts guide from the public conversations project.* Retrieved from www.publicconversations.org/docs/resources/Jams_website.pdf

Kelman, H. C. (1992). Informal mediation by the scholar/practitioner. In J. Bercovitch & J. Z. Rubin (Eds.), *Mediation in international relations* (pp. 64–96). London: Palgrave Macmillan.

Leavy, P. (Ed.). (2018). *Handbook of arts-based research.* New York, NY: Guilford Press.

Lock, A., & Strong, T. (Eds.). (2012). *Discursive perspectives in the therapeutic practice.* Oxford: Oxford University Press.

McNamee, S., & Hosking, D. M. (2012). *Research and social change: A relational constructionist approach.* New York, NY: Routledge.

Moghaddam, F., & Harré, R. (2010). Words, conflicts and political processes. In F. Moghaddam & R. Harré (Eds.), *Words of conflict, words of war: How the language we use in political processes sparks fighting.* Santa Barbara, CA: Praeger.

Monk, G. D., & Winslade, J. M. (2013). *When stories clash: Addressing conflict with narrative mediation.* Chagrin Falls, OH: Taos Institute Publications.

Pearce, W. B., & Littlejohn, S. W. (2011). *Moral conflict: When social worlds collide.* Thousand Oaks, CA: Sage Publications.

Shank, M. (2005). Redefining the movement: Art activism. *Seattle Journal for Social Justice, 3*(2), 531–559.

Staub, E. (1999). The origins and prevention of genocide, mass killing, and other collective violence. *Peace and Conflict, 5,* 303–336.

Stearns, D. P. (2017, June 18). Ending on a puzzling note. *Philadelphia Inquirer,* H3.

United States Institute of Peace. (2017). *Arts and building peace: Affirming the basics and envisioning the future.* Retrieved from http://www.usip.org

Vassiliou, A., & Dragonas, T. (2017). Sowing seeds of synergy: Creative youth work-shops in a multi-cultural context. In T. Dragonas, K. J. Gergen, S. McNamee, & E. Tseliou (Eds.), *Education as social construction: Contributions of theory, research, and practice* (pp. 192–212). Chagrin Falls, OH: Taos Institute Publications.

White, M., & Epston, D. (1990). *Narrative means to therapeutic ends.* New York, NY: W.W. Norton & Company.

Whitney, D., & Trosten-Bloom, A. (2003). *The power of appreciative inquiry: A practical guide to positive change* (2nd ed.). San Francisco, CA: Berrett Koehler Publishers Inc.

Wielzen, D. R., & Avest, I. ter (Eds.). (2017). *Interfaith education for all: Theoretical perspectives and best practices for transformative action.* Rotterdam, NL: Sense Publishers.

13 Orientation, disorientation, and reorientation in the context of plural moralities

Experiences of an LGBT refugee arriving in the Netherlands

Carmen Schuhmann and Robin Knibbe

Introduction

When we look at the issue of moral orientation of individuals in liquid modernity, we may identify crisis, 'being on the move,' and multiple cultural and religious worldviews as factors that are specifically challenging. LGBT (lesbian, gay, bisexual, transgender) refugees can provide crucial insights on how these factors affect individual lives, and on the question of how to remain resilient when all of these factors are strongly present in one's life: "Propelled by fear of violence and flight from stigma, impelled by desire for connection and belonging, the movements of people whose sexualities or gender defy and offend norms cover a complex spatial, social, and psychological terrain" (Jordan, 2009, p. 169). LGBT refugees are literally 'on the move,' migrating from their home country to new places. They also remain in a situation of crisis for a long time, leaving an unsafe setting and entering an unfamiliar environment. Finally, as they leave one country, enter the next, and are surrounded by other refugees, they have to deal with multiple cultural and religious perspectives. The fact that the moral atmosphere in their home country is so hostile and potentially dangerous – it is illegal, wrong, or despicable to be LGBT – adds salience to the issue of moral orientation: it becomes a matter of safety – of survival.

In this chapter, contemporary challenges of plural moralities are explored simultaneously in a theoretical perspective and in the lived perspective of an LGBT refugee arriving in the Netherlands. We find it important to integrate empirical data in our theoretical reflections in order to emphasize how living in a world of plural moralities may have a very real and potentially devastating impact on the lives of people in vulnerable positions. To this end we decided to make use of a case study, as case study research "investigates a contemporary phenomenon (the 'case') in depth and within its real-world context, especially when the boundaries between phenomenon and context may not be clearly evident" (Yin, 2014, p. 16).

We start by outlining a theoretical framework concerning the subject of plural moralities. We give a brief explanation of Taylor's (1989, 2007) ideas concerning 'orientation in moral space'; we then relate these ideas to theory of relational being (Gergen, 2009), and to dialogical self theory (DST) (Hermans & Hermans-Konopka, 2010). After stating our research question and explaining the research method, we describe our findings concerning the lived experience of an LGBT refugee, Grace, whom we interviewed about her arrival in the Netherlands. We elaborate on four themes that emerged as crucial for understanding Grace's experiences: her relation with other people; language; the legal system; and embodiment and physical space. We conclude by complementing the initial theoretical outline with a queer theoretical perspective by feminist writer Sara Ahmed (2006) that allows for a more comprehensive understanding of Grace's story.

Orientation and disorientation in 'moral space' – relational being and DST

According to Charles Taylor (1989), human existence can be metaphorically described in terms of orientation processes. Human beings attempt to orient themselves in a metaphorical space that Taylor calls 'moral space'; the space of existential questions or questions of life orientation. Orienting frameworks in moral space are 'believable visions of the good' (Schuhmann & van der Geugten, 2017) – culturally rooted visions of a good life that we commit ourselves to and that we believe we may move towards and thus integrate in our lives. Here, morality and 'the good' are understood in a broad sense, encompassing not only people's obligations towards others, but also notions of a life worth living, a life commanding respect, and a 'full' life. Taylor explains his idea of morality as follows:

> I want to consider a gamut of views a bit broader than what is normally described as the 'moral.' In addition to our notions and reactions on such issues as justice and the respect of other people's life, well-being, and dignity, I also want to look at our sense of what underlies our own dignity, or questions about what makes our lives meaningful or fulfilling.
>
> (Taylor, 1989, p. 4)

According to Taylor, orientation processes in moral space often do not require much reflection, and orienting frameworks are moral intuitions that largely remain implicit. However, disorientation may occur when, for instance due to life events, a cherished vision of the good is no longer 'believable' and no longer functions as an orienting framework. It seems no longer possible to move towards this good, to integrate it in one's life in the new situation, or the original good no longer seems to be a valuable good after all (Schuhmann & van der Geugten, 2017). We are 'lost' with respect to existential questions; we do not know how to live or how to go on. Taylor (2007) argues that, in a 'secular age,' the traditional orienting frameworks, provided by religion, have lost their self-evidence. Even when people are not confronted with specific unsettling events, orientation is anything but straightforward: "The developing 'disenchantment' of modern culture . . . has undermined so many traditional frameworks and, indeed, created a situation where our old horizons have been swept away and all frameworks may seem problematic" (Taylor, 1989, p. 26).

When we look at orientation processes in moral space from a perspective of relational being (Gergen, 2009), we see how complex these processes are in a globalizing world. According to this perspective, human beings are not separate: they come into being via the relations into which they are born and in which they are immersed instead of the other way around. Gergen (2009) emphasizes the Latin root of the term 'morality,' which denotes custom or convention within a community. What we consider to be 'good' – our visions of the good – is not a matter of individual predilection but of relational construction. "If we trace all that we hold meaningful in life to relationship, then we must also view relationships as the source of our visions of good and evil" (Gergen, 2009, p. 356) – and, we would add, of our visions of the good in a broader Taylorean sense. As there are countless relational contexts, there are countless context-related visions of the good, some of which may be incompatible with others. In particular, in our globalizing world, where we are immersed in increasingly complex relational webs, we are connected to a complexity of different visions of the good, some of which are incompatible with others: "For every relationship of which I am part, I am also part of another relationship for whom my present actions may be misbegotten" (Gergen, 2009, p. 359). In other words, in a world of 'plural moralities,' disorientation in moral space may easily arise from getting confused because of the plentitude of, sometimes opposite, directions that are indicated by different relational contexts that we belong to. Disorientation might even be seen as a condition of our globalizing world.

When we add the perspective of dialogical self theory (DST) to the picture, we see how living in a world of plural moralities not only threatens orientation processes in moral space but also provides us with potentially rich resources for orientation. According to Taylor (1989), finding our orientation in moral space is constitutive of our identity: "To lose this orientation, or not to have found it, is not to know who one is. And this orientation, once attained, defines where you answer from, hence your identity" (Taylor, 1989, p. 29). In particular, in an age of globalization, as our orientation in moral space is at risk, so is our sense of identity. The increasing range of available visions of the good corresponds to "an increased range of identifications and disidentifications available" (Hermans, 2014, p. 135), which relate to multiple potential 'I-positions.' In fact, Hermans (2014), founder of DST, remarks that "the self, as part of a changing society, is subjected to an increasing process of fragmentation" (Hermans, 2014, p. 135). This may lead to disintegration of the self or to walling oneself off from others as a form of self-defense (Hermans & Hermans-Konopka, 2010; Hermans, 2014). However, when we manage to bring diverse, even opposite, *I*-positions together in a more complex and integrative self, this may counter disorganizing movements. Here the notion of dialogue is essential: in DST, *I*-positions are seen as voiced, which allows for dialogical relations between them. In the perspective of DST, an adaptive identity is one in which decentering movements are balanced by the centering movement of bringing different voices corresponding to different *I*-positions into dialogue. New moral positions we encounter – potential *I*-positions – may be enriching when we manage to weave dialogical relationships between the new position and existing *I*-positions, resulting in a richer, more multifaceted and multi-layered self (Hermans, 2014). In terms of orientation, this gives us a more detailed view of the moral space in which we are orienting ourselves, a better understanding of our position in it, and a better picture of potential connections between various orientation points.

An LGBT refugee's lived experience of arriving in the Netherlands: a case study

Aim and research question

The aim of the case study was to describe challenges of plural moralities from an experiential perspective. We aimed at tapping into the lived experience of (dis)orientation in a particularly challenging context: the context of LGBT refugees seeking asylum in the Netherlands. The research question around which we conducted our case study is: How do LGBT refugees in the Netherlands (manage to) (re)orient during asylum procedure? Subquestions were: What are experiences of disorientation of LGBT refugees when arriving in the Netherlands? What obstacles do they face when attempting to (re)orient? What resources do they have for (re)orienting? These questions may also be understood as questions about 'moral/existential resilience': processes where people in extremely challenging life situations manage to reorient towards some vision of the good in the context of plural and clashing moralities (Schuhmann & van der Geugten, 2017).

Method

We explored the research question by means of a single case. In our search for a suitable case study for analyzing contemporary challenges in plural moralities, we asked a befriended counselor at the Worldhouse in Amsterdam (a diaconal house for undocumented refugees) whether he had encountered stories in his work that would illustrate the difficulties of orienting in moral space. He told us about the challenges LGBT refugees face when they arrive in the Netherlands. Grace was one of those refugees, and she was willing to be interviewed by us. Apart from getting a clear image of the difficulties of orienting in a place that is not your home country, Grace's story is particularly interesting with a view to questions of resilience, as our impression was that she can be described as a very resilient woman (by the counselor of the Worldhouse, she was actually described as such). She was a confident respondent in the sense that she was able and willing to share personal stories concerning challenging and sometimes traumatizing situations that she had experienced. She showed emotions while telling these stories without being carried away by them.

We interviewed Grace in the Worldhouse, a place that is familiar to her and where she has spent quite some time during her procedure. We aimed at exploring the 'lived moral universe' of Grace: the complex web of her moral intuitions that function as orienting frameworks, consisting of notions of a life worth living, a life commanding respect, and a 'full' life. We also aimed at detecting impediments and resources that had an impact on her quest for (re)orientation during asylum procedure. In order to tap into Grace's 'lived moral universe,' we based ourselves on the Biographic Narrative Interpretive Method (BNIM) and used a BNIM-type narrative interview design (Wengraf, 2001). According to Taylor (1989), orientation processes in moral space are narrative processes: "we grasp our lives in a *narrative*" (p. 47). Other authors also argue that moral life is intertwined with narrative self-understanding (Walker, 2007; Atkins, 2008). Following the BNIM method, we started by posing a single narrative question to Grace – *Can you tell us your story of arriving in the Netherlands* – and listened to her story without interrupting her. After about an hour, Grace stopped herself and asked us, *Do you have any more questions for me?* We repeated the initial question and asked whether there was anything important she wanted to add. After that, Grace talked for another hour in which we did not interrupt her. We then felt that we had a rich account concerning Grace's 'lived moral universe' and her sources of resilience, as the account included detailed narratives of how she had experienced certain concrete events. We therefore did not feel the need to ask Grace further questions concerning concrete events in her story, which would be the procedure in a regular BNIM interview (Wengraf, 2001).

We analyzed the interview by zooming in on narratives in the interview concerning concrete situations; here we looked for experiences that, against the background of Taylor's notion of orientation in moral space, could be understood as experiences of disorientation. That is, we focused on situations where Grace tells having the experience that her attempts to live a good life (good in Taylor's very broad sense of good versus bad, versus unworthy, versus unfulfilling) are challenged or fail. For each concrete situation, we described what moral visions and intuitions were at hand, what obstacles Grace faced in (re)orienting, and, when she managed to (re)orient, what were the resources she had for (re)orienting. From these descriptions, four themes emerged that play a major role in Grace's experiences of disorientation and in her attempts to reorient, and that are helpful for understanding Grace's resilience in severely disorienting circumstances.

These four themes are: relations with others, language, the legal system, and embodiment/location.

Grace's arrival in the Netherlands and the process of seeking asylum: outline of the story and its context

Grace is a gay woman from Uganda. Uganda is an extremely hostile environment for homosexuals, both politically and culturally. Homosexuality has been illegal since British colonial rule, which ended in 1950. In 2009 the Anti-Homosexuality Bill (AHB) was proposed, both aggravating the sentences and creating additional crimes. With this bill, homosexuals could be sentenced for life in prison. Originally it was intended to introduce the death penalty for homosexuality, but this was averted and replaced by a life imprisonment sentence. The same bill made it illegal to 'propagate' homosexuality, and made it obligatory to report gay activities to the police. In 2014 the bill was accepted. It reflects a widespread anti-gay sentiment in Uganda: a poll showed that 96% of the people in Uganda believe that homosexuality should not be accepted by society. Following the acceptance of the bill, there was a significant rise of state and non-state violence against Ugandan LGBT people. While there were 8 reported cases of human rights violations in 2013, after the introduction of the bill in 2014, there were 162 reported cases in a period of only four months. Life became increasingly dangerous for homosexuals in Uganda.[1]

Grace arrived in the Netherlands in November 2013. When she got off the plane, she had no idea where to go. *I just got into a bus I didn't even pick and I just got out somewhere.* After an extremely cold night at the bus stop, a woman who had seen her on the bus the day before took her in and cared for her while she was sick. Grace, not knowing the political or cultural situation in the Netherlands, was very careful not to disclose why she had fled her country. She was afraid that the police would lock her up, or that the couple where she stayed would kill her. *Every time they ask me I was just crying. How am I going to tell them? How? What if they also kill me in the night in my sleep. Just splash my head off. I said: no way I'm not going to tell them.* After a few days she was told to go to a center for asylum seekers in Ter Apel. There she was met by the police, who wanted to know what her reasons for fleeing Uganda were. After a long and stressful interview, she finally told the police that she had fled Uganda because she is a lesbian.

Then, the process of seeking asylum began. After her first interview, she was given a negative decision by the IND (the immigration and naturalization service in the Netherlands). She had a lawyer who then took her case to court. There, the negative decision was confirmed after long deliberation. Six months later, her case was reopened because the European court had noted that the Dutch government was not following European guidelines in the process. There was a new interview with the IND. Again, she got a negative decision. And again, her lawyer took her case to court, where the negative decision was once again repeated. She was given 28 days to leave the country. A counselor at the Worldhouse (a diaconal house for undocumented refugees) encouraged her to reapply for status and helped her to find a new lawyer. Shortly after, by accident, Grace found an old Ugandan newspaper from 2015, where there was a list called: 'a hundred LGBT people exposed.' She was on this list. This turned out to be an essential piece of evidence in her new procedure. She took the newspaper to her lawyer, who then took her case to court again. In April 2017, she was granted a status in the Netherlands.

Experiences of disorientation and processes of (re)orientation in Grace's story

(Dis)orientation in relation to others

Grace describes how, just after arriving in the Netherlands, she asks herself existential questions, phrased in terms of the orientation metaphor: *"Where is life going? Where is life leading me?"* Her words express a deep and unsettling sense of disorientation, which even leads to suicidal thoughts: *"Because when I just got here, something that was always popped up in my mind was jumping in the train. Why living? Why do I have to live? I looked home, it was so far. . . . You know, the best thing to do is to die."* It seems that, having left her 'home' and arriving in an unknown country, Grace sees no orientation point, no potential way of living. After her journey, she no longer has the energy to search for orientation and meaning in her life, and she is at the point of giving up altogether.

In terms of relational theory, Grace has left the relational contexts back 'home,' where her life was at risk, but is not (yet) immersed in new relational contexts that affirm her sexual identity. Consequently, she does not have access to ways of living that support her sexual orientation. From a viewpoint of relational being, when one is cut off from all relational contexts, life is impossible. Still, Grace describes a relational resource for overcoming – or at least not giving in to – these suicidal thoughts. She explains how, according to her family in Uganda, she is cursed and sick because she is a lesbian. Her family members would see her death as the logical consequence of her living as a lesbian. In their view, being gay is not a viable way of life: *They say: you see that? She had to kill herself. They say: you people, you die miserable.* When she feels like giving up, Grace responds to this moral position of her family members: *"I hope [I] disprove my family. I'm sure one day they will understand that we are also human beings like them and we are equal."* From this statement, we learn that Grace derives a sense of hope from the relational context of her family, even though her family members reject her. Turning against her family's superstition is not a negative act but one that provides her with a sense of direction concerning her desperate existential question 'why living?'

What is important here from the perspective of DST is that, in turning against the superstition of her family, Grace does not cut off the relationship with her family members but rather makes a move towards them. She doesn't agree with the moral position of her family, but she is confident that, one day, she will prove them wrong, and even make them understand her. So, she manages to build a connection between two diametrically opposed *I*-positions – the position of 'I as lesbian' and 'I as member of a family with superstitious notions concerning lesbians.' Her resource is the hopeful idea that moral positions may gradually change over time, that people may eventually change direction and reorient towards a vision of equality of all human beings. This creative turn from disorientation to orientation can be connected to the notion of moral imagination (see Alma, Chapter 4 in this volume). Alma states that moral imagination can create visions of change, of something that is not immediately present in the current situation. This can transform the people involved in a way that strengthens relationships. By imagining her family coming to terms with her identity, Grace creates a focal point that is worth living for and entails a choice for connection over enmity.

Apart from her family members, Grace also describes the role of people she has met in the Netherlands – people she feels supported by as they do understand her: *If my family doesn't [understand] and I have only one who supports me, I have a new family here! Every Dutch person is my new family.* So, another resource for reorientation are the people she meets who embody a counter-position to the rejection of her family, people who embody the vision that all human beings are equal, people who understand her and accept her. She extends the idea of family to these people and eventually to all people in the Netherlands, thus creating a new position within the set of positions 'I as member of a family'; 'I as member of a family who does understand me.' *"I am so happy about the Netherlands people. They are really welcoming. Actually they don't discriminate us, like people from Africa."* By extending the concept of 'family' to all Dutch people – not just the people she has actually met who understand and support her – Grace creates a strong and extended relational context of people who support visions of the good in which she is accepted and has a place. So, 'family' has a double role in Grace's process of reorienting in moral space in a situation where she has suicidal thoughts. On the one hand, she bridges the moral gap between herself and her family members in Uganda through the hope that one day they will stand on her side, and in doing so she finds a solid counter-thought to despair and death. On the other hand, she extends the idea of 'family' to include all people whom she feels share her moral position that people should not discriminate against each other.

Grace maintains similar strategies when she is confronted with people in the Netherlands who discriminate against her. She explains that, when attending gatherings of the Uganda House (a meeting place for the Ugandan community in the Netherlands), she sensed that people were talking about her and telling their children not to get in contact with her. In contact with fellow refugees, she also experienced hostile reactions to her being gay. For instance, her Syrian work-out buddy suddenly did not want to be seen with her after he found out that she was gay. Grace explains that at first these reactions towards her made her cry and feel down. She describes day-dreaming about making people understand: *"If I was the president of the world I could make people understand. [. . .] I can put them in one room and I would tell everybody: 'come on! You're not supposed to discriminate people.'"* Clearly, the situations where she experiences discrimination have disorienting potential as they undermine the believability of a vision of the good that seems crucial to her: the vision that people should not discriminate against each other but (as Grace said in an earlier quote) should cherish their equality as human beings. In trauma therapy, Grace is offered a different perspective on how to handle the discrimination, one that does not involve having the power to make those who discriminate obey her. There she is told that she can't expect to change peoples' feelings. In the end, she seems to take a perspective that is in between her initial response of wanting to change the way the people think and the advice from therapy to let it go. She does not turn away from people when they judge her: *"because when you hurt me, I will find a place to forgive you."* She creates a position of 'I as (eventually) forgiving' that allows her not to turn away from people who discriminate against, judge, and hurt her. She notices that when she manages to forgive judgmental people, these people eventually become friendly.

> [A]nd that's how I made friends. People in the first place, they judge you right away: 'o my gosh, it's a lesbian. She doesn't need to be close to me. She doesn't need to see that.' But in the end, you actually see them coming for some advice. 'Oh Grace, how could I do this? Grace, you need to tell me here. Grace how do you do that?' They come for advice and in my head I was like: 'if I had just your way, you would never understand how good you are. If someone does you wrong and you say: if you go! You would never understand.' You need to put your enemies closer, for them to understand you more, and then they become your friends.

Grace's final statement wonderfully captures the strategy that helps her stick with her moral vision of human equality without breaking off the relation with those that block her orientation towards this vision by discriminating against her.

In both situations described here, Grace makes a deliberate and conscious choice to stick to her own moral vision that all human beings are equal, even when others block this orientation. Here, her resource to (re)orient in moral space in disorienting situations is a deliberate strategy of cultivating hope and forgiveness in response to people who discriminate against and hurt her. This seems a good example of the relational ethic Gergen describes (see Chapter 1 in this volume). The alienation the people create by discriminating against her is met with a relational ethic, where Grace is actively involved in restoring a space where she can be seen as a good person, and people can be good to her in return.

In another situation, however, the resource that she uses for orienting towards a good life does not involve an actively chosen strategy but is more obviously relational. When Grace is in an asylum center at the beginning of her stay in the Netherlands, one of the professionals at the center recognizes that she is a lesbian and asks her whether she would like to join LGBT communities. Grace is very surprised: *"I was like: 'how does she know?'"* So she found her way to LGBT organizations because she was invited by someone who was attentive to her and saw that she might benefit from being part of LGBT communities. Grace explains that meeting with people who share and represent visions of the good that do not contradict her sexual identity was of vital importance to her and 'keeps her going:' *"What keeps me going is the fact that there are a lot of organizations, you know? . . . So the fact that you can't have a devil's mind all the time."* According to relational theory, visions of the good spring from relational contexts; sharing visions with others give them viability. In this situation, Grace is guided by an attentive other to relational contexts where people live according to visions of the good that she may share. Her resource for reorienting to a good life consists of a caring person reaching out to her and showing her a path to follow.

(Dis)orientation in language

Language plays an important role in the stories Grace tells both about experiences of disorientation and about her attempts to (re)orient in life in disorienting situations. In the first place, Grace's story illustrates how disorienting it is not to understand the language that is spoken in the places where one attempts to live: *"And then everything is in Dutch and when they say 'asielzoekerscentrum' [asylum center] you don't know what it is. So: 'where am I?'"* Grace has literally no idea where people take her or send her, when the destination is explained to her in Dutch. She cannot assess whether these are destinations that will support her attempts towards a good life or not, and she feels that she is at the mercy of people who do know the language: *"And later they say: 'You know what, we are just going to [show] where you can sleep.' So I was like [soft voice]: 'Where then?'"*

The importance of language in orientation processes is perhaps most obvious in a story that Grace tells about the first interview that she has with the foreign police department in Ter Apel. When Grace refuses to answer the question "Why are you here?" posed in English, she is assigned an interpreter who speaks her native language, Luganda. She keenly feels how vulnerable and dependent on good intentions of others this makes her, since she cannot check whether the interpreter translates her words correctly. Not knowing how the interpreter is connected to the situation, Grace fears that she may be a spy from home.

So they put [the interpreter] on the phone and she said: 'Miss, they want to help you, and if you can tell them . . .,' and I was like: Who is that one talking to me on the phone. I don't know who she is, where she is coming from? . . . So she took a really long time to explain to me: 'I am working for myself, I am not working for the government of Uganda, I am not working for the government of the Dutch people.' And I thought: What if she is lying to me? What if I told them, and the next day they will take me back? It's better for me to keep quiet. What if they are lying? What if they are tricking me?

In the interview, Grace finally takes the risky step to tell the police (and the interpreter) that she has fled Uganda because she is a lesbian: *And then I said in a very tiny tone: 'I'm here because I'm a lesbian.' And my heart went like boom boom boom. What's next?* Then she hears a very specific response from the interpreter. "*So the woman she had a funny tone, she said: 'hmm.' And I was like: o shit. You see, if somebody in Uganda says 'hmm,' things are not good.*" This 'funny tone' scares Grace: she assumes that her situation is really bad and that she is in danger. As she does not understand Dutch, the language of the people who will decide about her future, she cannot 'read' their linguistic clues about what will happen to her, which is very disempowering. In order to assess her situation, she is dependent on the interpreter, a woman she does not trust, and on the language – Luganda – that is frightening for her in relation to her sexual orientation. So, she assigns great importance to any clue the interpreter gives her concerning her chances to orient towards a good life – a life where she can openly live as a lesbian. The first clue she gets comes from the interpreter: the sound that means trouble in Uganda.

Grace also describes experiences where language plays a positive and empowering role in her attempts to orient. A while after arriving in the Netherlands, she joins Ugandan communities where she gets to hear and speak her mother language again: "*I was like: I was missing this. It was a relief.*" Grace also tells how, at the end of her procedure, the Dutch language too is related to a positive experience of belonging. In her last court appeal, at a certain moment she decides to bypass the interpreter and answer the judge in Dutch, a language she has now learned to speak. "*So I told him – he was talking in Nederlands [Dutch for 'Dutch'] – and I don't know how I got the courage. But I had Dutch lessons and I thought: I'm going to reply in Nederlands. And he said 'Whaaaat? I'm so proud of you! Three years and you can speak.' So he was so happy with that.*" It is clear here how valuable and encouraging this moment of recognition by a representative of the Dutch legal system is for Grace. This positive experience illustrates that offering refugees opportunities to learn the language of their arrival country has significance at an existential level. This directly affects refugees' capacity to orient and thus their sense of meaning in life.

(Dis)orientation with respect to the legal system

The very first thing that Grace told us in the interview concerned the great sense of relief that she developed during her stay in the Netherlands: *"It was a breakthrough. It's like you've been in a house full of fire, and you come out. The freshness you breathe."* This sense of relief results from the insight that in the Netherlands she has basic rights, also as an asylum seeker. Grace is surprised to find that a room, a bed, and food is arranged for her, that she can go to a doctor when she is sick. It is a revelation to her that in the Netherlands her rights are taken so seriously: during all of the asylum procedure, even when she may still be rejected, she has rights. Grace emphasizes that she is not used to that: *"Even if you go to court and the judge will say: mevrouw [Dutch for 'Ms'] Grace, it's your right to tell me or not to tell me, or to talk or not to talk. . . . You understand? Sometimes you say no, sometimes you say yes, and it's your right! . . . It's a wonderful moment, you know?"*

When we follow Grace's story chronologically, we find that it took her a while to learn that, in the Netherlands, she may trust legal authorities to respect her basic rights. She had fled from a country where the legal system labels her sexual orientation as illegal, as punishable. Grace's visions of the good concerning her sexual life are not compatible with legal visions in Uganda of what constitutes a good life, worthy of legal support. The enormous sense of relief that she talks about at the beginning of the interview demonstrates how dangerous and oppressive it was for Grace to live in a country where, as a lesbian, she is not protected but rather endangered by legal authorities. This sense of danger and oppression is still very much present in her appraisal of (representatives of) the legal system in the beginning of her stay in the Netherlands. She fled Uganda in the hope of arriving in a country in which she is not prosecuted for her sexual orientation, but she has few means of finding out whether this hope is justified. Her lack of knowledge of the Dutch legal system and the Dutch language makes it extremely difficult for her to situate the legal system as a reference point in moral space. When Grace is about to be interviewed by the foreign police department, she reacts to the police just as she would have in Uganda: *"So I was scared. One of those scary moments, seeing the police. So he said: 'Follow me.' Doors closing [claps hands, mimicking the closing doors]. So I thought: Oh my God, not to prison. . . ."* The disorientation that Grace experiences is related to not knowing what vision of the good the legal system represents, not knowing her position with respect to the legal system. When she is assigned an interpreter, who tells her that she can trust the police, that the police wants to help her, she does not know whether or not she can trust the interpreter. The message that the police is trustworthy is told to her in her native language, which is frightening for her in legal situations; she has no reliable means of finding out whether the legal authorities are friendly or hostile, whether her legal situation has improved by fleeing from Uganda. As long as she is not sure about the position of the legal system in moral space, she feels disoriented: scared and insecure. It is only later, when she obtains knowledge about the Dutch legal system, that she embraces this system as an important positive point of orientation because of the protection of basic rights that it provides. To her, the system represents the equality of people, independent of their sexual orientation: *"No, no, nobody's going to kill you or take you to prison. They may take you to prison for some other reasons, but they can't take you to prison because you are a lesbian."*

It is noticeable that, despite the long, difficult legal trajectory that Grace has gone through while attempting to obtain a legal status, she emphasizes only the positive aspects of the Dutch legal system. She declares that she does not wish to complain about the procedure: *"You can't say: oh, I came here, and I was rejected, and I was done this to. However much they reject, . . . they always tell you: you have a right. Which in my country [laughs], well I never heard of that, that I have a right to things."* In her story, having rights seems to be far more important than having status. Grace also points out that receiving her status doesn't make a major difference to her: *"I still feel the same. I haven't changed. I'm Grace."* When Grace talks about the trajectory of obtaining her status, she is almost nonchalant. She tells how, before her final hearing, people keep asking her whether she is ready. This makes her impatient and annoyed: *"I don't need to prepare myself! It is my personal . . . you know it's me. I'm talking my heart out. I don't need to prepare myself."* She tells with pride how, when the judge comes to collect her for his final decision, he finds her watching football instead of waiting miserably. It seems that her confidence that her rights are secured by the legal system gives her a certain peace of mind that helps her deal with the uncertainty of the legal decision concerning her status.

(Dis)orientation in physical space and the role of embodiment

In the interview, Grace describes moments of literal disorientation in (physical) space: she does not know where she is or where she is traveling to. Leaving Schiphol, she picks a random bus to get on, and gets out at the last stop, not having any clue where she is. There she stays until a woman she does not know picks her up and, after a few days, explains to her to what place refugees are supposed to go. Apart from orientation in physical space, we also find that physicality in the sense of embodiment is related to experiences of disorientation. In the interview, Grace often refers to experiences of disorientation in bodily terms. For instance, when describing a low point in her life, Grace explains to us how she was freezing: *"I couldn't feel my feet, I couldn't feel my hands and my nose, my ears."* She remembers getting a jacket from the unknown woman at one of these moments where she was extremely cold – clearly this gesture was of vital importance for her in a desperate situation. In order to elaborate on the meaning of (dis)orientation in physical space in relation to moral space, and on the bodily (physical) dimension of (dis)orientation in moral space, we zoom in on two (chains of) events in Grace's story.

When Grace is given a negative decision from the IND after her first interview and has 28 days to leave the country, she has a hard time finding shelter. She finds a place to stay, but has to leave there after a week. This is a moment of severe disorientation: *"I was being stressed and crazy. It was too much for me."* She then becomes seriously ill: she develops a fever, has terrible headaches, and is not able to talk. Here, we see that her capacity to orient in physical space depends on her bodily condition: Grace has to be taken into the hospital. When she is released from the hospital, she is taken in by an organization where she can sleep for one night. As she is not officially registered as being ill, she is told to leave after one night – according to the rules of the organization, an official registration of illness was necessary for staying more than just one night. Grace then goes to a place that she is familiar with: the central station in Amsterdam. Sitting in front of the station, looking at people walking by, she thinks, *"what am I going to do? What's next?"* Here, we see how orientation in moral space is intertwined with orientation in physical space. Without a place where she can find shelter, Grace asks herself how she may go on living. Her question can be read as a fundamental question of survival: she is ill, has been told to return to the country where her life is in danger, and has no place to sleep at night or stay during the day – "what's next" can be read as "is there a 'next'?" We saw something similar when Grace arrives in the Netherlands; she wonders whether she should go on living at all as, having fled a country where her life is at risk, she is not sure whether she will find a safe place in this new country. This points at the 'physical' basis of orientation: finding an orientation in moral space depends both on one's bodily condition and on having a safe (physical) place where one can find shelter. Grace's story also points at the role of coincidence in orientation processes: sitting in front of the station and despairing about her situation, she happens to be called by her contact person from a refugee support organization in Amsterdam, who wants to check on how she is doing. Hearing about her situation, this organization makes sure that she gets a room where she can stay and recover. So, Grace manages to survive, not through some internal process of planning and decision making, but because of the fact that her contact person happened to call at the right time and was able to provide her with a safe place.

A second event that emphasizes the physical basis of orientation in moral space occurs in the beginning of Grace's arrival in the Netherlands. By the authorities, she is sent to Heerlen, in the south of the Netherlands, to live there while waiting for her procedure to start. She soon finds out that in Heerlen there are very few people of the LGBT community. She describes how this prevents her from feeling at home: *"It was not really welcoming."* People from the asylum center, realizing that she feels lonely, ensure that several people from her region in Africa (Ugandans and Nigerians) are located at the center. After a while, however, these people are sent away to other countries: *"So again, life was miserable."* At that moment, Grace makes a conscious decision to attempt to leave Heerlen and move to a place where she expects to be happier: *I say: you know what? I am not going to live here to be sad. I have to explore more in Amsterdam. Everybody says: life is in Amsterdam for the LGBTI.* After asking around, she is able to move to Amsterdam. Here, we see three things that are important with respect to Grace's attempts to orient in moral space. First, we see how important being part of a community – either a community of people from her region in Africa, or an LGBT community – is for Grace: it seems an indispensable element of living a good life. Second, we see how a vision of a good life – an orientation point in moral space – may be related to an actual place – a geographical orientation point. Third, we see that when Grace does have information about where she may feel at home ("Everybody says: life is in Amsterdam for the LGBT"), she takes action to move to that place (in a literal sense). Here, her orientation towards a certain place is not a matter of coincidence – as it is in the first chain of events we described, where Grace has no clue of what might be a safe place – but an intentional act.

Conclusion: obstacles, resources, and resilience in the context of plural moralities

Looking at Grace's story in terms of contemporary challenges of plural moralities, we find that, although Grace faces severe challenges in life, these challenges are not in the first place related to a confusing multitude and fluidity of moralities that are available to her. They are primarily related to her clashes with people and institutions representing moral visions that rule out the possibility of living as a lesbian. In Uganda, the moral visions that are dominant in the legal system and in the view on life of Grace's family members include the view that homosexuals need to be incarcerated or even deserve to die. What we see is that living in a world of plural moralities does not necessarily imply that these visions of the good are 'available' to a person. Moral visions in which the value of life does not depend on sexual orientation are not readily available to Grace – she cannot simply live according to these visions as, in Uganda, this would mean risking lifelong imprisonment or even her life. They seem, however, to be available to her in the sense that she somehow got into contact with such moral visions and could imagine the possibility of fleeing to a country where homosexuality is not seen as 'wrong.' Here, getting into contact with plural moralities seems to be an important resource for envisioning the possibility of living a different, better life.

In terms of orientation in life, we found several experiences of severe disorientation in Grace's story; situations where she felt that a good life was beyond her reach. These include arriving at Schiphol and wondering whether it is better for her to die; several instances of literally not knowing where she is or where she might go to; her first interview with the foreign police department in Ter Apel; the moment she is told she has 28 days to leave the country and falls ill without having a place to stay; various experiences of discrimination. The problem in these situations is not that Grace does not know or cannot decide what would be a good life for her; her experiences of disorientation are related to her struggle to live a life according to her firm vision of what is of ultimate importance in living a good life. In this vision, the notion that people, regardless of their sexual orientation, should have equal rights and chances in life is an essential element. This is embedded in a broader idea of equality of all people in which there is no room for discrimination whatsoever. In Grace's story, there is no fluidity or ambiguity when it comes to this vision of the good. We do not learn from the story what relational context in Grace's life is the source of this vision; but we do learn that not only in Uganda, but also after arriving in the Netherlands, she encounters serious obstacles in her attempts to orient towards this vision of equality.

We found that the main obstacles that Grace faces in the Netherlands in her quest for a good life are in the first place related to a lack of knowledge – knowledge of the language that is spoken by people she depends on, knowledge of the legal system that determines her legal position, knowledge of what is located where in this new and unfamiliar country. Second, there are obstacles related to embodiment and location: feeling too ill to have energy to go on, to walk, to move, literally 'freezing,' or having no place where one feels safe and at home. The various people who discriminate against Grace may also be seen as blocking her attempts to orient towards the vision that discrimination is wrong. Eventually, however, she turns this obstacle into a resource, when she decides to act according to her own moral vision of equality by forgiving these people, not giving up on them, and staying close to them. More straightforward resources for (re)orienting towards a good life that appear in Grace's story are learning to speak Dutch and the different communities where she does feel at home, like Ugandan communities or LGBT communities. Grace does not always actively and consciously navigate towards resources; for instance, she is led to an LGBT community by someone who is attentive to her, who cares and reaches out to her. In other instances, too, resources have the character of being given rather than sought for, sometimes through coincidence. Several people reach out to her without her asking for it, for instance when someone happens to call her when she is ill and arranges shelter for her. One resource that, as she eventually recognizes, is available to her, is the Dutch legal system, which represents equal rights for all. A final resource is simply the passing of time, which seems to have healing potential for Grace. In relation to a moment of severe disorientation, where she did not know any more whether remaining alive was the best option for her, Grace tells us: *Yeah, but the fact that every day I lived here I became stronger and stronger and I said: you know what? You can do it.*

When we look at these findings in terms of what we called moral or existential resilience – processes where people in extremely challenging life situations manage to reorient towards some vision of the good (Schuhmann & van der Geugten, 2017) – we see that Grace's resilience cannot be understood as an individual process and accounted for in terms of inner strengths. Of course, her firmness in sticking to the vision that discrimination is wrong may be understood as an inner strength. However, we do not know in what relational contexts she came into contact with this vision. We also see that this firmness in itself does not save her from despair and suicidal thoughts. Grace also needs to live in a social and political context in which her vision is seen as legitimate, and she needs to be part of relational contexts or communities which support her vision of the good in order to be able to integrate her vision of the good in her life. Grace's story suggests that we need to go beyond an individualistic perspective and emphasize the role of relational and social contexts, of power structures, of embodiment, and of coincidence, in order to understand resilience of individuals in the context of plural and clashing moralities.[2]

Discussion: theoretical perspectives on moral orientation amidst plural moralities

Case studies, like experiments, are not generalizable to populations or universes, but to theoretical propositions (Yin, 2014). So, let us explore what the case study that we have explored teaches us about the theoretical perspectives of relational being and DST in relation to plural moralities. From the perspective of DST, we find different *I*-positions in Grace's story. In line with DST we see how, over time, *I*-positions shift in relation to each other. For instance, the position of 'I as safe,' which is at first incompatible with 'I as lesbian,' approaches this position later on: Grace starts to feel confident when speaking about her sexuality. We also see that, on several occasions, Grace builds bridges between apparently opposed *I*-positions and manages to come to a third position. We saw this, for instance, when she envisioned her family members as eventually making a turn towards her. Grace's story shows that understanding the language spoken by someone else is a prerequisite for understanding and adopting the other's position as an *I*-position. Not speaking Dutch cuts Grace off from potentially enriching experiences. Grace's story also shows that (metaphorical) *I*-positions may be connected to embodied positions in physical space. For instance, when Grace is ill, her position of 'I as safe' depends on having a room where she can recover.

In relation to the theory of relational being, we see that Grace needs to join relational contexts which support her moral visions in order to be able to live according to these visions. When she arrives at Schiphol, unsure of ever finding such supportive contexts, she suffers from suicidal thoughts. Grace's story shows the significance of being part of a community, particularly when she speaks about her eagerness to join Ugandan or LGBT communities in the Netherlands. However, we also see that access to relational contexts that support one's visions of the good is not self-evident. Power plays a role here; lack of knowledge of the Dutch legal systems and the Dutch language is disempowering for Grace. In terms of relational being, we may say that relations are partly mediated through language and power dynamics; living in a place where one cannot understand power structures or the dominant language seriously impoverishes one's resources for 'relational being.'

Throughout Grace's story, we see that knowledge about the culture, politics, and language of her surroundings is an essential precondition for orientation. Without this knowledge, Grace has limited tools to orient. An interesting additional perspective on orientation – both literal orientation and metaphorical, moral orientation – that captures this point is provided by feminist writer Sara Ahmed (2006). She points out that

> In order to become oriented, you might suppose that we must first experience disorientation. When we are orientated, we might not even notice that we are orientated: we might not even think 'to think' about this point. When we experience disorientation, we might notice orientation as something we do not have.
>
> (pp. 5–6)

When Grace arrives in the Netherlands, she experiences severe disorientation, and clearly is very aware of her difficulties to orient. In her story we see that she does 'think to think' about orientation. She wasn't in the easy position where orientation is self-evident.

Ahmed (2006) emphasizes both the normative and the embodied dimensions of orientation that also come to the fore in Grace's story. Ahmed illustrates this with the image of walking blindfolded in a room. It makes an enormous difference whether we are familiar with the room or not. If we do not know the shape of the room, orientation will be difficult, whereas we will be able to orient without even thinking about it in a room where we have lived for a while. In order to know the space in which we orient ourselves, we need in the first place knowledge of the social norms in our current situation. Norms influence what roads we are supposed or even allowed to take in social contexts; what lines to follow. "The lines that direct us . . . depend on the repetition of norms and conventions, of routes and paths taken, but they are also created as an effect of this repetition" (Ahmed, 2006, p. 16). In Uganda, there was no road for Grace to follow within existing social norms. In the Netherlands, she did not know how to find out what roads there are to follow. Knowing the space in which we orient ourselves is also related to embodiment: "Familiarity is shaped by the 'feel' of space or by how spaces 'impress' upon bodies." (Ahmed, 2006, p. 31). According to Ahmed's ideas, orienting ourselves in challenging situations requires a certain familiarity with the places where we find ourselves, and this familiarity also depends on our bodily experience of the space.

The emphasis on familiarity – bodily familiarity, familiarity with social norms and language – in relation to orientation is reflected by several episodes in Grace's story: for instance, the moment that Grace had her final hearing at court, and, now familiar with the Dutch language, decides to bypass the interpreter when she addresses the judge in Dutch. Compared to the situation where she was interviewed by the foreign police department and had to rely on an interpreter whom she did not trust, the contrast is enormous. Another episode concerns the switch Grace makes when embracing people in the Netherlands as 'familiar,' as family members who, in contrast to members of her biological family, support her sexual orientation. In the end, Grace's story of attempting to orient in a strange country can also be read as a story about the existential significance of 'feeling at home.' Grace leaves the familiarity of the country where she is born and has lived many years of her life – and that she still, occasionally, refers to as 'home' in the interview – but where she is not accepted and does not feel at home. She flees this 'home' in search for a place where she may find the familiarity connected to being welcomed, accepted, and actually feeling at home. In the words of Ahmed (2006): "The question of orientation becomes, then, a question not only about how we 'find our way' but how we come to 'feel at home' " (p. 7).

Notes

1 We retrieved the information in this paragraph from the following websites (consulted on 10 March 2018): www.pewglobal.org/2013/06/04/the-global-divide-on-homo sexuality/; www.theguardian.com/world/2014/may/12/uganda-anti-gay-law-rise-attacks; http://sexualminoritiesuganda.com/and-thats-how-i-survived-press-release/
2 Several recent approaches to resilience develop such a broader perspective on resilience; see, for instance, the work of Ungar (2011) on the 'social ecology of resilience,' or work by Jordan, Walker, and Hartling (2004) in which resilience is related to relational-cultural theory, and *The Resilience Handbook*, edited by Kent, Davis, and Reich (2014).

References

Ahmed, S. (2006). *Queer phenomenology: Orientations, objects, others*. Durham, NC: Duke University Press.

Atkins, K. (2008). *Narrative identity and moral identity: A practical perspective*. New York, NY: Routledge.

Gergen, K. J. (2009). *Relational being: Beyond self and community*. Oxford: Oxford University Press.

Hermans, H. J. M. (2014). Self as a society of I-positions: A dialogical approach to counseling. *Journal of Humanistic Counseling, 53*, 134–159. doi:10.1002/j.2161-1939.2014.00054.x

Hermans, H. J. M., & Hermans-Konopka, A. (2010). *Dialogical self theory: Positioning and counter-positioning in a globalizing society*. Cambridge: Cambridge University Press.

Jordan, J. V., Walker, M., & Hartling, L. M. (Eds.). (2004). *The complexity of connection: Writings from the Stone Center's Jean Baker Miller Institute*. New York, NY: Guilford Press.

Jordan, S. R. (2009). Un/Convention(al) refugees: Contextualizing the accounts of refugees facing homophobic or transphobic persecution. *Refuge: Canada's Journal on Refugees, 26*(2), 165–182.

Kent, M., Davis, M. C., & Reich, J. (Eds.). (2014). *The resilience handbook*. New York, NY: Routledge.

Schuhmann, C., & van der Geugten, W. (2017). Believable visions of the good: An exploration of the role of pastoral counselors in promoting resilience. *Pastoral Psychology, 66*(4), 523–536. doi:10.1007/s11089-017-0759-z

Taylor, C. (1989). *Sources of the self: The making of the modern identity*. Cambridge, MA: Harvard University Press.

Taylor, C. (2007). *A secular age*. Cambridge, MA: Belknap Press.

Ungar, M. (2011). The social ecology of resilience: Addressing contextual and cultural ambiguity of a nascent construct. *American Journal of Orthopsychiatry, 81*(1), 1–17. doi:10.1111/j.19390025.2010.01067.x

Walker, M. U. (2007). *Moral understandings: A feminist study in ethics* (2nd ed.). Oxford: Oxford University Press.

Wengraf, T. (2001). *Qualitative research interviewing: Biographic narratives and semi-structured methods*. London: Sage Publications.

Yin, R. K. (2014). *Case study research: Design and methods*. Los Angeles, CA: Sage Publications.

Epilogue

Hans Alma and Ina ter Avest

Leading question

'How can we further develop theory and practice regarding moral and spiritual leadership, and/or transformative dialogue in the public sphere, in order to strengthen a democratic way of living together in a context of plural moralities?' This is how we formulated our leading question for this publication. In the preceding 13 chapters, we have brought together reflections on this question that show us both its urgency and its complexity. Also, new questions came to the fore. An important issue several authors address is the tension between closing off from what is 'other' and unfamiliar, and opening oneself to values and ways of living that others bring to the common social space we all participate in. The authors agree on the importance of opening movements in the fields of organizations, education, migration, and citizenship. They also agree on the difficulties people encounter in the face of the uncertainties and ambiguities of our times. Uncertainty and fear are the backdrop of people's lives and, as different chapters indicate, can easily lead to fixed, top-down moralities being imposed on others. However, in the authors' thinking, the emphasis on the dynamic rather than the static is evident – the focus is on dialogical relationships and ethical ways of life, on processes instead of procedures and entities.

Throughout the contributions, a complex 'gridwork' emerges of intercrossing distinctions, also understood in terms of intersectionality. There are the basic social 'them' and 'us' distinctions, the different groups that constitute a plural society: indigenous persons and people with a migrant background, males and females, Moroccan Muslims and Turkish Muslims, baby boomers and millennials, just to name a few. There are many more dialectic positions one can think of. Distinctions between moralities are linked to these social distinctions; especially when we take into account the difference between first and second-order morality, and between surface and foundational values. Furthermore, there are levels of identity – like individual, group, humanity and local, national, global. The pressing question then becomes: how do moral and spiritual leadership, transformative dialogue, and the strengthening of a democracy-inspired attitude relate to this gridwork? What are the possibilities and risks of 'moral compasses,' where could they be rooted, and how might such a moral compass help us find our way in a world of plural modalities and moralities? More than giving clear-cut answers to these questions, the authors of this book help us to live with and through these complexities and ambiguities that often feel uncomfortable. However, from the authors' 'inconvenient truths,' possibly perceived as disruptive moments, innovative responses might pop up in the reader's mind.

The metaphor of rhizomatic processes (M. Gergen in Chapter 12) leads both to the perception of nodes of conflict as well as to the emergence of new forms of living and working together. Whatever seems to be the story at one point may need to be restoried at another point in time. Positioning, counter- and repositioning, telling and retelling are never-ending basic processes of personal and social life. The authors of this book alert us to recognizing the rhizomatic character of social dynamics and to acknowledging both people's pain and strength in struggling with the challenges and antagonisms they face. The authors are of the opinion that Hermans's dialogical self theory (Chapter 2) can help us to understand the processes of inclusion, exclusion and expulsion, and the transcendence of dichotomies both on a personal and on a societal level. K. J. Gergen's relational ethics (Chapter 1) with its four central components (*caring communication, conscience, creativity* and *continuation*) sets goalposts for finding our way in the complex landscapes of a globalized world. The need for creativity makes clear that we cannot travel without use of our imagination, which can find possibilities in our ever difficult reality and can build images of alternative courses of action (see Alma in Chapter 4). Imagination may be a core characteristic of a form of leadership that both cares for people and challenges them to move out of their comfort zone to build moral or existential resilience ('provocative guidance' – ter Avest in Chapter 5; 'pedagogy of interruption' – van der Zande and Bakker in Chapter 9). The imaginative capacity reminds us of the need to explore playfulness ('homo ludens') in living with and enduring complexity and uncertainty.

Conceptual concerns

As we made clear in the introduction to this volume, we did not want to give limiting definitions of what we understand by 'moral' and 'spiritual,' because we wanted to allow for free explorations of what plural moralities are about and what challenges for moral and spiritual leadership they pose. In broad terms, we made the following distinctions with regard to these and related concepts:

> Moralities are about people's notions of the 'good' as they are imagined, articulated, and practiced in daily life. Conceptualization of and explicit reflection on these lived moralities belong to the field of ethics. We will

see that several authors use related terms to do justice to the sensual and embodied dimensions of how people connect to the 'good' (aesthetics), to the ultimate concerns raised in this context (existential dimension), and to the experience of what people consider to be of ultimate importance, transcendent or holy (spiritual dimension).

(Alma & ter Avest, Introduction in this volume)

Reflecting on the contributions, we feel inspired to take a closer look at what meaning different authors attach to the concepts we distinguished in our introduction and how this relates to moral and spiritual leadership. The term 'moral' is used by all authors, and it is explicitly defined by K. J. Gergen in the following way:

the sense of 'good' functions as a primitive (we may find it 'good' to have peace and quiet); when the sense of good is codified or articulated we speak of it as 'morality' (it is a moral good that we don't disrupt others' wellbeing, for example, by playing loud music); and when we provide a conceptual account of why such morality is imperative, we enter the field of ethics.

(Chapter 1 in this volume, note 4)

In a similar way, Skeie distinguishes between 'ethical foundation' and 'moral rules': "they are different levels of preferences and arguments. If we differ in morals, we may address this on the level of ethics; and if we agree in ethics, we may still differ in morals." More specifically, he understands ethics "as the justification and anchoring of moral values" (Chapter 10 in this volume). Ter Avest, however, refers to the conceptual clarification of Heres (2014, pp. 34–35), who

interprets 'ethics' and 'morality' and their adjectives 'ethical' and 'moral' as synonyms that designate the group of normative judgments which appeal to generally accepted ideas about what is 'right,' 'good,' and 'just.' These normative judgments provide a frame of reference for evaluations, appraisal, and action.

(Chapter 5 in this volume, note 3)

When we look closely at the way the concepts of 'moral' and 'morality' are used by the other authors, we both find instances of conceiving them as synonyms of 'ethical' and 'ethics,' and instances of treating them as differing in level of reflection in the way Gergen and Skeie propose.

Things become more complicated when we add the notion 'existential.' Not all authors use this concept, and those who do relate it to people's search for meaning in life (Alma, who describes existential as touching "on the foundations of our existence"; Chapter 4), and to "ultimate questions about purpose and meaning" (van der Zande & Bakker, Chapter 9). Van der

Zande and Bakker connect it with the concept of life orientation, defined as "an existential positioning process pertaining to the meaning of the human being, the world and the meta-empirical, directed towards the horizon of the good life." Schuhmann and Knibbe also use the term life orientation when they speak of existential questions, and they relate this to Charles Taylor's use of the concept 'moral space.' In line with Taylor (1989), they explicitly choose for a broader conception of 'moral,' "encompassing not only people's obligations towards others, but also notions of a life worth living, a life commanding respect, and a 'full' life" (Chapter 13).

Only two authors refer to 'aesthetics' as a concept that is closely connected to morality and existential questions. Alma goes back to the root of the concept, "to 'aisthēsis' as knowledge of the sensible." She argues that "meaning-making is about how I sense the world, how my body relates to it, what feelings are evoked, and the understanding I gain from this general perception" (Chapter 4). M. Gergen sees aesthetic experiences as a way of coming to relational engagement. They "emphasize the sensual, engage the emotional and spiritual qualities of a conflict, and they invite embodied activities" (Chapter 12). Both M. Gergen and Alma stress the importance of the arts in coming to terms with plural moralities. According to M. Gergen, "artistic endeavors create opportunities for shared commitment, receptivity, serenity, and playfulness among the participants, regardless of their intellectual differences" (Chapter 12). She gives examples of how artistic initiatives work out in practice in building relational engagement, finding common ground, and engaging in transformative potentials.

As to the spiritual dimension of leadership, many authors conceive of this in terms of religion and worldview, without restricting these phenomena to institutional or dogmatic forms. Yet, we also find broader uses of the term spirituality. Alma refers to Connolly, who describes spirituality in terms of transcendence "as an intensification of everyday experience so as to amplify sensitivities, open the self or constituency to experimentation, or augment experimental ties across lines of difference" (Connolly, 2011, p. 39). Another aspect of spirituality is addressed by ter Avest, who speaks of "a point of reference for the ongoing evaluation of my actions. Reflection and action meet in an interpretation of spirituality as a practice-based life orientation" (Chapter 5 in this volume). It is important to notice that the notion of life orientation is mentioned by several authors in this volume as an important element in thinking about moral and spiritual leadership. We may conclude that Alma stresses the experiential quality of spirituality, whereas ter Avest and others stress the orientational quality.

Van Loon and Buster "make a plea to recognize that human beings have a *natural* inclination towards a vertical, transcendent dimension in life" (Chapter 6). They speak of this dimension in terms of mystery, wonder, childlike curiosity, miracle; they point to both the experiential and orientational qualities ("sense of direction") of the transcendent dimension. Much in line with terms like mystery and wonder, König (Chapter 7) reminds us of a potential tension between knowing and not knowing with regard to the spiritual and transcendent, as she quotes Richard Rohr (2002), who speaks of a liminal space. This, according to Rohr, is a unique spiritual position and can be described as a place of transition, waiting, and not knowing. Yet, König also speaks of "knowing in the in-between" that can be reached through other knowledge centers than the rational mind: emotional and intuitive ways of knowing that are facilitated through contemplative practices. This is also addressed by van der Zande and Bakker when they speak of spiritual lessons in terms of "pedagogical interruption." Through different forms of meditation, yoga, music experience, bibliodrama, haptonomy, theater, sport, and visual arts, students are drawn out of their comfort zone with the intention of stimulating reflection while focusing on the experiential learning and embodied knowledge of students.

Skeie (Chapter 10) mentions the personal or life story as a way to address spirituality in education. Again, in these stories, the experiential and orientational qualities of spirituality come to the fore. Without always relating them to spiritual guidance or leadership, several authors address the importance of (life) stories in reflecting on plural moralities. The chapters that take the perspective of dialogical self theory point out that in (life) stories, the voices of several *I*-positions can be distinguished, sometimes in dialogue, sometimes in confrontation. For these authors, stories have an important methodological function in their research and counseling practices. From a relational perspective, M. Gergen points out how important stories are in creating common ground, for "a personal story tends not to be challenged, which allows diverse opinions to be put forth without argument" (Chapter 12). Schuhmann and Knibbe (Chapter 13) see a personal story as a place where processes of dis- and reorientation can be found, thus addressing an important quality of spirituality, although they do not use this term.

Common themes running through the volume

Theoretically, we chose a relational and dialogical approach that is presented in the first part of the book. Kenneth J. Gergen (Chapter 1) and Hubert J.M. Hermans (Chapter 2) provide us with fundamental insights regarding relational processes and dialogical self that are the very basis of the answers this volume provides to our guiding question. Working with the two approaches requires us to reflect on how practices of collaboration influence dialogues within and between people and how a 'society of mind' can never be abstracted from ongoing social action.

Throughout the second part of the book (Developing Theory and Practice in Dialogue), we see a continuation of the lines that emerge in the Theoretical Perspectives of the first part. Thus, three dimensions or levels of moral and spiritual leadership come to the fore: (1) self-guidance or personal leadership (especially in the chapters by van Loon and Buster, König, and Schuhmann & Knibbe, who address the capacities for freeing space in the self, intercultural sensitivity, and moral or existential resilience); (2) guidance by a leader with followers or hierarchical leadership (addressed, yet nuanced by ter Avest in her discussion on good leadership); (3) relational responsibility (discussed by van der Zande and Bakker in terms of distributed leadership, by ter Avest in terms of a 'band of brothers,' and by M. Gergen with the help of the metaphor of the rhizome). It is interesting that the second dimension, that of a leader with her/his followers, is so little discussed in the practice-oriented chapters in this volume: this approach does not fit well with the relational and dialogical perspective we chose. Yet, we also see how the three dimensions sometimes blur and become more complicated through recognizing the dynamics of social life with its categorizations and power relations. Bringing theory and practice in dialogue, the articles in the second part of this volume point to complexity and intersectionality that add both depth and difficulty to our endeavor.

The concept of intersectionality is rooted in the 1970s in black feminism and critical race theory, arguing that it was very difficult to separate race from class from sex oppression because these phenomena are experienced very often simultaneously. According to Von Brömssen (2016) the word 'simultaneously' points to the heart of intersectionality, since it is all about different positionings in social life that cut across each other and – what is most important – constitute each other (Von Brömssen, 2016, p. 2). In theories on intersectionality developed in the 1980s and 1990s, it became clear that the position of women could not be described and analyzed by just studying one of the characteristics, but should be understood as "comprising multiple, converging and interwoven systems" (Crenshaw in Von Brömssen, 2016, p. 3). Intersectionality, in this line of thought, is about the interaction of different positionings in which power appears to play a dominant role. For the further development of our thoughts on leadership and plural moralities, it is of utmost importance to be aware that in the process of positioning – which plays a crucial role in dialogical self theory – positions cannot be separated and social roles are not simply additive. None of a person's positions is a matter of choice clearly related to or influenced by one specific location or image of a person's position in society. It is the complexity of positioning as a social power relation that cannot be neglected and should be included in theoretical and practical research on interwoven systems of living and working together in a context of plural moralities.

Conclusion

Schuhmann and Knibbe end Chapter 13 with the deep insight that the question of moral and existential orientation is not only about how we 'find our way'; the more urgent question might be how we come to 'feel at home.'

This brings us to a concise summary of what moral and spiritual leadership in an age of plural moralities is about:

> Facilitating and enhancing our ability to feel at home in the world – especially our competency in response to the complexity thereof – through education and social action that promote self-guidance (personal leadership) and relational responsibility, recognizing the multi-layeredness of the sources of knowledge and inspiration we use in our search for meaningful experiences and life orientation.

We do not present this as a tight definition. With the explorative exercises and 'examples of good practice' we offered in this volume, we hope to inspire the reader to respond to the complexities of leadership in a plural world. Our book is an invitation to work with the material presented and to enrich it with your own experiences and stories. It is an invitation to dance, with a playful exchange of who takes the lead – the voices of the authors alternating with your own voice as an experienced participant in a society of plural moralities. Rooted in this 'dialogical dance,' your own innovative actions might be like 'social yeast,' with impact that exceeds the numbers of the team you participate in.

References

Connolly, W. E. (2011). *A world of becoming*. Durham, NC, and London: Duke University Press.

Heres, L. (2014). *One style fits all? The content, origins and effect of follower expectations of ethical leadership* (PhD thesis). VU University, Amsterdam.

Rohr, R. (2002, January–February). Grieving as a sacred space. *Sojourners Magazine*.

Taylor, C. (1989). *Sources of the self: The making of the modern identity*. Cambridge, MA: Harvard University Press.

Von Brömssen, K. (2016). Is there a place for intersectionality in research on religious and values education? In J. Astley & L. J. Francis (Eds.), *Diversity and intersectionality: Studies in religion, education and values* (pp. 1–22). Oxford: Peter Lang Publishing Group.

Index